# Drugs in Afghanistan

# Drugs in Afghanistan

## Opium, Outlaws and Scorpion Tales

DAVID MACDONALD

Pluto Press

LONDON • ANN ARBOR, MI

First published 2007 by Pluto Press
345 Archway Road, London N6 5AA
and 839 Greene Street, Ann Arbor, MI 48106

www.plutobooks.com

British Library Cataloguing in Publication Data
A catalogue record for this book is available from the British Library

Hardback
ISBN-13    978 0 7453 2618 4
ISBN-10    0 7453 2618 8

Paperback
ISBN-13    978 0 7453 2617 7
ISBN-10    0 7453 2617 X

Library of Congress Cataloging in Publication Data applied for

10   9   8   7   6   5   4   3   2   1

Designed and produced for Pluto Press by
Chase Publishing Services Ltd, Fortescue, Sidmouth, EX10 9QG, England
Typeset from disk by Stanford DTP Services, Northampton, England
Printed and bound in the European Union by
Antony Rowe Ltd, Chippenham and Eastbourne, England

*Dedicated to the memory of Behar*

# Contents

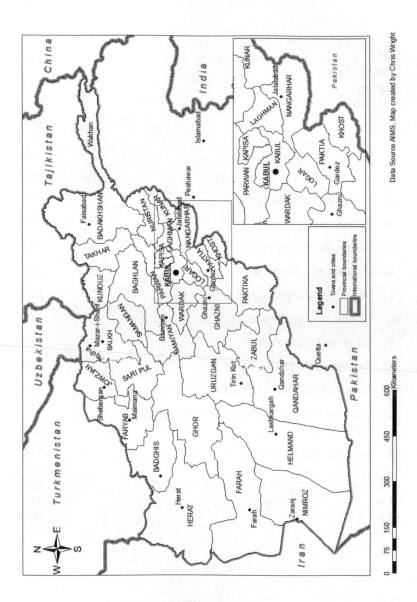

# Abbreviations

| | |
|---|---|
| AIDS | Acquired Immune Deficiency Syndrome |
| AK-47 | Kalashnikov automatic assault rifle |
| AKF | Agha Khan Foundation |
| AMF | Afghan Military Force |
| AMRC | Afghan Media Resource Centre |
| ANF | Anti-narcotics Force |
| ASNF | Afghan Special Narcotics Force |
| ATS | Amphetamine type stimulants |
| BBC | British Broadcasting Corporation |
| BCCI | Bank of Credit and Commerce International |
| CIA | Central Intelligence Agency |
| CND | Commission on Narcotic Drugs |
| CNPA | Counter Narcotics Police Afghanistan |
| DCCU | Drug Control Coordination Unit |
| DDR | Disarmament, demobilisation and reintegration |
| DDTC | Drug Dependency Treatment Centre |
| DEA | Drug Enforcement Administration/Agency |
| FDA | Food and Drug Administration |
| HIV | Human immunodeficiency virus |
| IDP | Internally displaced person |
| IDU | Injecting drug use |
| IDUs | Injecting drug users |
| INCB | International Narcotics Control Board |
| ISAF | International Security Assistance Force |
| ISI | Inter Services Intelligence (Pakistan intelligence agency) |
| IWPR | Institute for War and Peace Reporting |
| LEAP | Law Enforcement against Prohibition |
| LSD | lysergic acid diethylamide (a hallucinogenic drug) |
| NGO | Non-governmental organisation |
| NIFA | National Islamic Front of Afghanistan |
| NSP | Needle and syringe access and disposal programme |
| NWFP | North West Frontier Province |
| ORA | Orphans, Refugees and Aid (international NGO) |
| PNCB | Pakistan Narcotics Control Board |
| PTSD | Post traumatic stress disorder |

| | |
|---|---|
| RAWA | Revolutionary Association of the Women of Afghanistan |
| RPG | Rocket propelled grenade |
| RSA | Rapid situation assessment |
| RTA | Radio-TV Afghanistan |
| SAS | Special Air Service |
| SHCDC | State High Commission for Drug Control |
| SP | Spasmo Proxyvon |
| SUV | Sport utility vehicle |
| THC | Tetrahydrocannabinol (the main active constituent of cannabis) |
| TRIPS | Trade-Related Aspects of Intellectual Property Rights |
| UMRC | Uranium Medical Research Center |
| UNAMA | United Nations Assistance Mission in Afghanistan |
| UNDCP | United Nations International Drug Control Programme |
| UNDP | United Nations Development Programme |
| UNESCO | United Nations Educational, Scientific and Cultural Organisation |
| UNHCR | United Nations High Commission for Refugees |
| UNICEF | United Nations Children's Emergency Fund |
| UNODC | United Nations Office on Drugs and Crime |
| UNODCCP | United Nations Office for Drug Control and Crime Prevention |
| UXO | Unexploded Ordnance |
| VOA | Voice of America |
| WFP | World Food Programme |
| WHO | World Health Organization |
| WTO | World Trade Organization |

# Glossary

| | |
|---|---|
| Afs | shortened form of the Afghani, the currency of Afghanistan |
| *al-khamr* | intoxicants or drugs (originally meaning alcohol) |
| *andiwal* | friend |
| *ashar* | the use of reciprocal labour |
| *ashrar* | those who spread discord; a term used by the communist regime to describe *mujahideen* |
| *bhang* | herbal cannabis |
| *bhangawa* | drink prepared with herbal cannabis |
| *burshesha* | type of medicine made by *hakims* (often with intoxicating properties) |
| *chai khana* | tea room or tea house |
| *chando* | form of refined opium |
| *charas* | hashish |
| *charasi* | habitual hashish user |
| *chillum* | water pipe for smoking hashish (in Afghanistan) |
| *chowkidor* | watchman or guard |
| *cristal* | type of heroin |
| *dawa* | medicine |
| *daya* | midwife |
| *djinns* | spirits |
| *faqir* | Islamic (Sufi) ascetic holy man |
| *farman* | edict |
| *ghamza* | form of opium smoking |
| *girda* | crumbly powdered cannabis resin |
| *hakim* | practitioner of herbal medicine |
| *haram* | forbidden |
| *Hijra* | the Islamic calendar |
| *jihad* | holy war |
| *jirga* | a tribal council or assembly (Pashtoon) |
| *kafila* | caravan |
| *khans* | the equivalent of aristocratic feudal lords |
| *konjara* | animal fodder |
| *Kuchis* | nomadic tribespeople; usually referring to a tribe of Pashtoon nomads in Afghanistan |
| *lashkar* | tribal army |

| | |
|---|---|
| *Loya Jirga* | grand assembly or council |
| *madak* | pills made from opium mixed with water and rice or barley husks |
| *madrassa* | Koranic school |
| *majun/majoun* | edible mixture of hashish and other ingredients |
| *malang* | a Sufi ascetic or mendicant |
| *maliks* | community leaders or tribal elders |
| *mast* | state of intoxication |
| *mofarah* | intoxicating mixture |
| *mothad* | drug addict |
| *mujahid* | (pl. *mujahideen*) one who leads the faithful in holy war or takes part in holy war |
| *mukhadir* | intoxicant or drug |
| *narghile* | water pipe for smoking hashish |
| *nashaimawad* | intoxicating substance |
| *naswar* | a type of chewing tobacco |
| *Pashtoonwali* | the Pashtoon social code of conduct |
| *patou* | blanket |
| *pir* | spiritual leader (usually of a Sufi order) |
| *poder* | powder, a term used to refer to heroin |
| *poderi* | heroin addict |
| *puri* | weight just under 1 g |
| *riba* | usury, interest on loans |
| *rubab* | Afghan lute |
| *sadhu* | Hindu ascetic holy man |
| *saglahoo* | type of sea otter |
| *salaam* | loan as advance payment for a fixed amount of agricultural product |
| *serai* | traveller's lodging place |
| *shabnama* | 'night letter', often referring to a clandestinely distributed leaflet |
| *sharab* | alcohol |
| *Sharia* | Islamic law |
| *shirac* | high quality Afghan hashish |
| *shura* | village council |
| *tariak* | opium (Afghanistan) |
| *tarra* | home-brewed liquor |
| *tchilim* | type of water pipe |
| *thariac* | opium (Iran) |
| *topakai* | gunman or armed bandit |
| *toshak* | floor cushion |

| | |
|---|---|
| *Ulema shura* | the council of Islamic scholars, acting as advisers to the government |
| *usher* | traditional Islamic tax (10 per cent of all agricultural products) |
| *Wolesi Jirga* | Lower House of Parliament |
| *zamzam* | holy water from Mecca |
| *zina* | sexual activity outside marriage |

# Acknowledgements

Although this book covers many different topics related to drugs in Afghanistan, as well as other areas of the world, its essential focus is on the increasing number of Afghans who have turned to drug consumption to mask the pain of their existence in an impoverished and war-wracked land.

Over the seven years that I have visited and worked in Afghanistan, untold numbers of people have influenced this book, sometimes subtly, sometimes more overtly. But all have unfailingly, with good humour, grace and dignity, been willing to discuss their views and ideas on Afghanistan's many drug problems—usually over several cups of green tea.

Thanks are due to a great many: the staff of the few available drug treatment services in Kabul and Gardez; ex-colleagues in UNODC and the Ministry of Counter Narcotics in Afghanistan; residents of the UN Flower Street guesthouse in Kabul between August 2002 and September 2003; community members; families of drug users; and, most importantly, drug users themselves.

To the following friends and colleagues I owe a particular debt of gratitude. Their ideas, help and support in the development of this book have been invaluable: Barbara Bruckmoser, Anna Pont, Shirazuddin Siddiqi, Richard Will, Daud Sangarwal, Jamie Gairns, David Morran, Fariba Soltani, Professor Cindy Fazey, Dr Parveen Azam Khan, Dr. Nadeem-ur-Rehman, Karim Merchant, Khaled Mansour, Leda Stott, Harry Shapiro, Trevor Martin, Dr Nadine Ezard, Marc Theuss, Gary Poole, Professor Gerry Stimson, Anthony Fitzherbert, Zalmei Sherzad, Molly Charles, Robert Kluijver, Vyas Kirit, Robbie Jack, Wayne Bazant, Sayed Hassan, Robert Webb, Roger van Zwanenberg, the late Vicky Patterson and Chris Wright for the map.

Special thanks must go to my friend and colleague David Mansfield for his pioneering work in recording and analysing the complex dynamics and processes of opium cultivation and production in Afghanistan. In many ways this book mirrors his work by describing the equally complex processes and dynamics of drug consumption that in turn reflect more global concerns about the paucity of a prohibitionist stance of a war against drugs—especially drug users. The last thing the Afghan people need is another war.

Special thanks must also go to all my colleagues and friends in the field of drug demand reduction in Afghanistan, but particularly to Jehanzeb Khan, Mohammad Naim, Dr Mohammad Zafar and Dr Mohammad Raza who continue to fight the odds against the country's expanding drug problem in an exemplary and professional manner and with few resources at their disposal.

Finally a very special thank you must go to my ever loving and supportive family, Liz, Roseanna and Lucy, who during the beginnings of this book had their lives disrupted and were evacuated twice from our home in Islamabad, Pakistan, to Scotland. This happened once after 9/11 and again in June of 2002 after the spurious nuclear standoff between Pakistan and India. It provided us with the merest glimpse of what it must be like to be suddenly displaced from home and community, a situation that too many Afghan families have found themselves in over the last few decades.

However, while thanks are due to all the above for their contributions, the book reflects only my own views, any unforeseen scorpion tales are my responsibility. I can categorically say that the author does not guarantee the accuracy of the data included in this work except that based on his own personal experience and the research findings that he has been responsible for producing himself. Such is Afghanistan.

Perthshire, Scotland, July 2006
ds_macdonald@yahoo.co.uk

*Our obsession with fact and reason, a consequence of the scientific revolution, has allowed us to dismiss myth because it is not rooted in verifiable certainty. In doing so, we ignore the extent to which myth deals in emotional, rather than literal truths. Myth does not try to provide concrete answers, but it is better viewed as a flag for our lack of understanding. We hoist these flags in order to help us make sense of the incomprehensible, and to deepen our understanding of what it means to be human.*

Sunday Herald Seven Days, 23 October 2005

*The developed country does not, as Marx thought, show the backward country its future; the fragmenting countries show the integrating ones the dark side of their common present.*

Barnett R. Rubin, 1996,
*The Fragmentation of Afghanistan,*
Lahore: Vanguard Books, p. 5

# Prologue

Stories shift like sand in a place where no records exist.[1]

In March 1999 I was unexpectedly summoned to a meeting in the dry dusty city of Quetta, situated in Pakistan's southern province of Baluchistan, with Mullah Abdul Hameed Akhundzada, head of Afghanistan's SHCDC (State High Commission for Drug Control) based in Kabul. Akhundzada had arranged the meeting to discuss any plans UNDCP might have for drug demand reduction activities in Afghanistan.* A few months previously my appointment as the UNDCP international drug demand reduction specialist for Afghanistan had given me some negotiating power to make decisions about who should receive any available funding for the prevention of problem drug use in that country, the mullah's domain. Not that there was much funding available, however, as demand reduction featured low on the list of priorities for Afghanistan, and far below the twin gods of global drug control policy—law enforcement against the cultivation, production, trafficking and consumption of illicit drugs and the elusive search for sustainable alternative development and livelihoods for farmers in opium poppy and coca bush cultivation areas. It was deemed more politically expedient and of a higher strategic priority to prevent the supply of heroin to western countries than respond to its burgeoning use within Afghanistan itself.

The meeting was to be held in a temporarily converted bedroom on the second floor of a hotel in Quetta's noisy main bazaar. As head of the Taliban-led SHCDC, Akhundzada was an important man and held a powerful position in a country that at the time provided up to 75 per cent of the world's illicit opium. This was also a country with an extreme fundamentalist government officially unrecognised by every state but three (Pakistan, Saudi Arabia and the United Arab Emirates) except as a presumptive authority. Beds had been cleared

---

* In 1997 UNDCP (United Nations International Drug Control Programme) combined with the CICP (Centre for International Crime Prevention) to form UNODCCP (United Nations Office for Drug Control and Crime Prevention), although it also retained its own name. On 1 October 2002 UNODCCP became UNODC (United Nations Office on Drugs and Crime) including UNDCP. These different names are used where applicable throughout the text.

away and bottles of water and sweetmeats provided on a low wooden table surrounded by soft green armchairs. My two colleagues and I sat and waited for the mullah and his entourage to arrive. After an hour or so they swept into the room with rough black cotton cloaks matching their long untrimmed beards. Uniform black turbans were wrapped around their heads, the ends trailing down their backs to their knees.

My first impression of Mullah Akhundzada was startling. With his long black hair and dark enigmatic expression, his face looked remarkably similar to that depicted on an early poster of Jim Morrison, lead singer of the Doors, a 1960s American rock band. The only difference was a broad flat brown scar on the mullah's right cheek that he sometimes hid with his hand, the result of flying shrapnel during the war against the Soviets. That and the fact that he was an Afghan commander who controlled what amounted to a medieval fiefdom near Qandahar with over 200 armed men at his disposal.

The comparison between a man like Akhundzada and the old clan warrior-chiefs of Scotland was hard to resist. If a feather had been stuck in his turban, his clothes made of rough wool instead of black cotton, and a claymore belted at his side instead of an AK-47 slung over his shoulder, he would have looked and acted the part. An Afghan writing in 1928 compared his own country's highlands and 'clan system governed by predatory chiefs' to those of Scotland, although it has also been noted that Afghanistan typically evokes images of *Macbeth* rather than of the Scottish Enlightenment.[2] Indeed, the prevailing situation in Afghanistan, particularly after the Soviets were driven out in 1989, mirrors that of Scotland up to the seventeenth century when banditry, protection racketeering and feuding clans were commonplace until the pacification of the clan system wrought by the English invaders from south of the border. Rory Stewart, a young Scot who courageously walked from Herat to Kabul in January 2002, recounts how Afghans he met along the way defined their landscape by acts of violence and death in the same way that places in the Scottish Highlands are also remembered by acts of violence. The difference, however, was that in Afghanistan 'the events recorded were only months old'.[3]

Akhundzada's interpreter, a smiling and gregarious Qandahari, began every sentence with the phrase: 'His excellency the mullah Abdul Hamid Akhundzada proclaims that...' But such formalities were soon dispensed with and we discussed a wide range of issues around drugs and the ravages of war in Afghanistan. As Akhundzada was responsible for all drug control issues in Afghanistan, it was agreed that we would maintain contact with him and his office on matters concerning the prevention of problem drug use in the country. We had little choice if we wanted to offer any drug demand reduction activities inside Afghanistan. This was at a time when the uncertain communications and relationships between the international community and the Taliban authorities were adversely affecting aid and development assistance reaching the Afghan people.

After the official meeting was over and the mullah and his entourage had returned from another room where they had gone to say their prayers, vast amounts of Afghan pilau rice, roast lamb, naan bread, salad and soft drinks were brought to the room and we ate in silence. Over the ubiquitous green tea and sweets at the end of the meal, the mullah regaled us with stories about his days as a *mujahid* fighting against the Soviets. One particular story concerned the many *mujahideen* who were paid or rewarded for their fighting with hashish, which they often consumed before going into battle. When there was no hashish, Akhundzada claimed that some of them would cut the heads off snakes and the tails from scorpions, then dry and smoke them: 'I have seen this with my own eyes.'

His graphic account of the use of snake heads and scorpion tails as substitutes for hashish led my colleagues and me over the next three years to search for Afghans who had used such substances. While conducting an assessment of problem drug use in rural eastern Afghanistan in 2000, UNODC fieldworkers reported several accounts of people smoking preparations made from snakes and scorpions, although they never came across an actual user.[4] One informant suggested that there was a remote mountain village in Azro district to the southeast of Kabul where 'many people' killed scorpions before drying, crushing and smoking them. Our questions were legion: What type of scorpion? Did they use the whole scorpion or just the tail? What was the effect? How did people first find out about the supposed psychoactive properties, if any, of scorpions? Were such preparations taken mainly for medicinal or ritual purposes, or just to become intoxicated? What was the likelihood of toxic poisoning or even death? Or were these tales about using scorpion preparations just a myth?

In February 2001 we were informed about an ex-heroin addict living in Islamabad in Pakistan who had used preparations made from snake venom as an intoxicating drug. On interviewing him we soon discovered that he had been apprenticed to a *pir* who had shown him ways to be bitten by poisonous snakes without any apparent ill-effect. This had greatly enhanced his status among his friends and, anyway, he had felt a definite psychoactive effect from the snakebite, although this was not the main reason for taking the venom. Having been a drug user since the age of ten, when his mother first introduced him to hashish, he was more than qualified to report on this. At that time we had no conclusive evidence of the use of preparations made from snakes or scorpions for their psychoactive intoxicating properties in Afghanistan.

What such a search for users of snake heads and scorpion tails signifies, however, is that the search for the truth about drugs and their uses in Afghanistan, like many other topics in that country, is an elusive enterprise often clouded by exaggeration, rumour, innuendo, myth, half-truths and a sheer lack of reliable information. It is the Afghan equivalent of the contemporary urban legend spread by ancient Chinese whispers, or what can be referred to as a 'scorpion tale'. Visiting Kabul in the early 1920s, the American traveller Lowell Thomas described how information was conveyed 'by that whisper from sources unseen which wings its way from bazaar to bazaar in Central Asia'.[5]

The basic lines of communication haven't changed all that much in Afghanistan since then, apart from the odd satellite phone and the mushrooming of mobile phones in the main urban centres. The vast majority of the population still rely on a highly interpersonal oral tradition, receiving news primarily by word of mouth. Even before the Soviet invasion of 1979, only three of the 32 provinces were linked by telephone to Kabul the capital city. In Afghanistan the bazaar still functions as the mass media. As a character in a novel set during the struggle against the Soviets says, 'People come to the teahouses to hear things. That is why these places were called the Newspapers of Bricks.'[6] During the Soviet occupation the *mujahideen* spread news by means of *shabnamas* or 'night letters'. These were leaflets passed from hand to hand throughout the country and read and re-read to relatives, friends and neighbours by the few who could read. More recently the re-emergent Taliban has used *shabnamas* to spread underground anti-government messages in Qandahar, Kabul and other areas.

Undoubtedly the air of intrigue and mystery that seems to pervade much public discourse and political debate is fuelled by the fact that more than 70 per cent of Afghans aged 15 and over are illiterate and have little recourse to news apart from radio, accessible to less than half the population, and what they hear directly from others.[7] If conspiracy theories abound in Afghanistan, then they are at least in part, as the journalist Robert D. Kaplan notes, 'inflamed by illiteracy: people who can't read rely on hearsay'.[8] People also now increasingly rely on the radio for news, information and entertainment, Afghanistan has become a radiocentric nation. Apart from international radio stations such as the BBC and VOA, by January 2004 the central government had issued licenses for 30 independent FM radio stations, as well as 6 TV stations, although mostly in Kabul and with limited production capabilities and reception areas. By mid-2006 there were over 50 private radio stations, many in the provinces. In Kabul and Mazar-i-Sharif, 40 per cent of respondents maintained that the state RTA was the most trustworthy source of news and current affairs. At the same time, a UNICEF study in 2003 showed that 33 per cent of households in Afghanistan had no working radio and it is likely to be some time before there is a more developed Afghan media capable of shaping public attitudes and opinions.[9]

In December 2004 this was how a BBC correspondent described conditions inside the poorly resourced RTA newsroom:

The news team occupies a few rooms along a squalid corridor in one of the few buildings on the site that is still intact. The newsroom itself is a tiny sliver of a room furnished with a couple of ramshackle tables and a motley collection of plastic picnic chairs.[10]

In Bakhtar, Afghanistan's official news agency located in the Ministry of Information building,

The favoured method of communication is the fax machine, and I mean THE fax machine. There was just one, attended by two men in what appeared to be a small bedroom overlooking the street. The fax machine was rather hi-tech compared to everything else I was shown at Bakhtar.[11]

However, information, from whatever source, is not always reliable or immediately verifiable, although this does not mean that it should be discounted as the evidence to substantiate it may eventually be discovered. This is particularly true of scorpion tales because, as everyone knows, the scorpion carries a sting in its tail and no one wants to get stung. Media images, impressions and personal narratives are useful for complementing the more limited harder data that is available—although any source is always subject to a scorpion tale or two. This is particularly the case in trying to unravel the puzzle of what drugs mean in Afghanistan—a country that has never had any institutional mechanism for gathering national data in the first place. Certainly all official estimates and figures emanating from Afghanistan, right up to the present day and whether collected by government or international agencies, are subject to wide variation and should be treated with caution. Although they may be useful for indicating general patterns and trends, they are frequently reified into concrete numbers and 'facts' that carry significant political weight, determine social policy and influence foreign attitudes towards Afghans and Afghanistan.

Globally, however, and not without some irony, there are probably more scorpion tales about psychoactive drugs, that vast array of intoxicating substances that have carved their enigmatic trail through human history, than there are circulating in, and about, Afghanistan.

# 1
# Introduction

[Afghanistan] promises mystery, a movement back into time of medieval chivalry and medieval cruelty, an absence of the modern world that is both thrilling and disturbing.[1]

Our country is completely different from those that are 100 years ahead of us. The freedom these Afghans from the West have seen is not suitable for here.[2]

It is more appropriate to consider Afghanistan as a place of enormous complexity that has been subject to a constant state of flux throughout history rather than to view it as somehow caught in a time-warp, with life going on as it has always done.[3]

To outsiders it had seemed more of a fairytale than a real place: it had never been a single country but a historically improbable amalgam of races and cultures, each with its own treasuries of custom, languages and visions of the world, its own saints, heroes and outlaws, an impossible place to understand as a whole.[4]

In trying to describe, understand and explain drug use in Afghanistan useful comparisons and analogies can be made with other areas of the world. The golden chessboard that constitutes the global drug trade is all-encompassing and far-reaching. Apart from Afghanistan, I have worked in the drugs field in several such areas, for example, in southern Africa with Basarwa (Kalahari Bushmen), in Pakistan with Afghan refugees and even in Scotland with the urban dispossessed. Although the cultural contexts may be very different, common patterns and themes inevitably emerge and some aspects remain remarkably similar despite the separation of historical, geographical and cultural distance. This book has been written with a wide readership in mind: the specialist who is interested in drugs and their myriad forms and uses, the academic or development worker looking at the interface between Afghan history, politics and drugs and the general reader who is curious (and concerned) about how 'fragmenting countries show the integrating ones the dark side of their common present'.[5]

Afghanistan itself is a multi-faceted place, consisting historically of several distinct tribal groups with different social structures, hierarchies and styles of political leadership, not to mention culture and customs. It is a country of marked contrasts and complexities. There are still mountain valley communities three or more days' donkey ride from the nearest bazaar, untouched by the Soviet invasion or the tyranny of the Taliban, where life has changed little in centuries. In September 2005, election officials had to hire 1,200 donkeys, 300 horses, 24 camels and nine helicopters just to deliver ballot boxes to the remoter areas of the country. At the other end of the social spectrum, mobile phone shops compete for customers in the congested vehicle-clogged streets of the booming capital Kabul where 4x4s roar past grand new buildings sprouting up like mushrooms, funded (at least partly) by profits from the drug trade and other criminal activities such as extortion, protection racketeering and the diversion of money from international aid programmes.

Some years ago a colleague visited a small village on a high plateau near Kabul in the winter where he sat outside wrapped in a blanket drinking tea with the village headman, similarly clad to keep out the biting cold. A small child ran past wearing only a thin cotton nightdress. Noticing that the child was blue with cold my colleague asked, 'Aren't you concerned that the cold is affecting that child and he might get sick?' The headman laughed, shrugged his shoulders and replied, 'If he is strong he will survive, if he is weak he will die.'

This response was a simple acknowledgement of the harsh reality of daily life in a war-torn country where insecurity, extreme poverty, malnutrition and lack of healthcare is endemic in many areas. Apart from what is left of the close-knit extended family system after decades of war and social dislocation, there are few social safety nets available for the ordinary Afghan.

## THE CRITICAL SOCIAL DIVIDE

At the risk of over-simplification, two of the main competing social forces at work in contemporary Afghanistan can be described as traditional conservative Islam at one end of the spectrum and a more secular liberal modernity, with its emphasis on democratic processes such as the emancipation of women and individual human rights, at the other. Anybody who lives or works in Afghanistan will daily experience the increasing duality and tensions posed by these two competing forces. Abdul Rab al-Rasul Sayyaf is a warlord and founder of the *Ittihad-i-Islami Bara-i Azadi Afghanistan* (Islamic Union for the Freedom of Afghanistan) *mujahideen* group. Based in Paghman a few miles to the west of Kabul he is an elected member of the *Wolesi Jirga*. He is in no doubt about who Afghanistan belongs to. It belongs to the *mujahideen* who fought against the Soviets, not to members of the Afghan diaspora returning from neighbouring countries like Pakistan and Iran, as well as further afield from Australia, Europe and the Americas. Sayyaf urges that:

This nation is a *Mujahid* nation. Stones, trees, rivers, woods, mountains and deserts in this country are *Mujahideen*. This country exists because of the *Mujahideen*. This country was in Russia's throat, before the *Mujahideen* took it back out, by God's mercy. Then it was nearly destroyed by Taliban and terrorists and again the *Mujahideen* saved it. *Mujahideen* do not need posts and money, but the government needs the *Mujahideen*.[6]

An interview with Ismail Khan, the deposed self-styled Emir of Herat, one of the most famous, and probably most prosperous, of the Afghan warlords, provides an answer to the charge of how he feels about being described as a warlord:

During the Soviet invasion, I was called *Ashrar*, during the Taliban regime *Topakai* and now they call me a Warlord. The people who call me that do not have a good understanding of Afghanistan. Undoubtedly, guns shed blood but there is a difference between the gun one raises for protection of one's country and honour and the gun one raises to scare and harass. If we had weapons during the *Jihad*, it was to protect our rights, values, honour, freedom and independence and to ensure the security of our people, not to abuse them.[7]

Significantly, Khan does not say why he, like many other *mujahideen* commanders, retained a large standing army and its weaponry long after the *jihad* against the Soviet invaders had ended and a central government had been established in Kabul. While security of the populace may be one answer, the maintenance of personal power including a private militia secured by the huge profits derived from taxing the lucrative border trade with Iran, is perhaps a more appropriate one.

Nevertheless, both Khan and Sayyaf make the important point that it all depends which side of the ideological fence you are standing on. Looking at Afghanistan through a modern democratic lens, groups defined as warlords are often perceived as predatory violators of human rights who are more likely to prey on communities than to protect them. Many documented examples of this are cited in

Chapter 6. From the more traditional Islamic and pre-modern perspective of the warlords such activities can be rationalised by pointing out that the social relationships and structures of the 'new' Afghanistan as defined by foreigners and Afghan returnees are not the social relationships and structures that they live in, understand or even want.

The fate of Afghanistan will largely be determined by which of these ideologies comes to prevail in the country over the next few decades, or in what manner they become reconciled and integrated. Already some warlords and militia commanders have come to be perceived as legitimate autonomous local leaders, others have been removed from the power bases of their provincial fiefdoms and co-opted to central government posts or elsewhere, and some have been elected to the *Wolesi Jirga*. However, any legitimisation process will have to consider that while 'some of these leaders are responsible, most are old-fashioned warlords—in many cases the very same warlords whose depredations, including toward women, paved the way for the rise of the Taliban'.[8] The parliamentary elections held in September 2005 included 207 'commander-candidates' with their own private militias who had all been identified before the poll. Only 32 of them were disqualified from standing and a significant number of the rest were elected. Others, like Gulbuddin Hekmatyar, had never bought into the new democratic process in the first place.

In 2003 the former Afghan leader Maluvi Younis Khalis (who subsequently died at the age of 87 in July 2006) announced a holy war against US troops in Afghanistan, asking Afghans to resist the 'crusaders' as had their Iraqi brethren. Apart from calling the presidential election in Afghanistan 'a drama', he is also reported as saying, 'A puppet government has been installed in Afghanistan. It does not represent the aspirations of the Afghan nation. We consider struggling and waging a holy war against this government our religious obligation.' He also claimed that foreign 'invaders' had endangered Afghanistan's identity by introducing 'obscenity, vulgarity and an ideology of disbelievers'.[9]

Yunus Qanooni, a senior political and military adviser to the assassinated *mujahideen* leader Ahmad Shah Massoud and the chief rival to Hamid Karzai in the 2004 presidential election, as well as former Education and Interior Minister in the Interim Government and now an elected independent Member of Parliament, believes that the *mujahideen* are crucial to Afghanistan's future. He also believes that 'there is no place for secularism in Afghanistan', although he stresses the progressive and tolerant nature of Islam, rejecting out of hand its repressive reinterpretation by the Taliban.[10]

However, the dynamic of this critical social divide between a relatively westernised urban elite and a rural Afghan tribal society traditionally dominated by mullahs, *maliks* and *khans*, is not new, it started with the modernising reforms that King Habibullah tried to initiate in the early part of the twentieth century. His son Amanullah who succeeded him then began to develop programmes for the reform, secularisation and modernisation of the Afghan state and society until he was deposed by the bandit leader, Bacha-i-Saqao, in 1928.[11] Amanullah had returned from a 'Grand Tour' of several western countries, India, Egypt and Turkey, and had tried to initiate over-ambitious and unrealistic reforms such as the abolition of purdah, monogamy for government employees, a minimum age for marriage and curtailment of the mullahs' power. At the time one popularly held explanation given for this deviation from Afghan Islamic tradition was that Amanullah had embraced Catholicism during the tour and 'had become deranged through drinking alcohol and eating pork'.[12]

## ACROSS THE CULTURAL DIVIDE

The continuing polarity between the rules and regulations that govern human rights-based secular modernisation and the customs and traditions of conservative Islam was exemplified by the furore over the publication of a bestselling book by the Norwegian journalist Asne Seierstad called *The Bookseller of Kabul*.[13] While conducting research on the bookseller in question, Mohammad Shah Rais, whose books had been looted by the *mujahideen* and burned by both the communists and the Taliban, Seierstad was invited into his home as a guest with no restrictions placed on her with regard to which family members she could talk to. In her own words she became 'bi-gendered' with equal access to both the separate male and female worlds of the Afghan family. The resultant book mainly provided a detailed account of the social relationships in the family with Shah appearing as 'a cruel, tyrannical patriarch' who treated the women of his family like chattels and his sister as 'a virtual slave'.[14] It is a document, according to another journalist, of 'the appalling subjugation of Afghan women, their cultural invisibility, the hardship of their lives', although at the same time, 'Seierstad seems not to understand anything about Afghan pride or the social ruination of dishonour'.[15] Shah, understandably, felt let down by what he saw as a betrayal of trust, and accused Seierstad of impugning and defaming not only himself but the entire Afghan nation and he sued her in the European courts for compensation and damages.

Interestingly, it has been suggested that Seierstad's excessive use of journalistic licence may have led to her spinning a few scorpion tales of her own. A Norwegian professor of anthropology and Middle Eastern studies, Unni Wikan, has suggested that some of the book may not be authentic as it is doubtful that such insights into 'hearts and minds' was possible. Furthermore, 'she has revealed the secrets of the women which is shameful and dishonourable. It will be regarded as an affront for its lack of respect for Afghans and Muslims.'[16] Who knows what the consequences of such revelations may be for Shah and his family, now easily identifiable and open to gossip and ridicule.

This conflict between Seierstad and Shah symbolises the problem, and the unintended consequences, of interpreting Afghan cultural traditions and practices through the lens of a modern human rights perspective. While universal human rights are to be fully endorsed and respected, in many developing countries like Afghanistan they may make little sense, as concepts based on individualism may be culturally inappropriate, if not nonsensical and politically non-viable. Rights in such societies are more likely to centre on the extended family, the community and the tribe and the rights of the individual are not perceived as paramount. For most Afghans, human rights, as understood by people in the west, remain a distant and abstract notion. At the same time, it is hypocritical of the west to preach human rights for Afghanistan when the US has so flagrantly breached them in its treatment of individual prisoners at Bagram and other military prisons in Afghanistan (see Chapter 6 on outlaws and warlords), not to mention the unarmed civilians, including women and children, killed by US bombing in Bibi Mahru, Kili Sarnad, Lashkargah and Takhta-Pul, for example, during Operation Enduring Freedom. In May 2006 further coalition bombing resulted in the death of over 30 civilians in Azizi village to the west of Qandahar, an action unlikely to convert many Afghan villagers to western ideas about what constitutes human rights.

Another cultural event that symbolised the ideological struggle for Afghanistan's heart and mind was the entry of Vidsa Samadzai as Miss Afghanistan in the Miss Earth beauty pageant held in Manila in November 2003. Her onstage appearance in a bright red bikini caused outrage in Afghanistan and prompted the Minister of Women's Affairs to denounce Samadzai's actions as 'lascivious' and 'not representing Afghan women'.[17] A member of the Supreme Court in Kabul stated that her appearance in a bikini was completely unacceptable and unlawful in Islam, and the Afghan government, through its embassy in Washington, lost no time in publicly stating that her appearance in the pageant had not been authorised by them. Fears were expressed that Vidsa could have unwittingly undermined the cause of women's emancipation in Afghanistan as well as endorsing widespread perceptions of the moral corruption and excessive freedoms of western democracy.[18] In a country where most social events and celebrations are segregated by gender, all post-primary schools are single sex, the majority of marriages are arranged and women are still in purdah and shrouded from men who are not close relatives, this is hardly surprising.

## MEDIA WARS

A further example of this ideological struggle is the ongoing media war, where new innovative TV stations show programmes denounced by the more conservative members of the community, along with government officials. The Kabul-based TV station Tolo has been at the cutting edge by presenting MTV-style music shows, fashion shows and western films, with young male and female presenters working together on-screen. Tolo is rightly proud of its investigative journalism and has covered hitherto taboo news topics such as paedophilia, the power of warlords, illegal logging and corruption in government. In March 2005, Afghanistan's *Ulema shura* criticised Tolo and other TV stations for showing inappropriate programmes 'opposed to Islam and national values'.[19] Two months later a young female presenter, Shaima Rezayee, who had been forced to resign from her job at Tolo under pressure from clerics, was gunned down in Kabul, a real-life victim of the country's culture wars. A young male presenter, Shakeb Isaar, also received death threats from the Taliban and al-Qaeda, and Chief Justice Fazl-e Hadi Shinwari, branded him 'a corrupter of youth'. One of the founders of the programme, Mohammad Mohseni, made the following point: 'Look at the demographics of this country, it has one of the youngest populations in the world. The old conservatives fear becoming irrelevant. A few years down the line and they will have lost most of their power.'[20] This remains to be seen, a new generation of conservatives may well replace the old.

Human Rights Watch has reported that members of the press and the media generally have been harassed, intimidated and threatened in Afghanistan. Journalists have been physically attacked and some threatened with death as retribution for past and future publications and broadcasts. Such attacks 'have led to self-censorship as many journalists have decided not to publish critical or objective articles'.[21] In October 2005, the editor of a magazine called *Haqoq-e-Zan* (Women's Rights), Ali Mohaqiq, was jailed for two years for questioning Islamic law. Articles he had written that were critical of the harshness of some interpretations of the law were considered blasphemous, such as a provision that someone found guilty of adultery be sentenced to 100 lashes and that giving up Islam was a crime that should be punished by death. Mohaqiq was arrested after the Supreme Court sent a letter to the public prosecutor's office, also signed by the *Ulema shura*, complaining about him.[22] In February 2006, one of Kabul's four private TV stations, Afghan TV, was fined $1,000 by a special media commission, headed by the Minister of Information, Culture and Tourism, for screening 'un-Islamic' material. By that time two of the other stations, Tolo and Ariana, had established offices to control and self-censor their broadcasts, and Tolo blanked the screen during risqué music videos and films, mainly from India.[23] In June 2006 Afghan intelligence services issued a list of directives to Afghan journalists (international journalists were excluded) banning them from criticising the US-led coalition, representing the Afghan armed forces as weak or criticising the government's foreign policy.[24]

A central issue, then, is how realistic is it for a society steeped in such conservative traditions, laws and customs to adapt and change to a more modern democratic rights-based polity. While it has taken western countries hundreds of years to undergo a (continuing) process of democratisation and establish rights for women and other marginalised groups there is a western expectation that this can be achieved in countries like Afghanistan in little more than a few decades, or worse, that the process can somehow be fast-tracked. In terms of future political structures various possibilities exist, although it is likely that if international armed forces leave in the foreseeable future the country will relapse into some form of civil war.

Differing scenarios have been put forward by the ex-Finance Minister and now Vice-Chancellor of Kabul University, Ashraf Ghani, who has starkly outlined three of the leading contenders: (1) the country will become stable, relatively prosperous and western-friendly with a strong rule of law and internal disintegration and conflict a fading memory as the economy is driven by a growing private sector; (2) the country will become yet another 'failed state' lurching from crisis to crisis, stagnating in poverty and unable to repay its international debt; (3) the country will become a narco-mafia state, with all trade and industry, including drug production, controlled by criminal syndicates both Afghan and foreign, where there will be extreme disparities between the few rich and the mass of the poor and militias will continue to protect, and fight over the economic interests of the various 'mafias'.[25] But in trying to predict the future of Afghanistan, as Barnet Rubin has stated, 'There are too many imponderables.'[26] It would take a very large crystal ball indeed to predict what the country will look like even a few years from now.*

Afghanistan is yet again at a crucial juncture in its history, ready to choose, or have chosen for it through the influence and political machinations of external forces, some permutation of life between conservative Islamic tribalism at one extreme and consumer-driven secular modernism at the other. While over the last 15 years of internecine violence between a bewildering array of warring factions Afghans have already had a taste of one end of the continuum, they are only now beginning to taste, as well as resist, the other end, so aptly described by that great traveller and explorer of Islamic countries, Wilfred Thesiger:

The long-term effect of US culture as it spreads to every nook and cranny in every desert and every mountain valley will be the end of mankind. Our extraordinary greed for material possessions, the ways we go about nurturing that greed, the lack of balance in our lives, and our cultural arrogance will kill us off within a century unless we learn to stop and think. It may be too late.[27]

## CONTINUING DUALITIES

There are other related dualities to be found in Afghanistan. As Bergen (2001) suggests, there can be little doubt that many Afghans still

---

* To give but one example: the week I sent this manuscript to the publishers it was announced that the government was considering re-establishing the notorious Ministry of Enforcement of Virtue and Suppression of Vice originally set up by the Taliban, most likely to appease the conservative lobby. This would undoubtedly impact negatively on perceptions and treatment of problem drug users and push drug use further underground, making contact with drug users in need of help, particularly injectors, more difficult.

subscribe to a double-edged code of social behaviour not found in western societies, or indeed in many developing ones. On the one hand, Afghans are among the most polite and hospitable people on earth; on the other, they are a proud, ruthless and unyielding enemy if slighted or provoked:

They will carry hospitality to embarrassing extremes, but are implacable as enemies. If there has been an overriding feature of their history, it is that it has been a history of conflict—of invasions, battles and sieges, of vendettas, assassinations and massacres, of tribal feuding, dynastic strife and civil war.[28]

One British traveller journeying through Afghanistan in 1783 suggested that Afghans were 'generally addicted to a state of predatory warfare'.[29] Like Scotland, where 'Highland hospitality was traditionally inviolable, whatever the bitterness between guest and host',[30] *Pashtoonwali*, the Pashtoon code of conduct, is centred round hospitality and sanctuary, as well as revenge and retribution, particularly for insults to family honour that frequently result in blood feuds.

Afghanistan has long been a victim, as well as a resolute and brutal defender, of its strategic geographic position bridging the crossroads of south and central Asia. Unfortunately it has rarely been left alone to determine its fate, least of all by its immediate neighbours Iran, Pakistan and the central Asian states. Other foreign powers, the British in the nineteenth century, the Soviets in the twentieth century and now the Americans in the twenty-first century have all used force to try and build strategic partnerships with Afghanistan, peddling their various brands of civilisation, imperialism and ideology in the process. While invasions by outsiders have frequently resulted in feuding groups within the country banding together against a common enemy, old enmities and feuds are soon resumed after the invaders have been vanquished.

It has also been argued that the characteristics of modern *mujahideen* and militia groups, such as 'charismatic leadership, fierce local loyalties, shifting alliances, guerrilla tactics, gritty endurance and inborn xenophobia', originated with Bactrian warlords combating Alexander the Great and his forces over 2,000 years ago.[31] At that time, with a foreign empire stretching through Egypt, Turkey, Syria, Iraq and Iran, Alexander had to leave his largest army of occupation in what is now Afghanistan. Over 40 per cent of his infantry and over 95 per cent of his cavalry posted to foreign garrisons were left in Bactria (modern-day Balkh) in an attempt to pacify local warlords.

Tactics stemming from this period have been honed over the centuries and are still extant today, typifying the campaigns of modern Afghan militants: 'the element of surprise, the avoidance of warfare waged from a fixed position, the use of terror, the exploitation of weather and terrain, the application of primitive technologies to achieve unexpected results'.[32]

Even the national Afghan game of *buzkashi*, where two teams involving hundreds of horsemen chase a headless goat carcass around a large field, has been interpreted as a metaphor for chaotic, uninhibited and uncontrollable competition among Afghans, particularly in the political arena, as well as a commemoration of cultural heritage. As the original author of this metaphor, American anthropologist Whitney Azoy, explains, his view of the country offended some Afghanophiles because they were 'confounded by the emphasis on aggression, opportunism and maximisation of spoils'. However, as succinctly suggested in the preface to the second edition of his book, *Buzkashi: Game and Power in Afghanistan*, while *buzkashi* does not represent all of Afghan experience, it serves as 'an apt metaphor for ongoing political chaos since 1978'. Certainly it would be delusional to neglect it. As Azoy says, 'delusion will only invite a continuation of Afghanistan's agony'.[33]

Flying back to Dubai from Islamabad in August 1998, I sat next to a young Pakistani businessman who was in the oil business in the Gulf States. We started chatting, and I explained that I had intended to travel to Afghanistan to complete a consultancy for UNDCP but had been thwarted by the Americans who had reached there first as their Cruise missiles crashed into terrorist training camps outside Jalalabad in reprisal for the bombing of American targets in east Africa. Instead, I had spent the time in Peshawar interviewing drug users and NGO staff before being evacuated back to Islamabad. 'Ah!' he replied, 'The Afghan, your best friend and your worst enemy.'

While subscribing to such national stereotypes may be a dubious and sometimes dangerous pastime, this phrase neatly encapsulates the polar complexities of the Afghan character paraphrased by Bergen as 'medieval chivalry and medieval cruelty'. As Bergen further points out, there is in Afghanistan 'an absence of the modern world that is both thrilling and disturbing' that can easily seduce westerners into over-romanticised notions about the country and its people. While one female western journalist reported that, 'from schoolboys at play to University students, Cabinet Ministers to legendary commanders, Afghans were quieter, gentler and more self-contained than Americans',[34] she fortunately had not been privy to the other more martial side of the Afghan character, unlike many of her Afghan sisters who continue to suffer at the hands of warlords, commanders, their militias, and corrupt police.

## GLOBAL CONSIDERATIONS

While this book can do little justice to the complexities of the political dramas and the extent of human suffering performed on Afghanistan's stage over the past three decades, it seeks to illuminate the many seemingly unrelated and disparate, yet interdependent, factors that need to be considered to reach an understanding of the complexities of drugs and their uses in such a context. Inevitably it has to take liberties with the truth, a commodity hard to grasp in a country where scorpion tales abound and the boundaries between fact and fiction are frequently blurred. Public truth remains where it has always been, on the shadowy margins between media images and the ideologies of the powerful. The book's main purpose is to try and clarify what drugs mean in Afghanistan and to the people who consume them, why they use them, and the types of problems that arise from their consumption.

To understand how and why drugs are consumed by increasing numbers of Afghans it is also necessary to provide a glimpse of the convoluted dynamics and processes involved in the cultivation of opium and cannabis, the production and trafficking of heroin and hashish, the importation and availability of other psychoactive substances, and a brief description of the outlaw territory that is Afghanistan. Increasingly there is recognition that in the matter of drug control, both supply and demand issues are inextricably linked, as are producer and consumer countries. And while the demand for drugs stimulates supply, the availability of drugs creates a demand as more people use them and become dependent on them.[35] The consequences of these dynamics and processes reach far beyond the borders of Afghanistan. Through no accident of history it is a country whose tragic past shows us, as Rubin so eloquently states, 'the dark side of our common present' and, just perhaps, our common future. There are lessons to be learned here for drug control policies and strategies that stretch far beyond the boundaries of Afghanistan.

Indeed, Afghanistan holds up a mirror to the developed world and the anomalies and paradoxes inherent in its drug policies. For the better part of a century international drug control has been dominated by a western model based on prohibition and the criminalisation of drugs and those who use them. Punishment and imprisonment have been the lot of those caught in possession of substances defined as illegal. A criminalised economy and the rise of mafias and organised crime groups involved in drug trafficking and associated corruption and violence to protect illicit enterprises the result.

As a consequence of prohibition-based policies, in the US over 2 million Americans are currently incarcerated for non-violent drug offences, with over 1.5 million arrested each year for similar offences—more per capita than any other country in the world. Annually the drug war costs US taxpayers around $69 billion and there is a growing anti-prohibition lobby, including the organisation LEAP, consisting of current and former members of law enforcement who support drug regulation rather than prohibition. As LEAP say in their mission statement:

Despite all the lives we have destroyed and all the money so ill spent, today illicit drugs are cheaper, more potent, and far easier to get than they were 35 years ago at the beginning of the war on drugs. Meanwhile, people continue dying in our streets while drug barons and terrorists continue to grow richer than ever before. We would suggest that this scenario must be the very definition of a failed public policy.[36]

Even in Scotland the futility of prohibition is recognised by powerful groups such as the Strathclyde Police Federation which represents nearly all the 7,500 rank and file police officers in the area. In April 2006 the Federation called for the legalisation and licensing of all drugs including Class A drugs, such as heroin and cocaine, under the UK Misuse of Drugs Act.[37] At the same time, over 3,000 UK troops were preparing to head for Helmand province in southern Afghanistan, part of their mission being to support Afghan soldiers in the task of eradicating opium poppy fields and destroying heroin laboratories. Helmand produces nearly 20 per cent of the world's illicit opium. The effects of such a war against opium farmers and the inevitable rise of drug trafficking mafias will be explored in Chapters 4 and 5.

One of the main inconsistencies in global drug control policy is that its definition of 'drugs' does not include alcohol. As in all other Islamic states, Afghanistan has long considered alcohol one of the most harmful and forbidden intoxicating drugs, yet to the non-Muslim world it remains socially acceptable, infinitely available and legally profitable. Conversely, opium and cannabis, two of the three main drugs considered harmful and prohibited by UN conventions and international drug policy, have been used in Afghanistan for centuries for medicinal, cultural and recreational purposes. Chapters 9, 10 and 11 will consider the uses and misuses of opium, its derivative heroin, cannabis preparations and other psychoactive drugs such as alcohol and methamphetamines.

Those who use use illicit substances, whether in Afghanistan or elsewhere, are at the dubious mercy of traffickers and have no access to quality controlled regulated products that would help to minimise any resultant harm. Indeed, one of the challenges to the dominant prohibitionist paradigm is a public health model that recognises that many people who consume drugs are victims of circumstances such as impoverishment, war, social dislocation, conflict and insecurity. In Afghanistan, still 'a nation in anguish' as Chapter 3 illustrates, many people self-medicate with a range of psychoactive substances as a way of coping with chronic mental health problems such as anxiety, depression and PTSD. Ironically, such problems also exist, and are even increasing, in wealthy western societies. In the UK it has been estimated that 15 per cent of the population suffer from depression or anxiety,[38] and in April 2006 the Mental Health Foundation highlighted the use of alcohol to self-medicate emotional trauma, with 36 per cent of men and 16 per cent of women drinking above recommended limits and classed as having an alcohol use disorder. National Opinion Poll research carried out for the Mental Health Foundation found that 40 per cent of people drink alcohol to feel less anxious, 26 per cent to deal with depression and 30 per cent 'to forget their problems'.[39]

Apart from drugs like alcohol and cannabis and opium products, in a world perceived as increasingly fragile and unstable there is also a growing demand for the wide range of painkillers and tranquillisers produced by multinational pharmaceutical companies. While such drugs are marketed and sold through medical prescription in the west, it is in the largely unregulated and uncontrolled markets of the developing world that they are most likely to be misused, causing serious problems for consumers. Chapter 11 will explore the vagaries of the global pharmaceutical market and how they affect countries like Afghanistan.

Most importantly, much international discourse on 'the drug problem' is permeated by misinformation and dubious logic, or what LEAP calls 'drug war distortions'.[40] In the world of drugs all is not as it would seem. The types of scorpion tales to be found in Afghanistan have much in common with those to be found in other settings, reflecting the paradoxes and ambiguities underpinning global drug policy. This is no more so than in definitions and measurements of what constitutes the drug problem itself.

# 2
# Scorpion Tales

Because politicians demand figures, figures are produced but these often have very little to do with reality. At best they represent an overestimation or under-estimation of the true position, at worst a complete fiction.[1]

Estimates of drug consumption may be the most politicised and inaccurate of all modern statistics. As noted ever so wryly in a 1976 report of the House Select Committee on Narcotics Abuse, 'There is an old axiom which originated in the League of Nations...that a nation has as many addicts as it chooses to discover.'[2]

Addiction concepts have become a commonplace in storytelling, offering a secular equivalent for possession as an explanation of how a good person can behave badly, and as an inner demon over which a hero can triumph.[3]

The proverbial hospitality of the Afghans is also a form of defensive screen... The foreigner finds himself confronted by an endless series of evasions, procrastinations and side-stepping of the issue. The person who is responsible is always somewhere else, the horses are in the mountains and the truth is in the depths of the well.[4]

Scorpion tales are frequently found in journalistic accounts from Afghanistan, as the hard evidence needed to substantiate a story in such an insecure and often dangerous environment can be difficult to come by and 'facts' difficult to verify. It is highly unlikely that any journalist would ever have to invoke the right of qualified privilege in defence of their stories from Afghanistan. One news report from October 2002 alleged that the amount spent by the British government during the spring of that year on compensating opium poppy farmers in Nangarhar province in eastern Afghanistan for destroying their opium crop was between £25 and £37 million of British taxpayers' money. The article further alleged that the NGO sub-contracted to survey the land under poppy cultivation, used as the measure for compensation, was headed by a man whose cousin, Haji Rohullah, was the leader of an extreme Wahabbist sect in Wardak province adjacent to Nangarhar. Rohullah had previously been arrested in August 2002 by the US military for his alleged connections to al-Qaeda. The article concluded with a definite sting in the tail by posing the question of 'whether much of the British money may have been directed to al-Qaeda or its sympathisers'.[5] Such allegations based on speculation and guilt by association may have been responsible for this particular tale never receiving broader media coverage at the time. Nevertheless, journalistic accounts can alert us to issues and problems that can benefit from further investigation and research, just as the media moves off in its never-ending quest for new headlines and soundbites.

Afghanistan is naturally rife with hard-to-verify scorpion tales, and not just about drugs. People living in a country that has experienced almost continuous war, internecine conflict, social disruption and insecurity for over a quarter of a century develop out of necessity a wide range of survival strategies and tactics. Distorting, downplaying or exaggerating news or information for reasons of self-interest, self-benefit or self-preservation is understandably the norm. Many Afghans have become economic and political opportunists, as well as creative and innovative entrepreneurs, in order just to survive. If this includes changing or bending any perceived truth to their own advantage, then so be it. It has been suggested that for many years Afghans have lived in *Dar-ul-harb*, 'the house of war', where everything is considered military, although based on religious grounds. In such a context it is permissible to lie in order to deceive your enemy, something forbidden in ordinary life.[6] In such circumstances a few scorpion tales are only to be expected.

It has also been suggested that Afghans have learned how to redefine themselves within whichever social category is currently benefiting from foreign aid at the time. How to distinguish between a widow with no family support and a widow from a wealthier extended family network not in need of aid or support?[7] How many ex-combatants who have joined the national army and police remain loyal to the central state and how many retain their loyalty and allegiance to the clan, tribe, militia group or past commander?

## THE DATA VACUUM

In Afghanistan good research data has largely been replaced by 'the swopping of anecdotes': basically there has been a black hole as far as accurate information is concerned.[8] Even in 1980, just after the war started with the Soviet invaders, it was claimed that statistics on

Afghanistan were 'wild guesses based on inadequate data'.[9] A report published in 2002 suggested that

Afghanistan is one of the least researched countries in the world. A dearth of pre-war data, the inherent difficulties of conducting research in a war zone and the low priority accorded to Afghanistan before 9/11 by the international community have all contributed to this problem.[10]

The first ever UN National Human Development Report for Afghanistan in 2004 also stressed that, apart from security concerns, gathering data from provinces and villages was hampered by logistical difficulties such as an absence of roads, networks, knowledge and know-how on survey techniques.[11] Afghanistan is a country that is only now in the process of being popularly discovered by the international community.

A weekly newspaper that started in Kabul in 2002 contained a prominent column entitled 'People say…' acknowledging that much public debate in Afghanistan is conducted on the basis of rumour, innuendo and gossip. A copy of the paper printed on 5 December 2002 had 14 examples of 'People say…' To cite but two: 'People say—A very small part of the drugs and narcotics captured by security officials are burnt and the remaining part is sold again', and 'People say—Armed men are taking money from people for various reasons in many districts of Logar province.'[12]

This lack of reliable data has undoubtedly acted as a barrier to a comprehensive understanding and analysis of many pressing issues, as well as the development of realistic and culturally appropriate policies desperately needed to tackle the country's many serious socioeconomic problems. In part, the lack of any pre-war quantitative or 'hard' data, particularly from rural areas, can be attributed to the Afghan state at that time being largely dependent on external rather than internal revenue. This resulted in the rural economy and lifestyle remaining 'statistically unknown' and largely neglected by central government – to the extent, that is, that any effective central government authority existed outside the capital Kabul.[13] In several areas of the country effective central government authority and control continue to be tenuous at best.

## HOW MUCH DRUG USE?

The prevalence of drug use in Afghanistan, except for a very few areas, still remains unknown, although this does not mean to say that attempts have not been made to measure what is extremely difficult to measure with any real accuracy. In neighbouring Iran, with a much more developed infrastructure than Afghanistan, a psychiatrist has argued that 'Attaining a definite estimate of prevalence and incidence of substance abuse in Iran is not possible. Social stigmatization along with legal restrictions on substance abuse prevents drug users from admitting their act, offering clear data and referring to governmental sectors.'[14] Even in the US, with a well-resourced and professional research base, it is difficult to accurately measure illicit drug use. The government relies on surveys to determine the level of use and its own National Research Council has suggested that under-reporting is common because illicit drug use is a heavily stigmatised illegal activity: 'The existing drug use monitoring systems and programs of research are useful for some important purposes, yet they are strikingly inadequate to support the full range of policy decisions that the nation must make.'[15]

In July 2001 the Talib head of Qandahar DCCU, Alhaj Mufti Abdul Hakim, claimed that the DCCU had identified 6,000 persons 'seriously suffering of drug addiction' requiring urgent rehabilitation and 25,000 addicts at different stages of addiction who also required rehabilitation 'but have not yet reached that stage'. An undefined 'special methodology', not uncommon in Afghanistan, was used to identify these drug addicts, then came a plea for funding to establish a health clinic in Qandahar for the rehabilitation of drug addicts in the southwest region.*

From previous experiences with the Taliban, however, it can be safely assumed that their figures were suspect and that a substantial percentage of any such funding would have been diverted into their own pockets, irrespective of how many drug users required treatment.

In early 2001 a small grant was given by the UNDCP to the Taliban-led DCCU in Kabul to upgrade the drug dependency treatment Centre of the city's mental health hospital and to check whether the DCCU would be able to implement such a project before considering any future funding. The grant was intended to buy medicines for use during detoxification, as well as basic resources such as beds, mattresses and pillows. Some medical equipment was also provided

---

* A similar special methodology has also been used by regional powerbrokers who have not only encouraged poppy cultivation in areas under their control to attract development assistance, but have also exaggerated levels of poppy eradication in order to try and attract more assistance.

and three quotations were produced by the DCCU for all intended purchases. Arriving in Kabul in May 2001 to visit the centre, the first thing I did was to ask the recovering drug users if they had any complaints. To a man, they all pointed downwards to the beds and mattresses that they were lying on. The beds were simple metal frames with carelessly sawn wooden slats lying across them. These were the same beds that had been invoiced as 'orthopaedic beds' costing $115 each. More disturbing was the state of the mattresses that were of very poor quality and hardly half the width of a standard single bed, yet had been costed at $35 each. The patients were obviously having difficulty even lying on them, never mind resting comfortably or sleeping.

It was important that the Taliban be confronted about this and a colleague went to see the Deputy Head of the DCCU to complain, as Mullah Akhundzada was in Herat at the time. His reply was: 'You know Jehanzeb, you are a lucky man, nobody has spoken to me like this before, but I like you...' Although the threat was veiled it was serious and we felt it judicious not to pursue the matter, apart from insisting on the purchase of new mattresses that duly arrived a month later. In 2002, government investigators and auditors collected $3.8 million lost through fraudulent practices and retrieved from officials under the Taliban regime who, in spite of their 'often chaotic image', seemed to have kept good financial records.[16]

## DEFINITIONS, DEFINITIONS

While the truth may be distorted by personal agendas and vested interests, another major problem in trying to measure and understand drug use in Afghanistan, as well as other countries, is the definition of 'addiction' and what constitutes a 'drug addict', a 'drug misuser' or a 'drug abuser'. Many drug users in countries like Afghanistan and neighbouring Pakistan, even first-time users, are commonly referred to as 'addicts' when they may not be clinically dependent on drugs at all. As far back as the 1960s the WHO recommended that the term 'dependence' should replace 'addiction' and 'habituation', as dependence can exist in different degrees of severity, unlike addiction which tends to be seen as an 'all or nothing' disease.[17] As the WHO itself recognises, addiction continues to be a commonly used term by both professionals and the general public.[18]

Although some find it cumbersome to adopt, the term 'problem drug user' is much less pejorative and dehumanising than the more moralistic labels of 'addict', 'abuser' and 'misuser' and helps the drug user to retain some sense of humanity, self-worth and dignity. There are several different definitions of what constitutes problem drug use. One very focused and specific definition of the term is the 'intravenous or long-duration/regular use of opiates, cocaine and/or amphetamines'.[19] However, a more inclusive and broader definition of the problem drug user developed by the UK's Advisory Council on the Misuse of Drugs in 1982 is: 'Any person who experiences social, psychological, physical or legal problems related to intoxication and/or the regular excessive consumption and/or dependence as a consequence of his own use of drugs or other chemical substances.'[20]

This latter definition seems more appropriate, particularly in an impoverished country like Afghanistan, as it acknowledges the wide range of serious problems that can be associated with the use of different types of drugs, both in the short term and the long term. Such problems constitute not only the more obvious health-related ones, but extend to financial, social, legal and spiritual ones as well. Why stigmatise 38-year-old Sumera, who now lives in Kabul with the remnants of her war-shattered family, by labelling her a drug abuser? A widow who has seen her husband, brother and two of her sons killed in the fighting that has wracked the country, she is now dependent on opium and tranquillisers just to cope with the daily struggle of trying to bring up her four remaining children. This is not to deny that drug use is adding to her problems, but there is little to be gained by adding further stigma and shame to her burden by using labels like 'drug abuser' or 'drug addict' with the attendant risk of compounding her social exclusion as a widow who is head of a household without family support.

Keeping in mind such problems with definitions around drug use and that accurate measurement relies on a sound understanding of the quality being measured, throughout this book terms for problematic drug use will be used interchangeably. This reflects the different language used by different authors and, concomitantly, their own attitudes to drugs and the people who use them. However, when such concepts as 'addiction', 'dependency' and 'problem drug use', never mind the word 'drug' itself, are translated into other languages then assumed meanings can change. In Afghanistan the word *mothad* means an addict, with *poderi* commonly used to refer to a heroin addict. This latter term carries a definite stigma and has recently appeared because there was no word for someone who used a drug in powder form like heroin, commonly referred to as *poder*.

## FIGURES FROM AFGHANISTAN

In July 2003 the UNODC published an assessment of problem drug use in Kabul city. The report stressed that the lowest estimated number of drug users in Kabul as reported by drug users and key informants such as doctors, police, shopkeepers and mullahs was 62,643. This represented 23,995 hashish users, 14,298 users of pharmaceutical drugs, 10,774 opium users, 7,008 heroin users and 6,568 alcohol users. The report was careful to emphasise that the total figure was likely to represent a substantial underestimate, as many of those interviewed only provided estimates for the locality of the city where they lived and not for the larger target area that they had been requested to provide information about. Responsibly and realistically they did not feel able to provide estimates for areas of the city that they were not familiar with. Neither were they able to make judgements about who was a drug user and who was a problem drug user, although the inference was that anybody who used drugs had problems related to that use.

At the press conference for the release of the report a journalist exclaimed: 'These figures are ridiculous, there are 40,000 taxi drivers in Kabul and they all use hashish!' Not surprisingly he was unable to substantiate such an assertion with any evidence.

Nevertheless, he had a valid point. How can an accurate measurement be made of the number of problem drug users in a city like Kabul where no significant official public records are kept and drug use is largely a hidden activity? One reviewer noted that while the report provided valuable ethnographic information about qualitative aspects of drug use, 'The data on prevalence in the report obtained from both drug users and key informants would perhaps be better left unpublished.'[21] Given the way such figures were also misinterpreted by the media and public officials, frequently to become the commonly cited scorpion tale that 'there are 60,000 drug addicts in Kabul', this comment was somewhat prescient.

The figure of '60,000 addicts' has also been mistakenly extended to obtain a prevalence figure for the whole country. The logic is simple: if there are 60,000 addicts in Kabul with a population of 3–4 million (as far as this can be ascertained with any accuracy), then in Afghanistan with a population of around 24 million there must be 480,000 addicts. It is just a case of simple arithmetic, with such extrapolated figures being used as hard facts in many a debate about the country's 'drug addiction problem'. At one meeting of senior officials in Kabul a colleague heard a Deputy Minister state categorically that 'there are 60,000 drug addicts in Afghanistan'. He had obviously forgotten to do his sums correctly.

Another UNODC report published in February 2001 provided estimates of problem drug use in five adjacent rural districts in eastern Afghanistan, Khak-e-Jabar in Kabul province, Azro in Logar province, Hesarak in Nangarhar province, and Gardez and Sayed-Karam in Paktia province.[22] Again this report clearly noted the problems in trying to estimate prevalence rates in Afghanistan, particularly under a Taliban regime that was known to persecute drug users, thus forcing drug use to become an even more secretive and hidden activity. The report stressed that the resultant figures were likely to be an underestimation and that the traditional use of opium for medicinal purposes would be unlikely to be perceived or reported as a form of problem drug use, even though it was a common practice and could easily lapse into problematic use and dependency. Nevertheless, these cautionary warnings did not prevent the UNODC two years later from comparing its own limited data on 'opium abuse' (even though the study was emphatically about problem drug use) in 'Eastern Afghanistan' with national rates of 'abuse of opiates' in countries as diverse as Iran, North America, the Russian Federation and Pakistan. The resultant table provided a mish-mash of incomparable and largely meaningless data. Five districts out of nearly 50 in eastern Afghanistan were hardly representative or comparable with national data from countries with populations of well over 100 million. To cap this, the table, although ostensibly comparing rates of 'abuse of opiates among the adult population', in the case of central Asian countries contained data that included estimates of problem drug use that combined opiates with other drugs.[23]

## THE SEVEN DEADLY POLITICAL SINS

It is, of course, not only in Afghanistan that suspect methodologies and distortions of dubious facts contribute to the dearth of reliable information about the magnitude and nature of the drug problem. Professor Cindy Fazey, who worked for several years with the UNDCP at its headquarters in Vienna as one of the organisation's first demand reduction specialists, claims that globally many governments 'obscure the reality of the world situation of drug use and abuse' for a wide variety of reasons that she astutely encapsulates as the seven deadly political sins. Indeed, Fazey suggests that these sins may even be unavoidable due to the type of pressure put on the UN by representatives of member states of the CND for countries to provide information that they 'do not have, cannot give, do not want to give or do not have the resources to collect'.[24]

The first sin, 'the politics of necessity—or desperation', refers to the fact that many countries in the developing world have more pressing concerns than trying to find out the number of problem drug users and what to do with them. Until very recently this has certainly been the case with Afghanistan, a country beset by a vast range of disparate problems such as drought, malnutrition, grinding poverty, large numbers of armed ex-combatants, armed conflict and continuing insecurity for the majority of the population—not to mention the international focus on drug cultivation, production and trafficking. Although mental health, and related problem drug use, has now climbed to third place after mother–child health and communicable diseases on the list of priorities of the Ministry of Public Health, there are still few resources available to provide basic primary healthcare services across the nation, never mind specialist drug treatment services.

Another sin is 'the politics of corruption', typified by countries where politicians are either directly or indirectly involved in illicit activities, particularly the drug trade. In these cases politicians and others in powerful positions, such as the military, may try and divert attention away from their own criminal activities by maintaining that there is no drug problem or that it is not as bad as others, often outsiders, claim. In Afghanistan some commanders and local officials have been known to claim there is no drug problem in their area, while themselves benefiting from the supply of drugs to the local population. Staff of an NGO in Kabul offering services to women and children with drug problems have reported that situated next door to their centre is the house of a police inspector who is also the main neighbourhood drug dealer, selling heroin, opium and hashish to the centre's clients.

The process of denial constitutes yet another deadly sin, in which drug-producing countries in the developing world counter western blame for contributing to their drug problems by claiming that if there was no demand in these countries then there would be no supply. This is pertinent in the case of Afghanistan, where in the mid-1990s the Taliban authorities were initially more concerned with stopping hashish production than opium production on the grounds that opium, when refined into heroin, was a 'western problem' driven by demand mainly from European countries. Hashish, on the other hand, was perceived as the traditional Afghan vice and therefore merited more draconian sanctions against both producers and consumers. At that time, there was a denial that opium and heroin were already beginning to cause problems for many drug users in different parts of the country. Ironically, there were several reports of hashish users in Afghanistan moving directly to heroin use because the fumes of heroin smoke were much less pungent than those of hashish, thus reducing the risk of being traced, arrested and punished by *al-Amr bi al-Ma'ruf wa al-Nahi 'an al-Munkir* (the Ministry of Enforcement of Virtue and Suppression of Vice), the dreaded 'Religious police' of the Taliban.*

Even after the Taliban had dispersed following the US-led Operation Enduring Freedom, in April 2002 at a drug demand reduction seminar for members of the new post-Taliban SHCDC in Kabul, based on UNDCP initial assessments of the drug problem in Afghan communities, there was a distinct process of denial. Most participants believed that while there were serious drug problems in neighbouring countries like Iran, Pakistan and Tajikistan, Afghanistan itself didn't have a drug problem. Fazey also suggests that 'The admission by a country that it may have a drug problem is seen, sometimes, as some kind of moral failure—hence the "total denial"—and that the authorities have failed to control the situation.' This also happens at district and local levels. During the UNDCP assessment of problem drug use in rural eastern Afghanistan in 2000, the fieldworkers found that community leaders and village elders were reluctant to disclose information about drug use in their communities because they felt a sense of shame attached to that behaviour that would reflect badly on them.[25] There is, however, now a growing awareness that an increase in opium cultivation and heroin production has led to an increase in their availability and use among the country's many vulnerable groups.

Another deadly sin is 'the politics of the spotlight', or selective presentation, where some drugs, like the opiates, may be highlighted

---

* The Taliban's Ministry of Vice and Virtue, as it was generally known, was modelled on the *mutawwa'in*, the religious police of Saudi Arabia's long-established Committee for the Promotion of Virtue and the Prevention of Vice.

at the expense of others. There may also be information available about drugs in isolation and not the role that they play in the lives and lifestyles of people. While western governments may see the heroin coming from Afghanistan as contributing to a serious domestic drug problem, there is little recognition that in parts of Afghanistan opium itself has been cultivated and used for centuries as a medicine and for a range of other social and cultural purposes. There is also little recognition of the wide range of other drugs, apart from the opiates, that are used in Afghanistan and that lead to problems. Visitors from western countries frequently ignore or deny that hashish consumption can lead to serious problems in Afghan communities. Western sensibilities and perceptions of cannabis often neglect the fact that the hashish produced in Afghanistan is often more powerful than much of the hashish available in Europe, and daily consumption rates among Afghan users significantly higher than their western counterparts. Reports suggest that hashish use in such an impoverished country as Afghanistan contributes to severe financial problems for the family, leads to arguments and fights among family members over money spent on drugs, and exacerbates endemic health problems such as bronchitis, pneumonia, tuberculosis and other respiratory complaints.[26] A man spending $8 a month on hashish when the family income is only $40 is spending 20 per cent of available income that could have been used to purchase basic necessities like medicine, food and clothes.

### REPORTING DRUG USE

These deadly sins, however, not only manifest at the national level but also at the international level. The UNODCCP World Drug Report 2000, for example, was criticised for containing a wide range of such sins, especially when compared to the previous report of 1997.

Professor Emeritus Arnold S. Trebach, founder and past President of the Drug Policy Foundation based in Washington DC, acknowledged that while the 2000 report appeared 'rational and helpful' in providing a comprehensive review of official country reports on trafficking, consumption, prevention and treatment, it was also 'riddled with bias, irrationality, and outrageous errors'.[27] Apart from the report not dealing fairly with new innovations and experiments on 'the cutting edge of the drug field' and being 'in many respects a defence of the existing order of [drug] control in the world', Trebach argued that the claims made in the report regarding sharp reductions in drug production and consumption needed to be approached with a great deal of caution. Francisco Thoumi, the coordinator for the publication of the report, was so concerned about its inadequacies, and that his professional reputation would suffer if his name was associated with it, that he asked Pino Arlacchi, the then Executive Director of the UNODCCP, to remove his name from the report.[28] What deadly sins, then, did the report contain to merit such criticism and direct action?

A comprehensive critique by Professor Carla Rossi claimed that the report was neither objective nor comprehensive, and failed to achieve a balance between advocacy and credibility.[29] On the basis of a detailed technical critique of the report's underlying methodology, Rossi concluded that in several areas the data had been interpreted in an arbitrary and distorted manner. In particular she claimed that the data had been manipulated to promote certain policy approaches that excluded data from the Netherlands that would have supported the positive effects of harm reduction policies and interventions. These included Trebach's 'cutting-edge' innovations such as NSPs, provision of general health care for addicts and drug maintenance.*

Rossi's critique of data manipulation for policy ends was endorsed rather diplomatically by the European Monitoring Centre for Drugs and Drug Addiction (EMCDDA) who said: 'Where data produced by the EMCDDA are involved, notably on the prevalence of problem drug use and on drug related deaths, there is cause for concern over the way in which those data have been presented and interpreted in the World Drug Report.'[30]

Such critiques of the World Drug Report also signify a growing global paradigm shift in approaches to problem drug use and problem drug users, from abstinence and a rigid 'zero tolerance' enforcement of drug prohibition at one end of the spectrum (the so-called 'war on drugs' lobby) towards reducing the harms and risks that can accompany drug use at the other (the so-called 'harm reduction'

* The World Drug Report for 2005, compiled by the UNODC, has also been criticised as biased and unbalanced, again because it fails to even mention the successes of harm reduction policies and programmes and also for its 'use of inconclusive scientific evidence to demonise cannabis...identical to the preceding mistake that resulted in scheduling cannabis on the list of the 1961 Single Convention at the same level as cocaine and heroin in the first place' (Transnational Institute, 2006, Drug Policy Briefing No. 18: 'International drug control: 100 years of success? TNI comments on the UNODC World Drug Report 2006', Amsterdam: Transnational Institute, p. 4.)

lobby).[31] While there are vestiges of yet another drug war between the more extreme supporters of each camp, all the evidence suggests that this paradigm change has already produced more effective, realistic and humane services for problem drug users in countries such as Australia, Brazil, Canada, New Zealand and much of western Europe, particularly Switzerland, the Netherlands, Germany and the UK.[32] This has positively affected public health, especially related to the prevention of HIV/AIDS and other blood-borne diseases like hepatitis B and C spread through IDU. Countries like China and India with potentially huge populations of people at risk of HIV infection through IDU have also adopted harm reduction measures, including needle and syringe access and disposal programmes (NSPs) and information on safer injecting and other health-related issues. Indeed, it may be in the developing world where the two ends of the abstinence–harm reduction spectrum are best integrated regarding realistic and pragmatic services for drug users and not perceived as being somehow mutually exclusive.

Dost Welfare, a drug treatment centre in Peshawar in NWFP in Pakistan, catering for both Pakistani and Afghan drug users, while based firmly on an abstinence twelve-steps approach to drug addiction, sees no contradiction between this and the provision of a wide range of harm reduction interventions such as a drop-in daycare centre for street heroin users providing washing facilities, food, first aid and medical care, a safe respite from the dangers of the street and an NSP for IDUs. Services depend on the needs of the drug user, their family and the community, not on preconceived models of what constitutes addiction or drug dependency.

It is also notable that both Pakistan and Iran have adopted national harm reduction policies, including NSPs, in attempts to deal with the increasing public health problem of IDU and prevention of the spread of HIV and other blood-borne infections. In Afghanistan in May 2005 the Ministries of Counter Narcotics and Public Health jointly produced and approved a 'National Harm Reduction Strategy for IDU and the Prevention of HIV/AIDS'. On 17 December 2005 President Karzai also signed the new Counter Narcotics Law that mandated the establishment of 'health centers for detoxification, treatment, rehabilitation and harm reduction services for drug addicted and drug dependent persons'. By early 2006 three NSPs existed in Kabul city with plans for the scaling-up of such services to other areas of the country. While some critics have seen harm reduction as the 'Trojan horse' whose underlying intention is to achieve drug law reform and promote the legalisation of currently illicit drugs, in a world where HIV infection is often driven by IDU harm reduction measures remain the only pragmatic and realistic public health option that saves lives.[33] At the same time it should be recognised that harm reduction services can also be used effectively with non-injecting drug users.

Certainly the World Drug Report of 2000 contained unsubstantiated data regarding problem drug use in Afghanistan. While several global maps showing changes in 'drug abuse' have Afghanistan represented by the colour code for data 'not available', Map 9 entitled 'Changes in abuse of heroin and other opiates, 1998 (or latest year available)' shows Afghanistan as having a 'large increase', yet no reliable national, or even provincial, study had been carried out in Afghanistan that would have provided such data, although 'guesstimates' and anecdotal accounts might have suggested this to be the case—hardly the type of data to be included unacknowledged in a World Drug Report. Global Map 13, 'Abuse and trafficking of cannabis', shows an annual prevalence for 'level of abuse' of cannabis between 1 per cent and 5 per cent of the population. Again, there is no reference as to the source of this data, if indeed it existed at all, or any definition of what constitutes 'abuse' in a traditional hashish-producing country like Afghanistan.

The map also shows a thick black arrow from Afghanistan pointing north into central Asia. This arrow purports to represent a main trafficking route for herbal cannabis, yet in Afghanistan only cannabis resin (hashish) is used and produced from the cannabis plant after the flowering tops have been processed into *girda*, a light crumbly powdered resin that is then kneaded and moulded either by hand or by machine into the much darker and oilier *charas*. *Girda* itself is not typically used for smoking in either Afghanistan or Pakistan as it is said to cause headaches. The only preparation made from herbal cannabis is the drink *bhangawa*, made with a number of ingredients that can include milk, honey and spices. While there have been some anecdotal reports of pressed 'cakes' of herbal cannabis being produced around Mazar-i-Sharif in the north of Afghanistan, this hardly provides evidence of 'a main trafficking route' for herbal cannabis into central Asia and beyond.

Indeed one of the problems with such a generalised World Report is that, apart from including unsubstantiated and incomparable data, it glosses over the ground realities of the complexities of motivations for drug use, the many varieties and different preparations of drugs actually used, and indeed the very definition of what constitutes a drug. Later chapters will focus on the wide range of psychoactive drugs apart from opium and its several derivatives and preparations that are used in Afghan communities. This includes all psychoactive substances, plant-based or synthetic, including the problematic use of psychoactive pharmaceutical products such as analgesics and tranquillisers, and not just those drugs proscribed by law. Psychoactive pharmaceutical drugs are sometimes referred to as psychotropics, although in a more general sense the term 'psychotropic' means the same as psychoactive—substances that affect the mind or mental processes.

One of the greatest scorpion tales surrounding global 'drug' policy is that alcohol is not included as a psychoactive drug, mainly because its use, even to the point of intoxication and overdose, is socially acceptable and legal in the vast majority of Judeo-Christian societies. Talking about 'alcohol and drugs' is like talking about 'cabbages and vegetables'—it is not logical. The fact that alcohol is typically ingested by mouth and not snorted through the nose like cocaine or injected like heroin also contributes to this myth of alcohol as a non-drug. If the only way to take alcohol was to inject it and the only way to take heroin was to drink it, then there would be considerably more doubt in people's minds about what constituted the more dangerous drug. The process of globalisation means that cultural preferences for different drugs become more apparent and highlight how the western-led focus on the global criminalisation of coca, opium and cannabis products has distracted attention away from alcohol as potentially an equally harmful substance.

This is one scorpion tale not perpetuated in Afghanistan and other Islamic states where all intoxicants are *haram* under *Sharia*, particularly alcohol. In such societies a drug like alcohol is likely to cause serious problems because users are not culturally familiar with it or have experience of its effects. Also, because it is illegal and in short supply, home-brewed liquor (known as *tarra* in eastern parts of Afghanistan, the word imported by returning refugees from India and Pakistan) may contain methyl instead of ethyl alcohol, with often debilitating, and sometimes fatal, consequences for consumers. Overall, 'intoxicant' is perhaps a better word than 'drug' to describe any psychoactive substance because it suggests the potential a substance has for attaining a state of euphoria, usually expressed as 'getting high', for literally 'getting out of your head', for escaping from an ordinary everyday level of consciousness and for altering mood. As such it focuses on the effects of the substance rather than whether some substances that produce more or less the same general type of effect are legal or illegal in different cultures and societies during different historical periods. It also infers that all intoxicating substances, irrespective of legality, are potentially toxic or poisonous if taken in too great a dose.

## DANGEROUS DRUGS

What constitutes a dangerous drug is also relative. Unless processed incorrectly or adulterated, a drug is not independently dangerous in itself, this will depend on a wide range of factors. At the same time all psychoactive drugs, including alcohol, are potentially dangerous if used inappropriately and incorrectly; there is no such thing as a completely safe drug. A drug like diacetylmorphine (heroin) can be a wonderful drug when used to relieve the acute pain of terminally-ill patients in a cancer ward. It can be a living hell for a war-traumatised Afghan squatting in a bombed-out building in Kabul.

In 1986 at a meeting of a parents' support group in an economically and socially deprived area of Glasgow in the west of Scotland, most of those attending had suffered the death of a teenage son or daughter from an overdose of heroin. Their grief and anger knew no bounds—and they knew for a fact that heroin was 'an evil drug' that had caused the death of their loved ones. It was only when one woman mentioned that her dying mother was in a nearby hospice being regularly administered heavy doses of the same drug, diacetyl-morphine, to ease her suffering that they began to re-evaluate their position and look for other factors that may have contributed to the tragic and untimely deaths of their children.

On a broader stage, the first international UN Convention on Drugs, the 1961 Single Convention on Narcotic Drugs, placed plant-based drugs such as opium and cocaine, grown mostly in southern countries, under the strictest schedule on the assumption that they should be considered hazardous or dangerous until proven not to be. By contrast, during negotiations for the 1971 UN Convention on Psychotropic Substances, the criteria for what constituted a hazardous drug were reversed. For psychoactive pharmaceutical or chemical drugs, mostly produced by, or under licence from, multinational companies in northern countries, there needed to be substantial proof of harmfulness, otherwise they would remain uncontrolled.[34] Such double standards reflect the vested interests and profit motives of governments and multinational pharmaceutical companies rather than any intrinsic measure of what constitutes potential danger when it comes to a particular psychoactive substance.

What leads to a drug becoming dangerous or hazardous is a combination of why, how and where it is used, as well as the purity and potency of the drug itself, which is never guaranteed in an unregulated and uncontrolled illicit market. In Afghanistan, drug use can often take place in a context of imminent physical danger and personal insecurity. Inherent dangers also exist where people have little understanding of what constitutes a safe dose, safe methods of consumption, or information about the risks regarding dependency and overdose. In many reported cases people do not even know the type or name of the drug they are using, never mind its long-term effects. Heroin is frequently referred to simply as *poder*, and women using sedatives and tranquillisers refer to them as 'red pills' or 'yellow pills', without actually knowing which drug it is they are consuming.

If opium, heroin and other narcotic drugs were truly dangerous as substances in themselves, then it would be doubtful that they would play such an important role as analgesics in the pharmacopoeia of the majority of the world's countries. Nevertheless, given its low prevalence of illicit use in most developed societies, the ability of heroin to cause its users and the community a disproportionate amount of harm, such as risk of dependence, overdose and increased crime and the risk of blood-borne infections like HIV and hepatitis C for those who inject should not be underestimated.[35]

The report of the estimated world requirements for narcotic drugs, as compiled annually by the INCB, provides valuable insights about different national drugs of choice for medical and research purposes around the globe. In 2001, for example, it was estimated that the UK required 230.6 kg of heroin and 26 tonnes of opium for medical and research purposes—at the same time that both these drugs were designated as class A drugs under the UK Misuse of Drugs Act, incurring the highest penalties for unauthorised possession, trafficking and production.

During the same year, the UK also required three other narcotic drugs derived from the opium poppy: an estimated 20,170 kg of morphine, 42,000 kg of codeine and 100,000 kg of concentrate of poppy straw with 50 per cent morphine content.[36] At over 200 kg, the UK's medical and research needs for diamorphine (heroin) far surpassed that of the US, which only required 0.7 kg of the drug.

At the same time, however, the US led the world league table for estimated medical and research use of opium at 625 metric tonnes. (This lack of availability of a powerful analgesic like diamorphine, particularly for advanced stage cancer patients and older Americans living in long-term care facilities, has led to accusations of the undertreatment of significant and debilitating pain.)[37] Second in the table was India with 531 tonnes, followed by the Russian Federation with 200 tonnes. Interestingly, China, the country with the largest population in the world, consumed only 53 tonnes, perhaps a reflection of its reliance on more traditional herbal remedies—or synthetic analgesics.

## WORLD OPIUM SUPPLY

If the estimated world requirements for all opium-based narcotics, like opium, morphine, heroin, thebaine, codeine and concentrate of poppy straw, are added together, the total is greater than the highest level of annual opium production in Afghanistan, except perhaps for 2004 when the estimated opium production topped 4,000 tonnes. While the INCB reports that there are sufficient stocks of opium in the world for medical pupposes, they also recognise that the developing world is experiencing a severe shortage of opium-derived pain medications. This is accounted for not only by supply-related issues concerning drug dependency, drug diversion and restrictive national laws, but also deficiencies in national healthcare delivery systems and insufficient training programmes.[38]

According to the INCB, while ten countries account for almost 90 per cent of the world's consumption of morphine for medical purposes, 80 per cent of the world's population living in developing countries consume only 6 per cent of morphine distributed worldwide.[39] In 2005 such figures led the Senlis Council, a European drug-policy research institution, to carry out a feasibility study to look at the possibility of licensing Afghanistan with the INCB to sell its opium legally and fill this shortage.[40] While in principle a good idea, the Minister of Counter Narcotics in Kabul, Habibullah Qaderi, responded to the proposal by saying that,

The poor security situation in the country means there can simply be no guarantee that opium will not be smuggled out of the country for the illicit narcotics trade abroad. Without an effective control mechanism, a lot of opium will still be refined into heroin for illicit markets in the West and elsewhere. We could not accept this.[41]

Apart from such factors, what criteria could be used to license some farmers to take part in trials to cultivate opium poppy while their neighbours were denied licensing? In any case, it is unlikely that farmers would appreciate being paid the going rate for licensed opium produced for the licit market, a sum likely to be considerably less than farmgate prices for illicit opium. In India, the only country licensed to produce licit opium (the others only being licensed to harvest poppy straw and produce concentrate of poppy straw rather than the raw gum incised from the poppy capsule), the average price paid to farmers in 2005 was $26 per kilo. This was an insufficient amount to prevent diversion from the licit to the illicit market, and although there are no reliable estimates about diversion rates, in 2005 the government of India discovered and closed down six clandestine morphine base production laboratories in the country's main opium-growing areas. In Afghanistan the average farmgate price was $102 per kilo, almost four times as much, but still only providing a marginal income for many of the 309,000 families reputedly involved in opium cultivation.

While Afghanistan may be cast as a pariah for having the dubious distinction of being the main illicit opium producer in the world it is ironic that countries like Australia (mainly the island of Tasmania), France, Hungary, India, Spain and Turkey are profiting by cultivating opium products and supplying a legitimate world market for narcotic drugs. Even in regions of India where opium poppy is still grown illegally there is a strong lobby advocating legalisation of cultivation. In a situation symbolic for Afghanistan, the federal Indian government in 2002 was pressurised by officials in the northeastern state of Arunchal Pradesh to legalise poppy farming and to provide trade licences to save the livelihoods of thousands of farmers. Meanwhile, the Central Bureau of Narcotics planned to destroy hundreds of acres of illicit poppy in areas of India bordering Myanmar and Tibet where opium has been used traditionally in tribal rituals and consumed because local people believe it makes them strong and hard working.[42] What will they consume instead of opium if it is eradicated? What will Afghanistan's many opiate users consume if opium is eliminated from the country? If opium is eliminated and no longer available from other sources then drug users are likely to move to pharmaceutical substitutes and other drugs that can lead to equally harmful consequences. Ironically, and reminiscent of links between opium farmers and Taliban in southern Afghanistan, by early 2006 there were reports of farmers in the northeastern Indian state of Jarkhand growing opium hidden among their wheat crop and selling it to Maoist guerrilla fighters who smuggle it into Nepal and Bhutan to generate revenue for their long-running insurgency.[43]

The contradictions in current global drug policy, then, mean that the same drugs that provide the basis for the wealth and power of legal and successful commercial enterprises in some countries also provide wealth and power for illegal and criminal organisations in others. A decade ago the CND estimated that the annual global turnover of the illicit drug trade was $500 billion, over seven times the total international foreign aid given to the developing world.[44] Such distortions are also the case in a world whereby rhetoric and public discourse about drugs frequently mask the reality of people's experience and the nature of drugs and drug-taking itself, leading to interventions that can exacerbate the problem instead of solving it. An emphasis on supply-side strategies like law enforcement and criminalisation policies has led to a wide range of unintended consequences with huge socioeconomic costs, such as the rise of drug mafias, the criminalisation and imprisonment of minor drug offenders and the inflation of police budgets at the expense of prevention and treatment services.

## MEASURING COLOURS

Some of the greatest scorpion tales regarding the reliability of drug figures, however, are to be found in assessments of poppy cultivation and production in Afghanistan. According to the UNODC, in 2002 there were 74,000 hectares planted with poppy[45] while for the same year the US claimed there were only 30,750 hectares,[46] less than 50 per cent of the UNODC figure. This also meant that, according to US figures, by 2003 cultivation had doubled, as their estimate for that year was 61,000 hectares. For the same year the UNODC estimated 84,000 hectares, only an 8 per cent increase from 2002. By 2004, the UNODC estimated that 131,000 hectares had been planted with poppy,[47] while the US showed an unprecedented 238 per cent increase on its 2003 figure of 61,000 hectares to 206,700 hectares. Cultivation figures produced for individual provinces reveal even more discrepancies: between 2003 and 2004, UNODC figures showed a 25 per cent *increase* in cultivation in Ghor province, while the US figures showed a *decrease* of over 50 per cent.

Such discrepancies may be explained away by the use of different methodologies, the UN basing its figures on a combination of comprehensive ground surveys and analysis of images from commercial satellites, the US on a sample survey of Afghan agricultural regions conducted with specialised US government satellite imaging systems. However, they inevitably result in confusion about the 'truth' regarding opium cultivation and production in the country and present clear dilemmas for policy development, sealing the fate of opium farmers in the process. Ironically the ground data used to support image analysis are referred to as 'ground truth'. Without going into the complex technical differences between the two methodologies, it is important to recognise that both are measuring a socially visible, if sometimes not easily accessible (at least from the ground), phenomenon—cultivated fields of opium poppy remarkable for their bright colours while in bloom. How much more difficult, then, to try and measure a phenomenon like problem drug use that, far from being socially visible, is often purposely hidden not just by drug users themselves but also by the families and communities they live in who fear the shame and stigma that public awareness of such problems might bring.

Moreover, scorpion tales, flawed methodologies, a distinct paucity of hard data and a lack of comparability of data based on different methodologies aside, there is no doubting the human tragedy that has been the lot of the Afghan people over the last 27 years and that it has been a major contributing factor in the rapid increase of problem drug use in the country.

# 3
# A Nation in Anguish

Given present levels of aid and development, the best that the Afghan people can hope for is to move from misery to poverty with dignity.[1]

Afghanistan is today a shell of a state facing daunting development challenges and an accelerating insurgency.[2]

Psychological symptoms of drug dependence, such as compulsive regular use, can appear whenever the absence of a person, an object, a place or a situation creates a feeling of anxiety, stress or serious discomfort, often coupled with psychosomatic signs.[3]

## WHY TAKE DRUGS?

Apart from the authenticity and level of purity of a drug, as well as the quantity taken and the method of consumption, it is generally recognised that set and setting will to a large extent determine its effects on an individual. Set basically refers to a person's expectations of what effects the drug will produce, including any memories of past drug experiences, and the setting to the physical and social environment in which the drug is consumed. There is a marked difference between taking a drug in a comfortable and secure setting surrounded by good friends listening to relaxing music, and taking the same drug in a hostile environment characterised by physical and psychological insecurity and the omnipresent threat of gunfire.

A person's expectations about the effects of a drug will depend on the set of motivations, beliefs and values that lead up to the point of consumption. Sometimes a person just drifts into taking a drug without really thinking about why they are doing so, or what the consequences may be. Motivations for use often come later in the form of post facto justifications and rationalisations, usually for the benefit of others, such as an irate parent (or child), a schoolteacher, a mullah, a village elder or the police. Motivations also change over time during a drug-taking career; a person dependent on a drug like heroin may be primarily motivated to continue its use to avoid the pains of withdrawals rather than to experience the feelings of pleasure associated with earlier use. In western countries psychoactive drugs are increasingly perceived as being taken for recreational and social purposes, although not without associated problems and risks, just to enhance social activities and to have 'a good time'. At the same time it is also recognised that those disadvantaged groups on the margins of society, the socially excluded underclass, also take drugs to escape the daily grind of unemployment, poverty, boredom and the pressures engendered by an unavailable consumer hyperculture.

As well as underclass drug use, the privileged 'Prozac nation' uses both licit and illicit drugs as a psychic crutch in its search for the impossible dream of an elixir that will make life constantly pain-free and pleasurable. In his comprehensive social history of drug use, Davenport-Hines suggests that the reason why the US, the richest nation in the world, has 'such a persistent and pervasive drugs problem' is embedded in the 1776 Declaration of Independence and its fundamental belief in 'Life, Liberty and the pursuit of Happiness' that enshrines individual fulfilment and personal happiness as inalienable emotional rights and human entitlements:

The high expectations raised in the USA by a right to happiness were unrealistic, and have inevitably been confounded. Some Americans have numbed their disappointment by taking drugs: when the pursuit of happiness has failed them, they have gone in pursuit of oblivion.[4]

Other motivational factors exist for drug taking; for example, different types of functional drug use where a drug is taken specifically to enhance performance and build confidence as in sport, sex, work, a job interview or warfare. It has also been argued that 'the ubiquity of drug use is so striking that it must represent a basic human appetite', although this refers specifically to satisfying what has been postulated as a basic human desire to alter everyday levels of consciousness through drug use.[5] Apart from drugs there are many other ways and means to achieve this effect including religion, extreme sports, yoga and meditation.

## DRUG USE AND MENTAL HEALTH

While it can be claimed that there are as many reasons for taking drugs as there are drug users, in Afghanistan there exists a particular social environment, resulting from over two decades of war, civil disorder, internecine violence and social disruption. This provides an understandable set of motivations, although not the only set, for drug use among many Afghans. Such circumstances have put considerable strain on traditional coping mechanisms and survival strategies that have already been all but shattered by the destruction of the clan community, the extended family structure and the economy, leaving the vast bulk of the population vulnerable to a wide range of chronic mental health problems, particularly depression, anxiety, sleep disorders and PTSD.

A generation ago in 1985 a psychiatrist warned of the likelihood of high incidences of anxiety, depression and drug dependence in Afghan refugee communities in Pakistan—on top of the ones in broken communities inside the country itself. He suggested that for such communities, after having endured, at that time, only six years of war and conflict, 'the psychological repercussions and psychiatric illnesses produced as a consequence match no parallel'.[6] Over a decade later in 1998 a study of 80 women living in Kabul and 80 who had recently migrated to Pakistan as refugees found 97 per cent demonstrated evidence of major depression, 86 per cent had significant anxiety symptoms and 42 per cent reported symptoms that were commensurate with diagnostic criteria for PTSD.[7] A further study of mental health in a sample of 297 Afghan women with young children living in two refugee camps in the NWFP of Pakistan revealed that 36 per cent screened positive for a common mental disorder. Of this group, the vast majority, just over 90 per cent, had experienced suicidal thoughts in the last month with nine of the women rating suicidal feelings as their greatest concern.[8]

After 11 September 2001 and the terrorist attacks on New York, a survey of the city's residents found that levels of depression and PTSD had almost doubled since before the attack and that there had been a significant increase in drug use.[9] Since the attack, 3.3 per cent of the respondents had started smoking cigarettes, 19.3 per cent had started drinking alcohol and 2.5 per cent began using cannabis. This didn't include the existing smokers and drinkers who had increased their consumption rate by over 40 per cent. Another study found that in the year after 9/11, 4.5 per cent of New York residents surveyed took psychotropic medications because of the attacks and 13 per cent said they received mental health counselling.[10] Tragic and traumatic though the attacks in New York undoubtedly were, these figures put into perspective the likelihood of a far greater increase in mental health problems and resulting drug use among an Afghan population who have faced decades of trauma, conflict and war without the cushion of wealth, healthcare and social services available to the majority of American citizens.

The words of Horace Day written in 1868 on the effects of the American civil war on opium consumption are strikingly apposite for contemporary Afghanistan:

Maimed and shattered survivors from a hundred battle-fields, diseased and disabled soldiers released from hostile prisons, anguished and hopeless wives and mothers, made so by the slaughter of those who were nearest to them, have found, many of them, temporary relief from their sufferings in opium.[11]

Recent research has shown that after relatively short spells of combat duty 15–17 per cent of US troops in Iraq and 11 per cent in Afghanistan met the screening criteria for major depression, generalised anxiety or PTSD.[12] For their Afghan counterparts who fought the Soviets for ten years and then each other for several more years, the psychological and dehumanising effects can hardly be imagined. In a global environment increasingly characterised by a climate of fear and insecurity, whether real or imagined, the consumption of psychoactive drugs, whether licit or illicit, is only likely to increase:

Now we all lead global lives. Individually we cannot help feeling the effects of war, terrorism, oppression, corruption, greed, instability, poverty, misery, stress, unhappiness and ill-health. They have become an inescapable part of our own lives; they come closer and closer to home.[13]

According to various reports, after more than quarter of a century of almost continuous war and conflict, chronic mental health problems are now endemic among many in the Afghan population. In 2002, the WHO estimated that 20 per cent of the population, or approximately one out of every five people, suffered from mental health problems or some form of diminished capacity.[14] Also in 2002, the US Centers for Disease Control and Prevention, along with collaborating partners, conducted a national mental health survey, albeit with a limited sample of 799 adult household members aged 15 years or older. This study concluded that 78 per cent of respondents displayed symptoms of anxiety, nearly 70 per cent displayed symptoms of depression and 42 per cent the symptoms of PTSD; 62 per cent had experienced at least four traumatic events in the last ten years and, hardly surprisingly, for 83 per cent of the sample, feelings of hatred were high.[15] A report on the Public Health System in Afghanistan also recognised that there is currently a high prevalence of mental health problems in the country, and went on to state that 'there are undoubtedly many people in Afghanistan who would benefit from psychotropic medications. In fact, the abuse of these sedatives is widely reported.'[16]

While depression and other mental health problems appear widespread, particularly among women, and self-medication with a range of sedatives, tranquillisers and painkillers, both licit and illicit, a daily reality for many, the shattered public health system lacks the expertise and resources to deal with such problems.[17] Generally there is a shortage of trained and qualified medical staff that has led to untrained people claiming to be doctors and prescribing drugs or even carrying out surgery at unregulated private clinics. In 2004, Abdul Manan Saidi, then Deputy President of Law and Assessment in the Ministry of Health suggested that 'Even those people who were hospital cleaners in Pakistan and Iran have opened their own clinics.'[18] A 2001 report from Pharmaciens Sans Frontieres also stated that in Afghanistan,

Private doctors and pharmacies are available in the bazaar, but doctor's medical knowledge is poor, diagnosis uncertain and prescription often hazardous. The pharmacies are selling drugs of doubtful quality from China, Pakistan or India without being aware of the risks run by the patient.[19]

Mental health problems in Afghanistan are understandably often under-recognised and neglected in a country where just ensuring physical survival has become a daily imperative for much of the population, as well as a primary objective of humanitarian aid and development assistance. In early 2005, however, the new Minister of Public Health placed mental health higher on the public health agenda by establishing a mental health unit within the primary health care directorate that included a remit for drug addiction. At the same time, as with measurements of problem drug use, caution must be exercised in trying to estimate the extent of psychopathology in an environment like Afghanistan where western diagnostic concepts may not always be valid.[20]

### THE PROBLEM OF LOSS

Underlying many of the mental health problems endemic in Afghanistan is the central problem of loss. Some people will understandably turn to drugs to cope with the pain, both physical and psychological, of the loss of loved ones and family members, home, job, limbs, personal security and, in the case of refugees, their country.[21] It should be noted, however, that these mental health problems are largely determined by the circumstances that have prevailed throughout the country. As such, it has been suggested that the mental health needs of the population can best be served by a return to normal life as quickly as possible, in tandem with the development of education, homes, income-generating activities and increased security and stability.[22] A British psychiatrist specialising in PTSD has warned against the over-medicalisation of such mental health problems in a country like Afghanistan and any attempt against trying to solve them solely by importing experts in PTSD who may risk dislocating sufferers from culturally available resources such as traditional healers or family and community networks.[23]

An adviser working on issues of vulnerability and risk among children in Kabul has also warned against assuming that all children are overwhelmed or incapacitated by trauma. Although many have 'lived through events that most of us would not wish on any child', she found that children displayed fortitude and resilience as a result of caring and protective parenting that encouraged gratitude, overcoming fears, schooling and friendship, happiness through play and religious faith.[24] A report by UNICEF and Save the Children US also emphasised the need for a holistic psychosocial approach to children who have been affected by conflict rather than a focus on individual trauma counselling.[25] Such an approach should be based on the coping strategies already developed by children and their parents who have endured years of war, and should emphasise the strengthening of family support structures and the need for children to gain a sense of normalcy through access to school and play. On a broader note, 'The social fabric of Afghan society may have been brutally torn, but traditional mechanisms of caring for children are among the last elements to be compromised.'[26]

While the current plight of the Afghan people should not be downplayed, there is certainly a need to recognise that Afghans are also resilient and have proved themselves survivors, but are now desperately in need of the resources to reconstruct their communities and make a better and more secure life for their families in order to regain their mental health and equilibrium. How long it will take the majority of an impoverished population to gain these resources is another matter, and desperation can easily lead to the illicit cultivation of opium, as well as its consumption, by people who might not otherwise consider it. In 2003 a report by CARE

International compared Afghanistan to other post-conflict zones, producing a table of available 'aid per person' donated by the west. At the top of the table was Bosnia which received $326 per person, with Kosova receiving $288 and East Timor $195. Over the next five years it was estimated that Afghans would receive $42 per person. Other statistics also showed that while in Kosovo there was one peacekeeper for every 48 people, and in East Timor and Bosnia there was one for every 66 and 113 people respectively, in Afghanistan in 2003 there was one foreign soldier for every 5,380 Afghans.[27]

## WAR, CONFLICT AND LOSS

Underpinning the various losses mentioned above is the central and continuous loss of a very basic personal security and freedom that most people living in the relative peace and stability of western societies usually take for granted. As Joseph Nye of Harvard University has pointed out, 'Security is like oxygen. You tend not to notice it until you begin to lose it, but once that occurs there is nothing else that you will think about.'[28] In Afghanistan 'security is probably the most precious and the most elusive public good for most Afghans'[29] and was the 'longed for luxury' that was sufficient reason for most Afghans to support the Taliban regime, at least initially.[30] In August 2005 Jean Arnault, the UN special envoy for Afghanistan, warned an open meeting of the UN Security Council that 'Bringing extremist violence and other forms of insecurity under control will remain at the top of the agenda for the government, and for millions of Afghans for whom the most basic dividend of peace—security—remains a distant goal.'[31] Indeed, since 1979 when the Soviets invaded there has been no point when war and violence have not reigned over significant parts of the country resulting in the vast majority of Afghans experiencing a distinct loss of personal security.

The decade between 1979 and 1989 saw one of the most brutal wars in modern history. During that period the Soviets reportedly killed over a million Afghans and through their scorched earth policy, replete with atrocities (and arguably genocide against sections of the civilian population), aerial bombardment and mine warfare, forced nearly a third of the population, estimated at around 5 million, into exile as refugees, mostly in the neighbouring countries of Pakistan and Iran.

At the same time the war was under-reported mainly due to the tough terrain, the many dangers that faced journalists brave enough to venture into Afghanistan and neglect and disinterest on the part of the international community. As a result, the true story of this period in Afghanistan's history will never be told and the true numbers of dead will remain unknown, although figures of over 1.5 million Afghans killed are often quoted.[32] After the Soviet invasion, Afghanistan became another kind of place:

It went from an out-of-time land of myths and legends to an Orwellian territory of terror and destruction. Villages that had existed for thousands of years, that had seen Alexander the Great's armies and survived Genghis Khan's hordes, were eradicated, erased by jets and gun-ships in hours. Huge tracts of countryside were totally depopulated, turned into ghostly no-mans lands.[33]

Very few families were untouched by the violent death of a relative during that war or the subsequent violence and insecurity that have plagued the country. By 2003 this left Afghanistan with an estimated half a million widows, nearly 7 per cent of all women, plus their children, a particularly vulnerable and impoverished at-risk group for problem drug use.[34] An Amnesty International report from 1996 painted a bleak picture of the post-Soviet period in Afghanistan, particularly for women:

Local military commanders and factional groups fight for control in a country where laws are meaningless and systematic human rights abuses are a daily occurrence. Killings, torture, beatings, rapes, 'disappearances' and hostage-taking have all been conducted with impunity by the different factions in the conflict. And the victims are almost always ordinary civilians.[35]

During this post-Soviet period torture was reportedly endemic, age no barrier to cruelty, and rape condoned by faction leaders as a means of terrorising conquered populations and rewarding soldiers. Amnesty goes on to describe a particularly harrowing story of a young widow living in the Shahrara district of Kabul in the winter of 1994. Leaving her three children, aged between two and nine years, at home while she went to find food, she was arrested by armed *mujahideen* guards and taken to their base. There she was held for three days and repeatedly raped by over 20 men. When they allowed her to return home she found that her children had all died of hypothermia. It was little wonder that she then lost her sanity.

Subsequent Amnesty International reports on Afghanistan between 1997 and 2002 compiled a litany of human rights abuses by both sides as the Taliban battled with the United Front (later the Northern Alliance) in an attempt to take over the whole country. In 1997 it was reported that over 20 mass graves containing an estimated 2,000 bodies were found in the northern province of Jowzjan. The bodies were allegedly those of Taliban militia who had been taken prisoner and summarily executed by a local commander after being captured as they entered the city of Mazar-i-Sharif. The following year the brutal pendulum swung in the opposite direction when Taliban guards killed thousands of ethnic Hazara civilians after the Taliban military takeover of the city. Apart from those killed in their homes or the street, 'women, children and the elderly were shot while trying to flee the city'.[36] In 2001 during the fighting between Taliban and Northern Alliance forces in northern and central Afghanistan, Taliban forces subjected civilians to a 'ruthless and systematic policy of collective punishment', including summary executions, the burning and looting of houses, shops and public buildings and confiscation of farm land.[37] On a visit to Afghanistan in October 2002 the Pakistani lawyer Asma Jahangir, the UN special rapporteur on extrajudicial, summary or arbitrary executions, stated that the number of people executed in Afghanistan during the past 23 years was 'staggering'.[38]

In the Shomali plains of central Afghanistan, just north of Kabul city, it was academic whether the Taliban engaged in a deliberate scorched earth policy as part of an ethnic cleansing of the local population, or whether they destroyed homes and cut down age-old grapevines and mulberry and walnut orchards on the pretext that enemy troops were hiding there in ambush. Either way, it did not matter to the many families forced to join the ranks of those already displaced by internecine violence. In northern and western areas of the country many of these IDPs had no choice but to settle in unsanitary makeshift camps without adequate shelter, and frequently with little food or medical care. Impoverishment was so severe that reports from the north indicated that some families had little choice but to marry off their young daughters, some as young as six years, at far reduced dowries, basically selling their daughters so the rest of the family could survive.[39]

There can be little doubt that, for all the excesses of the Taliban, for many victims there was often little to choose between them and their predecessors, and immediate successors, the local warlords and commanders, in the brutality stakes. On an overland journey in May 2001 along the 140 km of corrugated and cratered road between Jalalabad and Kabul we passed a large restaurant standing at the roadside in Sarobi district. My travelling companions explained that the restaurant had been owned by a *Hezb-i Islami* commander infamous for forcing the occupants of every passing vehicle to 'stop and have lunch'. Their vehicles were then searched and they were asked to pay a 'tax' on any goods they were carrying. One recalled that his brother had been stopped and asked to pay $20 on a television set he had in his car. When he protested that the television belonged to someone else, the commander's reply was '$30!' The traveller again claimed that he did not have that amount of money. The reply was '$40!' At $60 the man eventually wised up and paid. I asked my companion what would have happened to his brother if he hadn't paid and he replied, 'the commander had a lieutenant called "Dog". If someone wouldn't pay, then this man ripped their flesh with his bare teeth until they did pay. You can see the graveyard up the road. That is what happened to people who didn't pay.' We then continued on our way and I reflected on what was most likely another scorpion tale, until in October 2002 the *Kabul Times* reported that 'Zardad, one of Gulbuddin Hekmatyr's commanders, kept his stooge, a human dog, underneath his niche and in case a driver or passenger refused to pay all his money, the dog bit his flesh till blood oozed from parts of his body.'[40] In 2004, Sarwar Zardad Faryadi, now an illegal immigrant running a pizza business in London, was arrested and tried on charges of murder, kidnapping, theft and torture by a British court under a 1988 convention allowing it to try crimes of torture that had been committed abroad. In April of the same year his lieutenant Abdullah Shah, the 'human dog', was executed in Afghanistan. In July 2005 Zardad, aged 42, was found guilty of murder, torture and hostage-taking and sentenced to 20 years in a British prison with a recommendation that he be deported back to Afghanistan after serving his sentence.

But the deprivations experienced by the Afghan population had started long before the Taliban appeared on the scene. In 1995, a year after factional fighting mainly between the militia forces of Rashid Dostum, Gulbuddin Hekmatyr and Ahmad Shah Massoud had reduced several neighbourhoods of Kabul to rubble and the Taliban had taken control of Qandahar, indicators provided by UNDP illustrated the grim plight of Afghans brought about by the war with the Soviets and the ensuing civil war between rival *mujahideen* leaders-cum-warlords. The infant mortality rate stood at 18 per cent, or 163 deaths per 1,000 births, the highest in the world at that time, and 1,700 mothers out of 100,000 died in childbirth (ten years later in 2005, UNICEF reported that this latter figure had marginally decreased to 1,600 per 100,000 women.[41]) Life expectancy for both men and women was no more than 43–44 years. Less than one third of the population had access to healthcare and only 12 per cent had access to clean safe water, resulting in many children dying of preventable diseases such as measles and dysentery. The destruction of a large number of schools during the war, along with social disruption, led to an illiteracy rate of 90 per cent for girls and over 60 per cent for boys.[42] In 2000 a report from Helmand, the largest province in the country, with a total population of over 1 million, claimed that only 18 per cent of males and 1 per cent of females over the age of 15 were literate.[43]

Such a life of deprivation was to become even more desolate under the next six years of Taliban rule. Their particular brand of authoritarian Islamic fundamentalism banned a wide range of what had been culturally acceptable forms of personal behaviour in many areas of Afghanistan, such as flying kites, dancing at wedding parties, listening to cassette tapes, trimming beards, playing drums and other musical instruments and displaying photographs or pictures of human beings. On one occasion an Afghan colleague was stopped at a roadblock in Kabul and searched by a young Talib guard who found a photograph of the man's family in his pocket. The guard became very angry, ripped up the photograph, threw the pieces on the ground and hit the man in the face. Television was banned because it constituted a form of western decadence, although alternative live entertainment was offered by holding weekly public executions and amputations in football stadiums in Kabul, Qandahar and other cities throughout the country. Safety and security had at last arrived in Afghanistan, maintained by a reign of terror and threats of arbitrary violent reprisals for the slightest violation of Taliban law.

## THE PLIGHT OF WOMEN

But it was the specific treatment meted out to women that initially drew most international criticism of the Taliban. Before they came to power, up to 40 per cent of doctors and 50 per cent of teachers in Afghanistan had been women. Under the Taliban, women became the 'vanished gender', effectively banned from public life with very limited opportunities for appearing in public places, and then only if accompanied by a male blood relative.[44] Women were forced to paint the windows in their home black to prevent them being seen. Even if they were permitted to appear in public they had to wear the *burqa*, a shroud-like garment that enveloped them from the top of their heads to below the ankles and only allowed a small mesh-covered opening to see and breathe. Women were reportedly beaten, stoned, whipped and even killed for violating these new laws. If a woman was caught wearing nail polish the ends of her fingers could be cut off and in several cases this reportedly happened.[45] At the same time, women were active in resisting the oppression of the Taliban by establishing underground beauty parlours and home schools for girls. Another form of resistance for some women was to join the Revolutionary Association of the Women of Afghanistan (RAWA) with some saying that being involved with RAWA in their struggle to resist the Taliban provided a social role that made them feel emotionally better and improved their mental health.[46]

While there may have been several contributing factors why the Taliban took such a brutal and draconian stance against women, Ahmed Rashid asserts that most Talibs, 'the orphans, the rootless, the lumpenproletariat', had been brought up in the totally male environment of the *madrassas* so that 'control over women and their virtual exclusion was a powerful symbol of manhood and a reaffirmation of the student's commitment to jihad'.[47] Restrictions on women's social movement and dress, however, did not start with the Taliban, they were an integral part of *Pashtoonwali*, the social code of the Pashtoons. Neither were they limited to Taliban-controlled areas of the country, but also applied to those non-Pashtoon areas in the north under control of the Northern Alliance.

Even though Afghan women in rural areas still wield considerable power and influence in household management, family decision-making and decisions regarding income generation and remain important agents of change, the almost total suppression of the human rights of women under the Taliban had many lasting consequences. Apart from the many restraints on personal freedoms experienced by women, the exclusion of women from most paid employment and the practice of forcing young girls into marriage with the Taliban had the severest impact.[48] Although a few female health workers were permitted to return to work, the vast majority of women were effectively banned from earning a living. In the case of the country's many widows and their children, this had a devastating economic impact and undoubtedly contributed to widows, as well as women generally, suffering from mental health problems and becoming a high-risk group for problem drug use as well as commercial sex work.

At the same time, it needs to be acknowledged that long before the Taliban came to power equal rights under law had never been guaranteed for women in Afghanistan, 'tradition and the conservative interpretation of Islam have long prevented women from enjoying legal and actual equality in the areas of marriage, divorce and inheritance, and the right to travel, to education and to work'.[49] Despite the democratic rhetoric, there is also little guarantee that in the post-Taliban future the majority of Afghan women will benefit from greater equality, even under new constitutions and their related laws. In April 2003, for example, it was reported from both Mazar-i-Sharif and Herat that forced chastity examinations were being carried out on girls by local authorities without informing their families in advance. Typically a woman arrested on suspicion of having had premarital intercourse was accompanied by the police to a clinic and given an internal examination. Indeed, over 75 per cent of women in Afghan prisons have been convicted of *zina*, engaging in sexual activity outside marriage, even though most were trying to escape from domestic abuse and oppressive households.[50] In August of 2003 in Kabul 1,000 women gathered to call for action to improve the security situation in the country. The women came together in the Women's Park, a walled garden reserved exclusively for women and children, too afraid to take their protest to the streets.[51]

## THE PLIGHT OF DRUG USERS

Drug users themselves were another social group singled out by the Taliban as deserving punishment for their behaviour.[52] In December 1996 in Kabul the Ministry of Enforcement of Virtue and Suppression of Vice passed a decree stating that 'to eradicate the use of addiction, addicts should be imprisoned and investigation made to find the supplier and the shop. The shop should be locked and the owner and user should be imprisoned and punished.' In Afghanistan, as in many other countries, criminals still go to prison *for* punishment, not *as* punishment, including being beaten, shackled and deprived of adequate food and bedding. A year later in 1997 there was a change in Taliban policy when the Supreme Court passed an edict which stated unequivocally that 'the addicts of illegal drugs should be referred to the hospital/treatment center to receive proper treatment. If an addict after receiving treatment and being rehabilitated restarts using drugs, in this case he will be entitled for receiving punishment [sic].' Ironically this edict failed to recognise that there was only one specialised treatment service for drug users in the country, that this was seriously under-resourced and that for many treated drug users relapse back into drug use is a normal part of the recovery cycle.

This policy of extreme criminalisation and persecution of drug users who previously had, at worst, been ostracised by the community led to many being traced, arrested and punished by the Ministry of Enforcement of Virtue and Suppression of Vice. One consequence was that drug use became a more hidden activity and drug users became even less socially visible than they already were, reducing even further any chances they might have for help from the few available healthcare services.

In 1999, a report indicated that there was little consistency in the way the ministry dealt with drug users in different parts of the country. Some were kept in prison for three months, others for six months, while a few were able to buy their way out of prison if family members could guarantee they would remain drug free. In Herat in the west of the country, reports indicated that 'arrested drug users are taken to the department's offices and beaten with 21 lashes. They are then imprisoned there unless they display drug withdrawal symptoms such as vomiting and diarrhoea when they are simply released back into the community.'[53] Such summary justice, often administered with a *durra* (leather strap), was not uncommon and was indicative of the Taliban's punitive and harsh approach to drug users, some of the most vulnerable members of the Afghan community. In Qandahar, drug users were reportedly imprisoned and 'rehabilitated' by a regular exercise regime and two cold baths a day, giving a new spin to the phrase 'cold turkey', where addicts experience the pains of withdrawals from drugs without any symptomatic treatment.*

Ironically the majority of the drug users imprisoned in Qandahar at that time had been brought from Pakistan by their families in the knowledge that there would be no drugs available in Qandahar prison, unlike Pakistani prisons where drug use was rife. In Jalalabad it was reported that on several occasions, even in winter, drug users

---

* In 2000 I visited a respected residential drug treatment centre in Peshawar and spotted an open pool of water about 6 m² in the garden. On remarking that this was a strange location for a water tank, I was told, 'Oh, no. This is a plunge pool for the recovering addicts, they love to have a cold bath as part of their treatment programme.' Several Pakistani NGOs reportedly use this 'water therapy' as part of their detoxification and treatment programme.

were simply thrown into the river as a punishment, or perhaps as a misguided form of treatment.

The ambivalent and paradoxical attitude to drugs held by the Taliban is also well-illustrated by a newspaper report of a young man interviewed in a drug treatment centre in Quetta who had once been caught by the Taliban at the border with Pakistan trying to smuggle opium. Four of his fingers were cut off, his face was painted black, and he was then paraded around town on the back of a donkey. Another young man in the same centre recounted how he was a fighter for the Northern Alliance when he was captured by the Taliban and imprisoned in Jalalabad. After some time in the jail he was taken to the frontlines where he was promised unlimited hashish. However, the hashish he was given seemed different from previous hashish he had taken: 'When I smoked the hashish, it felt different in my body. It made me feel powerful and fearless.' Later he discovered that heroin had been added to the hashish and that he was now dependent on the heroin and was quite willing to go and fight against his former comrades in the Northern Alliance—as long as the Taliban kept supplying him with heroin, which they did.[54]

### IMPOVERISHMENT, DEPRIVATION AND SOCIAL DISRUPTION

Apart from the mental health problems that have been outlined above, the main consequence of constant exposure to war, violence and conflict has been the almost complete decimation of the social fabric and economic infrastructure of Afghan society, to the extent that in 2000 a report stated: 'In short, presently the situation of Afghanistan barely allows people to survive as human beings.'[55] Afghanistan has been almost off the map of any human development index and, in the words of the 2000 UN Human Development Report, 'is worse off than almost any other country in the world'. In 1996 the UN Human Development Index had seen Afghanistan placed 169 out of 174 countries, but since then the country, along with Somalia, has been one of only two countries in the world unable to produce enough accurate data to be ranked in the UNDP's annual Human Development Report. In 2004 using whatever data was available, the first ever National Human Development Report for Afghanistan was published. It estimated that the country was ranked 173 out of 178 countries, with only Burundi, Mali, Burkina Faso, Niger and Sierra Leone receiving a lower ranking.

Over the last decade or so, any available social and economic indicators, particularly regarding women and children, make grim and disturbing reading. In 1998, UNICEF reported that acute malnutrition in children varied from 10–30 per cent, with stunting of growth estimated to be as high as 52 per cent. Child mortality rates of over 25 per cent were higher than all countries in the world, apart from Angola, Niger and Sierra Leone. In September 2002, it was reported that nearly 20 per cent of returnee children from Pakistan and Iran under the age of five passing through the encashment centre in Pul-i-Charki in Kabul were severely malnourished.[56] To compound these figures, it has also been estimated that 96 per cent of children have witnessed violence and 65 per cent have experienced the death of a close relative. Around 25 per cent of children do not even live to see their fifth birthday.

In May 2002 only 6 per cent of Afghans had access to electricity, what little power existed was rationed to hospitals and public buildings with very little trickling down to businesses and private residences, and then limited to only a few hours a day.[57] In Kabul, city power is still sporadic at best and there is a thriving business in the sale of diesel generators, although in a city like Herat a functioning public power supply has been restored. Whether people can afford to pay for electricity is another matter. By 2003 less than a quarter of the country's population had access to clean safe water and only 24 per cent of urban households had access to piped water.[58] This lack of clean water contributes to a range of illnesses such as dysentery, diarrhoea, cholera, polio and typhoid fever and is a major cause of child and infant mortality. Only 10 per cent of the population have access to sanitation and most piped water and sewerage networks have been destroyed or damaged. This lack of sanitation is exacerbated in urban areas by broken drains, the lack of solid waste disposal and the non-existence of sanitary waste disposal sites. In Kabul the ubiquitous dust, as fine as talcum powder, contains several micro-organisms injurious to health, including human faecal matter.

Throughout the country there has been a general degradation of the environment that has also affected people's livelihood, health and vulnerability. The more than 75 per cent of the population living in rural areas decimated by war and an extended drought that lasted until the winter of 2004 (then resumed in 2005) predominantly live in countryside suffering from widespread and serious degradation including, 'lowered water tables, dried-up wetlands, denuded forests, eroded land and depleted wildlife populations'.[59] It has been estimated that desertification due to drought, extreme heat and winds and severe frost conditions has reduced arable land by up to 50 per cent over the last 25 years.[60] Such factors have seriously hindered agricultural activity, depleted natural resources such as water for irrigation and trees for food and fuel and driven people into cities that have almost no basic public amenities or viable infrastructures to cope with increased populations. At the same time a US geological survey has already spent $17.4 million on assessing the country's mineral and energy resources that appear to be substantial and profitable. As part of the survey it was estimated that two geological basins in the north contain up to 1.6 billion barrels of oil and 15.7 trillion cubic feet of natural gas.[61] Afghanistan also has some spectacular scenery and the potential for ecotourism is almost unlimited, assuming a significant improvement in the security situation.

Nearly 25 per cent of urban housing is severely damaged or destroyed, although money, much of it allegedly from the illicit drug trade, has recently fuelled a building boom of mansion houses in the larger cities. During the Soviet occupation an estimated two thirds of all villages were bombed, leading to over 30 per cent of farms being abandoned and irrigation systems destroyed, with severe loss of livestock due to shooting or mines. This destruction of rural infrastructure and source of livelihood, coupled with the ongoing drought, meant that in late 2002 an estimated 4.3 million people in rural areas faced livelihood insecurity. Altogether during 2002 nearly half of all Afghans, the critically poor and the chronically vulnerable, were identified as requiring humanitarian assistance.[62] By September 2004 the situation had hardly improved, with the Minister for Rural Rehabilitation and Development, Mohammad Hanif Atmar, declaring that 'around 6.3 million Afghans are facing the threat of famine as the protracted drought is continuing…this year's drought is the severest one in living memory'.[63] He also reported that at least 4,000 families, over 20,000 people, had abandoned their homes in search of water and jobs, although the real figure was likely to be higher. In December 2004 WFP in Kabul reported that 40 per cent of the population lived below subsistence levels with 37 per cent being unable to meet their basic needs. Urgent help was needed in districts in 17 of the country's provinces, with 92 per cent of the population of Nimroz province, situated in the arid desert region of the southwest, needing food aid or other assistance.[64] The National Human Development Report for 2004 stated that 70 per cent of the total population were undernourished, 70 per cent lived under the poverty line of $2 income per day and the per capita income was $190 per year, increasing to $300 when the illicit drug economy was included.[65]

Throughout the country there are an estimated 800,000–1 million people disabled, some 4 per cent of the population, 200,000 of these disabled by mines, with such human impairment indirectly affecting around 22 per cent of the population through other family members. Afghanistan still contains more unexploded ordnance (UXO) than any other country in the world, with 732 km$^2$ known to be mined. During the US-led Operation Enduring Freedom, new areas also became contaminated. When ammunition dumps were bombed in major towns during the 2001 US air offensive, UXOs were spread up to a 5 km radius. Human Rights Watch also reported that there is still a threat to civilians from the thousands of unexploded 'bomblets' from dropped US cluster bombs. Between October 2001 and March 2002, 5 per cent of the 26,000 bombs dropped on Afghanistan were cluster bombs containing 248,056 bomblets, of which at least 12,000 remain unexploded.[66]

The Uranium Medical Research Center (UMRC) in Washington reported that US bombing with uranium alloyed precision-destruction weapons also resulted in high concentrations of non-depleted uranium in the urine of subjects tested in bombed areas. In Jalalabad the concentrations of non-depleted uranium were reportedly 400 to 2,000 per cent higher than normal populations, and between 100 and 400 times greater than in Gulf war veterans tested in 1999. The UMRC field team were 'shocked by the breadth of public health impacts coincident with the bombing' and reported that Afghans who were exposed at the time of the bombing reported immediate adverse health effects within hours of the attacks, as well as flu-type illnesses that started within a few weeks.[67] It was also reported by the UMRC that 'Radioactive, toxic uranium alloys and hard-target uranium warheads were being used by the coalition forces', including 'a new generation of deep-penetrating "cave-busting" and seismic shock warheads'. While not stating it directly, the UMRC implied that Afghanistan was used by the US as an experimental field-testing ground for a series of new uranium-based weapons.[68]

## THE OTHER SIDE OF THE POVERTY COIN

Such staggering levels of destruction, poverty and suffering experienced by the vast majority of Afghans stand in marked contrast to the comfort zone, or what has been described as 'the gilded café society of aid-workers, diplomats, businessmen, spies and westernised Afghans',[69] as well as a large international military force, existing in Kabul. In restaurants in the city a pizza can cost up to $10, almost one week's wages for labourers participating in cash-for-work schemes, and a meal (with wine) in a more upmarket establishment can cost $40–50 per person. In 2005 the new Serena Hotel opened in Kabul with room rates starting at $250 and up to $1,250 per night for the presidential suite.

In a country where alcohol is just as *haram* and illegal under *Sharia* as any other intoxicant (although not for foreigners under statutory law), foreign military and international exchanges sell a wide range of wines, beers, champagnes and spirits, as well as reputedly selling French perfume cheaper than anywhere else in the world. There is understandable and increasing resentment against what is happening to Kabul, nicknamed 'Kabulistan' in recognition that government writ does not extend much beyond the city limits and dubbed an 'island of westernisation', where many Afghans 'see unaffordable restaurants serving alcohol and internet cafes giving access to pornography while most of the capital remains in ruins'.[70] One Afghan complained that

There's a swimming pool in the central UN compound and regular parties and barbecues. Memories of a party held by the DHL courier group last November, when an opium pipe was passed around by UN staff, are still fresh...booze, pork chops, prosciutto, marinated steaks, shrimps, cigars and caviar are regularly flown into the two PXs [retail warehouses for foreigners] catering for westerners. Run by westerners themselves, none of their vast profit reaches the local economy. Now the German brewer of Bitburger Pils has a representative in Kabul signing up new customers. And Starbucks is here too 'for office or home delivery'. Again none of this investment is much use to us locals. True, a few Afghans are 'lucky' enough to get jobs cleaning, serving tea or gardening. But they keep asking for too much money and are causing inflation in the new Raj.[71]

Alcohol traded illicitly from military and other international exchanges onto the local market is now available to Afghans from many retail outlets in the city at inflated prices, and is openly sold in some restaurants to both non-Afghans and Afghans, in the latter case contrary to the law against the sale and consumption of intoxicants. In April 2003, after being open for only a month, Kabul's 'popular hangout for foreigners', the Irish Club (commonly referred to as 'the Irish Pub'), had to close its doors following warnings that it was going to be the target of a grenade attack: 'few places attracted as many people as the Irish Club. On Thursday nights—the day before the Friday Muslim Sabbath—hundreds of people thronged the bar and dozens of cars lined the street outside.'[72] In 2004, more discreet and upmarket venues selling alcohol opened up, including the Red Hot and Sizzlin' Steakhouse and Karaoke Bar, the Mediterraneo club and the Elbow Room, an American-style cocktail bar and restaurant. While such a large well-paid foreign contingent has had the knock-on effect of generally increasing prices of goods for locals, it has also allegedly led to an increase in the price of hashish in Kabul due to the demand for the drug from ISAF forces and other foreigners.[73]

Such 'foreign influences' have also led to charges of increased moral crime in Kabul, including prostitution rackets and alcohol sales organised by foreigners. While it may be legal for foreigners to purchase and consume alcohol in Afghanistan it is strictly illegal for local people who are Muslims. In August 2003 a newspaper run by the Northern Alliance called on President Karzai to crack down on these corrupt and non-Islamic practices and suggested that they were fuelling the spread of AIDS. President Karzai was further accused by the newspaper of failing to maintain Islamic standards, this type of moral crime being perceived as a serious threat to Muslims, particularly as it involved 'foreign organised crime'.[74] A backlash against immoral activities occurred in early 2005 when several foreign guesthouses and restaurants were closed down for allowing gambling, prostitution and the consumption of alcohol on their premises. In February 2006, reportedly through pressure from newly-elected members of parliament concerned about Kabul's widespread prostitution, 46 Chinese women working in the many Chinese restaurants situated in the more upmarket areas of Wazir Akbar Khan and Shar-e Now were arrested for prostitution and selling alcohol to Afghans: 'so synonymous have Chinese restaurants become with brothels in Kabul that it is not a good idea to tell anybody you are going for a Chinese meal—in case they get the wrong impression'.[75]

One other consequence of the large influx of foreigners with money to spend in Kabul has been the boom in property prices and rentals. In Wazir Akbar Khan, an area of the city much favoured by foreigners and international organisations, house rentals range from $2,000 to over $10,000 a month. One European country pays $30,000 a month in rental for the relatively small building housing its Embassy. The knock-on effect at the bottom end of the housing market has been crippling rentals throughout the city for local residents. A two-bedroom flat in Macroryan, the name of several crumbling complexes of Soviet-built four-storey apartment blocks throughout the city, is over $200 a month. In mud-brick slum areas it costs $30 a month for three rooms and access to a well, but with no electricity.[76] In 2005 most government officials and civil servants, including doctors, lawyers and teachers, were still paid only a standard $50–60 per month, with many having to supplement their income by taking other jobs or opening small businesses that increasingly took up most of their time and diverted their energies away from their government work. During the same period an Afghan driver working for the United Nations could earn over $400 per month with overtime and allowances.

However, at the same time as the people of Afghanistan have experienced such terrible hardships and inequalities as those outlined above, they have also shown remarkable resilience and displayed resistance to the various draconian regimes they have had to face. Community groups continue to reconstruct homes and mosques, repair irrigation and water supply systems and rebuild livelihoods, despite limited assistance from the government and international agencies. In some areas it has been suggested that the years of conflict may even have strengthened local identity 'in order to escape the predations of an illegitimate central state', although this may also help to engender suspicion and resistance towards any centralised authority, legitimate or otherwise.[77] In the face of adversity many Afghans have retained their dignity, sense of humour and hospitality, alongside a reputation for brutality and a penchant for their own particular tribal version of advanced Machiavellian politics. It is a country where social history is very much alive, if not well, in its present.

Much of the country's physical history and cultural heritage have been obliterated by the ravages of war, with the destruction of the giant Buddha statutes at Bamiyan by the Taliban and the continuing theft and plunder of the country's many important archaeological sites. In the 2005 parliamentary elections, Maulavi Mohammad Islam Mohammadi, the Taliban's governor of Bamiyan who oversaw the destruction of the Buddha statues, was elected as a representative for Samangan province in the *Wolesi Jirga*. Priceless artefacts such as jewellery, statues, frescoes, ceramics and 'the world's most important collection of Bactrian coins' are smuggled into neighbouring countries for onward sale to unscrupulous antique collectors in richer countries.[78] UNESCO has estimated the global industry in stolen Afghan antiquities at $32 billion.[79] During 2004 and 2005, British police and customs officials seized nearly four tons of plundered Afghan antiquities, including stone sculptures, Buddhist Gandharan statues, bronze weapons, and coins dating back to the third century BC.[80]

One of the main legacies of this tragic period in Afghanistan's history, from the Soviet invasion in 1979 to the rout of the Taliban in late 2001 and the uncertainties beyond, has been the development of social and economic conditions that have produced a set of very understandable motivations for people to use drugs, primarily as a means of coping with the painful daily reality of an impoverished and insecure existence and the all-pervasive legacy of war and conflict. One added ingredient necessary to ensure a rapidly increasing number of problem drug users over that period was the availability of a wide range of psychoactive substances, including opium and its more powerful derivative, heroin.

# 4
# Opium Cultivators*

The benefits of the dramatic increase in opium poppy prices are unevenly distributed. For those without accumulated debts and good yields, the current price of opium has been a windfall and led to an increase in conspicuous consumption in 2002. However, for those households with a high incidence of unpaid advances on opium among their accumulated debt, the dramatic increase in the price of opium since January 2001 will have had little impact, as many will need to repay this debt in kind.[1]

The drug economy threatens the very fabric of Afghan society. The authorities need to forcefully address this issue. The mission supports recent efforts by the government to work closely with international partners to develop a broad strategy to deal with the opium issue that focuses on education, alternative livelihoods, interdiction, eradication, and legal reform. At the same time, the staff recognize that eradication of opium production cannot be accomplished in isolation, and that it could have a significant economic impact—particularly on some of the most vulnerable segments of the population.[2]

For many poor people, poppy growing is not only the most profitable activity available, but also the only way of meeting their needs. In many ways it is a miracle crop. It matures quickly, allowing double cropping in many areas, it is more weather-resistant than wheat, is easy to store, transport and sell.[3]

It is only in the period since 1980 that Afghanistan has steadily developed as the world's leading producer of opium, although the opium poppy (*Papaver somniferum*) has been cultivated in several parts of the country for many centuries. Soldiers in Alexander the Great's armies may have introduced opium into the land that now

---

* Throughout this chapter I am indebted to David Mansfield for his pioneering work in providing such a comprehensive analysis of the complex dynamics and processes of poppy cultivation and production in Afghanistan. Apart from reports under his own name, he was also responsible for conducting the UNDCP's Annual Opium Poppy Surveys from 1997 to 1999 and developing, researching and compiling the UNDCP Strategic Study series, Nos 1–6 covering topics such as the role of women in opium poppy cultivation, the expansion of poppy into new districts, the coping strategies of opium traders and the role of opium as a source of informal credit.

constitutes Afghanistan or it may have been imported as a trade commodity from countries like Egypt and Greece where it was a popular medicine. A report by the British Indian Government from 1905 specifically mentioned that opium poppy was one of the main autumn-planted, spring-harvested crops in Nangarhar province in the eastern part of the country.[4] In the same year, the *Imperial Gazeteer* reported that opium was produced in the districts of the Herat valley, Kabul, Qandahar and Jalalabad, 'but not to any great extent'. At that time, apart from what was smuggled out illicitly, the export of opium to neighbouring countries, as well as the export of timber and all productions from Afghanistan's mines, was monopolised by the Amir Habibullah Khan.[5] Following this royal tradition, in the 1950s and 1960s it has been alleged that 'the relatively sparse opium trade was controlled by the Royal family, headed by King Mohammad Zahir. The large feudal estates all had their opium fields, primarily to feed domestic consumption of the drug.'[6]

In 1924 at the Second Opium Conference, organised by the Permanent Central Opium Board under the control of the League of Nations, Afghanistan reported poppy cultivation in the provinces of Badakhshan, Herat and Jalalabad (now Nangarhar). Eight years later in 1932, when estimates of opium production first became available, Afghanistan reportedly produced 75 tons, quite a significant amount given that the total population of the country at that time was no more than 10 million at most, and that a portion of this opium was designated for domestic consumption. For the next 40 years Afghanistan had rather a chequered career regarding opium production. Although officially prohibited in 1945, with annual production falling to only twelve tons by 1956, by the early 1970s Afghanistan was seen as a country where narcotics constituted a serious problem and the government was unable to control either production or trafficking to neighbouring countries.[7] It has been suggested that at that time drug users in neighbouring Iran consumed almost all of Afghanistan's opium, as well as smaller amounts produced in Pakistan.[8]

Certainly a catalyst for the expansion of opium cultivation and production in Afghanistan was the new bans and stricter drug control laws imposed in neighbouring Iran, Pakistan and India at the end of the 1970s, until that time primary sources of opium production in the region. Other catalysts included the governance vacuum in Afghanistan, the search by *mujahideen* groups for funds to buy weapons to fight the Soviets (and later each other) and increased cross-border movement by Pashtoon tribes involved in drug production.

However, while Afghanistan has become the world's leading producer of opium since 1991 it has not until recently been the main cultivator of the drug. Until 2003 this title belonged to Myanmar. Since 1990, Myanmar has consistently had more land under opium cultivation than Afghanistan, but with a poorer opium yield. In 2002, for example, for every 10 kg of opium produced per hectare in Myanmar there were 46 kg produced in Afghanistan.[9] This lower yield is due to several factors, including the effect of different soils and different climatic conditions on the growth cycle.

Although basically mountainous desert country, Afghanistan has always contained significant pockets of fertile arable land capable of producing a wide range of crops both for local consumption and export. By 1970, for example, Afghanistan provided an estimated 65 per cent of the world trade in dried raisins. However, with the advent of war other products that had been exported, such as natural gas, animal skins, cotton and carpets, all declined. While there is debate about whether pre-war Afghanistan had a mainly subsistence non-monetised rural economy or one that was more integrated into the market economy, the advent of war changed the livelihood strategies of many Afghans. As markets collapsed and the Soviets followed their scorched earth policy in rural areas, the rural economy that had enabled Afghanistan to be self-sufficient in food production and had accounted for 30 per cent of exports through agricultural produce 'retreated into subsistence production' and many rural inhabitants moved into the cities or fled the country and became refugees.[10]

## INCREASING POPPY CULTIVATION

Although agricultural production declined during the war with the Soviet Union, in the early 1990s it revived as refugees began to return and some investment was made in developing infrastructure.[11] The severe drought that occurred in 1998, and continued until late 2004, adversely affected this revival and encouraged the move to off-farm income generating activities, always an integral part of livelihood strategies in rural Afghanistan. One of the factors responsible for rural regeneration was the cultivation of opium poppy. In a major growing province like Helmand, opium played several roles in the farming system, as it still does in several areas of the country. It is a cash crop with a hard currency value and it is easy to transport and sell, rather than a subsistence crop in a country where over 80 per cent of farmers grow their own food. It is also relatively drought resistant. With limited water availability it generates higher marginal returns on available water, even although the opium yield is much less than on irrigated land. Opium poppy also serves as a break crop in rotation and provides an economic means for rigorous weed control.[12]

While emphasis is often placed on the unassailable profitability of opium poppy, this masks the complex and ever-changing dynamics of poppy cultivation that depend on a wide and frequently changing set of variables. For a significant number of farmers in Afghanistan these variables still create as many costs as benefits. The undoubted profits generated by the opium trade are not equally distributed along the trafficking chain, and it is the farmer, particularly the resource-poor farmer, who is likely to benefit least. This is especially the case in a country like Afghanistan where traditional land tenure structures and informal credit systems have consistently disadvantaged the poorer farmer and advantaged the richer farmer and landowner.

It is important to recognise that the majority of farmers in Afghanistan do not grow opium poppy, although there has been a definite increase in cultivation over the past 20 years, and that in areas where poppy is cultivated it is very rarely mono-cropped. In 2002 the amount of arable land under poppy cultivation was less than 1 per cent, and during the harvest of a drought-ridden 2000, that produced 3,276 tonnes of opium, only 8 per cent of arable land in poppy growing villages was used for opium cultivation. Indeed, not all farmers in these villages cultivated poppy. A year later in 2003 the UNODC estimated that poppy was cultivated on 1 per cent of the total arable land and 3 per cent of irrigated arable land with around 7 per cent of the Afghan population directly involved. Such direct involvement referred only to families growing opium and not to itinerant labourers, families involved in trading opium products and the many Afghans whose incomes derived from a wide range of commercial activities related to opium production or financed by opium money.

By the 2003–04 growing season, a study conducted in 16 districts in five provinces showed that on average 34 per cent of household cultivated land was used for growing poppy as against 59 per cent for wheat and 7 per cent for vegetables and fruit crops.[13] Although the UNODC reported that poppy cultivation had increased in Afghanistan from 80,000 hectares the previous year to a record 131,000 hectares in 2003–04, a 64 per cent increase, 54 per cent of farmers interviewed in the study allocated less than half their land to opium poppy and nationally only 3 per cent of arable land was cultivated with opium. Farmers were discouraged from cultivating only opium poppy due to concerns over food security, plus potential crop and market failure.[14] For the 2004–05 growing season farmers reported that they would only allocate 6 per cent of household cultivated land to poppy compared with the 34 per cent of the previous year. As the study noted,

While falling farm gate prices, low yields and concerns over food security have played an important role, the primary reason for lower levels of planting is the belief that the government is more serious this year in its intent to reduce opium poppy cultivation. In particular, it suggests that there is a growing view that the central government has greater jurisdiction over provincial and local authorities and consequently regional powerbrokers are more likely to comply with the President's desire to see a reduction in opium poppy cultivation this year.[15]

In Afghanistan generally, opium poppy cultivation is concentrated in 40 per cent of districts, although there was a rapid expansion to new districts cultivating poppy between 1995 and 2000. In planting season 2002 poppy was reportedly cultivated in 28 provinces compared with 18 in 1999.[16] By 2004 it was asserted that for the first time all 32 provinces were involved in opium cultivation, although in previous years some of these provinces had not been included in surveys of opium cultivation, making it difficult to know whether some of them had been involved in cultivation in past seasons.

## COSTS AND BENEFITS OF OPIUM CULTIVATION

Although there has been an increasing, if fluctuating, trend in opium cultivation, such figures beg the question that if opium poppy is so profitable, particularly in a context of abject rural poverty, why do all farmers not cultivate it? To answer this question it is necessary to look at the many factors that account for the great diversity in poppy cultivation found in Afghanistan. David Mansfield succinctly suggests that

Social and religious norms, as well as perceptions of morality, inform households in their decision to plant opium poppy. Access to land, water, and in particular, unremunerated and low paid labour, are important determinants in the level of opium poppy cultivation. The role of opium as a source of financial credit is also a particularly important motivation for its cultivation.[17]

In 2005 the credible threat of eradication of opium poppy crops added a new variable for the farmer to consider, at least in some areas of the country and for the first time since the Taliban's edict of 2000 banned all cultivation of poppy.

Within Islam the cultivation, production, trafficking and consumption of intoxicants like opium is *haram*, and in many deeply conservative and religious rural areas of the country this is perceived as a distinct cost when farmers weigh up the advantages and disadvantages of planting opium poppy. Some farmers will obey governmental edicts forbidding the cultivation of poppy and may even fear governmental efforts to eradicate their crop, while others will feel they have little choice but to continue the cultivation of poppy and resist and subvert any attempts to eradicate their crops. Apart from this, the decision to grow opium is largely dependent on the costs associated with obtaining labour, seed, fertiliser, farmpower, land and water. Although opium poppy can grow on poor-quality land with minimum water and no fertiliser, the yield is likely to be poor and may not be worth the effort—as long as there is no significant rise in farmgate opium prices. (Ironically, successful eradication and the concomitant rise in the price of raw opium in one season is likely to act as an incentive for some farmers to plant poppy the next season.)

Labour in particular can be costly as poppy is a very labour-intensive crop, requiring careful thinning and weeding in its early stages and expert lancing at harvest time to ensure maximum yield. One hectare of poppy requires approximately six times the number of person days of work compared to wheat. Experienced itinerant labourers, often blamed for the spread of poppy cultivation into new districts, are costly although efficient and practised in the specialised task of lancing and gathering the gum from the ripe poppy capsules: if the capsule is cut before it fully matures the yield will be reduced, if it is scored too deeply the resin will oxidise in the capsule and if it is not scored deeply enough the flow of resin is restricted.[18] In order to minimise such labour costs, the use of household labour is maximised, including the use of women and children, as well as the use of reciprocal labour arrangements called *ashar* that utilise the labour of other relatives, neighbours and friends who usually only receive food in return for their work. Staggered planting and the cultivation of poppies with different maturation cycles help to ensure maximum utilisation of family and reciprocal labour.

Throughout Afghanistan, opium has become a non-perishable, low-weight, high-value product that represents 'a commodity to be exchanged, not only for the purchase of food but as the means for achieving food security, providing the resource poor with access to land for agricultural production and credit during times of food scarcity'.[19] In a country with few secure financial institutions, basically it acts as the family's bank. For the landowner and resource-rich farmer, opium has presented an opportunity for profit that can be used to purchase property, vehicles and consumer items that might be considered luxuries in war-torn rural areas. For the sharecropper and the resource-poor farmer, however, opium has represented a basic means of family survival, although the very poorest may not even make a decent profit from their opium crop, even in a good year.

Households with no land, or not enough land to meet their basic survival needs, can only try to access land by entering into often exploitative tenancy or sharecropping agreements with landowners. Sharecroppers, for example, may receive only one third of the final opium yield if the landowner provides fertiliser, seed and farmpower, as well as land and water. One direct benefit for the sharecropper is that they can also plant crops such as wheat, maize and vegetables for consumption, as well as poppy, thus providing at least a minimum level of food security for their family. More importantly, cultivating opium will enable the sharecropper to gain access to credit, 'critical to household survival during the winter months when food scarcity is at its most acute'.[20]

But, credit 'facilities' made available for farmers to cultivate opium in Afghanistan can lead to a vicious cycle of debt and repayment, thus creating significant problems for the farmer and his dependants. While on the one hand the profit from opium can enable survival, reduce the harms and pains of poverty and facilitate access to essentials like food and medicine, it can, on the other hand, also ensnare the farmer in debt. It should be noted that survival in this case refers not only to food, clothes, housing and the repayment of existing loans, but also to other basic necessities such as healthcare. As one woman from Badakhshan in northeast Afghanistan stated, 'My daughter has had an operation for which we borrowed 15 million Afghanis. If we cannot produce opium to repay the loan, what shall we do?'[21] It is also important to recognise that 'luxury' in the case of Afghanistan is a relative term. In the words of a farmer from Kapisa in the east of the country, 'We are not cultivating opium poppy to have a luxury life. We have no food, no cloth [sic] and no shelter, the basic needs of a human being. Therefore, we are searching for the means at least to cover these needs.'[22] It should be noted, however, that debt in rural Afghanistan has long been ubiquitous across the social spectrum because 'at certain points—marriage, a family crisis, a major investment—families need capital'.[23] For many the vagaries of the opium market have exacerbated this debt.

In four districts of Nangarhar and Qandahar provinces in 1998 it was found that 95 per cent of 108 opium farmers interviewed had obtained a loan during the previous twelve months. This included landless households, owner-cultivators and landowners who employed sharecroppers or tenant farmers.[24] Most of these loans were based on an advance payment for a fixed amount of agricultural product, known as the *salaam* system. Although *salaam* can be provided for other agricultural products, 60 per cent of the farmers in the study had received *salaam* on their future opium crop. Typically the price paid as an advance is 50 per cent of the market price of opium on the day that the agreement is reached.[25] The farmers in the above study received 40 per cent less as an advance than the eventual harvest price, resulting in a much lower return than if they had been able to afford to wait and sell their opium after harvest. Such is the opium futures market in Afghanistan on the lowest rungs of the trafficking ladder.

In early 2003 in the south of Helmand province the governor, a member of the Akhundzada clan, forced the eradication of poppy crops thus effectively eliminating the competition while appearing to support the central government's ban on cultivation. As a result many farmers fell deeper in debt to local commanders, opium traders and money-lenders. At the same time farmers in northern Helmand did not have their crops eradicated and other members of the clan who controlled the production of opium in the north benefited from an increase in opium prices caused by the eradication in the south of the province.[26]

While for some the *salaam* system may appear little more than usury or *riba*, forbidden by the Koran, Mansfield cites its exploitative nature by giving the example of the 1997/98 growing season, when due to heavy unseasonal spring rains, households in Helmand and Qandahar provinces experienced shortfalls in yield of up to 70 per cent, resulting in an inability to pay off their *salaam* and an increase in debt.[27] In a study looking at the dynamics of the farmgate opium trade and the coping strategies of opium traders, 60 per cent of the opium traders interviewed had provided *salaam* on opium production.[28] By 2005, however, with changing structural and political conditions, research showed that many farmers had not taken *salaam* on their future opium crop, at least for the time being. In one study a farmer explained how

his advance payment of US$450 on five kgs of opium in December 2000 had been converted from opium to cash and back again over a three year period until he owed 50 kgs of opium by April 2003. His only option for repayment was to give his eight year-old daughter in marriage to his creditor.[29]

By 2004 it was estimated that there was 15,000 opium traders in the country, many offering *salaam*, although the exact number of traders remains unknown.[30]

This fluctuating credit dialectic between traders and cultivators, never mind the fluctuating fortunes of farmers and their families, is central to an understanding of opium cultivation in Afghanistan, and therefore to any attempts to prevent cultivation and introduce alternative livelihoods into poppy cultivation areas, including those areas of the country that may be at risk of starting to grow poppy. In 2003, in isolated and mountainous Ghor province, four days' drive to the west of Kabul, many of the poorest farmers, constituting most of the population of the province, had little choice but to plant opium poppy in the coming season. Ghor, like many other areas of Afghanistan, had been ravaged by drought and in 2003 farmers had planted poppy to pay off their accumulated debts. However, a late frost reportedly 'dried the bulbs before the opium gum could be scraped off. Nearly all of the harvest was lost. So the farmer's debts are still mounting, with much of the money owed to opium traders who will insist on a new planting next year.'[31] This cycle of debt and repayment is likely to continue for several years in impoverished rural areas of Afghanistan where farmers are at the mercy of unpredictable weather patterns and unscrupulous opium traders and have few alternative means of livelihood. Meanwhile in more prolific areas of production, many farmers are drawn to the opportunities provided by opium, despite the increasing risks, for capital accumulation and the conspicuous consumption of luxury goods.

Such evidence suggests that a significant number of poppy farmers in Afghanistan are balanced on a knife-edge of profit and survival on one hand and debt and impoverishment on the other. In weighing up the likely costs of poppy cultivation, an increasing number of cultivators, and particularly those already caught in the debt trap, may have to consider options such as fleeing or returning to neighbouring countries as economic migrants or refugees (an increasingly difficult option), selling assets including land, simply 'disappearing' with their families into other areas of the country or selling their daughters, some as young as seven or eight, for bride-price. While the practice of bride-price has long been customary in several areas of Afghanistan, cultural constraints have slackened and it has evolved into a commodity market where any man wealthy enough can buy young girls from poor families.[32] A season with poor rainfall and resulting poor harvests can throw even richer farmers back into the debt trap, although at the same time stockpiles of opium will see rising profits for big opium traders.

## PERSONAL DECISIONS

There are more hidden social costs associated with opium cultivation and production. Just after opium harvest time in July 2003 in the small market town of Jurm in mountainous and remote Badakhshan province the complexities began to emerge. Ahmed is the 15-year-old son of a local carpenter who is also a shopkeeper and small farmer. His father has been growing opium poppies for the past three years because 'there are too many carpenters in town' and he cannot earn a living from carpentry any more. For the three to four weeks of the poppy harvest, as well as the earlier weeding period, Ahmed has been off school for most of the time helping his father to collect the opium gum. For a seven-hour day between 5 a.m. and midday he is paid three tolas of opium (approximately 36 g) that he can sell in the bazaar for cash. Now he has saved nearly $600 and wants to use the money to take a correspondence course in English. Since harvest time started most children have been off school helping in the poppy fields. Even some of the teachers have joined them, particularly as it only takes a few days' work in the poppy fields to earn what they make in a month as a government teacher. In addition, civil servants in this area of Badakhshan have not been paid for the last four months. Ahmed, a bright boy who wants to go to Kabul University, is pessimistic about the future for himself and his schoolmates: 'If this opium continues none of us will ever amount to anything.' His younger brother Mohammad, who has also been off school collecting opium gum, is less pessimistic. He too has saved around $600 and now wants to buy a Russian-built Minsk motorcycle. A few years ago a new motorcycle cost $300, now it is $600, a reflection of the boom economy in the area kick-started by opium and the end of war between the Taliban and the Northern Alliance.

Local community leaders are concerned about the proliferation of motorcycles in Jurm. If poppy cultivation continues, the peace and tranquillity of an outstandingly picturesque area is likely to be shattered by the droning of hundreds of motorcycles revved up by their teenage owners, not to mention the roar of their fathers' 4x4 pick-up trucks and the resultant environmental and noise pollution. The bazaar, empty a few years ago, is overflowing with a wide variety of retail goods including satellite TVs and video recorders, but this is dependent on opium production. As with the expansion of opium cultivation in several other areas of the country, 'the short-term effect was to jump-start economic recovery and render the employment creation programmes of the aid agencies largely redundant'; local residents estimated that in 2003 Jurm district would produce upwards of 140,000 kg of opium worth over $32 million.[33] In the nearby town of Baharak opium was commonly used to barter for goods sold in the bazaar, and it was noticeable that most traders and shopkeepers kept a set of weighing scales just for this purpose.

By the time I left Jurm, Ahmed's father was still balancing his books. While he is grateful for the profits he has made from opium, he recognises the costs and the risks involved. Although for this last planting season he bought improved 'Jalalabad' poppy seed meant to produce double the yield of the local varieties, this has not been the case and his yield has been relatively low. While he, his children and other family members did most of the work in the poppy fields, apart from lancing the capsules, he had to hire labourers at a cost of over $10 a day just to get the rest of his farm work done. He also feels exhausted, as poppy cultivation is arduous and constant work. This is borne out by the local doctor who says that over the past few weeks many people have been coming to the clinic complaining of aches, pains and fatigue, the consequence of long hours of back-breaking work in the sweltering heat of Jurm's poppy fields. Ahmed's father will 'probably' grow opium again next planting season, as he sees no real alternative. Perhaps if international agencies did not import and distribute cheap wheat, keeping the price low, and there was a communal combine harvester that all the farmers could use to quickly harvest the wheat, he might consider it, but he doubts it. In 2003 the WFP, as well as other international agencies, allegedly put pressure on NGOs like Oxfam in Badakhshan to distribute wheat, resulting in lowered prices for local wheat crops and decreased incentives for farmers to grow a legal crop like wheat.[34] There may, however, be other more traditional and cultural reasons why farmers in areas like Badakhshan might want to continue growing opium, at least in smaller non-commercial quantities. In such areas by-products from the opium poppy apart from the resin are still in everyday use, including

opium oil which is used for cooking, konjara (winter fodder) given to the animals to build up their strength in cold days, dried stalks of opium poppy plants used as a fuel for cooking fires or as animal feed and opium soap of two varieties, one for washing clothes and the other for bathing.[35]

In Adraskan and Kushk districts in the parched desert lands of Herat province at the opposite end of the country from Badakhshan, villages have been growing opium just to survive. There are few motorcycles or 4x4s around, and no satellite TVs. They too are aware of the costs of producing opium. In one village, five women have lost sons to the Iranian border patrols who reputedly have a 'shoot to kill' policy when dealing with young Afghans trying to smuggle opium over the border into Iran. In another village there is hope a new crop is being tried: saffron, dubbed as 'Red gold' because it is so valuable. It is a hardy, drought-resistant, high-value cash crop that, unlike opium, takes little looking after once the initial planting has taken place. As one woman said:

Before, in my village we grew some poppy crop just to survive. But now poppy cultivation has stopped in favour of the saffron crop which is much better for us. It is legal and it doesn't damage people. On the contrary, according to local wisdom if you eat saffron, you feel good. It makes you cheerful. It's like eating a little piece of sunshine.[36]

The cultivation of oil roses and production of rose oil, yielding up to $3,000 per hectare, is one of the few other alternative cash crops to rival the profitability of opium, as roses can be easily cultivated in Afghanistan and rose oil easily transported to international markets at low cost. The Ministry of Rural Rehabilitation and Development has conducted a feasibility study for rose oil production and two international organisations have already started pilot projects to grow roses for essential flower oils to be sold in the global market for rose essence, a market worth $18 million a year. Rose oil is used in the perfume and cosmetics industries and it has been estimated that Afghanistan could capture 25 per cent of this market, with flower oils becoming a lucrative export. The main variety of rose used is *Rosa damascena* which is weather resistant and can hopefully withstand both the searing heat of an Afghan summer and the bitter cold of the winter. It is estimated that a hectare of roses would produce around 800 g of essential oil that could be sold for up to $5,000. While this may not be as much as a hectare of opium, assuming a good year's harvest, it gives a much higher return than other crops such as wheat at around $250 per hectare, and it is legal (although wheat is mainly grown for family food security and not as a cash crop). Like poppy cultivation, and unlike wheat cultivation, the cultivation of roses is a labour-intensive process, thus potentially providing a source of income for the labour currently employed in opium production.[37] But farmers anywhere are notoriously conservative and resistant to change and it is unlikely that Afghanistan's poppy fields will soon be filled with saffron and roses. Australian and German bio-engineers have also recently created another alternative to traditional opium poppy plants, mutated poppy plants that produce the alkaloids like thebaine and oripavine used in analgesic pharmaceutical drugs like buprenorphine (Temgesic), but without producing morphine that can be processed into heroin.[38]

## PREVENTING OPIUM CULTIVATION

Complexities such as those outlined above show some of the problems in developing sustainable policies to eliminate opium cultivation in Afghanistan. Mansfield suggests that attempts to develop realistic policies have been hampered by the information that these policies are based on. This is 'often little more than hearsay and anecdote' and is over-reliant on quantitative data that provides an aggregate scenario and a simplistic picture of 'the average farmer'.[39] He stresses that it is important to differentiate between the estimated 5–20 per cent of farmers who have access to family assets like land, livestock, irrigation and other means of income such as retail businesses, government salaries and remittances from abroad, and the 80–95 per cent who have no land or poor-quality land, limited access to irrigation and accumulated debts in excess of the value of their annual income. The former group are not dependent on poppy cultivation for their livelihood yet are less likely to have their crops eradicated because of their power, political connections and social status and are able to accumulate more assets and buy luxury consumer items. The latter group is dependent on poppy cultivation but more likely to have their crop eradicated, leaving them unable to service their existing debts and unable 'to obtain further loans for purchasing much needed agricultural inputs during the planting season or food during the winter months'.[40] In effect, according to one long-standing Afghan analyst, 'the predominant analysis of the opium economy has been wrong and has led policy makers in the wrong direction'.[41] A 2004 paper by the World Bank stressed that both Thailand and Pakistan took many years and a gradual sustainable approach incorporating comprehensive alternative development programmes before opium was more or less eliminated. In particular, a strategy based on eradication, apart from being difficult if not dangerous to implement, would create poverty and lead to political damage.[42]

The forced eradication of poppy certainly poses a range of ethical and political issues, as well as logistical and operational problems, for the Afghan government and its international partners. Because of the targeted nature of the eradication campaign in Nangarhar province during the 2001–02 growing season, just over half of farmers interviewed by UNODC surveyors reported that the eradication campaign had not affected their opium crop. However, 30 per cent of farmers interviewed claimed that their opium crop had been destroyed, with many of them saying that they were now deeper in debt. Only a very few had received any compensation for the destruction of their crop. As the UNODC study indicated, 'stories of corruption were widespread'.[43] In Nangarhar farmers had made payments, otherwise known as 'facilitation fees', to local and regional commanders to ensure that they would receive compensation after their crops had been destroyed. Those who did receive any compensation were paid at a much lower rate than that agreed. In other words the commanders simply kept most, or in many cases all, of the compensation money as well as the facilitation fees received from the farmers. In Helmand province farmers bribed government officials responsible for the compensation programme to increase the amount of land reported as eradicated, 'for instance one respondent in Nade-e-Ali reported that he paid $180 to an official to double the amount of opium poppy he had eradicated', resulting in a potential gain of $1,220.[44]

In 2002 the Director of the Counter Narcotics Directorate of the government's National Security Council, Mirwais Yasini, was reported as saying: 'We are committed a hundred percent to eradicating poppies. We know it won't be easy, but the decree is without reservation.'[45] A major problem in persuading farmers to obey the law, however, were the attempts to eradicate the poppy crop in the spring of 2002 (from planting season 2001) when many farmers claimed they received no compensation at all. Farmers in Qandahar threatened to grow double the crop in the 2002 planting season because they received no compensation money in the spring for the crop planted in 2001. But before the poppy planting season started in late 2002, a task force was established in the western part of Qandahar city, consisting of 100 armed personnel, 90 soldiers and ten commanders, with 25 each coming from Helmand and Uruzgan provinces and 50 from Qandahar province. UK Special Forces allegedly trained the commanders to intercept convoys of drugs and to find and destroy heroin laboratories and drug markets. After this training the task force also became engaged in poppy eradication. Each commander was paid $300 per month, while each of his men was paid $100. On top of this they were allegedly paid a 'bounty' of $5,000 for each successful mission. They were also supplied with vehicles, satellite phones and cameras, presumably to record their successes. On one mission to the Choto area of Helmand Province the task force returned empty-handed as the drug traders had fled the area before they arrived, presumably the result of a tip-off.

It was also reported that human rights abuses occurred during the eradication campaign in Qandahar province. Extortion, beatings and harassment were all used against opium farmers. Typically the farmer was told he had to pay a fine, pay up to $300 to hire the tractor to eradicate his own crops and spend a night or two in jail—unless he paid off the forces doing the eradication. However, on 31 October 2002 an operation was launched in Ghorak district in which 60 kg of opium was confiscated from several households—an operation carried out by the armed forces of the Governor of Qandahar and not by the task force. This suggested, at best, a lack of coordination, and at worst a power struggle to see who would claim the spoils of Afghanistan's new opium wars.

By 2003 the authorities had learned their lesson and no compensation was offered to farmers if their crops were eradicated. Other reports from January 2003 suggested a large increase in poppy cultivation in the northern provinces of Takhar, Baghlan and Badakhshan. Commanders in Baghlan were found distributing poppy seeds to farmers, saying that the UN would pay them money for the destruction of their fields, and if not they would receive money from selling their opium crop, a win-win situation if indeed the information had been true. In any case, some fields could simply be replanted after eradication of the first planting if this happened early enough in the growing season. A newly seeded field that is 'eradicated' by ploughing will likely be unaffected, unless the seed has already germinated, and will produce more or less the same crop that it would if it hadn't been eradicated in the first place. By 2004 eradication as a method of drug control became more realistic, only taking place during the latter stages of opium cultivation when the plant was almost fully grown. Unfortunately, this tactic allows the farmer no opportunity to re-seed his fields with another type of crop, possible if the plant is eradicated at an earlier stage in the growing season.

In May 2006 in Sar-i-Pul in the north of the country a student and a policeman were reportedly killed and nine policemen wounded in an armed clash with angry poppy farmers whose crops were being eradicated.[46] The students had been backing the police in their anti-poppy drive. Another report claimed that the two people killed were farmers and that three of the policemen were critically wounded.[47] In April 2005 in Maiwand district about 50 km outside Qandahar city, around 2,000 farmers blocked the highway with burning tyres in protest against the impending destruction of their maturing opium crops. In the ensuing confrontation between the protestors and the 600-strong government eradicators, accompanied and trained by private contractors from the US DynCorp company, several people were reportedly killed and others seriously injured. According to one press report, 'dense clouds of black smoke hung over the town from burning barricades, hundreds of shots rang out from gun battles, and American helicopter gunships flew low overhead'.[48] Some of the farmers complained of inequities in the eradication campaign, one said, 'it is only the fields of the poor that are being destroyed, not the fields of the rich'. The same farmer complained that while farmers had their crops eradicated, warlords were allowed to retain their stockpiles of opium and that crops would be spared eradication if the farmer paid bribes or shared kinship ties with the eradicator.[49] The police chief in Qandahar, spiritual home of the Taliban, claimed that local government authorities were being prudent in tackling the problem as they wanted to appease the poorest farmers 'who could be tempted to join the Taliban'.[50] Whatever the reasons, the eradication was a failure and its operations suspended.

By contrast, in the same year in Nangarhar and neighbouring Laghman province, one of the leading opium-producing areas over the last decade, cultivation fell by over 90 per cent. According to one report this was achieved by central government pressure on police chiefs and other officials at the district and provincial levels to reduce opium cultivation or lose their positons in the state admin-istration. Through a process of informal coercion, co-option and persuasion by the officials, as well as promises of compensation funded by international donors, farmers were convinced, if somewhat reluctantly, not to cultivate poppy. The threat of losing their official positions appears to have been a significant enough incentive for these officials, many of them former *mujahideen* commanders, to comply with government directives. On the other hand, deals may have been struck, and as the report states, at least in these two provinces 'there appears to be a growing understanding that being a warlord or jihadi commander is less secure and less lucrative than a position in the state bureaucracy', and that 'compliance with the ban on cultivation was explicitly seen as conditional on rapid compensation and rural development'.[51] By early 2006 it was almost inevitable that without adequate compensation and development for poor poppy farmers in southern provinces like Helmand province, the re-emergent Taliban would 'team up with drug barons' to offer armed protection to the farmers against government eradicators.[52]

Ironically, US government criticism of the ineffective strategies of President Karzai and the UK, as the lead donor nation for narcotics control in Afghanistan, was political fallout from the failure of the eradication campaigns up to 2005 in making any significant reduction in Afghanistan's opium production figures. An editorial in the *New York Times* stated that it required 'breathtaking audacity' for US government officials to blame the failure of the poppy eradication campaign on President Karzai because he wasn't a strong enough leader, especially when the US had neglected the opium cultivation situation for nearly two and a half years.[53] Indeed, over the past few years there had been growing concern over the US and the international community turning towards a strategy of crop eradication and also a growing recognition that without comprehensive development programmes, including alternative livelihoods, credit facilities, security and justice sector reform, farmers would only become more entrenched in the debt trap.[54]

Apart from human intervention in the shape of crop eradication, growing opium in Afghanistan is an occupation also beset by natural problems such as drought and a range of plant diseases and growth detractants such as worms, wilt, root rot, leaf blotch, green aphids and other insects. Fungi can also be a problem and poor crops have been blamed by farmers, particularly in Nangarhar province, on the deliberate spread, real or imagined, of the poppy fungus *Pleospora papaveracea* through aerial fumigation by the US military. This fungus was originally developed and tested in neighbouring Uzbekistan, with UNODC, UK and US funding and approval, with field trials taking place in Kyrgyzstan and Tajikistan. Certainly crop eradication by spraying with mycotoxins has long been part of the US-led strategy of fighting a global war on drugs. In the case of *Fusarium oxysporum*, used in Latin America to destroy coca bushes, it has been suggested that

The development of a capability to destroy drug crops with plant pathogens will inevitably provide a wealth of knowledge and practical experience that could readily be applied in more aggressive, offensive biological warfare targeting food crops. The Fusarium fungus is the root for many of the chemical/ biological weapons developed by the US, the Soviet Union, Britain, Israel, France and Iraq.[55]

In the words of an article published in *Scientific American*, 'the biowar against drugs is likely to be a poison chalice rather than a silver bullet'[56] and in any case reports on the effectiveness of aerial spraying of drug crops are not reliable or evidence-based. It would certainly be tragic if the Afghan government capitulated to US pressure to allow the aerial spraying of crops. Aerial defoliation of coca plantations in the Amazon region as part of the US-launched Plan Colombia that started in 1999 resulted in the destruction of fragile ecosystems, particularly aquatic ecosystems. The main toxic chemical used was Monsanto's Roundup SL, a combination of glyphosate and an agent called Cosmo-Flux 411F which causes eye and skin problems in humans. Roundup SL is prohibited for use in the US and was sprayed in Colombia by planes belonging to DynCorp, the same company involved in opium eradication in Afghanistan, as part of their 'aerial herbicide fumigation programme'.

Despite such natural and man-made problems and the edict passed by President Karzai in 2002 banning its cultivation, opium persists in several areas of the country, but particularly in Helmand province (at least for the moment). While there are no sustainable short-term solutions to the problem and it is recognised that there needs to be a carefully phased long-term strategy if opium is to be totally eliminated from Afghanistan, plans for eradication of current crops move ahead. While the Afghan government has a policy of no compensation for farmers whose opium crops are destroyed, as well as a sensible no-aerial-eradication policy, this has not always been the case and has led to significant problems and understandable confusion among farmers. As Ashraf Ghani, the Minister of Finance in the transitional government, now Chancellor of the University of Kabul, has stated:

Lessons from other nations show that today's quick wins can sow the seeds of future poppy harvests. Afghanistan's war on drugs will not be won quickly—nor can it be won without economic growth and political stability. Crop destruction "victories" will prove pyrrhic if Afghan farmers cannot find other ways to make a living and do not understand why drugs threaten their future.[57]

Indeed, the Taliban ban on opium cultivation in 2000 and its consequences, particularly for poorer farmers, is a salutary lesson in the problems inherent in any search for quick-fix solutions to the problem of opium cultivation and production. By contrast, and indicative of how life quickly changes course in Afghanistan, in November 2005 the re-emergent Taliban circulated *shabnamas* in the south of the country threatening households with death if they did not plant opium, as this would signify they were government agents.

## THE TALIBAN OPIUM BAN[58]

A continuing tendency in Afghanistan is for politicians of all persuasions to seek quick-fix solutions to complex social problems, journalists to seek quick soundbites to sell stories and commentators to focus on the 'success' of the Taliban ban in vastly reducing poppy cultivation in 2001. Such commentators often minimise or ignore the complex historical, political and socioeconomic motivations and dynamics that led up to it in the first place. This is not to mention the steady increase in opium cultivation and production that characterised the first five years of Taliban rule from 1995 to 2000. Such unidimensional views run the risk of encouraging comparisons between Taliban methods then and their potential replication for current poppy reduction strategies in Afghanistan, or elsewhere for that matter. The ban has been called 'the most effective drug control enforcement action of modern times', but this perspective neglects the fact that effectiveness needs to be premised on the use of methods and tactics acceptable within a framework of international law and human rights.[59]

Certainly focusing on whether opium cultivation and production aggregate figures for one year have risen or fallen makes little sense unless they are contextualised within much longer-term patterns and trends. A series of continuing, if diminishing, booms and slumps in poppy cultivation and opium production in Afghanistan is to be expected before poppy can finally be eliminated from the country. In neighbouring Pakistan it took over 20 years for poppy to be completely eliminated and even then, after UNODC in 2000 had officially declared Pakistan 'poppy free', cultivation has re-emerged at several new sites within tribal areas of the country bordering Afghanistan.

Having said this, and recognising that ascribing motivations to the Taliban for imposing the 2000 ban are speculative at best, there is little doubt that the ban was responsible for the dramatic reduction in opium cultivation and production as reflected in UNDCP's Opium Poppy Survey of 2001.[60] From 3,276 tonnes of opium in 2000, production fell dramatically to 185 tonnes in 2001. While this is not in dispute, it certainly needs contextualised and raises several important issues that need to be addressed before an effective drug control strategy can be developed in Afghanistan. Such a strategy needs to be evidence-based, replicable, sustainable and necessitates realistic long-term planning and commitment that cannot be evaluated using only a single year's 'success' or 'failure' as a benchmark. It also needs to be firmly based on human rights and the rule of law, particularly in a country struggling to establish a democratic polity.

Apart from being based on a suspect definition of what constitutes acceptable legal standards and their legitimate enforcement, the contention that the Taliban ban was 'the most effective drug control enforcement action of modern times' misses the point. It should not be the role of law enforcement to focus on eradication of poppy fields. Rather, its main role should be to focus on trafficking and drug processing and the successful arrest, prosecution and punishment of those engaged in such activities, no matter their official rank or social status. The approach to opium cultivators, particularly those on the bottom rung of the production ladder—the landless poor—needs to be based on a comprehensive strategy of alternative livelihoods integrated into a better-funded and more robust effort at reconstruction and state building, rather than on law enforcement.[61]

The tactics used by the Taliban to enforce their ban is also not in dispute. As with all repressive totalitarian regimes, a terrorised populace understood that summary justice and severe punishment, including the destruction of property, torture and death, would await any transgressor of Mullah Omar's total ban on opium cultivation. At the same time it has to be acknowledged that different tactics, largely dependent on local levels of Taliban influence and authority, were also used. For example, a negotiated settlement was reached with the powerful Shinwari tribe in Nangarhar province who had resisted the ban and was basically bribed by the Taliban not to cultivate opium.

The years 1994 to 2001 saw a radical shift in Taliban policy from initial tolerance, if not direct encouragement, of farmers cultivating poppy, resulting in a steady overall increase in cultivation and production levels up to 2000, as well as direct profit to the Taliban from the drug trade, to an enforced total ban by the end of 2000. It is unlikely that during this period the Taliban had some miraculous conversion to the more extreme dictates of *Sharia* resulting in the ban. There was enough evidence throughout their reign that their draconian interpretation of *Sharia* was already being ruthlessly applied, the whims of individual Taliban commanders nothwith-standing. The question is why the Taliban took so long to pass and enforce a ban on an intoxicant like opium known to be *haram* in Islam and that would have been consistent with their other 'law enforcement' activities.

In determining this it is important to remember that the Taliban were allegedly a strategic creation of the Pakistani ISI who equipped and trained them, along with material support from Saudi Arabia and at least tacit support from the US, to rapidly take over nearly 90 per cent of the country in little more than a few years. They were also not a homogeneous group, but consisted of several different, if overlapping, factions each with their own political agenda and vested interests. Some were simply economic opportunists and survival strategists, a legacy of a country ravaged at that time by 15 years of continuous war and internecine conflict. At the Taliban's core, however, was a group of Islamic fundamentalists dedicated to applying their own very strict and unique interpretation of *Sharia* as well as a relatively more liberal group that sought international recognition for purposes of political legitimation and consolidation of power—and their concomitant economic benefits. One example of such sought-after benefits was the $25 million per year for ten years for alternative development in poppy cultivation areas promised by the then Executive Director of the UNODC, Pino Arlachi. Given the Taliban's abysmal track record of public spending on development initiatives for the populace, however, much of this money, assuming that international donors would have given funds to a 'presumptive authority' internationally unrecognised except by three countries, would very likely have been spent on arms and sustaining the Taliban armies. While a few high-cost prestigious development projects might have been thrown in to impress donors, it was unlikely to provide any lasting benefits for the impoverished and suffering mass of the population. More importantly, there was a group within the Taliban that may have had other motives for establishing a total ban on opium—those profiting from the drug trade.

The Taliban always had an ambivalent attitude towards drugs, probably born out of their need for hard cash. On 10 September 1997, the SHCDC issued the following declaration (which notably failed to mention opium) through the ministry of foreign affairs:

The Islamic State of Afghanistan informs all compatriots that as the use of heroin and hashish is not permitted in Islam, they are reminded once again that they should strictly refrain from growing, using and trading in hashish and heroin. Anyone who violates this order shall be meted out a punishment in line with the lofty Mohammad and Sharia law and thus shall not be entitled to launch a complaint.

In 1999 Mullah Omar then passed an edict stating that opium cultivation should be reduced by one third. Over a year later on 27 July 2000 he announced a total ban on the cultivation of opium. During this period the Taliban took several other drug control measures. In 1999, 34 drug-processing laboratories/factories in Nangarhar were allegedly destroyed, with a further 25 destroyed in Helmand the following year, although law enforcement officials present at some of these events believed they were stage managed by the Taliban to impress foreign officials. A US anti-narcotics official was reported as saying that Taliban officials maintained 'poppy cultivation does not violate the principles of Islam, but that heroin processing, trafficking and the use of heroin is wrong for all Muslims [and therefore] all heroin must be intended for export to foreign non-Muslim countries.'[62] Indeed, it has been argued that 'the involvement of the Taliban in the drug trade was plain almost from the outset of their rule'[63] and that they were 'inevitably players in the international heroin trade'.[64] It has even been suggested that, prior to the announcement of the ban in 2000, the Taliban distributed fertiliser to farmers for growing opium poppy and did little to dissuade them from cultivating it, although the former point is most probably a scorpion tale.[65] Some individual Talibs (or at least men wearing black turbans) involved in opium production may have distributed fertiliser, and even poppy seed, but it was unlikely to be part of a more general Taliban strategy.

This was in marked contrast to 1994 when the Taliban took control of Qandahar and declared that they would eliminate all illicit drugs. However, it has been claimed that within a few months they 'realised that they needed the income from poppies and would anger farmers by banning it', so began the process of formalising the drugs economy to their own financial advantage.[66] In this instance 'formalising' may have meant little more than the decentralisation of funding for Taliban soldiers, with commanders permitted to draw on any economic activity that took place in their area. This included smuggled licit goods, gemstones and logging as well as opium. If the opium economy had been truly formalised then it could be supposed that opium cultivation would have been introduced to other areas under Taliban control. Soon after this, the Taliban began to collect up to 20 per cent of the value of all drug shipments made by traffickers, supposedly as a form of *zakat*, an Islamic tax where Muslims are expected to give 2.5 per cent of their annual disposable income and savings to the poor and needy. At the same time, individual commanders also imposed their own taxes for personal gain, to buy arms and to maintain their gunmen. In certain areas of the country, such as the east, some of these commanders like their *mujahideen* commander and warlord predecessors also continued to collect *usher*, the traditional ten per cent agricultural tax, on all agricultural production, with opium farmers paying this tax in raw opium.

On 2 April 2002 during a speech at the Institute for International Studies in Washington, Asa Hutchinson, the Director of the DEA, stated that the Taliban, 'in some instances', were involved in drug trafficking and had institutionalised taxation on the drug trade to the extent that they issued tax receipts when collecting the revenue from heroin traffickers. One receipt he recounted seeing said: 'To the honourable road tax collectors: Gentlemen, the bearer of this letter who possesses four kilograms of white good [sic] has paid the custom duty at the Shinwa custom. It is hoped that the bearer will not be bothered further.' Hutchinson also claimed that the DEA had received 'multi-source information' directly incriminating Osama bin Laden in the financing and facilitation of heroin-trafficking activities from Afghanistan, presumably with the collusion of the Taliban.[67]

It was no coincidence that the first drug banned when the Taliban came to power was cannabis. Its derivative hashish was considered to be an Afghan vice while opium and heroin were, erroneously, not perceived as drugs misused in Afghanistan and could be used by terrorist groups as a weapon against the *kafirs*, the unbelievers, of the west. Ironically, one result of the crackdown on hashish was to motivate users of the drug to move to smoking opium and heroin as their fumes are much less detectable than the more pungent hashish smoke, thus reducing the risk of being traced, arrested and punished by the feared Ministry of Enforcement of Virtue and Suppression of Vice.[68] When bin Laden had to close down lucrative construction companies following US pressure after the bomb attacks on US embassies in eastern Africa in 1998 it is believed he sought revenge by extending his *jihad* to include drug-running to the US and Europe.[69] For those given to conspiracy theories, it has also been alleged that he had 'unsuccessfully tried to create a super-strong form of heroin called "Tears of Allah" that would spread throughout the west like a biological weapon causing instant addiction and death'.[70]

The problem with publicly available information based on official intelligence reports is that such reports can be deliberately used for purposes of misinformation, disinformation and propaganda. As one BBC reporter says of Afghanistan, 'this is a country where rumour and propaganda are as important a currency as the dollar bill. All intelligence services are paid to lie and disseminate false information to damage and discredit their enemies.'[71] The tax receipts or 'chits' that Hutchinson mentions may or may not have been genuine. It has been suggested, for example, that the United Front (subsequently the Northern Alliance) forged such chits to discredit the Taliban at the same time that the Taliban forged similar chits to discredit the Front and show that they were capitalising on the illicit drug trade. The 'Tears of Allah' is a well-known scorpion tale and is unlikely to be true as there is no known drug that causes instant addiction.

Even those close to the inner *shura* of the Taliban were involved in drug trafficking and would benefit from a total ban on opium, thus substantially increasing opium prices and allowing the Taliban to sell their existing stockpiles for high profits. Perhaps the most infamous was Haji Bashir Noorzai who was considered by western intelligence agencies to be one of the top drug traffickers in Afghanistan, although how far he achieved this with the collusion of top Taliban leaders is unknown. It has been alleged that in the months before the ban his organisation purchased much of the opium in the country then profited when prices rose dramatically from under $100 at the end of 2000 to nearly $700 per kg by early September 2001.

The ban and its temporary nature, then, can on one level be interpreted as a deliberate strategy on the part of some influential members of the Taliban, or their associates, to profit from existing stockpiles and/or to offload stockpiles that had been building up over previous years. There was also, of course, the other side of the Taliban's win-win strategy. In 1998 the US concluded that there was 'evidence that the Taleban which controls most of Afghanistan have made a policy decision to take advantage of narcotics trafficking and production in order to put pressure on the west and consuming nations'.[72] As already pointed out, the legitimisation and acceptance of the regime by the international community as a result of the ban was always an unlikely outcome and not necessarily the sole motive for its implementation. According to law enforcement specialists, at that time there was thought to be a two- to three-year stockpile of opium in the country. As Antonio Maria Costa, the Executive Director of the UNODC, has suggested:

we should not forget that the Taliban ban only concerned cultivation, not trafficking, and this is symbolic and ironic, obviously because one of the reasons the Taliban banned cultivation of opium—cultivation, I stress—is because they had their warehouses full and they needed to reduce their stocks, above all benefiting from obviously higher prices, because there was no cultivation in 2000.[73]

Acccording to western intelligence sources, the Taliban-controlled Voice of Shariat radio on 2 September 2001, little more than a year after the total ban, announced that the ban had been lifted by the Taliban, although this cannot be confirmed.[74] While this was only nine days before 9/11 and the terrorist attacks on New York, this appeared to be coincidental. As the poppy planting season in many parts of Afghanistan starts around late September one of the consequences of the timing of the lifting of the ban was effectively to give the green light to farmers to resume poppy cultivation. Having said this, Costa's suggestion should not be taken literally to mean that the Taliban were the only actors involved in controlling the drug trade, and there is no agreement that the Voice of Shariat expressly lifted the ban.

If the Taliban's one-year ban in 'successfully' curbing opium cultivation had any global significance it was to clearly show the strict limits that need to be placed on any war on drugs where it is those on the lowest rungs of production, the poor, the dispossessed and the landless, that are most likely to be the victims; the civilian collateral damage. The last thing the Afghan people need is another war or a return to the terror tactics of the Taliban in search of a lasting solution for illicit opium cultivation and production.

The total ban of 2000 was initiated by the Taliban in the knowledge, at least by some ranking Talibs, that it could be no more than a temporary, and unsustainable, measure. The main consequence of the ban, apart from producing large profits for the Taliban, was to increase the debt burden of many Afghan farmers who had been permitted to grow opium unimpeded over the previous years. If the Taliban had continued with the ban they would have run the risk of a revolt from many of the farming communities left more debt-ridden because of the ban. In effect, the consequences of the ban affected the very sustainability that depended on the ability of farmers to sustain their own livelihoods without resuming poppy cultivation.

A member of the UN donors mission to Afghanistan at the time reported that the ban had led to serious consequences for the majority of small farmers: the inability to repay *salaam*; the sale of long-term productive assets such as livestock and land; the internal displacement of families; the migration of male labour, or indeed whole families, to neighbouring countries; and the inability of households to meet basic needs.[75] The World Bank reported that a combination of factors such as the ongoing drought and the sharply reduced incomes and loss of livelihood experienced by small farmers and itinerant wage labourers affected by the ban meant that malnutrition worsened and cases of starvation deaths were reported.[76] The ban also had secondary consequences, such as the impact on household fuel supplies through the loss of opium poppy straw, a valuable source of fuel and *konjara*, and the loss of other by-products of the opium poppy such as oil and soap.

Such consequences point to the many political issues and development problems involved in finding long-term, sustainable and effective solutions to opium poppy cultivation and production that necessitates taking into account the complex and convoluted dynamics involved in poppy cultivation in Afghanistan. In 2005 in Nangarhar province, research suggested that the dramatic reduction in opium cultivation in the 2004–05 season had a devastating effect on many farmers, their families and others in the community, particularly poorer households.[77]

The few examples cited in this chapter, then, illustrate the complexities for the authorities in trying to reduce and eventually eliminate opium cultivation and production in Afghanistan. There remains a distinct lack of law enforcement capacity to investigate drug-related crime and arrest, successfully prosecute and securely imprison drug producers and traffickers, particularly those at a high level with close links to warlords and top government officials. One of the main consequences of increased opium cultivation over the past few decades has been the increased production of heroin within the country, with a resultant increase in the availability of the drug on the local market in Afghanistan as well as its export to Europe and neighbouring countries in central and south Asia.

# 5
# Heroin Producers and Traffickers

By the early 1980s Afghanistan had become the world's second largest opium grower, the Pakistan-Afghan border was the leading source of heroin for Europe and America, and mass heroin addiction was sweeping Pakistan. In retrospect this rapid change seems the result of pressures in the global drug market, local political forces and covert operations. As in Burma thirty years before, the CIA's covert warfare served as a catalyst for the transformation of the Afghanistan-Pakistan borderlands into the world's leading heroin supplier.[1]

The heroin explosion emanating from Afghanistan is now affecting the politics and economics of the entire region. It is crippling societies, distorting the economies of already fragile states and creating a new narco-elite which is at odds with the ever-increasing poverty of the population.[2]

Despite what you might hear, we don't have sufficient evidence about drug trafficking groups and cartels and if and how they are linked and organised. Heroin laboratories are increasingly sited in remote and inaccessible areas. We don't even have the proper equipment and trained manpower to test the drugs that we do seize.[3]

Until the end of the 1970s the region's opium trade was primarily self-contained, with all opium products being soaked up by demand from drug consumers, mainly in Iran and to a much lesser extent Pakistan and Afghanistan. Although there was evidence of rising heroin production in Iran and increased cross-border trafficking, with small amounts of 'fairly high-grade heroin' being produced from Turkish, Afghan and Pakistan opium, in 1975 the US Ambassador to Iran, Richard Helms, argued that there was still no threat to western markets.[4] But by 1982 opium cultivated in Afghanistan was being converted into heroin in laboratories in Pakistan that supplied over half of the heroin reaching American and European markets. It has been claimed, although it may well be a scorpion tale, that

the first heroin laboratory in a tribal area [in Pakistan] was established by the Afghan Muhmand tribesman Haji Umar in Lakarho, Muhmand agency, in 1978. Haji Umar had a base in the heroin processing Herat province of Afghanistan, and when PNCB officials raided the laboratory Haji made his escape back there.[5]

A decade later in 1987 an estimated 100–200 heroin refineries were operating in the Khyber district of Pakistan's NWFP alone.[6] But 1995 proved a watershed year when the Pakistani army mounted a full-scale military campaign against heroin laboratories leading to a cross-border migration of laboratories and their operators from Pakistan into Afghanistan. By 2004 heroin produced from refineries that had mostly shifted into Afghanistan supplied over 75 per cent of Europe's heroin and almost all the considerable amounts of heroin available in neighbouring countries, although by this time 90–95 per cent of heroin in the US came from Colombia, Mexico and countries in southeast Asia. At the same time, according to police sources, the retail street price per gram of heroin in the UK had fallen from £74 in 1997 to £61 in 2004.[7]

The cataclysmic social and political upheavals in the central and southwest Asian region from 1979 onwards, the Iranian revolution, independence for the weak republics of Soviet central Asia and the CIA's decade long Afghan war that ravaged the country, destabilised Pakistan and mobilised radical Islam all contributed to a burgeoning illicit drug trade. In turn this increase in drug trafficking helped to finance a bloody civil war in Afghanistan after the Soviets left, as well as 'an eruption of ethnic insurgency across a 3,000-mile swath from central Asia to the Balkans'.[8] By the 1990s profits from Afghan heroin trafficked westwards and northwards to Europe helped to finance armed ethnic rebels in Bosnia, Chechnya, Georgia, Kosovo, Turkey and Uzbekistan. The heroin trade in effect had become consolidated, 'encouraging drug production, official corruption, mass addiction, and HIV infection. Through the alchemy of capitalism, mafias formed, ethnic separatists armed, and a culture of criminality crystallised.'[9]

In collaboration with a wide range of Albanian, Armenian, Italian, Turkish and other criminal groups and syndicates, several political movements profited from processing morphine and smuggling heroin, although this was by no means their only source of income. These groups included the PKK (Kurdistan Workers Party) in Azerbaijan, the Azeri Grey Wolves, the KLA (Kosovo Liberation Army) and the IMU (Islamic Movement for Uzbekistan). It has also been noted that Russian organised crime groups, apart from supplying arms to Ahmad Shah Massoud, acted as middlemen for the opium export trade, its transport north from Afghanistan facilitated by Russsian troops and border guards to the major transhipment point of Osh in Kyrgyzstan. The large profits from this drugs and arms trade have also undermined state institutions throughout central Asia, as well as funding criminal groups and some political parties.[10]

## CONTROLLING THE TRADE IN THE 1980S

Towards the end of the Soviet invasion and during the civil war that erupted before the Taliban took control of most of the country in the mid-1990s, *mujahideen* groups and warlords fought each other for control of territory where poppy was cultivated. Such factions became ever more dependent on opium production, transborder trade and smuggling to generate their own resources and to retain and expand their power.[11] As agriculture and trade began to pick up around 1987, *mujahideen* commanders became more involved in the opium trade and in some areas the vast profits from opium 'enabled commanders to turn themselves into powerful warlords, increasingly independent of external donors'.[12] It has been alleged, for example, that Younis Khalis, leader of a breakaway *Hezb-i Islami* group, battled with other groups for control of poppy fields as well as the roads and trails leading from them to his several heroin labs near the town of Ribat al Ali.[13]

Although by no means the only one, the most well-known and best documented case of a *mujahideen* leader being involved in the drug trade was that of Gulbuddin Hekmatyar, leader of *Hezb-i Islami*. During this time he was under the protection and patronage of the CIA and the main recipient of US funds-for-arms that were processed using the Pakistani ISI as a conduit. Although this period of Afghanistan's history abounds with scorpion tales, it has been asserted that Hekmatyar was:

the only leader to exploit opium profits systematically as a basis for a hierarchically organised party and conventional army. In the summer of 1988, expecting that the Soviet withdrawal would lead to decreased foreign support, he seems to have instructed his men to search for precious stones and to cultivate poppy. Unlike the warlord commanders who were content to sell raw opium at bazaars in Afghanistan and Baluchistan (where paper currency was weighed rather than counted), Hikmatyar seems also to have invested in some processing plants in partnership with Pakistani heroin syndicates.[14]

It has also been alleged that Hekmatyar and his men coerced farmers to increase opium cultivation, in the process using weapons that had been supplied by the CIA for the war against the Soviets. The opium was then sent to his heroin factories in the town of Koh-i-Sultan for processing.

In 1989 Hekmatyar also tried to take over opium production in the northern Helmand valley by fighting Mullah Nasim Akhundzada who controlled the valley's annual opium output of over 250 tonnes. Nasim, known as 'the King of heroin', reputedly issued production quotas to farmers who were coerced into growing opium by threats of murder or castration if they failed to obey the Mullah's commands.* He managed to repel Hekmatyar's forces, retained control of the valley and a year later was appointed as deputy defence minister in the transitional post-Soviet Afghan government dominated by *mujahideen* leaders and their proxies.

During this period Nasim made an agreement with the US Ambassador in Islamabad, Robert B. Oakley, to stop poppy cultivation in Helmand in exchange for $2 million in 'aid money' to be paid to him personally. The subsequent ban in 1990 tripled opium prices in Baluchistan province over the border in Pakistan resulting in Hekmatyar's forces again fighting to take over control of what was by this time a multi-million-dollar industry. That same year Nasim was assassinated, allegedly by *Hezb-i Islami* or others linked with the drug cartels, and his brother Rasul, a commander in the *Harakat-i Inquilab* faction, took over the family drug business and retained control over the Helmand valley, resuming large-scale poppy cultivation when the US failed to deliver the promised aid.[15]

During this period much of the opium smuggled into Pakistan's NWFP was sold to the then governor of the province Lieutenant General Fazle Huq, referred to by the Pakistani opposition as 'Pakistan's General Noriega'. It was then refined into heroin in labs in Dara Adam Khel and other centres in the tribal areas, and allegedly then transported to Karachi in Pakistani military trucks to be shipped to Europe and the US.[16] It was actually more likely to have been transferred by trucks of the National Logistics Cell, a commercial company set up by and affiliated to the military for the purpose of transporting commercial goods. During the mid-1980s the DEA had evidence of over 40 heroin syndicates operating in Pakistan, many of them involved in smuggling Afghan opium into Pakistan for refining

---

* In the planting season of November 2005 an informant reported that in Helmand local commanders had joined forces with the Taliban and were yet again coercing farmers into cultivating opium in order to collect a tithe on the harvest.

into morphine and heroin, with several enjoying close connections to the Pakistan military.

## CORRUPTION AND COLLUSION IN THE 1980S

One of the key unresolved issues from this period is to what extent the US colluded with and encouraged *mujahideen* groups in Afghanistan to grow opium to raise funds for the war against the Soviets. In 1980 Tom Carew, a British SAS soldier and the first known western agent to link up with the *mujahideen* and lead a series of military initiatives inside Afghanistan, provided the following account as part of a debriefing with his superiors, when he claimed that the reason he could not take out samples of Soviet weapons from Afghanistan was because all the available mules were 'loaded up to the eyeballs with opium':

I saw more than one thousand kilograms of opium being taken from Camp One near Wazir to Parachinar in Pakistan. Once the opium was inside Pakistan, it was escorted by the Pakistan military to a special section of the Mujahideen Camp, which was undoubtedly under Pakistani military control. My conclusion is that the Mujahideen are using the opium to fund their operations and obtain co-operation from Pakistan, and that the Pakistani military—or somebody in it—is taking a significant cut.[17]

At a further meeting where CIA agents were present, Carew was asked very specific questions about opium and told to completely ignore anything that he might see connected with opium during future missions to the area. This confirmed his suspicions that the *mujahideen* were moving the opium with the tacit cooperation of the CIA, although he suspected greater collusion.[18]

Despite the US backing of *mujahideen* groups with a CIA budget of $3.2 billion for their well-documented covert war, the Afghans contributed to their own war effort by engaging in the drug trade. However, it is unknown how much of the profits ended up in the personal accounts of *mujahideen* leaders and commanders in Pakistan's Habib Bank, BCCI in the Gulf States and other foreign financial institutions rather than being spent on the *jihad* against the Soviets. While the CIA/ISI axis allegedly pumped billions of dollars into the *mujahideen* groups in Afghanistan, at the same time supporting 'refugee warrior' communities in Pakistan and Iran, the Afghans, a proud and independent people, also saw an opportunity to finance their *jihad* by opium production, much easier in the anarchic and deregulated context of war.[19] At the same time as these *mujahideen* warlords were raising funds through opium production for their campaigns against the Soviets some were also lining their own pockets as 'they had bought houses and businesses in Peshawar, new jeeps and kept bank accounts abroad'.[20]

Various people had warned the US government about the risks involved in arming such groups and colluding in the cultivation of illicit drug crops. One was David Musto, a White House member of President Carter's Strategic Council on Drug Abuse who warned the Council that

we were going into Afghanistan to support the opium growers in their rebellion against the Soviets. Shouldn't we try to avoid what we had done in Laos? Shouldn't we try to pay the growers if they will eradicate their opium production? There was silence.[21]

Then in 1980 Musto and another colleague from the council, Joyce Lowinson, frustrated by the CIA and the State Department's attitude to the issue, wrote an opinion piece in the *New York Times* stating that

We worry about the growing of opium in Afghanistan or Pakistan by rebel tribesmen who apparently are the chief adversaries of the Soviet troops in Afghanistan. Are we erring in befriending these tribes as we did in Laos when Air America (chartered by the Central Intelligence Agency) helped transport crude opium from certain tribal areas?[22]

Another take on the issue was offered in a report in the *Philadelphia Magazine* based on an interview with an anonymous high-level law enforcement official in the Carter administration's Justice Department who allegedly said:

You have the administration tiptoeing around this like it's a land mine. The issue of opium and heroin in Afghanistan is explosive...In the State of the Union speech, the president mentioned drug abuse but he was very careful to avoid mentioning Afghanistan, even though Afghanistan is where things are really happening right now...Why aren't we taking a more critical look at the arms we are now shipping into gangs of drug runners who are obviously going to use them to increase the efficiency of their drug smuggling operation?[23]

At this time the DEA, an organisation claiming to be continually thwarted by the CIA, reported that *mujahideen* groups were very much involved in the drug trade to the extent that their incursions into

Afghanistan from their bases in Pakistan frequently coincided with opium planting and harvesting seasons.

## CORRUPTION AND COLLUSION POST-2001

It is ironic that 25 years later Afghanistan is still where 'things are really happening' and opium cultivation and heroin production is still an explosive political issue. The US more or less neglected Afghanistan after the Soviets left in 1989 until post-9/11 when they dumped millions of dollars into the hands of warlords.* The very same warlords allegedly involved in the drug trade but perceived as being crucial allies to the US in their purging of the Taliban and hunt for bin Laden and al-Qaeda. For the US government the primary concern was how best to use the five main factions and 25 sub-factions of the Northern Alliance forces as local proxies to carry out their war plans. However, as Bob Woodward reported in his detailed account *Bush at War*:

Worries about the Northern Alliance abounded. First, it was not really an Alliance, because the various warlords could probably with some ease be bought off by the Taliban. The warlords flourished in a culture of survival—meaning they would do anything necessary. Several were just thugs, human rights abusers and drug dealers.[24]

Just as in 1979 when the US was prepared to sacrifice the drug war to fight the cold war, now they were prepared to again sacrifice the drug war, this time to fight the war on terrorism. The apparent first strike in this new war was made on 26 September 2001 when a CIA agent was helicoptered into the Panjshir valley, home of the Northern Alliance, with a suitcase containing a first instalment of $3 million in cash.

Over the next few months, aided by more cash, arms and promises of airpower, the US soon found itself negotiating with a wide range

---

* The period between 1989 when the Soviets left and 2001 was not totally bereft of US political activity or funding in Afghanistan. Until December 1991 the CIA continued to fund Ahmad Shah Massoud and his militia group, later to form the Northern Alliance. In 1996 they again made overtures to Massoud in an attempt to buy back some of the Stinger missiles still unaccounted for and to persuade him to gather information about Osama bin Laden and his activities in Afghanistan (Steve Coll, 2004, *Ghost Wars: The Secret History of the CIA, Afghanistan and bin Laden, from the Soviet invasion to September 10, 2001*, New York: The Penguin Press).

of commanders and warlords in their latest fight. These included: Rashid Dostum, made Chief of Staff to the Commander-in-Chief of the armed forces, nominally President Karzai; Hazarat Ali, made Police Chief and Military commander of Nangarhar but who later resigned his post to become Member of Parliament for Jalalabad in 2005; Gul Agha Shirzai, self-proclaimed Governor of Qandahar in December 2001, before being moved to Kabul as a 'special adviser' to Karzai who then returned to Qandahar as governor before being appointed as governor of Nangarhar in late 2005; Haji Din Mohammad, brother of Abdul Haq who was killed by the Taliban just before the US invasion in October 2001, made the Governor of Nangarhar after another brother, Haji Qadir, had been assassinated in July 2002 in Kabul, then in late 2005 appointed as Governor of Kabul. Along with many other militia commanders and warlords these men were, rightly or wrongly, all perceived as being implicated in the drug trade:

Across Afghanistan, brutal commanders suddenly re-emerged to battle for territory, seize food shipments and smuggle drugs. Along the country's northern tier, the CIA mobilised Northern Alliance warlords, long active in the local drug trade, to capture Kabul and other key cities. In the southeast the agency delivered money to Pashtun warlords who dominated drug smuggling on the Pakistan border, to drive the Taliban out of their spiritual heartland.[25]

This US 'legacy of complicity' with groups engaged in the illicit drug trade that has subsequently helped to transform tribal warlords into drug warlords in several areas of Asia started over half a century ago in the 1950s in southern France when the CIA established a clandestine alliance with Corsican crime syndicates to restrain communist influence on the Marseille docks. Also in the 1950s the CIA supported the KMT (the nationalist Chinese Kuo Min Tang) in northern Burma, paving the way for the emergence of the greatest opium warlord in modern history, General Khun Sa of the Shan states. The well-documented activities of the CIA in Laos during the Vietnam war, where they financed and armed opium-growing Hmong tribesmen and Laotian military engaged in drug trafficking, 'facilitated logistics that shipped heroin to US forces fighting in South Vietnam'.[26]

The war against the Soviets in Afghanistan provided yet another covert arena for the CIA to engage in activities that helped to increase and expand the global drug trade, never mind the extensive civilian 'collateral damage' that was inflicted in the process. In all these cases complicity included protecting the CIA's drug warlord allies by blocking criminal investigations by the DEA or other law enforcement agencies and removing any constraints on trafficking.[27] It is hardly coincidental that during the ten years of war against the Soviets in Afghanistan the 17 DEA agents based in neighbouring Pakistan never made a major arrest or drug seizure, despite Afghan-Pakistani heroin accounting for 60 per cent of the US market at that time and the DEA identifying around 40 major heroin syndicates.

Apart from various warlords, militia commanders and ex-*mujahideen* leaders, there is also a range of government officials and 'businessmen' suspected of being involved in the drug trade inside Afghanistan. Perhaps the most infamous example of the latter group is Haji Bashir Noorzai who reputedly controlled much of the drug trade, especially around the time the Taliban were in power. Noorzai's criminal network provided explosives, weaponry and manpower to the Taliban in exchange for the protection of its opium crops, heroin infrastructure and drug smuggling routes.[28] Known to narcotics officers as the 'Pablo Escobar of Asia', Noorzai was popular and well-connected enough to be a member of the Qandahar provincial *shura* between 2003 and April 2005 when he was arrested on entry to the US and charged with conspiracy to import more than $50 million worth of heroin into the US and other countries. The Afghan police and authorities had no role in Noorzai's arrest. However, a few media reports pointed out that Noorzai had already been arrested by the US in late 2001,

knowing he was a major player in the illicit drugs business in the South and working closely with Taliban leaders at the time. He was soon released however because he was a useful intelligence asset and willing to collaborate in return for impunity. Nobody doubts his significant role in the heroin trade, but the indictment on which his arrest in New York is now grounded does not mention any case of drug trafficking that was not already known to US authorities when they released him several years earlier.[29]

Reading about Noorzai reminded me of being in Peshawar in 2000 when a prominent and respected Afghan who ran an NGO told me he possessed documentary evidence that proved the heroin trade in Afghanistan was controlled by two Afghan businessmen and Mullah Omar, leader of the Taliban. At the time I assumed this was just another scorpion tale. In October 2005, apart from Noorzai, two other Afghan 'businessmen' found themselves in the US, extradited there from Afghanistan to face federal charges of smuggling more than $25 million of heroin into the US and other countries. Haji Baz Mohammad was allegedly the leader of a drug-trafficking organisation that had close links to the Taliban and other Islamic extremist groups. Along with his co-accused Bashir Ahmad Rahmany, he stands accused of controlling opium cultivation in Nangarhar province, processing the opium into heroin and smuggling and distributing it in the US and elsewhere.[30] Mullah Omar's level of complicity and involvement in the drug trade remains unknown.

There is also little doubt that as the drug trade has become entrenched more public officials, from village and district police chiefs all the way to provincial governors and senior members of the central government, including the new parliament, have been involved in acts of corruption that facilitate the trade, as well as directly profiteering from trafficking itself. As Syed Ikramuddin, ex-Governor of Badakhshan province, later promoted to Minister of Labour and Social Affairs, and survivor of an assassination attempt, has said: 'Many of these policemen and commanders are former warlords who have disarmed and reintegrated into government jobs, and are now using their position to facilitate the drug trade and get rich.'[31] One media report estimated 'that 17 of the 249 new parliamentarians are drug smugglers; another 64 are believed to have links to mafia-like armed groups'.[32] Another report claimed that, 'According to some observers, as many as 60% of those elected to parliament last fall are linked to warlords and the drug traffic.'[33] In February 2006 the Minister for Counter Narcotics was reported as saying that even some Cabinet Ministers were deeply implicated in the drug trade and could be diverting foreign aid money into trafficking, although he declined to name individuals, pointing out that the corrupt justice system was unable to convert allegations and rumours into hard evidence.[34]

After a meeting between the Deputy Minister of the Interior, General Daud, and the German Defence Minister, Peter Struck, in September 2004 in Kunduz, it was reported that

They sat on the terrace, their delegations opposite each other, and exchanged pleasantries while Daud asserted that he considered drug cultivation a great evil that he intended to fight. As the regional leader and deputy minister of the Interior, he's charged with taking the fight to the opium industry. Struck was well aware of the fact that Daud might be involved in the opium business himself. At the meeting, he knew for a fact that the police officer sitting next to Daud was involved in the opium trade.[35]

In March 2006 General Daud filed a lawsuit for damages after Abdol Kabir Marzban, former governor of Takhar province and appointed by President Karzai as a senator, accused him of involvement in international drug smuggling and of supporting his brother in poppy cultivation in Takhar. While Marzban claimed that he had witnesses to substantiate his claims, Daud countered by claiming that he had recently arrested three drug barons in Yangi Qala district of Takhar, all allies of Marzban.[36]

In 2004 the drug trade accounted for 60 per cent of the country's GDP, continued to foster already endemic corruption among public officials and enabled nearly 10 per cent of Afghans to derive a livelihood. To all intents and purposes Afghanistan had become a narco state. While different accounts suggest widespread corruption, there is no consensus on how far this reaches into the corridors of central power. At the same time there is a problem in trying to deal with corruption among public officials in Afghanistan, as in other tribal societies, where traditions such as clientelism, familialism, nepotism and gift-giving are considered normative but actually constitute forms of corrupt behaviour within modern democratic moral and legal codes.[37]

While there is an abundant stock of scorpion tales regarding the identity of corrupt government officals, some in very senior positions, this is largely meaningless without an effective and impartial criminal justice system that can arrest, successfully prosecute and securely punish offenders. One report stated that

Officials at the national level are believed to be free of direct criminal connection to the drug trade. At the provincial and district levels, however, drug-related corruption is believed to be pervasive. This ranges from direct participation in the criminal enterprise, to benefiting financially from taxation or other revenue streams generated by the drug trade.[38]

Yet another report claimed that

Drug profits are financing local warlords and the political elite. There is evidently massive interpenetration of the opium business with central and local elites...Like any criminalised activity but on a massive scale given its size, the drug industry engages in corruption and undermines good governance through bribery. There is anecdotal evidence that many officials at all levels in government are benefiting from or are involved in drugs.[39]

Like the upper echelons of any group of people involved in serious criminal activities, however, top warlords and government officials are unlikely to be directly involved in the trade. This is left to those further down the chain of command. In December 2005 General Aminullah Amarkhel, the security chief at Kabul airport, accused senior Afghan officials of colluding with drug smugglers by releasing two female heroin smugglers that his men had caught 'red-handed' with 5 kg of the drug. Major General Sayed Kamal Sadat of the Ministry of Interior's Counter Narcotics Team admitted that the suspects had been released from custody, thus allowing them to inform other members of their smuggling ring who subsequently escaped to Pakistan.[40]

Echoing the concerns of the Minister of Counter Narcotics, Habibullah Qaderi, that some provincial governors and police chiefs were suspected of involvement in the drug trade, but none were being investigated because of lack of evidence, Ali Ahmad Jalali, who resigned as Afghanistan's Interior Minister in September 2005, reportedly told journalists that

Sometimes government officials allow their own cars to be used for a fee. Sometimes they give protection to traffickers. In Afghanistan, corruption is a low-risk enterprise in a high-risk environment. Because of the lack of investigative capacity it is very difficult to get evidence. You always end up arresting foot soldiers.[41]

By the end of 2005, the journalist Ahmed Rashid noted that 'Not a single drug baron—many of whom are well-known warlords, cabinet ministers, and commanders—has been ousted or convicted.'[42] In January of the same year the Afghan Supreme Court rejected a suggestion by President Karzai to grant a pardon to the country's drug traffickers, a court spokesman said that such a move would be against international norms and Islamic law. In March 2006, as poppy eradication teams moved into Helmand province, the country's main opium growing region, the new governor announced that drug barons should be given an informal amnesty and encouraged to invest their illegally earned profits in Afghanistan's economy rather than send them out of the country, 'We as a government will provide the opportunity to use their money for the national benefit...they must invest in industries. They must invest in construction companies.'[43]

### PRODUCTION OF HEROIN

In the late afternoon of a very hot day in June 2003 walking back to my guesthouse in the Flower Street area of Kabul, a favourite haunt of young western travellers in the late 1960s, I fell into conversation with two men sitting outside a small packing company. When the conversation inevitably came round to drugs, the elder of the two recounted that he had spent quite a bit of his life in Paris but his home village was in the Shinwar district of eastern Nangarhar province, just over 50 km from the provincial capital of Jalalabad and famous for its cultivation of opium. He recalled that in the summer of 1971 two Germans and an Italian had arrived in his village and set up what he claimed was Afghanistan's first heroin factory. (In 1978 the first heroin factory in the NWFP across the Pakistani border from Shinwar was also reportedly established by a German chemist in the Gadoon area of Swabi.)[44] The small amount of heroin manufactured in the Shinwar factory was then exported out of the country into Pakistan and onwards to the west. Whether this was the first heroin factory in Afghanistan or just another scorpion tale, over 30 years later one weekend in May 2003, Afghan government troops and local administration officials reportedly destroyed 16 heroin factories in Shinwar. During the raids the authorities met no resistance and no arrests were made, suggesting that the traffickers had been tipped off well in advance and had moved any heroin to safer locations.[45] In August 2003 Afghan and US troops destroyed another three heroin factories in Khogiani district to the west of Shinwar, but again no arrests were made.[46] In early June 2005 in nearby Achin district over 300 anti-narcotics police destroyed 35 heroin factories and seized 200 kg of opium and 20 kg of heroin.

These destroyed factories represented only a few of the hundreds of heroin-production facilities that have developed in several areas of the country. As opium cultivation and heroin processing began to decrease in Pakistan in the mid-1990s under US pressure and aggressive Pakistan military campaigns, so they inevitably increased inside Afghanistan. Heroin production moved into Afghanistan from NWFP and Baluchistan provinces, spreading from districts like Shinwar, where it had easily been shifted from Pakistan by the Afridi tribesmen who straddled the border and under the protection of the Taliban, into the Helmand valley and the northeast borderlands of Kunduz and Badakhshan provinces. In Nangarhar, 'The Taleban tolerated hundreds of heroin labs clustered around the city in exchange for a modest production tax of $70 per kilo.'[47] During the Taliban era, and beyond, heroin-producing facilities were operating in the border provinces of Badakhshan, Helmand, Kunduz, Nangarhar, Nimroz and Qandahar. During 2004 and 2005, around two thirds of the opium production was estimated to have been transformed into heroin before being smuggled out of the country, accounting for 417 tonnes of heroin per year.[48]

Such a proliferation of heroin production inside Afghanistan has guaranteed an increased supply of the drug for locals and those returning refugees from neighbouring countries where they first started its use. How many of their friends, colleagues and family members have also been persuaded, cajoled or threatened into taking heroin is unknown. The hundreds of Afghans who work in heroin processing, particularly boys as young as 10 years of age, are also at risk of becoming either heroin users themselves or contributing to Afghanistan's growing heroin problem by being paid in heroin and inevitably becoming small-time dealers supplying others with the excess heroin left after their own consumption.

A report from Nangarhar in 1996 claimed that drug barons were 'so concerned about the health of their workers that they had given them face masks to wear in the opium factories', although this was just as likely to have been aimed at maintaining productivity levels in factories producing heroin rather than just processing opium.[49] While the fumes from processing opium can be very pungent, in heroin production facilities, workers who continually inhale heroin dust run the risk of becoming dependent as well as sick through inhaling the fumes from toxic chemicals. In mid-2006 a Ministry of Public Health spokesperson reported that around 2,500 people, both men and women, who had worked in heroin factories 'have now developed various lethal diseases', including 'skin, stomach, liver, asthma, blood deficiency, mental weakness and diarrhoea problems'.[50] Several cases of drug dependency among drug production workers have been reported by treatment agencies. Certainly with the increase of heroin production in the country and an increase in border patrol capability some traffickers are likely to take the low-risk option and sell onto the local market at a reduced profit. Little of this heroin available for drug users in Afghanistan appears to be of very high quality, although ultimately only reliable testing can determine this.

## PROCESSING HEROIN

The process of extracting morphine from opium is relatively simple, requiring only a few chemicals and some empty containers like cooking pots and 50-gallon metal drums. Depending on the size and location of the factory, other equipment used can include press machines, diesel generators, air-pressure machines, water pumps and water storage tanks. Water and raw opium are boiled in the drum, the opium dissolves and insoluble material like straw and leaves settle at the bottom leaving the brown liquid opium. Removing other materials that have been added to the raw opium to increase its weight, and thus its profit, may prove more difficult. Farmers and traders have been reported adding black tea, *gur* (black sugar), raisins, rice flour and the agricultural fertiliser diammonium phosphate to raw opium.[51] As the solution cools, lime (calcium hydroxide or carbonate) is added to the mixture which is then siphoned off through a filter such as a burlap sack. The resultant mixture is then heated again, although not boiled, ammonium chloride is added and the solution allowed to cool.

Once cooled it is poured through cloth filters where lumps of solid morphine base remain on the cloth and are dried in the sun to leave a light-brown coloured powder. This crude brown morphine base can be purified further into white morphine base by dissolving in hydrochloric acid, adding activated charcoal then reheating and re-filtering, several times if necessary. Some ammonium hydroxide is then added and the mixture allowed to stand for an hour or so before filtering again. Anywhere between 6 and 10 kg of opium are needed to produce a 1 kg block of morphine base or 1 kg of heroin, although this will depend on the particular 'recipe' for making heroin, as well as the quality of the opium used and the heroin produced which can vary considerably.

Processing this morphine hydrochloride into brown heroin is also relatively simple, although very pure high-grade heroin may require a more skilled 'chemist' or 'cook'. The key ingredient is the chemical precursor acetic anhydride, easily detectable by its pungent vinegar-like odour. After pulverising the morphine block, the resultant powder along with the liquid acetic anhydride is heated in a sealed pot to a constant temperature of 185 degrees Fahrenheit forming diacetylmorphine (heroin). After cooling, water, activated charcoal and sodium carbonate (soda ash) are added and the heroin precipitate filtered and dried. This crude smokable form of brown heroin base can be further refined using a more sophisticated method that requires chemical solvents such as acetone, chloroform and ethanol (ethyl alcohol). This will result in a purer injectable form of white heroin, although this is still likely to include additives like caffeine or chalk powder. It has also been suggested that adding caffeine can enhance the bioavailability of heroin produced for smoking, thus making for a better 'mix'.[52]

While stored opium can retain its potency for several years, assuming that it is packed properly, heroin powder, depending on various factors, can start to deteriorate almost immediately. If the heroin is properly prepared and stored and of a 99.5 per cent purity level it can keep almost indefinitely without degrading. However, for adulterated heroin not kept in tightly sealed containers at an ambient temperature and stored in the dark, degradation can be quite marked. Most Afghan heroin is reputed to be chemically basic (heroin base) and not easily water-soluble. Being heat stable and vaporisable it is a form of the drug that lends itself to consumption by inhaling the fumes rather than by injecting. It is estimated that it takes around nine months for such heroin products made in Afghanistan to reach the streets of western Europe, including stops for further refining on the way.

Heroin laboratories in Afghanistan do have the capacity to produce over 90 per cent pure heroin. Typically white export-quality heroin, whatever the level of purity, is packed in 1 kg brown paper wraps, then sealed in a plastic bag before final wrapping in white cotton cloth. The cloth may be stamped showing the date and place of manufacture along with a motif such as a cluster of palm trees, a flying bird, '555' or '999'. This latter symbol may allude to the purity of the drug as 99.9 per cent, an impossible achievement in Afghanistan's heroin laboratories. Packing and labelling frequently takes place away from the laboratory in a facility that produces wholesale heroin destined for the next link in the trafficking chain.

Cheaper lower-quality heroin for the local and regional markets that still gives a marked psychoactive effect is also produced, perhaps achieved through using psychoactive additives like phenobarbitol or diazepam (see Chapter 11). Some of the drug seizures made in Afghanistan during 2002 were reliably and randomly tested and found to be very poor quality or even fake. Some samples of heroin were cut with 73 per cent paracetemol and 13 per cent caffeine, while others contained no heroin at all, only cutting agents such as paracetemol, phenobarbitol, diazepam and chloroquine, an anti-malarial drug. Most of the opium was very poor quality with less than 5 per cent morphine content and traces of the opiates noscapine, papaverine and thebaine. Either the authenticity of seizures and subsequent destruction of drugs in Afghanistan must be questioned, or there are considerable amounts of inauthentic drugs on the domestic market, although the purity of drugs is unlikely to be consistent year to year.[53]

Heroin processing, then, depends on the availability of several other ingredients apart from opium, particularly the precursor chemical acetic anhydride. Until the fall of the Taliban at the end of 2001 opium markets or 'drug bazaars' situated in places like Ghani Khel in Nangarhar province, Maiwand in Qandahar and Kajaki, Nowzad and Lashkargah in Helmand, contained literally hundreds of small and large shops trading opium, with the larger bazaars functioning as wholesale supermarkets for those engaged in heroin processing and production. In Ghani Khel up to ten tonnes of opium could be purchased at a time. One bazaar was held in a large compound where customers could buy any of the ingredients necessary to produce heroin and in any amounts. Apart from opium, hundreds of sacks of charcoal and calcium carbonate and other products containing lime could be seen stacked up next to large drums of acetic anhydride.

These chemicals could then be transferred to a do-it-yourself heroin 'laboratory' or 'factory', although these terms misrepresent what is increasingly a very basic small-scale cottage industry operating in house compounds by a few people where they can be easily dismantled for assembly elsewhere or quickly left behind if the need arises. Until the demise of the Taliban, however, the larger factories mirrored the drug bazaars in scale, they were well-armed with rocket launchers, 5–50 calibre machine guns and AK-47s, had upwards of 30 employees, relied on UHF radio and satellite phone communications and had a daily production capacity of over 100 kg of morphine base and 100 kg of brown heroin. During 2004, a total of 88 'rudimentary heroin laboratories' were destroyed by Afghan law enforcement agencies.[54] By September 2005 the ASNF had destroyed over 120 drug-processing facilities, as well as over 140 tonnes of opium and more than 35 tonnes of precursor chemicals. In that month one of the drug bazaars raided was Kajaki, still operational since 2001. Ironically, throughout 2005 local authorities continued to impose taxes on such bazaars in Balkh, Farah and parts of Badakhshan deriving substantial income from the illicit drug trade.

## SMUGGLING AND TRAFFICKING

Smuggled drugs come in all shapes, sizes and disguises. There is often an assumption made that a seizure of heroin along the trafficking chain, particularly at border controls, is high-quality pure heroin although this is not typically the case. Indeed, the drug seized may have low heroin content or may only be morphine base. Most field drug-testing kits only detect the presence of an opiate, not whether it is morphine or heroin or the percentage of heroin content that can be as low as 1 per cent. In fact other substances will react positively to some tests, including certain types of cough medicine and narcotine, an alkaloid found in opium. Some field tests of seized substances in Afghanistan have also been positive for 'cocaine', but the test used also reacts positively to methaqualone (Mandrax), a much more likely substance, as it was one of the main additives to heroin in the 1980s in Pakistan. Many field-tested drug samples are not sent for a more thorough analysis in laboratories because there may be resistance to this from law enforcement officials themselves. In Mazar-i-Sharif it has been rumoured that police who have no drug-testing kits bring in drug users to test the seized drugs on themselves. On both sides of the Afghan–Tajikistan border drug seizures are often destroyed on site, some are not even tested to ascertain their level of purity. If 10 kg of 'heroin' are seized and the traffickers arrested, then law enforcement officials will want to prosecute on that assumed basis, not on laboratory reports that show, in fact, only 2 kg of pure heroin have been seized, the rest of the contents being inert additives, a point not lost on defence lawyers.

Heroin, and even morphine, is certainly a much better smuggling option than opium as it has almost a tenth of the volume for the same, or a higher, profit. Many ingenious ways have been devised to smuggle drugs like heroin, morphine base and opium across Afghanistan's infamously porous borders. Sitting in a police chief's office in Pakistan looking at the blurred photograph on his wall of three camels carrying heavy loads of opium across the mountainous border between Afghanistan and Pakistan I naively asked, 'Is this the usual size of a camel train smuggling drugs and other contraband?' After his laughter ceased, the officer replied, 'Of course not, there can be over 200 camels in a train!' Apart from large camel trains, there is an alternative role for the poor camel, as well as other animals, in drug smuggling operations. In November 2004 at a checkpoint in Nain the Iranian police sliced open the stomachs of six camels that had been transported in a truck. They found 18 kg of opium in four of the camels.[55] A few months later in the same area police found 38 kg of opium hidden in the stomachs of nine sheep and goats. At the other end of the smuggling spectrum, consignments of well over 100 kg of heroin and larger quantities of morphine are routinely smuggled over Afghanstan's borders into neighbouring countries.

There have also been reports of small wraps of heroin concealed in hollowed-out almond shells, where the individual shell is filled with a small quantity of heroin then the two halves of the shell glued back together. The almonds are then packed in boxes where maybe every tenth almond conceals heroin. The time and meticulous care and attention it takes to do this, apart from the labour involved, illustrates the tenacity and ingenuity of heroin smugglers, motivated of course by the vast profits to be made from the trade. Small wraps of heroin have also been attached to empty cotton reels that are then wound with thread, sealed with plastic and labelled for the retail market. Heroin has also been smuggled hidden in pillow stuffing, the heels of shoes, hardback book covers and tubs of hair conditioner. In 2003 US authorities arrested nine Afghans living in the New York area and charged them with importing more than 8 kg of heroin, worth $500,000, over an 18-month period. Most of the drugs had been concealed inside heat-sealed plastic tubing sewn into the seams of traditional Afghan womens clothing.[56] It has also been reported that Afghan and Pakistani drug traffickers have used flocks of homing pigeons to smuggle heroin. Up to 10 g of the drug are stuffed into a bullet shaped capsule and fastened to a leg of each of the pigeons. 'The hungry and thirsty pigeons are released from Afghanistan and in one to two hours fly to their lofts in Pakistan where the heroin capsules are collected by the traffickers.'[57] Who knows, they might even be lucky enough to reach their destination without being shot down by hungry border tribesmen.

## DRUG SEIZURES

Seizure figures of opium and heroin from Afghanistan and neighbouring countries such as Iran, Pakistan and Tajikistan are less than reliable and may reflect the activities and methods of law enforcement officials or hidden political agendas more than any real increase in the amount of drugs being trafficked or a true reflection of trafficking routes. But such figures can still provide some evidence of broad trends in trafficking and cross-border smuggling. The Pakistan ANF figures for seizures of opium and heroin between 1995 and 2003 by all agencies: for example, police, customs and frontier corps, showed an interesting pattern that suggested an increase in heroin production inside Afghanistan during that period. From 1995 to

1999 the annual figures for seizures of opium exceeded the figures for seizures of heroin, but between 2000 and 2003 it was the opposite, with more heroin seized each year than opium. Given that most of the seized drugs had come from Afghanistan, if these figures are reliable then they would suggest that there has been an increase in heroin production in Afghanistan since 2000. However, while these drugs may technically come from Afghanistan, the tribes that live adjacent to the Durand line that officially separates Afghanistan from Pakistan do not recognise this border. Effectively the heroin produced close to the border on either side of this line comes from a no-man's land where the respective nation states have little authority. In these areas, whether the heroin originates from either country is largely irrelevant. As the former Director General of ISI, Hamid Gul, says, 'the Durand Line is just an imaginary border, not a physical border'.[58]

Such drug seizure figures are also used for political purposes. In the mid-1990s the Russians approached the UNDCP with evidence, mainly from satellite imagery, that there was a substantial increase in smuggling of both opium and heroin from Afghanistan into the Central Asian Republics and onwards into Russia. While the UNDCP executive director Pino Arlachi accepted this anaalysis and sought extra funding for drug control projects in central Asia to counter this supposed increase, such 'evidence' also conveniently legitimised the Russians increasing their military presence along Afghanistan's northern border, something they had wanted to do for years. Why would drug traffickers neglect well-worn smuggling paths and networks of contacts that facilitated the movement of opium and heroin by the 'Balkan route' to Pakistan, Iran, the Gulf states and onwards to Turkey and Europe? While there may have been an increase in law enforcement in Pakistan, and particularly Iran, that would have encouraged a switch to more northern routes, the success of large-scale drug traffickers relies mainly on the corrupting of public officials and corruption is endemic in these countries where official-trafficker ties are well established.

According to many law enforcement officials, most of the heroin from Afghanistan is still trafficked through the traditional routes rather than north through the central Asian republics and Russia, notwithstanding the substantial increase in demand for heroin in the old Soviet states such as Kazakhstan, Kyrgyzstan and Tajikistan, as well as Russia itself. Police sources, as reliable as any can be, suggest that only around 20 per cent of Afghan produced 'heroin equivalent' opiates are trafficked by the northern route, the rest by the Balkan route, although all drug trafficking routes are flexible and constantly adapting to local conditions and changes relating to market demand and law enforcement measures. In 2005 the UNODC itself reported that about 30 per cent of Afghan produced morphine and heroin, though only 25 per cent of all opiate drugs, was being shipped through Central Asia, while the bulk was 'still exported via Pakistan and Iran to Turkey (directly or via Iraq)'.[59] Apart from overland routes, drugs from Afghanistan are also trafficked by air and by sea from Iranian and Pakistani coastal ports.[60] Within Afghanistan changes in patterns of drug production are also reflected in changing trafficking patterns. In 2002 an increase in opium cultivation in Badakhshan in the extreme northeast of the country resulted in a corresponding 200 per cent increase in drug trafficking north through neighbouring Tajikistan.[61]

In the same year in the provinces of Badakhshan and Takhar, bordering Tajikistan, local 'non-official' commanders involved in trafficking allegedly kidnapped Tajik citizens as hostages until the drugs had been successfully smuggled into Tajikistan. According to local people, this was a common practice in the border area between Afghanistan and Tajikistan. While the locations of some of the 18 heroin factories reportedly operating in Badakhshan province in 2003 were secret, 'others are astonishingly open. One commander built his right on the main road. The governor's response was that he knew he did not have the force to stop it, but please would the commander move it a little further away from the roadside.'[62] Conversely in late 2002 it was reported that in Shaida district, newly created out of part of Baharak district, people had attacked a group of drug traffickers and had confiscated six vehicles, a large quantity of heroin and three satellite phones. The next day the forces of Commander Qari Wadood tried to return the heroin and equipment to the traffickers, but met resistance from local people. After requesting assistance from the governor, forces were sent to the district to confiscate the heroin and the equipment, destroying a heroin laboratory in the process. In the same month, speaking at a press conference in Moscow, Konstantin Totsky, director of the Russian federal frontier service, criticised the international forces failure to prevent drug production in Afghanistan, despite the fact that they allegedly knew the location of every drug plantation and laboratory in the country. In 2002, he claimed, nearly 90 drug smugglers attempting to illegally cross the Tajikistan–Afghanistan border were prevented, with 65 people detained and over four tonnes of drugs confiscated. Heroin accounted for 25 per cent of the confiscated drugs.

At least up to 1998, it was reported that opium smuggling across this border was still a 'people's activity'. The resultant capture of hundreds of small-time couriers who lacked the resources to bribe border officials enabled the Tajik authorities to report the seizures of several tonnes of opium each year. On the other hand, although heroin was 'everywhere' in Tajikistan, its lucrative trafficking was in the hands of well-protected professionals who were able to literally buy smuggling routes, resulting in the amounts seized being insignificant compared to what was actually transported across the border.

By early 2004, the *Financial Times* reported that British special forces had engaged in a covert programme, called Operation Headstrong, to secretly train an elite team of Afghan commandos to destroy heroin factories and 'confiscate drug caches and shipments' in the Badakhshan area. On 2 January 2004 this task force raided a heroin factory ten miles north of the provincial capital Faisabad, arresting several of the workers and seizing one and a half tonnes of opium. A support aircraft then bombed the factory, destroying it.[63] Another report claimed that during the raid ten people had been detained, one man had been injured and two AK-47s had been confiscated.[64] At that time the task force was not a proper law enforcement body and did not have the skills or a mandate to prosecute, their role was purely disruption by destruction of drugs and factories, leaving no evidence for purposes of prosecution in the courts.[65]

Heroin, mostly of Afghanistan origin, but also from Pakistan and Tajikistan, also accounts for up to 20 per cent of the heroin that enters the northwest Chinese province of Xinjiang, a trend that is increasing according to the DEA.[66] The unstable security situation in Iraq has also led to the emergence of a new trafficking route for Afghan heroin. While traffickers have been moving consignments of heroin from Iran across northern Iraq into Turkey for over a decade, there have been reports of heroin now being trafficked through Baghdad and southern areas. Increasingly heroin and other drug trafficking from Afghanistan spreads like a fan throughout the region, involving more and more countries, criminal groups and corrupt officials. West African organised crime groups, already active in regional drug smuggling, have now moved into Afghanistan itself. During one week in September 2005 four Nigerians were arrested at Kabul airport attempting to smuggle around 18 kg of heroin hidden in shoes, books, CD cases and tins of tomatoes. In the same month a Ghanaian national was arrested at Delhi airport in India en route to Abidjan in the Ivory Coast with 5.5 kg of heroin he had procured in Kabul.[67]

## OTHER PLAYERS

There have also been allegations made about the involvement of US military personnel in the drug trade, conjuring up the ghosts of complicity, corruption and criminality from the Vietnam era. On 12 July 2004 the alleged suicide of 25-year-old US army specialist Juan Torres at Bagram airbase north of Kabul raised the spectre of US military personnel involvement in drug trafficking in Afghanistan. According to the army, he was found in a shower/latrine with a self-inflicted gunshot wound to the head. In the few days before his death he had phoned his parents and fiancée back in Houston and had sounded upbeat and excited about his return after a year on duty in Afghanistan. His father recounted how his son had told him over the phone, 'Daddy, there are so many drugs here. I tell the people "Don't use the drugs".'[68] He was in good health, had a good job waiting for him at home and was making plans for his wedding in August.

Several military colleagues of Torres suggested to his family that there had been a cover-up. The army had retained the suicide note allegedly found at the scene, as well as the weapon, pending completion of an investigation. The Pentagon initially told the family that Juan had died of 'non-combat related injuries' but released no details. A soldier who had been at Bagram told the family that drugs (unspecified) were rampant at the base and she had seen 'drug sales taking place in a room at the base, with large amounts of cash on the table'.[69] Other soldiers were afraid for their lives if they talked about the incident, with witnesses ordered to burn much of Torres's personal belongings and reports of his rifle being sent to Fort Hood in the US instead of being retained at Bagram for the investigation. A few months earlier, in April 2004, an investigative journalist reported in the *New Yorker* that 'Since the fall of 2002, a number of active-duty and retired military and CIA officials have told me about increasing reports of heroin use by military personnel in Afghanistan, many of whom have been there for months, with few distractions.'[70]

While there have been no reports of US or other international military personnel involved in the trafficking of drugs out of the country, Afghan warlords, commanders and militias (as well as corrupt officials) have played several key roles in trafficking activities, as well as contributing to an increase in problem drug use. Working outside the law, they have frequently created social conditions that breed fear, insecurity and terror, thus increasing the likelihood of fellow Afghans turning to drug use as a coping strategy. At the same time, warlords underpin the opium economy, while also undermining good governance and weakening the state,[71] by providing protection and security for traffickers and dealers, taxing drug shipments, encouraging bribery and corruption among officials at all levels, and collecting *usher* from poppy cultivators. Some warlords are more directly linked with drug production, sponsoring and funding processing facilities such as heroin factories, controlling opium bazaars and the raw materials for heroin production like acetic anhydride and ammonium chloride, as well as running trafficking enterprises themselves.

But not only have the predatory activities of warlords and their militias helped to engender a climate of fear and insecurity, thus exacerbating mental health problems for many, and increasing risk of problem drug use, they themselves have constituted an at-risk group for problem drug use. There is little doubt that those working outside the law have played an integral role not only in the increasing supply of drugs but also in their demand and consumption.

# 6
## Outlaws and Warlords

If you were to roam the world from the Arctic goldfields of Kotzebue Sound to the pearl fisheries of Thursday Island, you could find no men more worthy of the title 'desperado' than the Pathans [Pashtoons] who live among those jagged, saw-tooth mountains of the Afghan frontier. They obey neither God nor man. Their only law is the law of the rifle and the knife.[1]

Warlord power is inextricably tied to the economy of war that has developed over the last two decades. This war economy relies heavily on poppy cultivation and opium production; gems (mainly emeralds from the Panjshir Valley and lapis lazuli from Badakhshan), arms smuggling, and the unregulated trade in legitimate goods.[2]

The situation [in 2006] is a reflection of the country's immediate past, where the breakdown of central government power led to the emergence of local leaders and warlords who wielded power and set up patronage networks through access to foreign aid, weapons, tax revenue, natural resources, and the illicit narcotics trade.[3]

In January 2003, a report by the International Crisis Group emphasised the serious shortcomings with regard to the rule of law in Afghanistan and the means of implementing that law:

Afghanistan's legal system has collapsed. Never strong to begin with, it has nearly been destroyed by 23 years of conflict and misrule. There are few trained lawyers, little physical infrastructure, and no complete record of the country's laws. Under successive regimes, laws have been administered for mostly political ends with few protections of the rights of individuals to a fair trial. Although the country has signed up to most international agreements on human rights, abuses have been widespread and military commanders have enjoyed impunity.[4]

In such a statutory law and order vacuum, where rule by the gun still prevails along with a predatory frontier ethos, a byzantine network of regional warlords, local military commanders and sub-commanders has developed throughout the country, based on a mix of previous tribal, clan, ethnic, political and criminal groupings. After the Soviets left in 1989 Afghanistan consisted of several major *mujahideen*-based factional groups plus many splinter groups that formed hyperarmed networks of power.[5] It is likely to be many years before this shifting but entrenched network of allegiances and alliances can be replaced by a functioning national legal system based on justice and the rule of law. In May 2003 in an interview with the UN News Agency IRIN, the Chief Justice of Afghanistan, the cleric Fazl-e Hadi Shinwari, was reported as saying that 'the warlords and their gangs of gunmen are a big challenge to the supremacy of the judiciary and the rule of law. They often reject our judgments and interfere in our affairs.'[6] To compound matters, the state justice system, such as it is, criminalises and excludes offenders, whereas the traditional system of customary law aimed at the reconciliation of disputants and the reintegration of offenders back into the village or tribe, although this frequently lapsed into acts of violent retribution.[7] Methods of non-violent conflict resolution that do exist have to a great extent been decimated by the social destruction wrought over the last few decades.

In 1845 a French soldier serving as a general in the Anglo-Indian army in Afghanistan remarked that

There is no nation in the world more turbulent and less under subjection; the difficulties in rendering them submissive to a code of just laws would be almost insurmountable…they hate all governments which introduce law and order into a country, or enter into peace with their neighbours; to do so in their eyes is an attack upon their rights, which deprives them of pillage, and consequently the best part of their revenues.[8]

While conditions of peace and order have existed for short periods and colonial caricatures are best avoided, a propensity to pillage and revolt has indeed been a constant thread throughout most of Afghanistan's turbulent history of the past 200 years. The fact that it is a landlocked country surrounded by nation states, both regional and global, that have desired to control its destiny and held predatory aspirations on its territory has been a major factor in the development of its martial history and ongoing warrior culture. Afghanistan has continually had to defend itself against outsiders during those periods when its tribes were not feuding and warring with each other.

When a Pashtoon tribe was called into battle by their *jirga* each family that contributed its men and weapons to the *lashkar* expected to be rewarded by whatever booty it could capture.[9] In the mid-1800s when British India was at its height, its armies in the area between India and Afghanistan were confronted with a mix of Pashtoon tribes 'whose traditional occupations were the imposition of tolls on travellers, cattle raiding, the capture of merchants for ransom, and other activities of a predatory nature'.[10] Ahmed Rashid's description of Uzbek clan history right up to the present day as being 'a long litany of blood feuds, revenge killings, power struggles, loot and plunder and disputes over women' presents a tribal microcosm of much of Afghanistan.[11] After the Soviets left and the civil war began, the militia forces of Rashid Dostum, the most famous Uzbek warlord in Afghanistan, earned the sobriquet *gilam-jam*, or 'carpet snatchers'. This is 'an Afghan way of saying "stripped down to the floor"; Dostum's forces were *gilam-jam* because they looted everything in sight, including, literally, the carpet'.[12] An Afghan friend says that it implies more than this, it relates to armed forces who wipe out everything and leave no one alive to hold the carpet down. Then it can be folded and removed.

When Dostum's militia, along with those of Ahmad Shah Massoud, Gulbuddin Hekmatyr and several other commanders, finally entered Kabul in 1992 and took over control of the city and the country from the communist regime of Dr Mohammad Najibullah they accomplished something that the Soviet invaders had not—the destruction and looting of several parts of the city. The Kabul museum was ransacked of priceless antiquities and national treasures while armories, government offices, shops in the bazaar and private houses were looted. More ominously, 'when there were no valuables left, the looting gunmen would steal people'. Such unfortunates were kidnapped for ransom, with thieves failing to honour any traditional code, so that 'purdah was routinely violated, along with the women themselves'.[13] During this period, starving street dogs in Kabul started to eat dead human bodies lying by the wayside then began attacking live humans as a source of food.

In 1929 after King Amanullah had been forced to abdicate, in part because an uprising of tribesmen in Nangarhar had seen the army turn against him, his eldest brother Inayatullah took over for a mere three days before an illiterate Tajik outlaw and bandit leader called Habibullah, more commonly referred to as the Bacha-i-Saqao (the 'son of the water carrier') captured the throne. After only nine months in power, that saw Tajiks rule in Kabul for the first time (much to the chagrin of the Pashtoons) and that was 'characterised by anarchy, pillage and terror', the Bacha was overthrown and executed by the Pashtoon forces of Nadir Shah, Amanullah's cousin.[14] Such convoluted tribal politics had seen the Bacha's Tajik colleagues plunder the national treasury and Nadir Shah's army loot Kabul to buy off Amanullah's supporters. When the country fell under the more autocratic rule of Nadir Shah it led Richard Maconachie, the British Minister to Kabul, to send a dispatch to London in January 1931 stating that

Throughout the country the advantages of anarchy seem to have been better appreciated than its drawbacks and the tribes are asking themselves why they should resign the freedom which they enjoyed the past year and submit again to a central authority which would inevitably demand payment of land revenue, customs duties and bribes for its officials and possibly the restoration of arms looted from government posts and arsenals.[15]

Since 2002, regional warlords and militia commanders have continued to deprive the newly established central government of much-needed revenue from taxes or customs collections levied on imported goods at border posts, as well as resources like aid shipments. The collection of *usher*, the 10 per cent tax on all agricultural products, collected in kind, was banned by President Karzai shortly after he was elected in October 2004 but this has largely been ignored by regional warlords and commanders. In the north of the country there have been reports of farmers being threatened for failing to pay *usher*. One farmer who could not pay was reportedly 'badly beaten and warned if he did not pay the tax he would be killed and his property would be occupied'.[16] Such activities have helped to weaken the central government even further, limited its powers mainly to Kabul, and encouraged lawlessness and banditry. The US government has been blamed for colluding with warlords by depending on them and financing them, rather than disarming and disabling them in their search for al-Qaeda and the re-emergent Taliban.[17] An article written in the *Washington Post* in April 2003 by Mahmood Karzai, brother of the President and founder of the Afghan-American Chamber of Commerce, Hamed Wardak, the Afghan Vice-President of the Chamber; and Jack Kemp, former US Congressman and Republican candidate for Vice President, claimed that 'Unfortunately the re-emergence of these warlords is directly related to US financial and military support, which is the sole source of their power. This power allows the warlords to treat public funds as personal largesse.'[18] They further claimed that by maintaining the political status quo that resulted in the weakening of central government power such warlords continued 'to exercise their political and economic policies autonomously—policies based on nepotism, tribalism, ethnocentrism, closed markets, price controls, conflict of interest, corruption, inequality and injustice'.[19]

In May 2003 President Karzai held a meeting with provincial governors and threatened to resign if they did not start sending customs and other public revenues to the central government. This resulted in only $20 million out of an estimated annual revenue of over $200 million being forwarded to Kabul by Ismail Khan, the Governor and self-styled Emir of Herat. One report claimed that the minister of finance, Ashraf Ghani, flew to Herat in a military plane, along with his metallic-grey Mercedes SUV, to try and elicit funds for central government as they risked running out of money to pay officials. After visiting several mosques in his quest, Ghani met with Khan who allegedly said: 'He [Ghani] came to me and said, "there is no money in the central bank", so I gave him the money', whereupon Ghani and his Mercedes flew back to Kabul with $8 million in cash and $12 million in the form of 700 million Afghanis, nearly enough to pay the government's entire wage bill for a month.[20]

Afghanistan is a country where many in the population remain victim to the rule of regional warlords, their commanders and militias characterised by predatory behaviour, protection racketeering and summary justice. There is often a heavy price to pay in Afghanistan for 'protection' and the tenuous conditional security provided to communities by such armed groups. Until 1994 and the appearance of the Taliban, the maintenance of security was the main business of large numbers of combat troops, regarded by Conrad Schetter as 'war enterprises' adapted to a market of violence within an economy of violence.[21] After the demise of the Taliban, who had managed to monopolise the economy of security in most of Afghanistan up to late 2001, there was no shortage of re-emergent well-armed combat troops, militias, commanders and warlords who were happy to fill the security vacuum. The UN National Development Report for Afghanistan for 2004 noted that 'wartime capital accumulations are typically obtained through brutal, primitive measures, such as slavery, oppressive working conditions, fear and force' and posed the question of whether activities related to the war economy in Afghanistan such as smuggling, resource extraction and drugs were responses to the stresses and strains of war or would have been carried out anyway under normal conditions.[22]

## OUTLAWS AND WARLORDS

There appear few examples in Afghanistan's history, past or present, of what Eric Hobsbawm refers to as 'social banditry' where unsolicited citizen protection and support occurs and progressive and socially redeeming links with the population are developed, usually as a prelude to seeking legitimation and political status.[23] One historical exception, at least until he was gripped by the reins of power, may have been the aforementioned Bacha-i-Saqao who was described in a letter to Sir Francis Humphrys, head of the British delegation in Kabul, by Mr Best, a delegation secretary, as follows:

He might well be called the 'man of rumours', because he is the hero or the villain of every fantastic tale in the bazaars of Afghanistan...He practically blocked the main road to the north between Kabul and Charikar, but his efforts seemed directed only against the King and his Government, ordinary individuals and traffic being allowed to go free. This distinction was so marked that the Bacha quickly earned for himself a sobriquet akin to that of Robin Hood.[24]

While it has also been suggested that Mullah Omar initially emerged as a Robin Hood figure who helped and supported the poor of southeast Afghanistan against rapacious commanders, the Taliban's increasingly oppressive regime and repressive behaviour soon dimmed this image.[25] Certainly by the time the Taliban seized power in Qandahar in 1994 Afghanistan had degenerated into a fighting, feuding 'maelstrom of shifting alliances' where 'southern Pushtun warlords and bandits continued to fight each other for territory, while continuing to sell off Afghanistan's machinery, property, and even entire factories to Pakistani traders. Kidnappings, murders, rapes, and robberies were frequent as Afghan civilians found themselves in the crossfire.'[26] Seven years later when they were deposed, the Taliban's legacy consisted of virtually nothing in the way of development, help or support for the suffering and impoverished mass of the population.

The illicit drug trade afforded one opportunity for such socially redeeming links to be established with the population, but this never happened. Almost without exception none of the profits of the trade were invested in wider benefits to the community:

in none of the poppy growing areas we have visited were there any signs of investment of even a small proportion of poppy income in things of public good, not even roads, which would benefit the traders themselves, let alone schools, clinics or drinking water.[27]

As the new Interim Government tried to come to grips with the country in 2002 several militia groups were paid by the Ministry of Defence and to some extent followed a centralised military hierarchy.

Warlords included over half a dozen regional leaders who controlled territory and troops, with some of them nominally functioning as corps commanders under the Afghanistan government, but effectively independent, while others lay entirely outside the government.[28] By the end of 2005, despite over 60,000 former combatants having been disarmed and reintegrated by the UN-backed DDR programme, it was estimated that there were around 2,000 illegal armed groups operating outside any legal or government structure.[29] This is hardly surprising considering that during the war with the Soviets each *mujahideen* group and political faction had a commander in each province and a sub-commander in each district of each province—the basic structures and networks of armed groups had been formed over two decades earlier.

Ironically, the first major warlord to be dealt with by President Karzai's national army, with considerable military backup from American forces, was Ismail Khan who had at least developed ambitious public works projects in Herat such as an electricity supply, new roads and public parks. However, with control over Herat and the nearby Shindand airbase being an important strategic objective of the US imperative to establish a substantial regional power base next to Iran's eastern border, Khan had little chance to resist. Other warlords like Rashid Dostum are likely to have been motivated to stand in the 2004 presidential elections against Karzai in order to try and legitimise their power and in the hope of gaining important and potentially lucrative posts in the new government. In early 2005 when Dostum was made Chief-of-Staff to the Commander-in-Chief of the Afghan armed forces, nominally President Karzai, there were calls by human rights organisations for his trial, as well as those of other commanders and warlords, for gross human rights violations.*

Although one report stated that in some parts of the country commanders have been elected by *shuras* of tribal elders as 'tribal leaders' and have good relations with local communities, claiming a modicum of grassroots support, the same report went on to state that 'the support that commanders receive from tribal elders is often

---

*    In 2006 a UN report emerged documenting human rights violations and atrocities that had been committed by communists, *mujahideen*, Soviet and Taliban fighters during the war and conflict wrought on Afghanistan since 1979. The report had been scheduled for release in January 2005, but was delayed. Deemed too sensitive for publication, it contained the names of several warlords and commanders still in positions of power, including the new parliament.

reluctant, or more pragmatic than genuine', and that 'tribal elders lamented their lack of control over the young men that are the *andiwal* or gunmen of the Warlords'.[30] At the same time, there have been attempts to co-opt more powerful warlords into the government to bring them under some central control. In July 2004, several provincial militia commanders were given governmental positions, presumably in an attempt to reduce their power ahead of the October presidential elections. One of these men was Atta Mohammad, a powerful Tajik warlord from Mazar-i-Sharif allied to *Jamiat-i Islami* and a bitter opponent of Rashid Dostum, who was made Governor of the troubled northern province of Balkh. Whether such attempts had the intended effect is doubtful. As one commentator noted, 'This was more a case of punishment by promotion than a serious effort to reduce their influence.'[31] By 2005, however, both Atta and Dostum had ostensibly laid down their arms and disarmed their militias as a prelude to building political power bases before the parliamentary elections scheduled for September of that year. According to a western diplomat in Kabul, 'It's a case of keep your friends close and your enemies closer. Dostum needed to have a role in government because they can't arrest him or get rid of him.'[32]

Apart from co-opting major warlords into government, a bigger development challenge is how to bring the many illegal armed groups into the government fold. While some are already motivated and want to disarm and return to civilian life, others are likely to continue with their profitable predatory activities. In the 1970s, prior to the Soviet invasion, a future prominent member of the Peshawar-based *mujahideen* group *Mahaz-i-Milli Islami* (NIFA), Haji Latif, was reputedly the leader of a gang of Qandahar brigands and had served 21 years in prison for murder. He allegedly ran a protection racket, extorting money from rich merchants and then distributing some of the money to the poor and needy. This gained his gang the reputation of being seen as a 'benevolent mafia', while NIFA officials rationalised his criminal past by defining him as a type of Robin Hood figure:

His gang was called *Pagie Louch*, Farsi for 'bare feet', because along with special prayers and magic incantations, its initiation rites involved walking barefoot on a bed of hot coals. New members also had to suffer nails to be driven into their heels without showing pain.[33]

Small benevolent gestures by such men, however, often serve as heroic attempts at self-legitimisation with the result of distracting attention from their more ruthless predatory activities.

While the concept of warlord has generally been the subject of much debate, any formal definition needs to include the following basic characteristics: the possession of autonomous force; the control of a base region; the use of force as the final arbiter; the reliance on personal rather than impersonal patterns of rule; and, a ruthless and extractive attitude towards society and the economy.[34]* However, as a leader in the *Kabul Times* rightly stressed, in Afghanistan there is a need to distinguish between former *mujahideen* who took up arms against the invading Soviet army as a religious obligation without expecting any financial gain or reward, and others who retained their weapons and their fighters after the war finished in order 'to enhance their personal prestige or for material gains' through warlordism and predatory criminal activities.[35] Others, in common with a British House of Commons report, have dismissed the pejorative use of 'warlordism' and 'warlords' in Afghanistan as a creation of the western media, preferring the term 'local military commanders'. The report may indeed be correct in concluding that, 'Afghanistan's "warlords" or commanders are both a large part of the problem and an essential part of the solution.' Nevertheless the fact remains that the essentially extractive relationship they have to their fiefdoms (referred to in the British report as: 'malign activities' like poppy cultivation, drug trafficking, human rights abuses, smuggling, misappropriation of tax revenues and obstructing reconstruction works), their ultimate reliance on the rule of the gun and their victimisation of many ordinary Afghans within their power bases merits the label of warlord.[36]

## PREDATORY ACTIVITIES

Throughout Afghanistan, a hierarchy of groups outside any statutory control, literally living outside any law except that which they confer on themselves, carve out large swathes of territory into fiefdoms, make and break alliances, compete for power and resources, challenge the central government's authority, and hold much of the populace, in rural areas particularly, at their dubious mercies. In Bamiyan province in early 2003, for example, a local commander was someone who had ten to twelve soldiers under his command, although a differen-

---

* At an international counter-narcotics conference held in Kabul in February 2004, the Governor of Qandahar province, Mohammad Yusuf Pashtun, defined a warlord in Afghanistan as anyone who misused his power, whether a businessman, a gunman or a Governor.

tiation was made between 'small' and 'big' commanders.[37] Such a commander had enough armed men to control two to three villages and would usually be seeking an alliance with a bigger commander. The predatory activities of these commanders included the appropriation at gunpoint and threat of force of land and buildings for their own use and setting up illegal checkpoints on main roads where 'tolls' would be extracted from passing vehicles. A small combi bus with around 16 passengers would be asked for $10–15. Not a lot of money, but with several checkpoints on one road this could prove very expensive for the passengers. As another source of income, opium poppy was also cultivated in secondary and tertiary valleys, increasingly in hidden side valleys away from the main roads. It was commonly reported that young girls were kidnapped to become 'wives' of commanders and their soldiers. If the girl became pregnant she was relegated to serving and other household duties and another girl kidnapped. At least this was preferable to what happened in neighbouring Uruzgan province where it was reported that young girls were kidnapped, raped and then sold on to other commanders.

Perhaps the most common predatory activity was a form of protection racketeering, the acquisition of commodities as payment for the 'insurance' necessary to ensure the security of households and property.* In poor communities, however, there was not much to take, maybe no more than some improved seed, bought in the bazaar or donated by an aid agency. But in a double cropping zone like Khamard district there was a lot more to take. While 'smaller' commanders would just take it, 'bigger' commanders expected a contribution as their right because they were offering protection and security in exchange. They reputedly sent their boy soldiers into the villages to collect such payments.

---

\* In the Scottish Highlands in the late seventeenth century, landowners paid a fee, or 'mail', to members of local 'Highland Watches' to protect their cattle from being stolen by raiders. In a lawless land, other individuals and some Highland villages also had to buy their security by paying an annual tribute to the chieftains who plundered them. Such a fee was usually paid in black cattle (black *meall*) and hence acquired the name 'blackmail', while fees paid in silver were refered to as 'whitemail'. One captain of the local Watch, basically a Highland commander (formally the war leader of his clan) later turned outlaw, Rob Roy McGregor, became a cattle dealer himself and soon 'began to operate a very profitable blackmail protection racket of his own'. (Bernard Byrom, 2005, *Old Comrie, Upper Strathearn and Balqhuidder*, Catrine: Stenlake Publishing, p. 39.)

The use of such boy soldiers is common throughout the country. In December 2002, the UN named Afghanistan, along with Burundi, the Democratic Republic of Congo, Liberia and Somalia, as a country where warring factions still forcibly recruited and deployed children under 16 to fight. It was estimated that there were over 8,000 boy soldiers in Afghanistan, many still in the employ of armed groups such as those in Bamiyan province. Even in Kabul city it is not unusual to see young teenagers walking around in paramilitary uniform with AK-47s hung casually over their shoulders. By early 2005 UNICEF had demobilised around 4,000 of these boy soldiers aged between 14 and 17 years in 15 provinces, providing them with opportunities for education and training as well as medical and psychosocial assessment.

A report by Human Rights Watch in 2003, ominously entitled 'Killing you is a very easy thing for us', provides a detailed account of the many predatory activities of warlords and their commanders in southeast Afghanistan and other parts of the country and the consequences for ordinary Afghans.[38] It is notable that some of these activities were also allegedly carried out by police and military forces allied to warlords and political leaders and under their protection. It is the sheer range of the activities that illustrates the power of such groups, some from within the law itself, working outside the law for their own self-aggrandisement and benefit: armed robbery and home invasions; arbitrary arrests, torture, kidnapping and ransom; rape of girls, women and boys; extortion and beatings of shopkeepers and taxi, truck and bus drivers; illegal seizure and forcible occupation of land; political intimidation; attacks on independent media and women's rights advocates; forced restrictions on social activities and human rights abuses of women and girls. There are of course no statistics available that would reveal the scale of these activities.

Apart from first hand accounts by individual victims of such terror, the report provides examples of the social effects of such activities at the community level. Late one night in west Kabul a taxi driver was asked to take a pregnant woman to hospital. On his return he was arrested by the police, then beaten and jailed for three nights until his family paid a ransom of $70 to have him released. After this incident, nobody in the area would risk driving a sick person to the hospital at night, depriving residents of a much-needed service.[39] Several residents of Paghman, a district close to the west of Kabul, reported that they had to keep guard dogs so that they didn't have to stay awake all night in order to patrol and protect their properties.

The only problem was that some were scared of the dogs themselves and also had to spend scarce family income on feeding them. As one person said, 'you must keep yourself hungry to feed these dogs'.[40]

Abuses against women and girls by armed men were well articulated by another informant from Paghman when giving information to a Human Rights Watch investigator:

Look—these people, these armed men, have been busy with war for a long time; war with the Russians and then war with themselves. Now they are addicted to war. Their lives are dependent on war. They had their incomes before, and were passing their luxurious lives by receiving extraordinary incomes from war, by looting and thieving. Now the fighting is over, and because they are addicted to drugs and are drunk on them, they have nothing except a gun in their hands, and when they see a girl outside, they may do something wrong.[41]

Another report from southern Afghanistan cited arbitrary arrest and imprisonment in private prisons, torture, extortion, seizure of businesses and even land. Merchants and wealthy people who were not under the protection or patronage of commanders were often targets of extortion, on some occasions being imprisoned and tortured until their families paid the ransom.[42] However, while the occasional kidnapping of internationals in Afghanistan can make world headline news, the many regular kidnappings of Afghan nationals go largely unreported.

In Badakhshan province in the extreme northeast of the country, commanders created a military structure called the *jabha* based on the recruitment of local men and taxation of the population, where 'Leadership has come with the gun (as opposed to consent) and commanders have a vested interest in the continuation of weak central authority in which there are few restraining influences on their local "fiefdoms".'[43] They also have a vested interest in maintaining the opium economy as it provides an important source of income for such self-financing groups. Such activities as those above have also been reported as basic to commanders and their foot soldiers or militiamen in other parts of the country. The revenue from opium and its trafficking contributes significantly to the wages of these combatants.

Since the Taliban lost control of the country in late 2001, clashes between commanders, political factions and ethnic groups for control of territory and resources have been consistently reported, leading to an increased risk of insecurity and possible crossfire injury for civilians. As only one example of many such incidents, in a remote area of Samangan province, Dar-i-Suf, in January 2003 there was fighting between *Harakat-i-Inquilab-i-Islami* and *Hezb-i Wahdat* forces, allegedly leaving four *Hezb* soldiers dead. A few months later in April, spring and summer being considered the traditional fighting season in Afghanistan, serious fighting erupted in Maimana in northern Faryab province between *Jamiat-i Islami* and *Jumbesh-i-Milli Islami* factions. This resulted in the deaths of 14 soldiers and two civilians. Serious human rights violations in Badghis province resulted in even more civilian deaths during the same month. In Akasi village 38 civilians were killed and 761 homes and 21 shops were looted. A UN spokesperson said that among the victims who died were three women and twelve children who reportedly drowned in a river: 'Some reports say that they threw themselves in the river to escape the gunfire while others said women jumped in to avoid being abused by soldiers.'[44] The local commander allegedly responsible for the deaths, Juman Khan, and his men were pursued by a coalition of local factions who then summarily executed 26 individuals whose bodies were found with their hands tied behind their backs. The prior events that may have engendered these conflicts included 'compulsory taxation of the local population by soldiers and armed individuals not wearing any recognised uniform, and extortion of money and food, and confiscation of money and cattle'.[45] If people failed to comply with these demands they were reportedly beaten, tortured, accused of being Taliban and, in some cases, summarily executed.

In February 2004, fighting erupted between the militias of the local police chief Qari Ziauddin and the district chief and local mayor of Argo district, just north of Faisabad the capital of Badakhshan province, that resulted in the deaths of twelve people including civilians and militia gunmen. The trouble started because of a feud over who should control the lucrative road tax levied on local opium and heroin traffickers. At the time, Badakhshan was one of the leading opium cultivation areas in the country and constituted a major smuggling route for illicit drugs into neighbouring Tajikistan en route to Russia and Europe.[46] In June 2004 there were reports of fighting with heavy weapons between Hazaras and *Kuchis* in Wardak province over ongoing land disputes. During the same month, fighters from the *Hezb-i Wahdat and Jamiat-i Islami* factions clashed in Mazar-i-Sharif over a property dispute, leaving one dead and two wounded. Allegedly 150 *Jamiat* militiamen wanted to take over a disused military barracks in the west of the city, but were fired on by local *Hezb* supporters who claimed that this was their property and that they had the title deeds to prove it.[47]

Such armed conflicts caused by disputes over land and property are likely to continue in Afghanistan for many years, despite well-worn traditional practices of conflict resolution through negotiation and arbitration and the demobilisation of militias or their co-option into the national army. In the end there is always recourse to the law of the gun. During the social upheavals of the last few decades, the property and lands of many refugees and IDPs have simply been taken over by men with guns who resist attempts to return such lands and properties to their rightful owners. Written title deeds may be non-existent, forged or lost and, in any case, there are many old scores to be settled, enmities to be resolved and economic interests to be consolidated. In August 2005 land and water disputes led to six deaths and 20 woundings in Nangarhar and Laghman provinces alone. In the former case, a man, his wife and son were killed and two children wounded after the enraged nephew of a rival family and other armed men broke into their house at night after an argument over a long-standing watercourse dispute. In the Badi Abad area of Laghman, only 15 miles from the provincial capital, a clash erupted as families of Allah Gul and Qayum Akhundzada exchanged fire over a piece of land. They were later joined by men of their respective clans resulting in the killing of three people.[48]

## RESPONSIBILITY FOR LAW AND ORDER

In such a context it can be difficult to ascertain who is responsible for law and order, not only in remote areas of the country, but also in the capital Kabul, protected by an international force of 4,500 ISAF troops as well as local police. On 11 December 2002 the *Kabul Times* carried a story paradoxically headlined, 'Armed men arrest two policemen in Kabul'. This referred to an incident in the Khairkhana district of the city when police stopped and challenged 'an Afghan warlord' about the lack of permits for his armed bodyguards and the tinted windows of his vehicle. The chief of the police precinct dealing with the incident reported that,

It was 8.45 am that the bodyguards of Amanullah Guzar, commander of No. 01 Jehadi section of Defence Ministry attacked three policemen in Sarwar Kayanat Square when they stopped Amanullah's vehicle and inquired about the licence of his bodyguard's guns and the permit for his black tinted car windows.

After the police had opened fire the armed bodyguards, reportedly dressed in commando uniforms, had returned fire wounding one policeman and arresting two others.

By 2005, when many newly demobilised militia fighters had joined the police force and national army, incidences of crime and armed banditry throughout the country had reportedly increased although there were no official statistics to substantiate or repudiate this. In Qandahar thousands took to the streets in protest over the inability of the authorities to prevent a spate of child kidnappings and demanded the resignation of the governor and police chief. For ordinary Afghans, 'armed robbery, kidnapping and intimidation have displaced the Taliban as the principal security problem. The line between cops and robbers is becoming increasingly blurred.'[49] Security reports commonly cite incidences of armed men dressed in police uniforms committing criminal acts, although whether these men are genuine police or impostors is never clear. It has been reported that senior officers in the national police suspect that organised criminal groups who have been involved in armed robbery, kidnapping, drug trafficking and other serious crimes are supported by powerful members of the government. The President's spokesperson, Jawed Ludin, acknowledged that such criminals existed in the ranks of the national police itself, aided and abetted by senior government officials.[50] According to human rights activists, 'In some areas, militia fighters have followed their commanders into the local police force, turning it into a private army in police uniform.'[51] A project coordinator for Civil Society and Human Rights Network, a coalition of over 30 Afghan groups, has claimed that this whole process has been unwittingly facilitated by President Karzai's policy of shifting warlords and militia commanders around the country from their own fiefdoms and criminal rackets into powerful official positions such as provincial governors and police chiefs in other areas where they have less personal authority and influence. This has enabled them to cooperate, network and form criminal alliances at the same time that human rights groups have pressed for these warlords and militia commanders, several of whom are now senior government officials, to be prosecuted for war crimes and human rights violations.

In May 2005 two Afghan journalists reported that in several provinces local people had complained that the police were not much better than the criminals they were meant to be apprehending and still maintained links with armed militias:

Most complaints come from herders and farmers whose crops and flocks are 'taxed' by local gunmen. Local residents say these gunmen use threats, beatings or torture and operate under the protection of the local police... About 450 kilometres to the southeast, in Kunar province near the Pakistan border, herdsmen fought a three-day skirmish in March against the forces of local commander Haji Sardar. Fed up with his tithe of every twentieth goat and every tenth sheep, they burned his compound and ran him out of their village, Mazar Dara. 'There were no casualties, but their centre was set on fire, and the commander escaped along with his friends,' village elder Malik Gulan told IWPR.[52]

In February 2005, armed members of the Ministry of the Interior forced their way into the private house of Edward Girardet, a journalist who has been reporting and writing on Afghanistan for over 20 years. He was at home having a dinner party with his family and some friends. Girardet's subsequent letter of complaint to President Karzai talked about the growing concern over lawlessness and corruption within the ministry and how the officials had engaged in forced intrusion, physical assault, violent intimidation and a refusal to identify themselves properly. Eventually he was arrested, manhandled into a vehicle and held for nearly two hours before being released with no apology. His letter accepted that the officials may not have been adequately trained or lacked the professional expertise to uphold responsible law and order, although he also commented that they may have taken their cue from US security forces acting more like an occupation force than a peacekeeping force by condoning armed intrusion into houses in the name of public security. Most crucially Girardet noted that, 'Many Afghans who have been mistreated or otherwise abused by elements within the Ministry of Interior do not have connections capable of intervening in their favour as do foreigners like myself.'[53]

In cities like Kabul armed robberies are also frequently reported, often with large sums of money stolen. During one night in February 2003 over $250,000 was stolen from the UNICEF office by over 20 men dressed in military uniforms and armed with AK-47s. They allegedly forced their way into the building and loaded the main safe onto a UNICEF vehicle and simply drove away with it. In early 2005 within a few weeks of each other, two of the eleven new banks that had opened since 2002 were robbed of substantial sums of money, both allegedly 'inside jobs' involving members of the militias hired to provide security. In February 2006, a group of armed men dressed in police uniforms killed a policeman and injured a 14-year-old girl while making off with $320,000 stolen from a vehicle belonging to the Habib bank.[54]

If it is generally accepted that military training, techniques and experience are the best background for would-be armed robbers then there is no shortage of such technical experts in Afghanistan. The hijacking of vehicles is also frequently reported, and in several cases the occupants have been brutally killed, even if they did not resist. If vehicles are not hijacked or robbed, they are always vulnerable to being stopped at illegal checkpoints where a toll is demanded. On 30 January 2003 50 armed horsemen tried to block a road near Mess-i-Ainak in Logar province, allegedly in protest against the authorities removing 40 illegal checkpoints in the area. There have also been reports of drug traffickers using the cover of vehicles with false logos of UN agencies and international NGOs to smuggle drugs. Both types of organisation are usually afforded privileges and immunities that preclude the searching of their vehicles by the authorities. In January 2003 a vehicle bearing the logo of an international NGO, Mine Dog Centre, was apprehended by security police near the Salang tunnel in Baghlan and found to contain 50 kg of narcotics. After the vehicle failed to stop at a checkpoint, police opened fire killing one of the occupants and capturing another. Ironically, there have also been reliable anecdotal reports of drugs being transported in police vehicles that have been seized by the CNPA of the Ministry of the Interior then released back to the traffickers after pressure from various government officials.

### TOOLS OF THE TRADE

Central to all these predatory activities are the tools of the trade: guns and other weaponry. In February 2003 President Karzai, speaking at a donors' conference in Tokyo, emphasised the need for the disarmament, demobilisation and reintegration of the estimated 100,000 armed militiamen that made up Afghanistan's many private armies at that time.[55] In other words, for every 200 civilians in the country there was an armed militiaman aligned to a regional warlord or local commander mostly operating outside the rule of law. Generally it is difficult to estimate how many armed men are aligned to various factions and militias in Afghanistan as this can change depending on need and circumstances. A commander from the re-emergent Taliban when asked how many Talibs there were, revealingly replied: 'Today there are 50, tomorrow there could be 500, it depends on how many we need. You see, the Taliban are everywhere and they are nowhere.'

Certainly guns have been a way of life in Afghanistan for much longer than just the last few decades of conflict and war. Permanently disarming men who have made their living by the gun and have no other trade or skills will be a long and difficult process if it is to be sustainable. Guns are commonly fired into the air at weddings, the birth of sons and other cultural occasions, as well as used to settle disputes with neighbours, other family members or other clans. It has also been claimed that 'Afghan men say they love their guns as much as their wives.'[56] While this may or may not be true, carrying guns in public in many tribal areas of Afghanistan is certainly a symbol of status and manhood, often seen as necessary for the protection of self, family and property in a lawless environment. Afghanistan's age-old gun and warrior culture is well expressed in the words of a popular folk song: 'If you don't know who I am, when you come to the battlefield you will know that I am an Afghan.'[57] Driving along almost any road in rural areas you can often see men of all ages going about their daily business while carrying a wide range of different types of weaponry. In the spring of 2003 on a journey north from Kabul to the Salang tunnel and the Hindu Kush, as soon as the mountains were reached most men walking along the roadside carried a gun. Many of the guns were old-fashioned muzzle-loading muskets called *jezails*, longer than most of the young boys who struggled to carry them.

In the biography of Samiullah Safi by the anthropologist David Edwards, Safi recalls a confrontation that took place in the 1940s between his father Sultan Muhammad, a famous Pashtoon tribal leader from Kunar province, and General Daud of the national Afghan army. The general had been called into Chaga Serai, the provincial capital, after the local government treasury was looted by Pashtoon tribes as part of a continuing uprising against the Afghan state, known as the *Safi Jang* (Safi war). After the general told the elders of the tribe that he had the authority to take away their guns as if they were wooden walking sticks, Sultan Muhammad directly challenged this perceived insult and threat to disarm the tribe by admonishing the general in front of his men. The reason for this challenge is explained by Edwards:

Taking away a tribesman's rifle was morally equivalent to raping the women of the family. A man's rifle was categorised along with his land and his wife as his namus, which can be translated as both the substance of a man's honour and that which is subject to violation and must be defended.[58]

During the two nineteenth-century Anglo-Afghan wars the Afghans defeated the invading British armies and appropriated their weaponry for themselves. Then at the end of the century, during the reign of Abdul Rahman Khan, the Iron Amir, the British used Afghanistan as a buffer state to stabilise and maintain the northwest frontier of British India as part of their 'Great Game' strategy in Central Asia. During his reign the British 'lavished weapons and cash' on the Amir, and in the 15 years between 1880 and 1895 he purchased significant weaponry through British grants and the open arms market. According to a British India Office missive of the time, he was 'presented with 80 guns [cannon], 17,342 shots and shells, 33,302 rifles, 3,200 carbines and 21,308,000 cartridges'.[59] In the many souvenir and carpet shops crowding Kabul's Chicken Street, you can still find old British-made Lee Enfield rifles and Wilkinson steel bayonets in their original scabbards from this period, as well as oddities like nineteenth-century French army officers' sabres. One shopkeeper claimed that these old weapons had been kept in locked government armouries until the early 1990s when *mujahideen* groups and criminals broke in and looted them.

While guns have always been an integral part of Afghan culture, as they have been in many other lawless frontier lands, it was only during the ten-year Soviet occupation that there was a massive proliferation of modern weapons of all kinds. Initially hundreds of thousands of Lee Enfield .303 rifles flooded into the country, quickly followed by Chinese-made AK-47s, large quantities of RPGs, 60-millimetre Chinese mortars and '12.7 millimeter heavy machine guns in batches of two thousand or more'. As one CIA agent involved in the delivery of weapons to the *mujahideen* reputedly said at the time, 'Can it possibly be any better than buying bullets from the Chinese to use to shoot Russians?'[60] America's third world allies also profited from selling old or surplus weapons via the CIA and the Pakistani ISI to the *mujahideen*. As well as the Egyptians offloading weapons that had been sold to them by the Russians, 'Turkey sold sixty thousand rifles, eight thousand light machine guns, ten thousand pistols, and 100 million rounds of ammunition—mainly of 1940–42 vintage.'[61] Saudi Arabia, through its intelligence service, GID (General Intelligence Department), preferred to bypass the ISI and the CIA and donated large sums of cash-for-arms directly to *mujahideen* groups. While most of the infrared homing surface-to-air Stinger missiles supplied later in the war to these groups by the US were allegedly bought back at up to $150,000 per missile after the Soviets left, many powerful weapons remained, as well as the men who had some experience of using and servicing them.

While Afghanistan may retain its gun culture, and carrying a gun is still a passport to adult society for many men, there is a difference between the villager keeping a gun for his family's protection in a lawless land and celebrating events like weddings and births and men who make their living through guns for hire to the highest bidder.[62] In April 2003 the UN launched its DDR programme that planned to disarm and demobilise a maximum of 100,000 militia members, 'a compromise between the defence ministry's claims of 250,000 and UNAMA assessments that the true number was closer to 45,000'.[63] While 45,000 members of the AMF were to be decommissioned, over 65,000 'Afghan irregular fighters' from an estimated 850 unofficial militias still remained outside the scope of the formal DDR process.

By February 2005 the DDR programme reported that around 38,000 AMF had been disarmed. While around 18,000 former fighters had joined the ranks of the new national army, this was far short of the total 70,000 that needed to be recruited. It is still by no means certain that all soldiers will remain committed and loyal to their national duties rather than to future 'duties' that might be demanded or expected of them by the tribe, ethnic group, clan or their previous militia commander. Between January and May 2006 the desertion rate in the newly formed army fell from 25 to 13 per cent, still high even though salaries had been increased. Such figures may reflect a reluctance to fight alongside foreigners against fellow Afghans, a move to a higher-paid position as a fighter or simply mirror more traditional patterns where fighters who joined militias were permitted periods of extended leave.[64] While there may be a genuine desire on the part of fighters tired of war to disarm and return to a more settled civilian life, many gunmen continue to align themselves with regional warlords, local commanders and the Taliban or band together in small groups of predatory outlaws. Others have joined the ranks of the national army and police. Indeed, it has been claimed that 'Commanders can employ their former militiamen as police, maintain patronage links with sub-commanders, and protect their economic interests.'[65]

Until it learned better, the DDR programme itself had been difficult to implement with some commanders forcing their men who entered the programme to hand over the $200 they received for turning in their weapon. A defective low-quality AK-47 could be purchased in the arms bazaars of Pakistan border towns for as little as $45, although a high-quality model could command $250. Arms dealers in Darra Adamkhel, Miran Shah and Landi Kotal reported an increased demand for cheap hand-made AK-47s from representatives of Afghan commanders, allegedly to distribute to their men to hand in as part of the disarmament process, thus making a tidy profit and at the same time allowing the fighters to retain their original guns.[66] In late 2004 it was estimated that there was over 100,000 metric tonnes of ammunition of varying types in the country. This national estimate was based on indicators such as the 600 Russian Kamaz trucks full of ammunition found in the northern city of Mazar-i-Sharif.[67]

## FOREIGN INFLUENCES

In the 'new Afghanistan' warlords have also played an important role in political decision-making, starting with the very first democratic process, the *Loya Jirga*, held in June 2002. To what extent their participation in this *Jirga* was elicited and co-opted by third parties from foreign powers or their proxies is not known. According to a UN colleague who was directly involved in the organisation of the *Loya Jirga*, but later resigned from the UN:

The delegates, after having gone through an electoral process that was probably the most democratic and representative one that Afghan history has ever seen, were blatantly disenfranchised. After having being told for months that they were to decide on three matters—the Head of State, the structure of government and the key posts—they were not allowed to decide on any of these issues. Instead, their voices were silenced (and drowned) by the last minute admission of governors, warlords and secret service gooks who kept a careful eye on them...The UN, maybe following the cue given by the US special envoy, had seemingly given in to threats by some of the factional leaders that they would not accept the results of the *Loya Jirga* if the latter would be contrary to their interests. Peace had prevailed over justice it was said, implying that the demand for justice would throw the country into renewed conflict. Implying, in fact, that the two can be separated, that one can have peace without justice.[68]

Human Rights Watch has also reported how various military factions and warlords increased and legitimised their power during the *Loya*

*Jirga* by threatening, intimidating, imprisoning and allegedly killing candidates to prevent them from running as Jirga representatives.[69] It is perhaps ironic that three years after the *Loya Jirga* took place the UN High Commissioner for Human Rights, Louise Arbour, and the Afghan Independent Human Rights Commission pressed President Karzai to bring war criminals, including several prominent warlords, to justice after a long era of human rights abuses. While Arbour stressed that it was important 'to address past and present human rights violations so as to ensure that those responsible for egregious abuses do not succeed in wielding power', a survey conducted by the Commission reported that many Afghans have suffered so much at the hands of human rights violators that they see the last two decades as 'a seamless era of terror'. The report concluded that lasting peace and stability in the country can only be achieved by bringing perpetrators to justice and holding them accountable for past crimes.[70]

Even before the *Loya Jirga* was held it was reported by the International Crisis Group that 'Political leaders and local warlords were able to carry out arrests, threats and even murder their opponents, including elected delegates.'[71] In any case, Afghanistan's political fate had been decided long before the first *Loya Jirga*. In early October 2001 Colin Powell, the US Secretary of State, clearly laid out the State Department's plans for Kabul, and by extension, the whole country: 'Let the UN administer it or maybe the OIC administer it. Make a center for humanitarian assistance, and make it the site for the Loya Jirga...we'll turn it over to Brahimi and the UN.'[72] This was stated at a meeting a few days after Donald Rumsfeld, the US Secretary of Defense, had given his daily report on military operations in Afghanistan, including the brief that a decision had been made not to bomb the Taliban's drug labs and heroin storage because of the risk of collateral damage.

Ironically, it has not only been local warlords and commanders who have operated outside the law in Afghanistan. The several detention centres set up by the US forces post-9/11 to detain al-Qaeda and Taliban suspects were not established or operated under the Geneva conventions, had no legal process and supported conditions that included sleep and sensory deprivation, sexual humiliation, stress positions, dietary manipulation and the use of dogs to instil fear and terror. Released detainees from US 'facilities' in Bagram, Qandahar, Jalalabad, Asadabad, Gardez and Khost have made repeated allegations of torture and mistreatment to the UN, Afghan officials and Human Rights Watch. It has also been reported that terrorist suspects detained in Afghanistan by US forces were subject to a process known as rendition where they could be transferred to third countries such as Egypt, Jordan, Morocco, Syria or Uzbekistan known to practice torture. In 2006 a Council of Europe report found that several European countries, including Germany, Sweden and the UK, had colluded with the CIA by acting as stopover or staging points for rendition flights.[73] The report also suggested that secret interrogation and detention centres were operating in eastern European countries like Romania, Poland and Bulgaria, although there was no conclusive proof. Banned by the UN, illegal interrogation techniques were allegedly used to extract information that was then used by US intelligence forces. In short, 'the entire system operates outside the rule of law'.[74]

In December 2004 Human Rights Watch wrote an open letter to Rumsfeld regarding the allegations of serious abuse by US military personnel and the failure of his office 'to make public the results of investigations into past abuses and take adequate steps to hold abusers accountable'. In the letter they cited the case of the Criminal Investigative Command of the US Military in Afghanistan who, in May 2004, completed a classified report on deaths in US custody that recommended 28 personnel be prosecuted in connection with the deaths on charges that included negligent homicide, maiming, maltreatment, assault consummated by battery, conspiracy and dereliction of duty. By the end of the year only one person had been charged in connection with the deaths, and by mid-2005 Specialist Glendale Wells was the first US soldier since 2001 to be convicted of abuse in Afghanistan. He was sentenced to a derisory two months in prison for pushing a detainee called Dilawar against a wall and doing nothing to prevent other soldiers at the US Bagram air base from abusing him. Dilawar was a 22-year-old taxi driver. He died at the base in December 2002 after repeated beatings by US guards while chained to the ceiling by his wrists and waist while standing with his feet on the ground.[75] According to a US Army report from July 2004, an autopsy showed that Dilawar's legs were so badly damaged that amputations would have been necessary if he had lived. In June 2005 President Karzai's spokesman said: 'We think the punishments given to those who have severely violated human rights are very light and unexpectedly lenient.'[76]

More surprisingly to Human Rights Watch, Captain Carolyn A. Wood, who had been head of the interrogation unit at Bagram from

July 2002 to December 2003, was not among the 28 recommended for prosecution. It was Captain Wood who had drawn up 'the harsh interrogation techniques that interrogators later used at Abu Ghraib prison in Iraq, techniques which she had previously approved in Afghanistan according to an Army lawyer who testified before Congress in May 2004'.[77] By early 2006 three US military personnel had their charges relating to the deaths of Afghan prisoners in US custody dismissed and four others had been acquitted.

The behaviour of the US military has frequently mirrored that of the warlords and commanders by operating outside the law with impunity and a disregard for basic human rights and dignity. On frequent occasions US soldiers have been criticised for ignoring the very strict social code of *Pashtoonwali* by breaking into private house compounds without permission and searching the women's quarters. US detention centres are no less forms of penal fiefdoms than the private jails of the warlords where, justified by the global war on terror, human rights violations are reportedly rife. As Fahim Hakim, the deputy head of the Afghan Independent Human Rights Commission was reported as saying, 'They came to liberate us, to make us free of this intimidation and oppression, but this will be overshadowed by this sort of behaviour.'[78] In July 2005 after over 1,000 protesters had staged a demonstration outside the Bagram base 80 km north of Kabul, angry at the arrest of several nearby villagers, a local resident, Shah Aghar, said: 'We have supported the Americans for years. We should be treated with dignity…they are arresting our people without the permission of the government. They are breaking into our houses and offending the people. We are very angry.'[79]

Echoing the sentiments of an increasing number of Afghans, a local newspaper likened the culturally insensitive behaviour of American troops to colonialists, protesting that they had promoted ethnic discrimination, bombed indiscriminately and detained and tortured innocent people.[80] The UN National Human Development Report for Afghanistan for 2004 was also critical of the US-led military engagement saying that it had neglected the longer-term threat to security posed by inequality and justice and had instead helped to create a climate of fear, intimidation, lawlessness and terror.[81] Nader Nadery of the Afghan Human Rights Commission was quoted as saying that 'Afghanistan is being transformed into an enormous US jail. What we have here is a military strategy that has spawned serious human rights abuses', while an unnamed government minister said: 'Washington holds Afghanistan up to the world as a nascent democracy and yet the US military has deliberately kept us down, using our country to host a prison system that seems to be administered arbitrarily, indiscriminately and without accountability.'[82]

In April 2005 a UN Human Rights monitor was removed from duty after his report accused the US military, as well as factional warlords, Afghan police and security forces, of acting above the law 'by engaging in arbitrary arrests and detentions and committing abusive practices, including torture'.[83] The report covered many aspects of human rights violations in Afghanistan and expressed concerns about inequities against women, abduction and trafficking of children, illegal seizure of property, lack of due process and social and economic abuses against minorities, displaced people, the poor and the disabled. The post of Cherif Bassiouni, a well-respected Egyptian professor of law from DePaul University in the US who was appointed as an independent human rights monitor for Afghanistan by UN Secretary-General Kofi Annan in April 2004, was scrapped after pressure from Washington. According to a US official who asked not to be identified, one of the reasons that the post was cut was because the human rights situation in Afghanistan 'is no longer troubling enough to require it'.[84]

Since early 2002 one of the largest growth industries in Afghanistan has been private military companies, or as they prefer to be called private security contractors.[85] With no agreed governing regulations, little corporate social responsibility or public accountability at least one group of these contractors has also operated outside the law by running private makeshift jails in Kabul where captured Afghans were tortured for information about the whereabouts of Osama bin Laden. In July 2004 three alleged American 'bounty hunters', Jonathan Idema, Brent Bennet and Edward Caraballo, were apprehended in Kabul and charged with hostage taking, torture and running a private prison in a house in the city. Although they had no official authorisation from the US government, the release from custody of four Afghans who had been helping Idema, all of whom were employees of the Afghan Ministry of Defence, suggested that they may have had some type of official sanction from the Afghan government. In the convoluted world of Afghan politics, Maulawi Siddiqullah, a Supreme Court judge and the first person 'arrested' by Idema along with several other members of his family, later suggested to a journalist that the whole case could have been resolved if his family had been paid $20,000 in compensation. After publicly requesting Idema to prove the legitimacy of his operation, and before sentencing him to ten years in prison, the judge who presided over the case, Abdul Basit Bakhtiari, seemed to congratulate Idema by saying: 'You have saved the life of Minister Qanooni, and the people you have arrested were terrorists and Al Qaeda.'[86]

Among the interrogation techniques allegedly used by Idema's group, the self-styled task force Sabre 7s, were hanging men from the ceiling and dousing them with freezing water. The three men claimed that, while not employed directly by the US government, they had been in close contact with the CIA and their 'mission' was approved by the Pentagon. The US government later acknowledged that Idema and his group had indeed been in contact with the US military but denied they had been working for them. Idema and his two accomplices were found guilty of running a freelance operation to capture, imprison and interrogate al-Qaeda suspects and they were sentenced to jail terms. By March 2005, however, Idema and Bennett had their ten-year sentences cut to five and three years respectively and Carabello, an Emmy award-winning documentary film-maker, had his sentence reduced from 8 years to 2. Unlike other prisoners in Kabul's notorious Pul-i-Charki jail, where thousands of Afghans were tortured and summarily executed during the communist regime of the 1980s, and the Afghans held in Bagram and other US 'facilities', the American prisoners heard the news on satellite TV in the comfort of their carpeted cells. The presence of such mercenary forces has also served to help alienate the local population from other foreigners coming to Afghanistan offering genuine support and aid: 'Private contractors lawlessness and abusive practices are creating increased resentment of the US presence among Afghans, who compare these contractors to Soviet troops.'[87]

This continuing litany of predatory behaviour and human rights abuses by warlords, commanders, militias, foreign security contractors and other groups working outside the law has created a set of social conditions that inevitably breed fear, insecurity, terror and resentment among many in the Afghan population. It is reasonable to assume that this, along with extreme impoverishment and other nightmares left by war, can only increase the risk of Afghans turning in desperation to drug use for refuge as part of a daily strategy to cope with the resultant stress, anxiety and depression. While the warlords underpin many activities in the drugs economy, thus contributing to the increased availability of opium and heroin within the country, as well as generally undermining good governance and weakening the state,[88] their behaviour also dramatically impinges on the set of motivations that increases the risk of someone using drugs. It has not always been so in Afghanistan's long history of drug use, as will be shown in Chapter 7.

# 7
# Drug Use in Afghanistan's History

## THE GOOD AND BAD OLD DAYS

In October 1504, Zahiruddin Muhammad Babur, the founder of the Mughal dynasty, took control over Kabul, Ghazni and their dependent districts in what is now central Afghanistan. Also known as 'the Tiger', this descendent of Genghis Khan and Tamerlane had ridden down from the central Asian steppes into Kabul and would go on to conquer Hindustan and control an empire that stretched from the Deccan to Turkestan. In his detailed autobiography, the *Babur-Nama*, Babur provides an interesting account of the use of intoxicants by himself and his warrior retinue, as well as the inhabitants of central Afghanistan, at that time. Predominant among these appears to be the consumption of alcohol. In his younger days Babur was renowned as 'a great drinker', although as he became older 'he preferred intoxicating confects and, under their sway, used to lose his head'.[1] These confects refer mainly to *majun*, a preparation made mainly from hashish, sometimes with added opium, and a range of other ingredients including honey, dates, oil and spices. Various forms of *majun* (or *majoun* or *majum*), literally 'mixture', are still prepared in many hashish-producing countries stretching from Morocco to Afghanistan and beyond.

Throughout the *Babur-Nama*, Babur provides an account of the production and consumption of beer, wine, cider and *araq*, a type of liquor made from the fermented juice of rice or the date palm, in several districts of central Afghanistan. While Kabul wines were described as 'heady', those of the Khwaja Khawand Said hill-skirt were considered famous for their strength. Wines from the city of Ghazni are also mentioned. In Kafiristan, now the Afghan province of Nuristan bordering northwest Pakistan, Babur reports that 'wine is so commonly used that every Kafir has his leathern bag (*khig*) at his neck and drinks wine instead of water', although this is qualified by the translator who says that Kafir wine was of poor quality and usually diluted with water.[2]

Over 300 years later, in 1888, Sir George Scott Robertson, another imperial traveller who visited Kafiristan, substantiated this. After watching the biggest man in the village jump into a vat to tread the grapes, Robertson reported that the liquid was siphoned off into goatskins and the grape residue later made into cakes. Although the first sweet grape juice tasted 'very pleasant', in eight or ten days,

it becomes sour by fermentation, and is then wine. There is no process of straining, and the fluid is most uninviting in appearance. Probably it is to remove the scum from near their lips that the Kafir always blows into the wine-bowl before drinking. The wine is usually poor and thin, but even then is diluted with water. Wine which has been left for two or three years was, however, clear and sometimes distinctly strong. Some Europeans think ordinary Kafir wine pleasant to drink. I have never seen a Kafir drunk.[3]

This practice of diluting wine with water, as in Roman times in Europe, had two principal functions. By adding alcohol it made the water safer to drink and also turned it into a thirst-quenching beverage that could be drunk in large quantities without becoming too intoxicated.[4] In Kunar, to the northeast of Kabul, a beer called *bir buza* was made from rice, millet or barley and fermented by a yeast substitute (*kim*) made from the roots of herbs. Babur and most of his men found this particular type of beer 'too bitter and distasteful' for their liking, preferring to eat *majun* instead.

Recalling sharing 'a few well flavoured and quite intoxicating confections' with two friends, that had left them too intoxicated to attend evening prayers, he confessed that 'If in these days I ate the whole of such a confection, I doubt if it would produce half as much intoxication.'[5] On another occasion, reminiscent of scenes from the English poet William Wordsworth's poem 'The Daffodils' with its reference to 'a host of golden daffodils', Babur and his friends sat at sunrise on a mound and ate *majun*: 'While under its influence wonderful fields of flowers were enjoyed. In some places sheets of yellow flowers bloomed in plots, in others sheets of red flowers in plots, in some red and yellow bloomed together.'[6] This rather lyrical scene stands in marked contrast to the more frequently reported scenes where Babur and his warriors fought battles and skirmishes with local Afghan tribes, building pillars and pyramids with the heads of their enemies, and then relaxing in the evening after the fighting with alcohol or *majun*.

While there are few specific references to opium in the *Babur-Nama*, Babur describes how he had to take it medicinally because of earache and 'the shining of the moon', a reference to what was then the widespread fear of moonstroke, the nighttime equivalent of sunstroke. As a result, and expressing a not uncommon reaction to the first use of opiates, he recounts that 'opium sickness gave me much discomfort next day; I vomited a good deal'.[7] Certainly it would appear that Babur and his men were well acquainted with the different effects of drugs and their social consequences. There is a continual tension expressed between those who preferred to drink alcohol and those who preferred to eat *majun*. Reflecting on an argument that had broken out at one particular party, Babur proclaimed:

Said I, 'Don't upset the party! Let those who wish to drink *araq* drink *araq*; let those who wish to eat *majun* eat *majun*. Let no-one on either side make talk or allusion to the other.' Some drank *araq*, some ate *majun*, and for a while the party went on quite politely. Baba Jan the *qabuz* player had not been of our party (in the boat); we invited him when we reached the tents. He asked to drink *araq*. We invited Tardi Muhammad Qibchaq also and made him a comrade of the drinkers. A *majun* party never goes well with an *araq* or a wine party; the drinkers began to make wild talk and chatter from all sides, mostly in allusion to *majun* and *majunis*. Baba Jan even, when drunk, said many wild things. The drinkers soon made Tardi Jan mad-drunk by giving him one bowl after another. Try as we did to keep things straight, nothing went well; there was much disgusting uproar; the party became intolerable and was broken up.[8]

Some centuries later in 1829, on the death of his father Shah Mahmood, another Afghan leader, Kamran Mirza, who battled to become the self-styled King of Herat and surrounding areas, retired behind the walls of his citadel and commenced 'a life of drunkenness, opium-eating, and every Eastern vice'.[9] Shah Mahmood, himself a drug user, had earlier been punished by Kamran for supporting a revolt against him by the Popalzai tribe, 'by depriving him of his wine during one whole month, which to him was a terrible affliction'.[10] In 1879, an English cavalry officer living in Kabul reported that several types of liquor were for sale, sub rosa, in the Shor bazaar under the name of *sharab*. While he described most of these liquors as being like the fortified wine or 'the most fiery "military" port' found in the officer's mess, he also reported that 'the strongest vintage of all has a mixed flavour of gin, vinegar and methylated spirits'.[11] Some 30 years earlier, General Ferrier of the British Army had reported that it was strictly forbidden to either make or drink wine in Kabul or Qandahar, although it was permitted in Herat where one Yar Mohamed 'has monopolised the right to make it, and this has brought him in a considerable profit by farming that right at a very high price to others.

As to the consumption of it, he is one of the greatest wine-bibbers in that city or the principality.'[12]

During the same period, Ferrier also noted that Afghans 'frequently smoke the *tchilim*, a kind of water-pipe, but very inferior to the *narghile* of the Turks, or the *kalioon* of the Persians'.[13] He does not say what they smoked in the *tchilim*, although tobacco, hashish and various combinations of both were reportedly common. Talking about Kabul in the late eighteenth century, Martin commented that

Women smoke the chillum (*tchilim*) as well as men. It is shaped like the hookah but has a straight stem instead of a flexible one. The tobacco is of country growth, and is very rank smelling, more resembling a burning oil rag than anything else.[14]

In the early 1800s, an Englishman journeying from Balochistan to Qandahar with a group of Afghans encountered a Balochi chief and his men who stopped the group and demanded a 'road tax', much like contemporary militia commanders:

With the insolence of men in authority, they commanded the *kafila* to halt, and called for the chillum and tobacco. The Afghans waggishly filled the chillum with *chirs* [hashish] and the Baloches, unaccustomed to it, as if by enchantment, fell asleep and the *kafila* left them snoring in happy oblivion on the ground.[15]

At the end of the nineteenth century in the border regions that separated Afghanistan and the British Indian Empire it was reported by colonial travellers that Islamic *faqirs* and *sadhus* were 'addicted' to smoking a mixture of hashish and tobacco in chillums. In 1908, an English medical missionary who had lived in Afghanistan for 16 years wrote that the *faqirs*, or wandering Muslim Holy men that he likened to the Hindu *sadhus*,

are much addicted to the use of intoxicants (they rarely use alcohol), and *charas* [hashish] and *bhang* [herbal cannabis] are constantly smoked with tobacco in their chillums. When thus intoxicated they are known as *mast* and are believed by the populace to be possessed by divinity.[16]

In the 1920s in Kabul, an American traveller, explorer and showman, Lowell Thomas, noted that the wandering dervishes, known as *mast malang*, were 'steeped to the eyes in hemp'.[17] Certainly Thomas would have been able to verify this, because before travelling to Kabul he had visited Peshawar in what is now the NWFP of Pakistan to find among the 'beggars, thieves, clowns, fakirs and bobbed-haired bandits' that inhabited the Old Town, many purveyors of hashish.

His characterisation of Peshawar as a city of 'a thousand and one sins' contains several graphic descriptions of the use of hashish. At that time it could be bought from government excise commissioners as well as street sellers, but at a higher price and of lower quality. His Pashtoon friend Abdul Ghani sat on his balcony above the street of the storytellers and smoked hashish in his *narghile*:

Taking a lump about the size of a sixpence, Abdul mixes it with his tobacco and puts it in the receptacle of his water-pipe. Then on top of the mixture of tobacco and *charas* he daintily places a red-hot piece of camel-dung from a smoking brazier...slowly and rapturously he inhales the carbon dioxide, essence of camel, nicotine, hemp, hubble-bubbling through the water of the pipe. He draws the smoke deep down into his lungs. Then, as he coughs it up again, he passes the tube over to me.[18]

While Thomas and his travelling companion, the photographer Harry Chase, as first-time users, describe the effects of hashish as though they were riding on a rather bumpy magic carpet, Abdul describes the experience as a 'delicious dreaminess' combined with an increased appetite for food. While the effects of the hashish were accompanied by constant coughing, it was deemed better than *bhang* (more usually *bhangawa*), a drink made with herbal cannabis, water, milk and sugar that led, according to Abdul, to 'a most unpleasant red-eyed form of intoxication with none of the brightening effects of *charas* or the conviviality of wine'.[19] Abdul then tells a story that astutely illustrates the varying effects of different drugs:

It was the year that Habibullah Khan was foully murdered in his sleep in Jalalabad. The tribesmen along the caravan route were more truculent than usual, and three travellers pushing on ahead of the camels of the *kafila*, or caravan, with which they had crossed Afghanistan from Mazar-i-Sherif, were trying to make the two final stages between Landi Kotal *serai* and Peshawar in one day. But night was already upon them when they left the eastern end of the Khyber, and upon their arrival at the Bajauri Gate they found it closed and locked. One of the three was a whisky-toper, the second was an opium smoker and the third a *charasi*. They were very anxious to get into the city and sat down outside the gate to drink and smoke and talk the matter over. Said the whisky-drinker, 'Let's break down the gate!' The opium-fiend toasted his pill, yawned, and said, 'No, let's go to sleep now and wait till morning.' Then spoke the *charas* smoker, inspired by a few drafts from his *narghile*: 'I have it. Let's crawl through the keyhole.'[20]

Abdul also describes the use of another drug called *post*, reputedly a favourite of the Mogul Emperor Jahangir, consisting of laudanum (a tincture of alcohol and opium), *araq*, sugar and cardamoms. Thomas himself noticed that only the richer men in Peshawar smoked opium, although generally it was mostly eaten rather than smoked. Initially mistaking the continuous coughing of hashish smokers for those 'in the last stages of galloping consumption', he went on to compare hashish users with 'snow-sniffers' or cocaine users in the US who he suggested had only a limited life, 'with only the first half a merry one'. He believed that in the end the '*charas* cougher' was taken to an asylum 'where he finds a row of *charasis* and joins the chorus of coughers'.[21] A similar moralistic view of hashish smokers in Peshawar in the 1920s was offered by Morag Murray Abdullah, a young Scotswoman married to the son of a Pashtoon chieftain, who commented: 'these drugs provide the most highly coloured foretaste of what the hereafter is supposed to be and a speedy way of attaining it'.[22]

## ISLAM AND INTOXICANTS

Throughout the Muslim world 'religion defines culture and the culture gives meaning to every aspect of an individual's life'.[23] Although open to slightly different interpretation in different Islamic states the official cultural position on intoxicants appears to be quite clear—total prohibition. According to the Koran and the *Ahadith*, the authenticated accounts of the life of the Prophet Mohammad, *al-khamr* (intoxicants) were forbidden and their use *haram* as they clouded the mind and distracted it from the path of God. *Al-khamr* itself comes from the root word *khamara*, meaning 'to cover', so anything that covers or clouds the mind is prohibited, including anything that alters the state of mind, for example substances like hashish, heroin, valium or cocaine. Alcohol, however, was considered by the Prophet as the most harmful of all the intoxicants, ranking above both opium and hashish, because more than any other drug used at the time it caused people to lose control, literally, of their mouths through verbal abuse and bad language, and their hands through violence to others, and was therefore seen to cause harm to other people, not just to the self. Abdullah ibn Umar in the *Ahadith* narrates that 'Allah has cursed wine, its drinker, its seller, its buyer, its presser, the one for whom it is pressed, the one who conveys it, and the one to whom it is conveyed' (Abu Dawud, Book 26,

Number 3666). The *Ahadith* also succinctly states: 'If a large amount of anything causes intoxication, a small amount of it is prohibited' (Abu Dawud, Book 26, Number 3673). At the same time, there are frequent references to the pleasures of drinking alcohol in the works of the famous Afghan Sufi mystic Rumi, although this is recognised to be largely metaphorical in nature where the state of intoxication represents the state of the follower when they are intoxicated with the love of the divine—not with alcohol or other drugs.

An American engineer, A.C. Jewett, who spent eight years installing a hydroelectric plant at Jabal-us-Siraj to the north of Kabul between 1911 and 1919, one of the first attempts at modernisation under the Amir Habibullah Khan, made an interesting observation regarding the use of intoxicants in Afghanistan; in particular, alcohol:

The soldiery and the mirzas are greatly addicted to this water pipe called a chillum, in which country tobacco is smoked and the smoke drawn through water before it is inhaled. Charas, which is Indian bhang or hemp, is smoked also, but those who use it to excess become imbecilic after a time. In fact charas smokers are called charasis, much the same as one would say drunkards. Snuff is imported mostly from India, and many use it, plastering their mouths so full that when they speak they sound as if they were stuffed with cotton. Others eat opium, although the use of opium is not prevalent. Needless to say, there is no doubt but that one of the best things Mohammed did was to prohibit the use of alcohol.[24]

Interestingly, from contemporary considerations of harm reduction practices in Islamic countries, in original Koranic injunctions concerning alcohol, a friend who is an Islamic scholar suggests that there were three stages proposed by the Prophet for stopping alcohol use. The first stage was to refrain from alcohol before praying or going to the mosque, to ensure sincerity of purpose. The second was to reduce over a period of time the amount of alcohol used before the third stage of stopping altogether was reached. It has also been asserted that there have been three distinct historical stages or levels of injunctions against drugs in Islam.[25] Initially the consumption of *al-khamr* was discouraged though not rejected outright, in recognition that consumption was deeply rooted in pre-Islamic culture. This is expressed in the following stanza (Al Baqarah: 219) when the word *al-khamr* was first revealed in Medina between the first and second year of the *Hijrah*: 'They ask thee concerning wine and gambling, say: "In them is great sin and some profit for men but the sin is greater than the profit".' The second injunction stated that *al-khamr* should not be used as it will interfere with prayer and the *ibadah* (An Nisa: 43): 'O ye who believe approach not prayers in a state of intoxication until ye can understand all that ye say.' In this case the injunction, which came around the fourth year of the *Hijrah*, demanded total abstinence before praying, 'the consumption of intoxicants is thus forbidden for specific period and purpose. Since Allah commanded a Muslim to pray at least five times a day, the indulgence in *al-khamr* became increasingly more difficult.'[26] Five years later the final verdict categorically prohibiting the consumption of *al-khamr* came when Allah decreed (Al Maidah: 90): 'O ye who believe. Intoxicants and gambling. Sacrificing to stones And (divination) by arrows Are an abomination Of Satan's handiwork. Eschew such (abomination) That ye may prosper', and (Al Maidah: 91) 'Satan's plan is (but) To excite enmity and hatred Between you, with intoxicants And gambling, and hinder you To admit us to the company Of the righteous.'

In modern Islamic states under both statutory law and *Sharia*, the use of alcohol and other intoxicants is *haram*, so stages of reducing the use of *al-khamr* are not proposed. Nevertheless, within the original tenets of Islam a harm reduction approach would appear to have been permissible. It is notable that both Iran and Pakistan, both staunchly Islamic cultures, have embraced harm reduction policies in their national drug control strategies, including NSPs and, in the case of Iran, drug substitution treatment using controlled buprenorphine and methadone as heroin replacements, as realistic public health measures to control the spread of HIV, hepatitis C and other blood-borne viruses. The first National Drug Control Strategy for Afghanistan, signed by President Karzai in May 2003, also stated the necessity for 'provision of harm reduction services to injecting drug users as a public health measure to prevent the transmission of HIV/AIDS and other blood borne diseases'. In May 2005, the Ministry of Public Health and the Ministry of Counter Narcotics jointly approved the National Harm Reduction Strategy for IDUs and the Prevention of HIV/AIDS that endorsed a wide range of harm reduction interventions.

## BEFORE THE SOVIET INVASION

While the use of intoxicants may be forbidden by Islam, during his travels with Bruce Chatwin in 1970, the traveller Peter Levi observed that in northern Afghanistan at least, 'hashish is the opium of the people', although Afghans he encountered also recounted with 'cold disapproval' stories about the consequences of addiction.[27] Travelling through Qandahar in the south of the country Chatwin and Levi were continuously pestered to buy hashish, including a liquid form of hashish, presumably hash oil, that smelled worse than methylated spirits: 'every kind of smuggling device was for sale, strings of hash beads, hash belts, hash-heeled shoes and for all I know hash codpieces'.[28] Interestingly, while travelling in the high mountains of Nuristan at an altitude of around 8,000 feet, Levi saw Fly Agaric (*Amanita muscaria*) mushrooms growing on the steep hillsides and assumed they were 'the chief source of hallucinogenic drugs at this level', although he cited no evidence for their use in Afghanistan, and none has emerged since.[29]

A straw poll of older Afghan colleagues and friends enquiring about their first knowledge and understanding of hashish and opium use revealed that there were distinct cultural norms and social constraints largely controlling the consumption of such substances. However, since the late 1970s these norms and constraints have gradually been eroded due mainly to the intense social disruptions resulting from war and conflict and the effects of the Afghan diaspora outlined in chapters three and eight respectively. Almost all had been given an opium preparation as a child or had seen it given to other family members as a medicine. One recalled that an uncle had brought some to the house to be used for the alleviation of cough and flu, but had stated that it should only be taken 'in quantities not exceeding a quarter of your smallest fingernail', and that water should never be drunk after its consumption. Another was reminded of sheltering from rocket fire in a ruined building in a village in Logar province as he and his family were fleeing to Pakistan in the early 1990s to escape the civil war in Kabul when his wife developed a severe toothache. An old woman in the village gave her some opium to relieve the toothache, saying 'I am giving you something very precious.' Such tales suggest that opium was ubiquitously recognised in Afghanistan as a useful and powerful medicine, but only to be used sparingly and judiciously.

The use of hashish, however, was another matter. It was recognised as an intoxicant and used as such by various groups throughout Afghan society although there was some disapproval and stigma attached to its habitual use. A British Army surgeon writing about the Yusufzai tribe in the 1860s said:

Opium also is used to some extent, and so are the different preparations of Indian Hemp [cannabis], but mostly in the plain country and only among the abandoned and debauched who are pointed at as disreputable characters and a disgrace to their names.[30]

Most colleagues could recall a 'famous *charasi*' in their childhood village who was treated and tolerated much as the neighbourhood drunk might be in western countries. Although considered normal, he was not really reliable or to be trusted or to be married to your daughter. Such perceptions also depended on the status of the user. One man recalled a visiting hashish-smoking mullah being tolerated for several months before eventually being thrown out of his village. Interestingly, two colleagues recalled how relatives who were wrestlers had used the drug. One claimed that 'when you inhale hashish smoke your opponent looks like a mouse', while the other claimed it gave him strength, although he believed that to take hashish your body had to be 'wet', so he ate *ghee* (clarified butter) to provide the oily wetness needed to counteract the hashish. This practice appears to be common among many hashish users who 'believe that smoking without the ingestion of lipids is harmful as only fat can absorb the drug's toxins and prevent mental and physical complications'.[31]

Writing in 1976, a psychiatrist at Kabul University noted that while problem drug use did exist in Afghanistan,

We do not have many problems with drugs. Our drug abusers appear to be of a more peaceful nature and have a general public reputation for passivity or cowardice. It appears certain that there is no basic relationship between crime and drug abuse.[32]

Between 1965 and 1974 only 24 opium addicts were admitted to the country's one mental health hospital located in Kabul. Initially the psychiatrist's first impression was that Afghanistan only had a small number of opium addicts, originally becoming involved with the drug through self-medication. He later revised this, estimating from various sources that there were nearly 100,000 opium addicts in Badakhshan province, representing nearly one in three of the province's total population and 'approximately 80 per cent of the whole opiate dependent population throughout the country'.[33] Reasons for such a high and continuing prevalence rate in certain districts of Badakhshan will be examined in Chapter 9. Hashish users on the other hand were 'scattered diffusely' throughout the country so their numbers could not be estimated, and were most prevalent among people of the lower classes and income groups like 'hermits, taxi drivers, truck drivers, tea-house dwellers, prisoners and in cheap restaurants'. In the larger cities like Kabul, Herat and Qandahar the use of alcohol had also emerged as a problem, but was restricted to a few members of the upper class, higher income groups and the western educated class.

In the late 1960s and early 1970s young western travellers stopped off in Afghanistan as they headed overland through the Khyber Pass to India, Nepal and beyond, or back home through Iran, Turkey and on to Europe. From all accounts, many of them, the self-styled WTs (world travellers) or hippies, spent some time in Afghanistan and a main attraction was the ease of obtaining and using hashish and opium. As one of the estimated 5,000–6,000 young travellers staying in Kabul at the time recalled, 'On Chicken Street you could buy opium from a little man in a red turban...and the best hashish in the world came from Mazar-i-Sharif, in the mountains not far away.'[34] The wife of an American official resident in Kabul at the time noted that for these hippies 'One of Kabul's draws was that hashish could be purchased for less than ten cents a day.'[35] According to another commentator many had little interest in Afghanistan and the Afghans, 'Foremost in most of their minds was hashish (which was plentiful in Kabul).'[36] By word of mouth to other travellers on the so-called Hippy Trail drug tourism had come to Afghanistan. At the same time some of these travellers were responsible for first importing heroin from Iran into Afghanistan, as well as LSD and other drugs from western countries. Some succumbed to disease, drug overdose or traffic accidents, their graves can be found in the European cemetery in Kabul, while a few resorted to prostitution to maintain themselves and buy their drugs.

## WAR AND CHANGING PATTERNS OF DRUG USE

After nearly 25 years of almost continuous war and conflict contemporary accounts of drug use in Afghanistan are very different from the tales provided by the various travellers of history. Many groups in the population are vulnerable and at risk of becoming problem drug users and for Afghans generally there is very little accurate or realistic information available about the nature of drugs and their effects and the potential dangers and risks from intoxication, dependency or overdose, as well as drug-related financial and social problems. For many, heroin is simply *poder*, an unknown powder made from the more familiar opium poppy and pharmaceutical drugs are referred to by the colour of their tablets or capsules, their name and long-term effects largely unknown. Many of the urban young I have spoken to seem blithely unaware of the risks of alcohol intoxication and dependency. Hashish is the drug that people have most knowledge about and even then they may be unaware of possible harmful effects to health and family relationships. While there is some understanding of the medicinal effects and uses of opium there appears to be little understanding among many of how easy it is for this medicinal use to lapse into problem use and dependency.

Cultural beliefs about drugs and their uses abound but are largely uncharted. Heroin addicts, for example, have consistently reported that they believe the only way to be 'cured of heroin addiction' is to have a complete blood change. Links between opium or hashish use and religious and spiritual beliefs are left unspoken, a taboo subject in a country where the use of all intoxicants is *haram*. The common belief in rural areas of the presence and power of *djinns* or spirits may affect the way a person views, uses and experiences drugs but there is little information about this. The easy availability of a wide range of drugs has certainly contributed to the problem, although restricting the availability of one drug can easily lead to the search for a substitute drug, perhaps more harmful than the one it has replaced. Polydrug use, where someone takes more than one drug either at the same time or in quick succession of each other, is becoming more common, the added risks and dangers of this type of drug use largely unknown, even to health professionals.

Historically, the development of problem drug use in Afghanistan has been constrained by a mixture of social, cultural, religious and legal factors. These have now largely fragmented, although traditional cultural patterns of more controlled use still remain, but frequently risk lapsing into problem use. This is particularly the case with opium, still used as a panacea for a wide range of ills, although it is now being replaced in many areas by the overuse of analgesics and tranquillisers, as well as other non-psychoactive pharmaceutical drugs like antibiotics. At Siahak, during the last stages of his overland walk from Herat to Kabul in January 2002, Rory Stewart recounts staying the night with a group of Hazara soldiers, when the commander

showed his status by laying out pills labelled Drotravine [Drotaverine], Metanemic Acid [Mefenamic acid] and Rowatex [Rowatenix]. He ate one of each before offering them around and everyone, except me, took a handful.

Then he drank from a bottle, which had a picture of a brain on one side and an oxen plough team on the other. It looked veterinary.[37]

In the darkness of his surroundings Stewart had either misspelt the names of the drugs or these were counterfeit drugs spelled wrongly on the packaging. Either way, such indiscriminate self-medication with powerful psychoactive pharmaceutical drugs appears increasingly common, in this case with Drotaverine, derived from the opiate papaverine and a smooth muscle relaxant, and Mefenamic acid, a non-steroidal anti-inflammatory and painkiller. Rowatinex is used in the treatment of renal and urinary disorders.

In many cases it is not easy to identify problem drug users, particularly women, as drug consumption is typically not a public or socially visible activity. Traditional conservative attitudes to the consumption of intoxicants have been compounded by the draconian tactics of the Taliban regime that targeted drug users for punishment, often severe, and helped to push drug consumption further underground. Over the past five years, however, there has been a noticeable and visible increase in the number of street heroin users in central areas of Kabul city, although this has not reached the marked level of visibility of street heroin use in Pakistani cities like Peshawar, Quetta and Karachi (as described in Chapter 8).

A study published by the UNODC in 2003 on problem drug use in Kabul indicated that heroin use was spreading in the city.[38] This study reported an estimated 7,000 heroin users, although this was a minimum estimate and the number was likely to be much larger. An estimated 500 of these were injecting heroin. According to data from the DDTC in Kabul mental health hospital, 710 drug addicts were treated during 2003, of whom 148 were heroin addicts. Although only three were injecting, such drug users are often a notoriously difficult client group to reach and attract into treatment. Information for the same year from the Nejat treatment centre in Kabul stated that 178 males who had received residential treatment included 23 drug injectors, three of whom were women. This means that injecting is already a problem in Kabul, as it is in other parts of the country, with attendant risks of HIV/AIDS transmission through sharing injecting equipment and engaging in high-risk sexual behaviour. By early 2006 the HIV/AIDS Unit of the Ministry of Public Health had tested around 300 IDUs in Kabul as part of a longer prevalence study. While less than 4 per cent tested positive for HIV, over 40 per cent tested positive for hepatitis C, another disease easily transmitted through sharing injecting equipment. Currently there are limited harm reduction services operating in Kabul, including NSPs, but these urgently need scaled-up to prevent a possible explosion of HIV among IDUs. In addition, there is a cultural acceptance of the practice of injecting drugs. Many Afghans do not feel that they have received proper treatment from a doctor unless thay have been given an injection.

## HIGH-RISK GROUPS

A particular at-risk group for problem drug use is women who carry the legacy of some of the worst social indicators in the world. As the UN Human Development Report for Afghanistan for 2004 states, 'The feminisation of poverty, serious malnutrition, exclusion from public life, gender-based violence, rape, lack of basic health facilities, illiteracy, forced marriage and routine denial of justice are just some of the many human security concerns faced by Afghan women.'[39] In May 2005 Amnesty International published a report on the plight of women in Afghanistan emphasising that entrenched feudal customs lead to women being treated as chattels. Even after the demise of the Taliban, women are still being murdered, raped and imprisoned with impunity and a complete lack of official retribution.[40]

There are sub-groups of women who are even more at risk: for example, widows who are heads of households and without the benefit of family support. In 2002 Physicians for Human Rights surveyed a sample of the 50,000 widows in Kabul who were also heads of households and found that 65 per cent had suicidal tendencies and 16 per cent had already attempted suicide.[41] Another sub-group is commercial sex workers, although no reliable figures exist of how many women are forced into commercial sex work through desperation engendered by extreme poverty. One tentative estimate of 60,000 nationwide may be an underestimate, and an NGO worker who interviewed commercial sex workers in the Shor bazaar area of Kabul claimed that all of them were 'addicted to heroin, hashish, cigarettes or *naswar*—a green tobacco substance that is mixed with calcium carbonate and has a narcotic effect'.[42] A study of groups in Kabul at high risk of contracting sexually transmitted infections, including HIV, interviewed 122 female commercial sex workers, 90 per cent stated that poverty was their main reason for starting commercial sex work.[43] A high-ranking police officer reported that in the 1980s there were over 300 brothels in Kabul, mostly in the red light district of the Old City known as *Kharabat*, later destroyed during the civil war of the early 1990s.* This resulted in the dispersal and spread of commercial sex work, both male and female, to other parts of the city. Its recent increase has also been attributed to the rapid urban growth caused by impoverished returning refugees and IDPs trying to rebuild their lives and make a basic living for their families.

Habiba Surabi, the Minister of Women's Affairs for nearly three years under the transitional government and appointed in 2005 as the Governor of Bamiyan province, the country's first ever female Governor, believes that Afghan cultural traditions 'binds the hands of women like chains'.[44] Forced marriage, child marriage, trading of women between tribes to settle disputes of honour and lack of security and safety due to the behaviour of warlords and commanders increase the likelihood of many women seeking refuge in tranquil-lising and sedative drugs to cope with the resultant stress, boredom and social alienation. There is no data available on women who are domestically confined or segregated who use drugs clandestinely without the knowledge of other family members.

Another group at risk is youth. While there have been some improvements in the education system and more young people, mainly males, are now attending school, there are likely to be few sustainable jobs or employment opportunities suddenly opening up within the country for a future mass of newly literate youth. Indeed, education may be seen by many as a way out of Afghanistan rather than a means of contributing to its development. The spectre of the Iranian situation where there is an educated and literate youth population with an unemployment rate of at least 20 per cent and a high prevalence of heroin injecting looms large on Afghanistan's western border. Ironically, a particular risk group may be those young educated urban Afghans who have returned to their country after being brought up as refugees in Pakistan or Iran where they enjoyed a sense of freedom and avenues of self-expression and employment opportunities not found in Afghanistan. With one foot in each country, their identity crisis runs the risk of being reconciled through drug use, particularly alcohol.

---

* The *Kharabat* area was better known as the city's music ghetto because of the hundreds of musician-families living there, rather than for prostitution, then more commonly found in the Shor bazaar area. Musicians did not enjoy a good social standing and *Kharabat*, a common word used by Sufis, literally means 'materially ruined, spiritually rich'.

When two high-level Afghan police officers report independently of each other that up to half of all police in local police posts take hashish, alcohol and/or opium to while away the time when on night duty, this signifies another high-risk group.[45] In 2006 it was reported that many police in Helmand province were regular users of hashish, with Colonel Asadullah Sherzada of the police headquarters confirming that some of his men were smoking hashish: 'I own that some policemen are drug addicts, but can anybody suggest to us the people who are not smoking charas?'[46] When an NGO in Kabul were debating whether to develop a drug treatment centre run by the police, an ex-policeman laughed and said that the police were more likely to need a treatment centre for themselves as many of them had problems related to drug use.

Certainly men who have been engaged as combatants in the various wars and conflicts throughout the country pose another high-risk group for problem drug use. Many may have started their drug-using careers by being provided with or paid in hashish when fighting with the *mujahideen* groups against the Soviets. Indeed, throughout history there have been many accounts of the use of various drugs by combatants. In eleventh-century Persia, Al-Hassan ibn-al Sabbah, the 'old man of the mountains', led a group of the Ismaili sect of Shi'ite Muslims called *hashishi*, 'the hemp eaters', who

allegedly incorporated the use of hashish into their violent reprisals against political rivals. They are said to have consumed hashish in order to induce ecstatic visions of paradise before setting out to face martyrdom, and in this intoxicated state launched suicidal attacks on challengers to their tribal hegemony. The word 'assassin' also derives from the cult of Al-Hassan, although in early European usage it meant devotee and only later acquired the meaning of murderer.[47]

Such a tale also led several nineteenth-century European writers to claim that the word 'assassin' had been derived from the word 'hashish'. However, while the traveller Marco Polo reported that the assassins of the sect did use a drug, this was not identified as hashish or necessarily linked to their violent acts. Unfortunately the link associating cannabis and violence had been formed in the public mind and has been exploited to the full in the war on drugs ever since, particularly in the anti-cannabis diatribes of Harry Anslinger, Chief of the United States Federal Bureau of Narcotics between 1930 and 1962.[48]

Whatever the reason, many *mujahideen* reputedly took hashish before going into battle with the invading Soviet forces. Whether they simply took the drug to calm their nerves and allay their fears and anxieties or to prime themselves for action is not known. On one mission with the *mujahideen* in eastern Afghanistan early in the war against the Soviets, Tom Carew, a British Special Forces soldier, wanted to leave camp but when he went to look for his *mujahideen* colleagues he 'found them all, sitting around getting stoned out of their brains on opium'.[49] The legacy of such drug use among combatants in Afghanistan's wars since 1980 is clear to see among groups of ex-combatants who are now heroin users living in places like Kabul and Gardez. On the other side of the battlefield, Soviet soldiers in Afghanistan between 1979 and 1989, many of them young conscripts, increasingly turned to drugs, particularly opiates, to cope with the stresses and strains of fighting against the *mujahideen*. It has been claimed that drug use among Soviet soldiers in Afghanistan resulted in their stimulating demand on return to Russia and inevitably increasing drug trafficking from Pakistan and Afghanistan into the Soviet states.[50] There have also been claims made that a deliberate strategy of the US, by means of the broader Operation Mosquito, was to spread drug addiction into the Soviet army and by extension into Soviet society.[51] In conjunction with the *mujahideen*, the CIA may have used drugs to purposely undermine the Soviets. As one *mujahid* said, 'We try to poison the Russians with it...they sell opium and hashish mostly but now also heroin to the Russian soldiers in exchange for guns and to poison their spirit.'[52]

Over the past decades one of the most vulnerable groups at risk of becoming problem drug users has been Afghan refugees in neighbouring countries where problem drug use is already prevalent. The local drug-using practices adopted in the vulnerable refugee camps and urban sprawls in neighbouring Pakistan and Iran have had a significant impact in Afghanistan as increasing numbers of refugees have returned home bringing their drug habits with them. At the same time it is important to avoid scapegoating returning refugees as being responsible for the country's increasing drug-use problem, particularly IDU. Such cursory examples as those above make it all too evident that many groups in the vulnerable war-shattered Afghan population constitute a high-risk group for problem drug use.

# 8
# Neighbours and Refugees

As the country which linked east and west, China with India and Persia, the European north with the Asian south, carrying the silk road which stretched, a full year's march, from Peking to Rome, everything had come to, or through Afghanistan.[1]

More than half of the world's total opiates abusing population is in Asia (8.5 million people) and all indications are that abuse is increasing in this region...the countries with the highest levels of opiate abuse are found in Asia, notably along routes where the drugs are trafficked out of Afghanistan.[2]

Nearly 50% of heroin users interviewed had first started to use heroin in either Iran or Pakistan. Twenty five percent of opium users had first started in Pakistan and a further 13% had started in Iran. Of the pharmaceutical drug users who reported where they first started to use these drugs, nearly 25% said Pakistan. By contrast, only 7% of hashish users had started to use hashish outside Afghanistan.[3]

After the Afghan tribes had overcome repeated attempts by the British to invade and control their territory in 1838 and 1878, the Amir Abdur Rahman and the British emissary Sir Mortimer Durand reached a political settlement in Kabul in 1893. This resulted in the creation of modern Afghanistan as a buffer state with the imposition of arbitrary state boundaries designed to assuage British India, Persia and Russia.[4] The new boundary, still referred to as the Durand Line, effectively divided the territories of the Pashtoon tribes homeland in what was then British India's North West Frontier Province (NWFP) and the Baluch tribes of south west British India, creating borders between Afghanistan, British India and Persia that are still not recognised over a century later by many of the tribesmen living on either side of the border. This situation has undoubtedly facilitated the development of cross-border drug trafficking networks based on close tribal and family ties, as well as seasonal migrations over the borders. Since the early 1970s the Afridi Pashtoons of Khyber agency in NWFP have dominated trafficking in collaboration with the Shinwari and Ghilzai tribes living in Afghanistan.[5] Such close cross-border ties also aided the flow of many refugees from Afghanistan to its neighbouring countries after the Soviets invaded in 1979.

By 1981, only two years after the Soviet invasion, almost 4 million refugees had fled the country, an estimated 2.3 million to Pakistan and another 1.5 million to Iran, as well as a smaller diaspora that reached central Asia, Europe, Australasia and North America.[6] The Afghans, proud of their heritage as a warrior nation and not easily cowed, had been terrorised by the Soviet Mi-24 Hind helicopter gunships, a force they had no answer to until much later in the war when the US began to deliver Stinger missiles to the *mujahideen*. Within a few years well over a third of the population had left the country, one of the largest mass migrations in modern history, with an estimated 3 million Afghan refugees in Iran and almost a similar number in Pakistan.

Most refugees fleeing to Pakistan ended up in camps along the Pakistan-Afghanistan border that functioned as military bases for the several *mujahideen* factions that made frequent forays back into Afghanistan to fight the Soviets, although many later moved to Karachi and other urban areas. By contrast, most Afghan refugees in Iran settled in the poorer neighbourhoods of urban areas rather than in the camps or refugee villages that were more common in the border areas of Pakistan and that had at least attracted limited assistance from the international community. After the Soviet withdrawal in 1989 a voluntary repatriation programme was started and a few years later the governments of Pakistan and Iran, who had shouldered most of the burden of supporting the refugees without any major international assistance, 'began to harden their attitudes to the continued presence of Afghans in their countries'.[7] Increasingly Afghans seeking refugee status in Pakistan and Iran were perceived as economic migrants and by 2000 refugee status in these countries was no longer granted on a prima facie basis.

By September 2005 the Pakistani government estimated there were still over 3 million Afghan refugees in the country with 1.8 million of these in NWFP. The government then ordered the closure of all refugee camps in the tribal areas of NWFP, ostensibly because of security concerns. Refugees were given a deadline to leave the country by 15 September and all refugees had to undergo an iris validation test aimed at preventing them re-entering through the porous borders separating the two countries. Nevertheless, from all accounts many of these refugees still remain in Pakistan.

Such a brief overview cannot adequately convey the intensity and complexity of the mass movement of Afghans back and forward over their borders between 1979 and today, or the diversity within the refugee population. Apart from fleeing the Soviet invasion, many Afghans continued to seek refugee status in neighbouring countries during the civil war between *mujahideen* factions in the early 1990s and the draconian regime of the Taliban between 1995 and 2001. Others continue to engage in traditional cross-border seasonal migration mainly between eastern areas of Afghanistan and the western tribal areas of Pakistan.

By early 2002, after the Taliban had been defeated and President Hamid Karzai became the leader of the Interim Government in Kabul, there was a strong impetus from several quarters to return large numbers of refugees to Afghanistan. While approximately 300,000 had returned between November 2001 and March 2002 without any official assistance, by the end of October 2002 a further 1.5 million had been assisted by the UNHCR to return from Pakistan and 220,000 from Iran, with a further 10,000 from Tajikistan.[8] A mass of people returned to a country characterised by a broken infrastructure, insecurity, limited resources (apart from opium) and few job opportunities which was not even able to sustain its existing population. Indeed 'Many returnees were complaining that they had been encouraged by promises of assistance to return to a situation in which they were worse off than in the country of asylum.'[9] UNHCR policy still only encourages the facilitation of voluntary repatriation of refugees to Afghanistan rather than its promotion, acknowledging that the situation in the country is still not safe and that many returns may not be durable. One report suggested that the main beneficiaries of the refugee return were not the returnees themselves but the major institutional actors involved:

For the Afghan government it could be seen as a vote of confidence strengthening its hand as it endeavoured to exercise authority over rival local power holders. For the US and its allies, it could be seen as a retrospective justification of the overthrow of the Taliban. For the governments of Pakistan and Iran, it represented a reduction of what they saw as the unfair economic burden of hosting Afghan refugees. And for UNHCR, it emphatically demonstrated its 'relevance' to the international community.[10]

After the large number of returnees during 2002, the spring of 2003 saw much lower numbers returning to Afghanistan, partly because many refugees thought they would be unable to return in conditions of safety and dignity.[11] At the same time, 'asylum fatigue' had, understandably, begun to creep into both Pakistan and Iran that led to pressures being placed on refugees to return to Afghanistan. Sayida, an Afghan woman who had just arrived in Herat from Mashad in Iran in April 2003, told Amnesty International: 'We were insulted a lot in Iran and harassed almost every day. Even if our children were allowed education, they are not allowed to get jobs. Every day we were psychologically and spiritually sick.' Mohammadin, recently returned from Mirpur in Pakistan in the summer of 2002, claimed that 'Since Karzai came into power, the police in Pakistan have increased their harassment of Afghan refugees. I finally decided to bring my family back to Afghanistan before the police took all our savings.'[12] Ironically the same Amnesty report cited allegations by the local representative of the Afghan Ministry of Refugees and Repatriation from Jowzjan province that 2,000 families had left the country in 2003 because two rival factions, *Jamiat-i Islami* and *Jumbesh-i-Milli Islami*, were 'forcibly recruiting men and boys to participate in the internecine fighting'.[13]

According to UN estimates, in January 2005 almost a million refugees were still in Iran with more than a million in refugee camps in Pakistan and 'an unknown but substantial number' living in cities across Pakistan. Although many of these refugees were forecast to return to Afghanistan during 2005, the then UN High Commissioner for Refugees, Ruud Lubbers, warned at the end of a four-day visit to Afghanistan that the pace of returns should not be speeded up.[14] This warning was based on reports that Iran was forcing refugees to return to Afghanistan by stopping their entitlement to healthcare, only allowing refugee children to attend Iranian schools if they paid an unaffordable fee and making it more difficult for registered refugees to obtain proper documentation without which they were no longer registered. In its defence, the Bureau for Aliens and Foreign Immigrants Affairs in Tehran rejected claims that Iran was forcing Afghan refugees to go home by saying that they were trying to make a genuine distinction between legal refugees and Afghan illegal migrants.

Whatever the push and pull factors influencing their decision to return to Afghanistan, the refugees from Iran, Pakistan and Tajikistan were returning from countries with significant populations of problem drug users and a very high prevalence of heroin addiction. Reports from drug treatment agencies in Afghanistan, as well as the few research studies available, show that a significant number of Afghan drug users started their drug use in these neighbouring countries, particularly Pakistan and Iran. While the international attention on drugs in Afghanistan has focused almost exclusively on the cultivation and production of opiates and their export to regional and western markets, one of the major social consequences of the regional Afghan diaspora has been largely neglected: the re-entry into Afghanistan of a drug using population who can unwittingly pass on their often uninformed understanding of drugs and methods for consuming them to the local population.

## DRUG USE IN IRAN

Iran is a middle-income country of 69 million people characterised by high rates of urbanisation, migration and unemployment, estimated at 16–20 per cent but likely to be much higher. It has a GDP per capita of $7,000 with an economy over-reliant on the production and export of oil. Figures for 2004 showed that 28 per cent of the population was under the age of 14 years, the median age was 23.5 years and life expectancy was 70 years.[15] There is a high literacy rate of 86 per cent for men and 73 per cent for women, while 97 per cent of eligible children enter primary school, with more than 90 per cent completing primary education. In 2001 a study conducted among Shiraz University students reported that at some time in their life 52 per cent had smoked cigarettes, 25 per cent had tried alcohol, 21 per cent opium and 12 per cent cannabis, although only one student had tried heroin.[16] By 2005 the UNODC reported that Iran had the highest prevalence of opium and heroin addiction in the world, with 1 in 17 of the population a regular drug user and 20 per cent aged between 15 and 60 a problem drug user. Such drug use cuts across education, class, age and economic barriers, with the middle-aged middle-class as vulnerable as socially deprived youth.[17]

Historically, Persia, renamed Iran in 1935 and then the Islamic Republic of Iran after the 1979 revolution, had been a major opium producer and cultivator, with an annual 600 tons of opium produced by the end of the nineteenth century and a peak in production of 1,350 tons by 1936. At that time exports of opium from Iran 'accounted for 40% of the world's medical morphine and earned 15% of Iran's foreign exchange'.[18] Opium smoking, a customary pastime for many in a population that 'accepted recreational drug use without reservation', was banned by the government in 1910 and made more expensive by the imposition of taxes in 1928. Both policies had little effect, however, and in 1949 when the US Bureau of Narcotics opened an office in Tehran, its resident agent

discovered the worlds most elaborate drug culture. Drawn from all regions and social classes, Iran had an addict population of 1.3 million, or one opium user for every nine adults—a rate only exceeded by China. Consumption was particularly high in the eastern opium-growing provinces adjacent to Afghanistan where up to 80% of the adults were addicts.[19]

Concerned about the high prevalence of opium addiction, in 1955 the Shah imposed a complete ban on opium, although this was rescinded in 1969 when opium cultivation was resumed to allow the sale of opium to registered addicts. While an apparent acknowledgement that prohibition had not worked, the move drew severe criticism from the UN's division of narcotic drugs and the US government. Indeed, it has been suggested that the Shah's restrictions on opium availability helped the emergence of an illicit heroin industry that supplied addicts who didn't register for government-supplied opium. The US ambassador to Iran in 1974, Richard Helms, estimated that Iran had about 30,000 heroin users supplied by Tehran heroin laboratories that were producing low-grade heroin from Turkish morphine base.[20]

By 1976 there were 170,000 officially registered opium addicts in Iran, with almost 50 per cent over the age of 60. This figure represented 50 per 10,000 of Iran's population and was believed to account for between one third and one half of the total addict population.[21] It also suggested a humane drug regime that permitted older people who had used opium for many years the comfort afforded by regulated doses of opium for the aches and pains of old age and to avoid suffering withdrawals. At that time it was mandatory for addicts under the age of 60 to seek treatment for their addiction, most being treated with a flexible reduction and substitution regime with either methadone or an 'opium pill' developed by the Iranian ministry of health that contained 80 mg of opium and 8 mg of chlorpromazine (Largactil), a powerful sedative and antipsychotic. On some occasions other psychotropic drugs had to be prescribed to counteract the side-effects of Largactil, such as a dry mouth, constipation and movement disorders.

After the Islamic revolution of 1979, opium cultivation in the country was again banned and the following year it was more or less eliminated. This provided an added impetus for opium cultivation in Afghanistan to fill the supply gap, and dramatically changed patterns of drug use in Iran. The traditional system of providing cards to opium users to access government controlled opium was abolished and drug users were given coupons for opium tablets for up to two and a half months to help them reduce their usual dose. They were given six months to stop completely after which they were sent for mandatory detention and treatment, or to prison. In effect, drug use had been criminalised by the new regime, leaving drug users at the mercies of the illicit drug trade. As Alfred W. McCoy points out in his comprehensive book on the politics of heroin, the CIA reported 'that drugs were being sold openly on Tehran's streets and the Revolutionary Guards, with many addicts in their ranks, did "not interfere with the dealers"'.[22]

Twenty years later in 1999, an RSA[23] of drug use conducted in ten major urban sites estimated that there were 1.2 million Iranians suffering 'severe forms of drug abuse', constituting two per cent of the country's total population, although an Iranian psychiatrist noted that the RSA could not directly address the issue of nationwide prevalence though 'cautious inferences can be made'.[24] Of the 1,472 drug users interviewed during the RSA, 60 per cent reported that opium was their first 'drug of abuse', both *thariac*, smoked in a pipe or orally ingested after dissolving in tea, and *shireh* and *sukhte* (opium derivatives obtained by boiling the residue of smoked opium which accumulates inside a pipe), both usually smoked in a pipe but sometimes injected as 'blackwater opium'. The use of codeine-based cough syrups and analgesics purchased from pharmacies was also reported and another study has claimed that cocaine and synthetic drugs are increasingly available, although not in amounts significant enough to warrant official concern and in amounts insignificant compared to the availability of opiates.[25] Nevertheless, all drug epidemics start with low availability and just a few users, with both capable of escalating rapidly given the vagaries of the global illicit drug market and smart marketing strategies employed by international drug trafficking cartels.

Of the drug users interviewed in the RSA, 94 per cent also had a history of smoking cigarettes and 33 per cent had a history of drinking alcohol. During the last month 73 per cent had used opium, 39 per cent heroin, 30 per cent opium residue and 13 per cent hashish, with 16 per cent having injected their drugs; 30 per cent of the sample had injected at some point in their drug-using career, with a mean age of first injecting of 26.3 years, and half of these had shared injecting equipment. Apart from heroin, both opium and opium residue were injected: typically 'an aqueous solution was prepared by heating the opium or the opium residue in a cooker and then the solution drawn into the syringe filtering through a cotton wool'.[26] Injecting was mostly reported as intravenous, usually in the veins of the arms and legs and the deep veins of the groin and sometimes in the veins of the testes. In 2004 a drug treatment agency in Kabul reported a few cases of male Afghan heroin users returned from Iran who injected in the veins of the groin and penis. In 2001 it was estimated that 67 per cent of the rising HIV transmission rate in Iran was caused by drug injectors sharing equipment, with needle-sharing being of particular concern throughout a prison system where more than 50 per cent of inmates were incarcerated for drug-related offences.

Iran had introduced mandatory drug screening before marriage, as well as preceding applications for government jobs and obtaining official licences. According to the RSA, in the late 1990s around 2 per cent of those screened under this scheme tested positive for opiates. Although such official figures from the RSA are high, it has been suggested that they are in fact an underestimation of the problem. National AIDS experts have estimated that there are up to 3.3 million drug addicts in Iran with 'addiction' being defined as repeated and continuing drug use over a period of nine months.[27] At the same time, an Iranian psychiatrist has suggested that despite some useful indicators of problem drug use, 'Attaining a definite estimate of prevalence and incidence of substance abuse in Iran is not possible. Social stigmatization along with legal restrictions on substance abuse prevents drug users from admitting their act, offering clear data and referring to governmental sectors.'[28]

## DRUG USE IN PAKISTAN

In 2004, Pakistan was a much more impoverished nation than Iran with a population of 159 million and a GDP per capita of only $2,100, an 8 per cent official unemployment rate and substantial underemployment. With a life expectancy of 63 at birth in 2004 (compared with Afghanistan's 44.5 at birth), 46 per cent of the population aged 15 and over were literate, with males having a literacy rate of 60 per cent and females 31 per cent.

In Pakistan there have been considerable discrepancies between different national assessments of problem drug use conducted over the past three decades. In 1980 the number of heroin users in the country was considered to be negligible, but by 1983 it had risen to nearly 100,000. Numbers then escalated rapidly and by 1993 there were an estimated 1.3 million heroin addicts out of a total 3 million drug users. The most recent national assessment, however, conducted by the UNODCCP and the Narcotics Control Division of the government's ANF in 2000, provided an 'upper estimate of approaching 500,000...calculated as the number of chronic heroin abusers (including drug injectors)', as well as an explanation why the number of heroin 'addicts' had fallen by a staggering 62 per cent since the last national assessment in 1993. As the report almost apologetically stated:

This figure is lower than previous estimates but still represents an extremely serious heroin abuse problem in the country. When an analysis of population levels and the demographics of heroin use in Pakistan is conducted, it is extremely difficult to see how higher levels than this would be credible.[29]

According to the 2000 report, problems with previous national assessments included the failure to clearly delineate between different 'drugs of abuse' and an over-reliance on key informants as the main data source. The 2000 report itself took a more comprehensive methodological approach that included interviews with drug abusers and data from prisons and drug treatment centres, as well as interviews with key informants. At the same time, the report claimed that other estimates (sources unspecified) 'have suggested that the total number of drug abusers may have reached four million by 2000'.[30] A UNDCP report from1998 providing an overview of previous attempts to measure the drug problem in Pakistan noted that results from the previous assessments could not be generalised because of the small sample size and the under-representation of groups like occasional drug users and people of high economic and social status. Female drug users had not been included in the previous assessments at all.[31]

Whatever the unreliability and variability of estimates of drug prevalence, all indicators suggest that Pakistan has a very serious drug problem, particularly with the injecting of heroin and, unlike Iran, a wide range of pharmaceuticals. By 2005 an estimated 27 per cent of Lahore's drug injectors were HIV positive, testimony to the failure of scaling up the city's limited harm reduction services. With a population of 130 million in 1999 it was estimated that 1.7 per cent of the population aged 15 years and above used opiates, mainly heroin, while 1.2 per cent used cannabis. Nearly 20 per cent of the country's prison population was estimated to have been incarcerated for drug abuse, possession of drugs and other drug-related offences. While many younger problem drug users may have ended up in prison because their families were unable to cope with their drug use, it is ironic that many of the drug users in Qandahar prison in Afghanistan at that time were young Pakistanis who had been brought there by their families who knew there were no drugs in the Taliban-run jails, unlike Pakistani prisons where drugs were rife.[32]

Although it was not nearly to the same extent as Iran, the area of British India that in 1947 became Pakistan had for several centuries produced opium both for domestic consumption and export. But from independence in 1947 up to 1953 Pakistan imported most of its opium from India and sold it to registered users and *hakims* through the centuries-old vend system in government licensed shops. After 1954 and up to 1979, under the International Opium Protocol of 1953 the UN permitted opium production, first in Punjab then in NWFP.[33] Like Iran, such a measured and pragmatic response to problem drug use, with opium addicts being able to obtain licit opium from government retail outlets, changed in 1979 with the imposition of Islamic law and the enforcement of the Hudood Ordinance by the military government of General Zia ul-Haq. This effectively ended the lawful and regulated production, sale and consumption of opium, alcohol and *charas*. Sudden closure of government-licensed opium shops resulted in the unregulated and uncontrolled production and selling of opium. Approximately 100,000 chronic opium addicts were left without their drugs and inevitably some turned to heroin as a substitute, their behaviour criminalised in the process. At the same time the Iranian revolution restricted the flow of opium from Afghanistan and Pakistan west across the Iranian borders and this forced traffickers to seek alternative routes such as overland to Karachi and its international seaport. En route some heroin traffickers took the opportunity to create local markets for their product.[34]

## OTHER NEIGHBOURS

A fact-finding mission sent to the central Asian republic of Tajikistan in 2000 found a range of drug-related problems.[35] With a high unemployment rate, particularly in towns in southern Tajikistan near the border with Afghanistan, and a malnutrition rate of 6 per cent, it was estimated that up to 30 per cent of the population of this ex-Soviet satellite state were dependent on the illicit drug business for their living. Generally in the several former Soviet central Asian states,

The breakdown of governance, rapid development of a large urban underclass living in wretched conditions and the establishment of thousands of new companies with minimal commercial supervision has created ideal conditions for growing drug markets. Heroin has now become the opium of the people.[36]

In Tajikistan it was reported that there was no shortage of heroin, with the drug being cheaper than vodka, as well as the drug of choice for many, especially school-age youth. Some users had tried to detoxify themselves with alcohol but this reportedly led to more cases of overdose deaths. The high quality of heroin in Tajikistan, presumably export-quality from Afghanistan, meant that it did not have to be 'cooked', but could be directly mixed with water and injected. Other reported methods of use were snorting it straight from the packet or smoking it mixed with tobacco, with a few users inserting the fine powder under their eyelids.

It was estimated that 30 per cent of heroin users preferred injecting, with many doing so in groups of three or four and sharing needles and syringes. The syringe was commonly flushed out between uses, not to prevent infectious diseases like HIV and hepatitis, but to avoid the violent shaking caused by mixing different blood types. Researchers estimated that the HIV prevalence rate among Tajikistan's IDUs had risen between 2001 and 2004 from 4 to 12 per cent.[37] Interestingly, from the perspective of developing drug use trends in neighbouring Afghanistan, the decision whether to smoke or inject heroin depended on how much money was available to buy drugs, the level of availability of the drug and how quickly the user wanted a 'hit'. Between 1992 and 2000 the UNDCCP estimated that there was an annual 28 per cent increase in the number of 'registered drug abusers' in Tajikistan, with an estimated 50,000 by 2001, representing 0.8 per cent of the total population.[38]

In 2002, an examination of used syringes in Tashkent, the capital of Uzebekistan bordering northern Afghanistan, revealed that 45 per cent contained blood that proved to be HIV positive. By 2005, it was estimated that around 75 per cent of people in the country infected with HIV were IDUs.[39] It has also been estimated that there are between 65,000 and 90,000 drug users reflecting a rapid increase in the consumption of heroin, opium and hashish over the past decade.

## DRUG USE AMONG AFGHAN REFUGEES

Several reports have emphasised the high rate of problem drug use among Afghan refugees still living in Pakistan and returnees from both Pakistan and Iran. In the case of Tajikistan there are only anecdotal accounts from NGO and government workers in Badakhshan province of an increase in heroin use, including injecting, among youth returning from Tajikistan. Although not yet substantiated, in 1999 the Afghan authorities and several NGOs reported that heroin addiction had also reached 'alarming proportions' in south-western Farah province situated next to the Iranian border because of returning refugees who had started their drug habit in Iran.[40] The same report claimed that a recent UNDCP pilot study of Afghan street heroin addicts, some as young as 13 years of age, in Quetta in Baluchistan Province of Pakistan showed that 4 per cent were currently injecting and that needle-sharing was becoming more common. In 2003 a research study of IDUs in Quetta showed that of 143 Afghans interviewed 18 per cent injected drugs, with nearly three quarters of this group sharing injecting equipment.[41]

It has also been reliably reported that in fortified heroin laboratories in Girdi Jungle and Jungle Pir Alizai refugee camps located in remote areas near the Afghan border in Baluchistan, young Afghans were paid to test the quality of the heroin on themselves. In 2002, a fieldworker visiting the same camps looked for indicators of growing drug use. Apart from observing some youths under the influence of heroin and learning that many of the men had crossed the border into Afghanistan to work in the heroin laboratories where many sampled the product and became dependent, the most significant indicator came during a meeting with the camp *shura*. When asked if drug use was a problem in the camp they unanimously replied: 'Let's put it this way, if we want one of our daughters to marry a young man in the camp the first thing we do is check to see whether he is a heroin addict.'

An in-depth study of problem drug use in rural eastern Afghanistan in 2001 interviewed 100 key informants with most of them claiming that the problematic use of opium was increasing in their districts, in part due to returning refugees. It also revealed that of the 99 drug users interviewed, 33 per cent who used hashish had started in Pakistan, and that of the 23 opium users six had started in Pakistan and three in Iran, while seven out of the eight heroin users had started in Pakistan. While this means that up to 40 per cent of those interviewed reported that they started their drug use in a neighbouring country, the report warned that, although indicative, the figures were too limited to be of statistical significance and that 'Several of these drug users were economic migrants to other countries rather than refugees escaping war and conflict.'[42] Asadullah, a heroin injector living in Kabul in 2003 who started his heroin use in Iran, claimed that many Afghans there worked on construction sites to fund their drug use: 'Almost all the builders in Iran are Afghan, and many take heroin.'[43]

A study of 200 problem drug users in Kabul in 2003 reported that of the 128 who used opium, 32 had started in Pakistan and 17 in Iran, nearly 40 per cent; 17 of the 74 heroin users had started in Pakistan and a similar number in Iran, nearly 50 per cent. One heroin user said:

When I was in Iran my neighbour encouraged me, he said, 'smoke heroin to know the taste of life'. I found it was more powerful than opium and started using it instead. At first I felt ecstatic, now I have been using it for five years and addicted and am using it for body pains and diarrhoea.[44]

Thirty-nine people in the study had also used alcohol, with ten of these starting in Pakistan, Iran or another country.

In November 1998, two fieldworkers were conducting preliminary research into problem drug use in Akora Khattak refugee camp near Peshawar when they were approached by a woman who invited them into her family compound. There they were confronted by a group of more than 50 women aged between 13 and 66 years of age, all drug users seeking help, some desperately, for their drug-related problems. This provided an opportunity for UNDCP to conduct an in-depth assessment with the women prior to establishing a comprehensive drug treatment and prevention programme for both female and male users in the camp.[45] The majority of the women were polydrug users who daily used a combination of opium and pharmaceutical drugs, particularly tranquillisers and painkillers, with 17 of the women using Valium on a daily basis. Thirty per cent had also used hashish at some point in their lives and two women had tried heroin, one starting in Kabul in 1997. Nearly two thirds of the women had started using opium in Afghanistan before becoming refugees in Pakistan, understandably, given that most had only come to the camp from Kabul within the last two to three years. Virtually all the women who currently used opium had started it as self-medication for a wide range of physical and mental problems, in particular depression, anxiety, insomnia and PTSD. It is unknown how many of the women in the study have now returned to Afghanistan. In 2003, Pakistan authorities closed Akora Khattak, although some families may have moved to other camps or Peshawar city rather than returning to Afghanistan.

In 1999, UNDCP fieldworkers identified a group of about twelve male Afghan heroin users who lived and used their drugs in a small cave in the Hayatabad area of Peshawar. Reliable sources also suggested that there were large groups of Afghan refugee heroin users in Quetta in Baluchistan, some as young as 13 years old and some also living in caves in the hillsides outside the city. On a visit to Quetta in 2000, we drove out of town and found several heroin users hiding and living in caves to avoid harassment from the police. A comparative assessment was then conducted of Afghan street heroin users in both cities.[46] At one end of the spectrum this included men who were jobless, homeless and had little or no contact with their family. Many lived on the street, often in dangerous and unsanitary conditions, with several obviously mentally disturbed and war-damaged. At the other end were drug users who bought and used heroin on the street but had the option of homes and families to return to each evening. There were also other types of Afghan heroin users in both cities who used their drugs exclusively in more private settings such as their own homes, but they proved a difficult group to contact and appeared, at least for the moment, more controlled in their drug use.

Very few of the respondents reported the use of pharmaceutical drugs such as tranquillisers and painkillers which contradicted informal reports from drug users themselves, as well as reports from treatment agencies in Peshawar, that Afghan street addicts used considerable quantities of these drugs. However, users may have perceived such drugs as purely 'medicines' for dealing with any adverse effects of heroin or withdrawal pains and therefore not included them in answers to questions about 'drugs'. Street drug users are unlikely to be aware of the potential dangers of using heroin along with pharmaceutical drugs, particularly those with a depressant effect.

Most of the drug users in the study reported smoking or inhaling as the main method of ingesting heroin, although another report warned that, while there is no national data available, there are injecting users in Afghanistan who risk spreading HIV/AIDS.[47] Although only 6.3 per cent of the respondents had reported drug injecting, 43 per cent of this group had shared injecting equipment, on average with four to six other users at one time. Research conducted a few years later on

Pakistani and Afghan drug users in Quetta identified them as being at high risk of contracting HIV, with only 16 per cent of the study participants having even heard of HIV/AIDS.[48]

Significantly higher proportions of Afghan drug users, when compared to the Pakistani research participants, were more likely to have used an opiate as the first illicit drug, to have other drug users in the family, to inject drugs and share needles. Furthermore, they were also less likely to know that sharing needles could spread disease. None of the Afghan drug users in the study who had sex had ever used a condom. Of 672 Afghan drug users registered with a treatment NGO in Quetta between July 2001 and August 2003, 12.5 per cent had a history of drug injecting and half of this group had shared syringes.[49] In 1995 a prescient UNDCP report suggested that Peshawar, and by extension Quetta, would increasingly become a heroin 'distribution point' for Afghan drug users, as well as a 'free zone for unchecked drug use (mainly heroin)' and a 'trendsetter' for urban drug use in Afghanistan.[50] Certainly there are signs that patterns of drug use found in these two cities are now being replicated in Kabul.

Overall, the return of drug-using refugees from neighbouring countries has had a significant impact on the extent and patterns of drug use within contemporary Afghanistan. The relatively free flow of people across the borders continues and is not only likely to increase the opportunities for the spread of socially communicable blood-borne viruses like HIV and hepatitis, but also an increase in problem drug use. During the 1980s and 1990s there has generally been a diffusion of heroin injecting in the developing world, a transition to the use of more dangerous drugs and more hazardous routes of administration.[51] This globalisation of drug injecting has left Afghanistan surrounded by countries that have extremely high rates of drug injection. It is almost inevitable that such habits are now becoming increasingly reported within Afghanistan itself. Compounding these problems is the lack of accurate information and understanding about the effects of drugs and the risks involved in using them, particularly opium, a commonly used but much misunderstood drug, as well as its derivative, heroin.

# 9
# A Tale of Two Opiums

Its [opium] medicinal value is undeniable, and in the Indian sub-continent it has been used for treating complaints including insomnia, nervous irritability, dyspepsia, diarrhoea, dysentry, neuralgia, neuritis, rheumatic pains, influenza and coughs, apparently with no problems of addiction.[1]

What should I do without opium? It keeps me warm in the cold of winter and lets me forget the misery of our meagre existence in these high snow-covered mountains.[2]

Perhaps the key to understanding heroin is to recognise that for most of these compulsive users, it serves as an antidote to a wretched existence—lives that might be full of pain, might be too complicated to manage, or,—conversely—empty of any meaning whatsoever. Heroin promises neutrality. It promises nothing.[3]

In 2000, when colleagues were developing basic information in the two major Afghan languages about the nature of drugs, their short and long-term effects and the dynamics of drug dependence, they immediately encountered a problem. There was no clear generic term for 'drugs' in either Pashto or Dari. The translators of the original English-language version of a basic information booklet about drugs promptly returned the text as being 'untranslatable'; it just did not make sense to them. There were two distinct terms, *dawa* and *nashaimawad*, that translated respectively as 'medicines' and 'intoxicants', but there was no general term for 'drug' as understood in the English language, whether legal, illegal, socially approved, plant-based or synthetic. A more commonly used term for intoxicants, as well as for narcotics, in the ubiquitous phrase 'narcotics control' found in most official Afghan policy documents, is the Arabic term *mukhadir* (although the term 'narcotic', strictly defined, excludes stimulant drugs). Such terminology is further complicated by the use of other Arabic terms such as *musakir* and *muftir* where the former means a substance that renders the user unconscious and the latter refers to anything that makes the body weak or the state of being intoxicated.[4] Apart from terminology, the provision of accurate, unambiguous and factual information in the Afghan context can also be problematic as an 'intoxicant' like opium has traditionally been used as a medicine in many parts of the country for centuries while a 'medicine' like Valium can be used as an intoxicant and can easily lead to dependency.

As it turned out, such local terms as *dawa* and *nashaimawad* provided much more culturally relevant definitions than the generic 'drug' and corresponded more closely with the complex realities of opiate consumption in Afghanistan. They reflected the dual nature of opium: on the one hand a very useful analgesic medicine for a wide range of illnesses, on the other a powerful intoxicant used for other more social purposes. This duality is also reflected in a definitive anthropological work on Afghanistan, published in the early 1970s, that cites both cannabis and opium as medicinal plants, with the former defined as a 'narcotic used as painkiller and timekiller', and the latter as 'a narcotic: a pastime and painkiller'.[5] The problem with opium (and its derivatives), perhaps more than with any other type of drug, is its dual nature, on the one hand a very effective painkiller, on the other an intoxicant that can easily seduce the user into dependency. It is for good reason that opium has been referred to as 'the heavenly demon'.[6]

By the early nineteenth century in several areas of Europe,

Laudanum was regarded as the indispensable tool of medicine. It was the aspirin/Valium of its day, used both to kill pain and sedate. It was considered the answer to diarrhoea, coughs, menstrual cramps and the discomfort of colicky and teething babies.[7]

During this period the use of opium products like laudanum, basically a tincture of opium in alcohol but often with other added ingredients, was more or less socially acceptable. Apart from being used by artists and poets to enhance their creative spirit, it was also taken on a regular basis by many ordinary people who used it as a household remedy or as a palliative for the hardships of life.[8] Opium was almost the perfect drug, if taken in small regular quantities, to endure the drudgery of daily existence, enabling the user to shrug off the aches and pains of manual labour and to suppress appetite when food was scarce. In Afghanistan it is still used for these purposes, although 'small regular quantities' can easily increase in amount and regularity and result in dependency. In neighbouring Turkmenistan opium was traditionally used by mountain shepherds and crop collectors in the cotton fields, enabling them to endure hard physical labour:

The mild stimulatory effect of raw opium if taken orally (due to the presence of alkaloids with strychnine-like effect and slow absorption) also allowed its use as a means for better adjustment during hard physical labour or in a difficult psychological situation.[9]

## THE BADAKHSHAN EXPERIENCE

In 1995, a UNDCP Assessment and Strategy Formulation mission to Afghanistan suggested that while opium use was extensive in the northeast of the country, it 'does not appear to be dysfunctional…and forms an important tool in the "survival kit" of the population, which has to survive in what can best be described as extremely hostile living conditions'.[10] Since that time and even before, such functional opium use has increasingly become dysfunctional for individuals, families and communities, especially in more isolated areas of Badakhshan province in the extreme north east of the country.

The Wakhan Corridor in Badakhshan is the narrow high-altitude strip of land that runs 200 km from Ishkashim district eastwards towards the Chinese border. Measuring 20–60 km in width, it is wedged in by the Pamir mountain ranges on the Afghanistan-Pakistan border to the south and the river Oxus bordering Tajikistan to the north. It is an inhospitable place where the small population of just over 10,000 Wakhis, Shegnanis and Kyrgyz lead a precarious existence, sharing their territory with snow leopards, lynx, brown bears and wolves. The economy of settled areas of the Wakhan is based on subsistence agriculture, while the Kyrgyz people are yurt-dwelling semi-nomadic herdsmen. Food insecurity, isolation, chronic rural poverty and a lack of medical facilities mean that malnutrition and hunger lead to almost continuous illness, and contribute to lathyritis, an incurable paralysis of the lower limbs caused by excessive consumption of grass pea, one of the few available plant foods.

One of the most intractable problems in the Wakhan is chronic opium addiction that affects 'all ages and both sexes, almost exclusively among the Ismaili population of Wakhis and Shegnanis living along the frontier, though addiction is also reported as a problem among the Kyrgyz of the little Pamir, who are Sunni moslems'.[11] While opium is not grown in the Wakhan, apart from a few plants for medicinal purposes, it is easily available from other areas of Badakhshan. Such chronic opium addiction in this part of Afghanistan goes back well over 100 years, although the situation has more recently been exacerbated 'by the increased isolation caused by national conflict and by the increase in opium production in other districts of Badakhshan by the Tajik and Uzbeq farmers'.[12] Such dependency on opium remains part of the survival strategy of people living in extreme conditions, where the drug can produce feelings of warmth by dilating blood vessels and aiding circulation. Papaverine, an alkaloid found in the opium poppy, acts as a vasodilator, as does THC (tetrahydrocannabinol), the major active chemical in cannabis. Opium can also act as an appetite-suppressant and helps to stave off hunger.

In Afghanistan generally, 'Opium has always been a part of the farming system in high altitude hardship areas where it plays a role in helping people cope with the endemic winter food shortages.'[13] Impoverished people faced with a choice between spending their little available money or other resources on food (assuming it is available) or a mood-altering drug that will alleviate hunger are likely to choose the drug. It has a double benefit: suppressing appetite *and* making them feel better at the same time. Food just takes the hunger away. In 1995 in southern Africa I worked with another group of similarly impoverished people living a daily struggle on the edge of a precarious and insecure existence, the Basarwa (Bushmen) of the Kalahari Desert. Restricted by the government of Botswana to settlements and banned from their traditional hunter/gatherer lifestyle, many Basarwa made the same choice as the Ismailis in Badakhshan by staving off hunger and misery with large quantities of another intoxicant, alcohol that has similarly decimated their communities and culture:

In the case of the Basarwa, it can be claimed that they are self-medicating on alcohol to alleviate their progressive suffering, both as individuals and as a people. They are helped in this by their compatriots in poverty who manufacture, distribute and sell liquor.[14]

In many ways this situation parallels the outsiders who have come into Ismaili communities in Badakhshan to trade opium, with reports of land and other family resources now being bartered for the drug. Such patterns of self-medication to mask hunger in impoverished communities can also become institutionalised by the state. Among groups of impoverished sugar-cane cutters in Brazil, for example, it has been suggested that hunger has become medicalised through the clinical prescription of tranquillisers and appetite suppressants rather than food in order in order to mask the structural source of rural suffering. For the rural poor it is 'a medical-technical solution to their political and economic troubles'.[15]

An Afghan psychiatrist writing in 1976 suggested that the lives of people living in Badakhshan's thinly-populated valleys were dominated by illness, frustration, lack of employment, boredom and poverty. In such a context, opium played a triple role of relieving pain, reducing motivation to satisfy primary needs such as food and sex, and causing indifference and passivity to their aimless and non-productive lives. It is a 'nice comforter, soothes idleness and regression and produces a state of passive dependence'.[16] It is also a habit that has resulted in untold misery and suffering for many families and communities in the province, keeping them bonded in debt to opium traders. Various prevalence estimates have been made of opium addiction in eastern districts of the province suggesting a problem of 'epidemic proportions', with one NGO reporting in 1998 that 'at least between 20 and 30%' of the local population were opium addicts.[17]

More recently AKF, an NGO focusing on aid and development for communities in Badakhshan and other northern provinces, has conducted a piece of ground-breaking action research in Lower Wakhan, Ishkashim and Zebak districts of Badakhshan. The resultant report conservatively estimated that over 15 per cent of the population of these three districts were habitual opium users. As the report stated: 'Opium addiction is chronic, extensive and historically entrenched.'[18]

The research findings, based on interviews with 129 male and 48 female opium addicts aged between 14 and 75 years in 19 villages in the three districts, showed that the dynamics of opium use in these communities is every bit as complex as the dynamics of opium cultivation and production in other parts of the country. Indeed the two are inextricably linked. Almost none of the communities cultivated opium themselves and were often reliant on outside opium traders, known as *tashkilis* (a term literally used to refer to government officials but pejoratively used by locals to describe opium or other commodity traders), for a regular supply of the drug. Many of the traders also dealt in other high value-for-weight commodities such as tea and soap. Traders, both male and female, would either visit family homes on a regular basis to sell opium, often arriving on horseback, or householders would trudge many miles to the nearest bazaar to purchase it. Many families found themselves in debt to these traders, in several cases bartering their land for opium. In some villages up to half of all land had been given up to the traders, in other cases livestock and other assets, including children, had been sold to pay off opium debts. In one case traders took the door, window frames and roof timbers from a house to clear a debt. Most insidiously, some opium addicts who had lost their land were then forced to work on this same land in a bonded labour arrangement where they paid back their debts by working, or were 'paid' in opium for their labour. Some Ismaili communities have attempted to resist the traders but have been bullied and threatened with violence. In some cases armed traders have returned to carry out reprisals, in one case reputedly pulling teeth out with pliers. In Khandud, the district capital of the Wakhan, there were up to 30 households of Badakhshani traders who lived in some degree of social segregation from the indigenous people (the Wakhi), separated by wealth and possibly ethnicity.

While opium has reputedly been used in Ismaili communities for centuries there is now a taboo against its use since the Agha Khan, the *Imam* (spiritual leader) of the global Shi'a Ismaili community, declared a *farman* against its use, as did the Shah of Panjah in the Upper Wakhan. However, some Ismaili scholars have suggested that opium use may have originally been encouraged and legitimised by the religious leaders, the *pirs*, who themselves became intoxicated on opium during religious rituals in order to become spiritually closer to God, although this is seldom openly talked about or even acknowledged in these communities.[19]

Generally there is a lack of medical facilities and services in Badakhshan so people readily turn to opium as a panacea 'for 100 diseases', although the study also reported that 22 per cent of the opium addicts used tranquillisers concurrently, some to mitigate the symptoms of opium withdrawal. Even where people do have access to basic medication provided by a healthcare clinic there is no pharmaceutical analgesic (except morphine) that can compare to opium in its ability to dull pain. Women in particular suffer from very poor health caused by years of poor nutrition, extreme cold weather, inadequate heating and clothing and constant cycles of pregnancy. One woman reported that after her husband died she started using opium because of body aches caused by sleeping on the cold floor over a period of many years. She was too poor to afford any floor covering. Women take opium for a variety of conditions, including arthritis, diarrhoea, stomach pains, eye problems, boils, during pregnancy and for complications during labour. However, opium dependency itself was reported as contributing to failed pregnancies and complications during pregnancy. According to local *dayas*, newborn babies of opium-dependent mothers were often very weak with a faint heartbeat, yellowish skin and an excess of mucous blocking their respiratory tracts.

On a visit to Badakhshan a community leader informed me of another reason why young women may become addicted to opium in these communities. If men who are already addicted to opium marry a woman who does not use it they will try to make their new wife addicted to the drug. As the men are sexually weak due to their addiction, they want to sexually weaken their wives in order that they can easily satisfy the wives' now weakened sexual desire. One local district administrator believed that the population of his district had remained the same for several years because opium addiction had created a low sex drive among users. He also believed, wrongly, that it led to infertility in women.

Opium is also given to children when they are sick, and to keep them quiet and calm. In some cases a child dependent on opium has to be given a dose of the drug before going to school. A local *daya* introduced researchers to an 11-year-old girl in Ishkashim who had been addicted since birth through pre-natal exposure and was allegedly using up to 7 g of opium a day. With rising opium prices, the *daya* claimed that the girl had financed her opium habit for the last two years by prostitution. Opium is also used in Badakhshan to curb children's hunger and to help them sleep and is traditionally administered by 'puffing' opium smoke into the children's airways, although it can also be dissolved in water or given orally in small pieces. Apart from some Turkmen communities in the north, this is probably the only other part of Afghanistan where significant numbers of opium users consume the drug by the traditional method of inhaling the fumes through a straight long-stemmed pipe while lying on the ground. In the AKF study, 90 per cent of users smoked opium this way rather than ate it. In Afghanistan this form of smoking opium in small groups is sometimes referred to as a *ghamza* session.[20]

## OPIUM USE IN OTHER AREAS

In many other areas of Afghanistan, apart from Badakhshan, opium is given to young children either as a medicine for sickness or as a pacifier and means of control to enable women to carry on with their domestic duties uninterrupted by the crying or demands of children. The drug is frequently given in the form of the juice from boiled poppy pods, although opium resin is also used directly, particularly among communities of Turkmen carpet weavers. A 1994 report on opium use in Nuristan province in north-eastern Afghanistan claimed that small amounts of opium were given to young children to relieve coughs and that the children of opium addicted mothers became addicted through the breastmilk (although the child would become dependent on opium in utero). According to the report, this could lead to further problems:

If an addicted mother is unable to find opium for her use then the child begins to cry and cannot sleep. Such a mother will calm her child by either rubbing a small amount of opium on her lips and then putting her lips over the lips of her child, or by inserting a grain-size piece of opium into the child's anus.[21]

A reliable report from a doctor working in Balkh records how during the two- to three-week period of the opium harvest in 2003 many cases of acute opium intoxication in children aged between six months and 15 years were brought to the hospital.[22] For the younger children this was possibly the result of inhaling fumes from drying raw opium, for older children involved in collecting the harvest it may have been the result of handled opium being absorbed through the skin or tasting the opium. In Maiwand district of Qandahar province in 2005 an opium farmer reported the following case:

A student of nine years of age brought some opium into school and distributed it amongst five of his fellow pupils. They all ate it and became unconscious. The headmaster of the school and the teachers took the pupils to hospital where they subsequently recovered. The headmaster then expelled all the children involved from school.[23]

Two health centres for women and children in Qandahar province reported that in rural areas over 50 per cent of children were given opium or the boiled juice of the poppy pod for medicinal purposes and to pacify and sedate them so that the mother could continue with her work.[24] A local doctor in Qandahar also claimed that he knew of 'at least ten child deaths' that had resulted from an opium overdose.

However, opium being given to children to pacify them so that mothers can continue their work is not a recent phenomenon nor is it specific to Afghanistan. It was also reported in nineteenth-century England when *The Second Report to the Commissioners* of 1842 cited cases of poor working women, particularly those who did textile work in their own homes, having few alternatives but to 'dope' their children with opium products. Some years later in 1869, *Mrs. Beeton's Book of Household Management* warned that 'Preparations which are constantly given to children by their nurses and mothers, for the purpose of making them sleep, often prove fatal.'[25] Many such proprietary preparations, like Atkinson's Infants Preservatives, Mrs. Winslow's Soothing Syrup, Godfrey's Cordial and Street's Infant Quietness were readily available over the counter from any pharmacist or other retailer.

A group of 50 Afghan women in Akora Kattak refugee camp outside Peshawar who self-medicated with opium and a variety of other drugs cited mental pain caused by the anxiety, depression and sadness triggered by war as the main reason why they had started to use opium, mostly by eating it. One woman said: 'I started eating opium with tea over six years ago in Laghman. I lost my husband, brother and son in the fighting and took opium to rescue me from depression.'[26] While quite a few of the women had also started taking opium for a range of physical ills such as respiratory problems, toothache and general body pain, all of them had continued to take it because of their chronic mental health problems, often expressed as 'sleep problems'. The women were now all regular users and dependent on opium, but they appeared to be relatively stable and none of them described any signs of tolerance having developed where they would have had to substantially increase their daily dose. In fact two thirds of them expressed some degree of control over their opium use and reported that they would intentionally and temporarily increase their dose if they were particularly upset or stressed. For many, painful war-related memories acted as a trigger to increase the dose. One woman said, 'we had land and a beautiful garden in Shakardara and had a happy life there. When I remember those days I become very upset and take more opium.'[27]

A third of the women had tried to give up opium at some time in their past, some more than once, but none had been successful for longer than 40 days before returning to opium use. Most restarted because they experienced withdrawal pains and now nearly all of them complained of health problems such as stomachache, headaches, tremors and prolonged monthly periods that they attributed to their opium use, although these may also be symptomatic of poor general health, a general high level of tension or the effects of other drugs that they take. Although the majority of the women only took small daily doses of opium and managed to maintain a relatively stable family life, most of them reported financial and social problems as a result of their opium use. They might only have spent an average of $8 a month on purchasing opium, but this constituted nearly a quarter of their monthly family income. Irrespective of the type of drug purchased, drug use among these women and many other impoverished Afghan drug users can have a devastating effect on family finances, leading to arguments and fighting with other family members. 'One woman said, "it has affected our family income. I feel shame because it is my children's money that I spend on opium", while another stated "it has damaged us financially. My son always quarrels with me and wants to stop giving me money".'[28]

For some groups of opium users, there is evidence of a more controlled functional use of the drug, although among these groups dependency is beginning to cause serious health problems. In May 2003 I visited a *serai* in the bazaar of Aqcha in Jowzjan province around two hours' drive northwest of Mazar-i-Sharif, and market town for the surrounding Turkmen communities. It looked as if it had not changed much over the last century. Indeed the Aqcha *serai* was evocative of the description of a *serai* given by Frank Martin, chief engineer to the Amirs of Afghanistan between 1895 and 1903:

The *serais*, which are stationed at intervals along the route, are intended for the use of the caravans, and they are made in the form of a square, with a high wall surrounding it, and the rooms are built against the inner side of the wall. There is a verandah outside the rooms, under which the packages carried by the caravans are stored for the night in bad weather, and which also forms a shelter for the camels and pack-animals.[29]

There were no camels in the Aqcha *serai* that day, but the square cobbled courtyard was full of donkeys and mules plus a few horses, their owners in town for the weekly market. The small low-ceilinged rooms were full of turbaned men sitting around drinking tea poured from delicately patterned china pots. Some were also smoking opium, although it was difficult to know how many in the dark and poorly lit interior of the *serai*. The *chowkidor* was a 58-year-old man who claimed he had been smoking opium habitually for 40 years. Although he looked liked an archetypal opium addict with a thin, drawn face and sunken hollow cheeks, he seemed otherwise fit and healthy and claimed that the only problem he experienced from using opium was constipation—and the pain of withdrawal when there was no opium available or he had no money to buy it.

Turkmen communities such as those around Aqcha have long had the reputation of being inveterate opium users, as well as traffickers of the drug along the border areas with Uzbekistan and Turkmenistan. In 1995 it was estimated that Aqcha had 24 opium-smoking 'dens', and in the nearby village of Mengajek 14 per cent of the population were habitual opium users. Those using it on a regular basis consistently confirmed that they were able to work much harder while using opium than they could without it.[30] There is still no shortage of opium in the area, as it is frequently taken by Turkmen carpet weavers, men, women and children, to help them work longer hours and to endure the often back-breaking pain of sitting at carpet looms for extended periods. In one carpet factory in Mazar-i-Sharif, several women were seen taking opium and most of the young children running around were given opium to quieten them and allow their mothers to work harder at the carpet looms. Liquid opium gum was rubbed on the top lip, earlobe or forehead of the very young children.

In some eastern provinces and across the border in NWFP in Pakistan, Pashtoons have developed different preparations of opium for smoking. *Chando* is a form of opium refined by boiling with water, several times if necessary, to remove impurities. The traditional method for using *chando* is to lie horizontal holding a long pipe with a bowl at the end held over a flame. Opium on the end of a needle is then inserted into the bowl and the fumes inhaled through the stem of the pipe. Another opium preparation is *madak*, primarily used by poorer people who cannot afford *chando*. Charred rice or barley husk is mixed with opium and water until the water is absorbed and pills of *madak* can be formed. These are then smoked through a water pipe or a small clay *chillum* made solely for the purpose.[31]

Although there is no reliable data, anecdotal reports suggest that in Afghanistan opium is increasingly used by those who have easiest access to it—cultivators and producers. Workers hired to lance and collect the opium gum are often paid in opium that can then be traded for cash or bartered for required goods and services, although some opium may be retained for personal use. Poppy seeds containing the chemicals tryptophan and phenylalinine that have a mild calming/sedative effect, as well as other chemicals, are regularly eaten as a snack by many working in the poppy fields, including children. In many countries these seeds are also added to a range of breads, pastries and confectionaries (except Singapore where they are illegal) and the oil from the seed is much prized by artists as it does not yellow like linseed oil.

### ENTER HEROIN

Over the past few decades another opiate drug has emerged in Afghanistan and all indicators suggest that its use is increasing and causing concern—heroin. As with other drugs, heroin users come from several different groups within the community and use heroin in different ways for different purposes.

Many miles from Afghanistan, Fraserburgh is a small fishing town in the bleak northeast of Scotland with a population of just over 13,000 and the reputation for having a high prevalence of heroin use, among the highest in the UK. While the town contains pockets of deprivation and long-term unemployment, it is also an affluent and prosperous community. As a local doctor noted, 'Drugs have no social barriers and often the more money there is, the greater the problem.'[32] Young men working on the fishing boats in the dangerous waters of the North Sea with high disposable income to spend after weeks at sea may want more than the legal kicks that alcohol provides and are likely to be targeted by heroin dealers. On the other hand over three quarters of heroin users interviewed reported that they started drug use because of difficulties in finding work and/or lack of diversionary schemes.[33] Couple this with local dealers who have good connections in Glasgow and further south and you have a set of specific factors that led to a serious drug problem that affected almost everybody in this small-town community, as well as the town's reputation, economy and social standing.

The 130 km of road south from Kabul to the market town of Gardez in Paktia province could not be further from the windswept waters of Fraserburgh. It passes through high dusty plains and narrow green valleys, where in the early spring of 2003 the new grapevines were marked by brown withered leaves due to the unseasonal cold weather, before winding its way up through stark jagged mountains and onto the even higher plains of Gardez. The low wide black tents of *Kuchis* were visible in the distance, their herds of sheep and pack-camels grazing on the plains, the smoke from their campfires rising vertically in the windless sky. Small boys with long flat-ended shovels filled in holes in the road in the hope that the drivers of passing vehicles would toss them some money. But while towns like Fraserburgh and Gardez may be geographically and culturally poles apart they share a common problem. It is hard at first glance to realise that the old garrison town of Gardez, with its central fort now housing the jail and police post, is an Afghan equivalent of Fraserburgh, with a localised set of circumstances making it one of the highest per capita heroin-using towns in the country.

In 2000 during the Taliban era, the UNDCP conducted an assessment of problem drug use in five districts of three provinces in rural eastern Afghanistan, including Gardez. During the assessment the fieldworkers visited the town and were told that there was a group of heroin injectors living there. Two doctors who had treated heroin addicts in the town suggested that heroin use was on the increase, one stating that 'if they cannot find heroin they will come to my clinic and ask for a Sosegon (pentazocine) injection.'[34] While the UNDCP already had reliable information about drug injectors in the main cities, this was the first reliable report of drug injecting in a small market town. Over a year later, Gardez, the provincial capital of Paktia province, was to become one of the main targets of US bombing in their hunt for al-Qaeda and the Taliban. After the Taliban were forced to leave the area, it then became a lawless anarchic place contested by at least three commanders and their militias, all vying for power and control. My colleagues and I always wondered what had happened to the drug injectors after the bombing. Did they remain in Gardez, go elsewhere, or had they been killed in the fighting?

In May 2003 I asked a friend who was going to be stationed in Gardez to enquire whether there were any problems in the town with drug injecting. Within a day she had sent an e-mail to ask for help as local doctors reported that armed men were coming into their clinics, putting guns to their heads, and demanding either drugs or help to treat their drug dependency, both equally impossible options given the almost complete lack of resources and healthcare services. A few weeks later UNODC staff visited Gardez, the first stop a meeting with the new chief of police who had arrived from the police academy only a few days earlier. After producing two heroin users who were being held in the police cells, the chief and his staff told us that there were at least 300 heroin smokers in Gardez and 'over 200' injectors of heroin, frequently mixed with Avil (pheniramine), an antihistamine, or Largactil (chlorpromazine) a major sedative. The police claimed that if the users couldn't find heroin, or had little money, then they would inject the cheaper pharmaceutical painkiller Sosegon imported from Pakistan and available in pharmacies for only 20 Afs (less than $0.50) an ampoule. Valium (diazepam), cheap and easily available, was also sometimes injected. During the time of the Taliban, ampoules of morphine could also be found in the bazaar, although their sale was later banned. Apparently morphine ampoules were again available but their sale was now kept hidden.

Our next visit was to the local hospital where one of the commanders responsible for security in Gardez, a swarthy Pashtoon with a long black beard almost down to his waist and a turban set at a rakish angle like a Barbary Coast pirate, had rounded up 14 heroin users from the bazaar so that we could meet them. Eventually we negotiated to speak with three bedraggled looking men, who were led into the hospital director's office. Displaying the track marks from recent injecting on their forearms, with one of them sitting on the floor slowly rocking back and forwards with a pained look on his face and desperately in need of a 'hit', they recounted how they had been thrown out of their family homes and were now living on the dusty streets.

Leaving Gardez it was impossible not to be reminded of an old spaghetti western movie, with gunmen lounging lazily in the glassless window frames of burnt-out buildings or lolling on the gun-barrels of tanks, just hanging around waiting for something to happen. As a result of the visit, the government's programme to disarm, demobilise and reintegrate ex-combatants was alerted to the problem of drug dependency among ex-combatants and the dangers for the programme in exchanging the drug-dependent fighters' guns for money that most likely would be spent on drugs. Subsequently a 15-bed drug treatment centre was established in Gardez, and by June 2004 there were 28 addicts from 14 provinces being given treatment, with others arriving daily looking for help and having to camp outside the gate waiting for a spare bed.

## THE USER'S TALE

On a hot sultry day in Kabul in 2003, a meeting was arranged with a heroin user to take photographs of him injecting. These were needed for the cover of a publication so that Afghans (as well as international donors) would graphically understand that injecting drug use did not only happen in neighbouring states like Iran, Pakistan and Tajikistan, but also in their own country. Two female workers from a drug treatment NGO took us to a neighbourhood in southwest Kabul to visit a heroin injector they had been counselling for some weeks. We arrived at the narrow gated entrance to a high-walled dusty courtyard to be met by a small girl of around six years of age. She grabbed my hand and kissed the back of it, a traditional mark of respect given to elders. After I had given her an impromptu kiss on the back of her hand, we were led through the courtyard and up a steep staircase into a bare fly-infested room where several women and small children crouched on the floor. After some discussion they took us into the room next door where the husband of one of the women lay on the floor on a thin dirty mattress. He had already injected his heroin, so we just sat and talked with him about his plight. After being a heroin addict for two years he had developed stomach cancer and was now unable to hold down food, even milk. He was obviously very ill and looked as if he was dying. His family thought he had contracted the cancer because he had started injecting heroin, so at least we were able to assure them that this was unlikely to be the case. We did not take any photographs. Given the situation, there was only one thing to do, give the family some money that we knew would most likely be spent on purchasing painkillers, most probably heroin, for the man, rather than on taking him to a doctor.

We then arranged to visit the NGO's treatment centre to take some photographs of another drug user injecting. While we still had some doubts about the ethics of this, it was necessary to have such photographs in order to attract the attention and publicity that would hopefully result in much-needed resources to provide services for injecting drug users. We were conscious that we were setting up a contrived scenario, but at that time there was little chance of finding a drug user in Kabul who would be injecting heroin in a public setting, unlike neighbouring Pakistan where in several cities drugs are injected in public places. The NGO had made the arrangements for the man to come and discuss the proposal with us.

An injector for over five years, for the past few months Ahmed had started to inject in the small veins in his feet and in his groin, his main veins having long since collapsed. He arrived on his bicycle and then stated that he would only agree to his photograph being taken if the NGO would take him into their residential treatment programme on Saturday, two days away. We told him that we could not arrange this as it was his responsibility to negotiate with the NGO to enter their programme independently of our taking his photograph. As he had been attending their weekly pre-treatment counselling sessions for some weeks and appeared motivated to stop using drugs, the NGO agreed to take him in but only in two weeks' time when the next vacancy was available.

A colleague and two doctors and a social worker from the NGO then accompanied Ahmed and me to the bombed-out ruins of the building next door, located in the part of southwest Kabul where most of the fighting took place between *mujahideen* groups in the early 1990s. This had resulted in the destruction of almost all the buildings in this part of the city. Ahmed then crouched in a corner, made a tourniquet out of a strip of rubber, and found a vein in the back of his forearm near the elbow. Most of the veins in his inner forearms were collapsed and he had an abscess almost the size of a cricket ball on one arm. He then cooked up the heroin in a spoon by adding lemon juice and lighting a crumpled sheet of paper to heat the mixture. The centre had provided him with a clean needle and syringe and he proceeded to slowly inject the muddy yellowish mixture, drawing back blood into the syringe to flush it out before injecting it back into his arm. For what seemed like an eternity he just left the syringe full of blood dangling from his arm before finally re-injecting it.

During all this time I had been concentrating on taking photographs of the injecting procedure. Suddenly Ahmed started to cry, ashamed of what he had just done. The NGO staff and my colleague also started to cry, the emotional weight of watching a fellow Afghan who had come to this stage in his life injecting heroin in a ruined building in a bombed-out area of what had once been a beautiful city was just too much for them to bear. Although tears filled my eyes, I had been too busy trying to take the photographs to become so emotionally involved and now I was more concerned about Ahmed's welfare. I took him by the arm and we all slowly walked back to the centre where he just hopped on his bicycle, waved goodbye, and set off home. It wasn't until the next day when I learned he had arrived home safely that my sense of guilt left me.

Five weeks later we visited Ahmed at the treatment centre where he had completed a three-week residential programme. He had undergone a remarkable physical transformation and looked like a completely different person, with colour in his face, which had filled out considerably, and his arms were almost completely healed, the abscess gone. He was smiling and thanked us for helping him to come off drugs. Now the problem was that he had nothing to do and no source of income, although he reported that his relationship with his family and friends was much better. We felt an onus of responsibility to help him with this, as the NGO was only just setting up vocational training and income-generating opportunities to help prevent its recovering addicts from relapsing into drug use. Luckily we had a contact in a carpentry and furniture-making training programme nearby and he was placed there. Before he started the programme I asked him about his life. The following is the story he told.

Ahmed was born in Kabul in 1973 and had attended school up to the age of 14. He then trained as a welder, had a well-paid job in a factory and also played for a prominent Afghan football team. When he was 18 he started to drink Russian vodka, easily available in Kabul at that time where it was sold openly in shops in the bazaar. He only drank it about once a month in the company of friends and liked the effect, although he did not like becoming too intoxicated. In 1995 he left Kabul because of the intense fighting in the city to become a refugee in Tehran where he found employment as a welder in a factory. One day, after about six months, he felt tired and a workmate suggested that if he smoked some opium he would feel better and not so tired. He then tried it, found it gave him strength, and continued to smoke it for a year when he switched to eating it, a more cost-effective method as none was wasted by literally going up in smoke. After another year he found that he had become dependent and developed a tolerance so that he had to increase his dose to feel even slightly intoxicated.

The only way he then felt he could avoid the pains of withdrawal was to inject. The first time an Iranian friend, a baker and fellow addict, injected him, showing him how to inject for himself. Although he injected with others, he never shared needles and syringes as he had been told that he would become ill if he did this. Before injecting, the opium or opium residue was simply boiled with water to prepare 'blackwater opium', a substance more commonly injected in Iran and Tajikistan than in Afghanistan. His main problem during this period was an inability to play football because he had no strength in his legs and his knees gave him trouble. He had also been caught twice using opium by the Iranian police. The first time he had been smoking opium in his room when two policemen burst in and arrested him. The factory owner he worked for arranged to have him released and told him that he would have to pay back the considerable sum that had been paid for his release. He worked at half salary for the next year, and then came to learn that it was the factory owner who had informed on him in the first place in order to exploit his cheap labour. Some time later he was walking in the bazaar when he was stopped and searched by two policemen who found some opium on him. They gave him a choice: he could go to prison, be forcibly returned to Afghanistan, or give them some money 'for tea'. He paid the tea money.

In 2002 Ahmed returned to Kabul and started to inject heroin three times a day for the simple reason that at that time street heroin in the city was cheaper to buy than opium. The same amount of money would buy a day's supply of opium or two days supply of heroin. Such 'heroin', it can be assumed, was cheap because it was cut with other psychoactive substances like diazepam or phenobarbitol and had low heroin content. Unless there is reliable testing of street heroin there is no way to guage what percentage of the drug is actually heroin and what percentage is psychoactive additives, toxic substances and/or inert fillers. He also supplemented the heroin by smoking hashish, around 20 g a week, because he felt that the heroin was not as strong as the opium he had been used to injecting in Iran.

Injecting this heroin caused him several problems, particularly abscesses and collapsed veins in his arms. He became very weak and was unable to walk, and this motivated him to try and give up. He also owed money to his brother and friends, given to him to buy drugs, and felt very bad about this. Four months previously he had gone to a doctor in Kabul in an attempt to give up heroin. The doctor had prescribed ampoules of the painkiller Sosegon, and although this had given him some relief, after a few days he felt some pain and returned to heroin use.

## OTHER PLACES, OTHER USERS

We later learned that Ahmed had relapsed and started using heroin again. While he was only one of an estimated several thousand heroin users in Kabul city, his experiences were perhaps typical of many young Afghan heroin users returning from neighbouring countries where they had first started to use opiates. A study of 200 problem drug users in Kabul found that 37 per cent used heroin, including three women, with half of this group starting in Iran or Pakistan and another 35 per cent starting in Kabul itself.[35] While, like Ahmed, most had used for six years or less, 20 per cent had used for more than seven years and five men for over 20 years. All the users were habitual, taking heroin on average two to three times daily, although half of them had given up at some point but started again. Only 7 per cent injected their heroin; the majority took it by the method known as 'chasing the dragon' where the powder is heated on a piece of tin foil and the fumes inhaled into the mouth through a narrow tube. At the same time, workers in a Kabul drug treatment centre reported that they had come across heroin 'doctors' in the city who injected other addicts and were paid for this service with heroin. The 'doctor' would use a large 10 cc syringe and inject 1 cc into each of eight to ten addicts in turn without changing the needle. In 2004 the centre started a small needle and syringe distribution scheme, handing out around 200 syringes a month, as well as condoms, to both drug users and female commercial sex workers.

The study also revealed other methods of use, although these were reported by key informants like health workers, taxi drivers and the police rather than the drug users themselves:

A few mentioned that heroin was also sniffed directly through the nose or taken by a method known as *sekhi sang* where a metal spike or thin knife blade is heated in a flame until very hot, then applied to a small quantity of the drug. The resultant fumes are then inhaled through a narrow tube. One person mentioned that he had seen a man with a head wound rub heroin into the wound until it was absorbed.[36]

The method known as *sekhi sang*, reminiscent of the 'hot knives' method of using hashish in some western countries, has also been reported as a way of using opium.

Almost half of the group in the study said they had started to use heroin due to the influence of friends, family members, work colleagues or room mates, although 'Such "influence" covered a wide range of behaviour including being forced, being persuaded, being encouraged and being offered free heroin.'[37] The other main reasons for starting heroin use were to help cope with illness and just sheer ignorance. They had no idea what heroin was, the problems that regular use would inevitably lead to or its addictive properties. Heroin was simply *poder* and could have contained anything. Such lack of knowledge and understanding of the drugs they are using have undoubtedly compounded the problems of many Afghan drug users. A few said that they took it because of sadness and loss, to work better, for sexual reasons or just to become intoxicated. The reasons for starting to use a drug, however, are seldom the same as those given several years later for its continued use. The vast majority of the 74 heroin users interviewed now used heroin primarily because they suffered withdrawal pains if they tried to stop. The others who continued to use 'for medical reasons' like aches and pains and diarrhoea, were most likely experiencing the withdrawal symptoms felt by their fellows.

Certainly there has been no shortage of heroin available in many areas of Afghanistan, although it can be speculated that very high export-quality heroin is seldom available at the retail end of the market because it is too expensive for local drug users and will fetch larger profits outside the country. Cheaper forms of both white and brown heroin are both available. The drug has become just another profitable commodity to be sold in the bazaar. Apart from the inevitable user-dealers who subsidise their own habit by selling to other users, several shops in the bazaar in Kabul are reputed to sell heroin over the counter just as they sell other consumer goods. Heroin is also sold by street beggars hired by drug dealers for the purpose and in houses and areas of the city where gambling takes place. In Herat one enterprising soft-drink stallholder erected a tent next to his stall so that customers could use the heroin that they bought from him 'in comfort'.

In Kabul in early 2006 there were three main types of street heroin sold, the best quality off-white injecting heroin was known as *cristal* and cost $4 a *puri*, a weight just under a gram but variable depending on the seller. The next quality was known as *gulbutton*, literally 'flower button', allegedly because it was darker in colour than *cristal*. The lowest quality, costing $2 a *puri*, was simply known as *button*. A year earlier drug users reported that white heroin from Badakhshan was of better quality than the brown heroin imported from Pakistan through Jalalabad. This latter 'heroin' may be a form of the chemical cocktails referred to in Chapter 11. It has also been reported that 1 kg of brown heroin is mixed with 0.5 kg of opium then boiled and reduced to form a concentrated opium/heroin mix—confusingly also referred to as *cristal*—that is then sold and ingested using the 'chasing the dragon' method.

Many of the men and boys who work as labourers in heroin producing factories are likely to become dependent on the drug, either voluntarily or involuntarily. While some begin using the freely available heroin by snorting or smoking it, for others just being in an environment where they unintentionally but inevitably breathe in the heroin fumes on a daily basis during the production process is enough. It has been claimed that when these men return home at night they can simply shake the *patou* they have had wrapped around them all day, breathe in the resulting heroin dust, and fall into a drug-induced sleep.

Apart from reliable research data on heroin use in Kabul and among Afghan refugees in Peshawar and Quetta, there have been reports, some more reliable than others, about heroin use in Herat, Qandahar, Badakhshan and other parts of the country. Of particular concern are increasing anecdotal accounts of heroin use in the major opium cultivating and heroin producing districts of Nangarhar province. In 2004 there were an estimated 1,000 heroin users in Shinwar district alone. If the source of this information had been anybody other than a respected drug treatment worker, who came from Nangarhar and had been a heroin user himself, it would have been tempting to dismiss this as just another scorpion tale. Reports have also come from workers in Badakhshan province that heroin use is on the increase there, particularly in Shegnan district, an area where there are several known heroin factories and close connections exist with communities in Tajikistan just over the border where heroin use, particularly injecting, is rife.

The different types of user described in this chapter show that there are many sides to the opium/opiate problem that necessitate different types of intervention and treatment responses. In the more remote corners of Badakhshan and other parts of the country where opium is used as a medicine and part of a wider survival strategy what would happen if opium cultivation was eliminated from Afghanistan and opium no longer available? Several days walk from the nearest pharmacist or clinic, some isolated communities would have no access to painkillers and if they did they might obtain pharmaceutical drugs that are as problematic and almost as dependence-producing as opium. Afghanistan's heroin users will also face problems if there is a reduction in supply because elimination of opium poppy cultivation is successful. Evidence from other parts of the world where there has been a rapid reduction in heroin supply suggests the likely transition of non-injecting drug users to injection of heroin or substitute pharmaceuticals. In Madras in India the scarcity of heroin and easy availability of pharmaceutical substitutes such as buprenorphine (Temgesic) was mainly responsible for the shift from heroin smoking to injection of pharmaceuticals.[38] Ironically buprenorphine has just been added to the WHO's global list of 'essential medicines', at the same time as it remains an illicit drug of choice for some drug users. Nearly 30 years ago, Joseph Westermeyer reported that after anti-opium laws had been passed in southeast Asia and Hong Kong opium smokers switched to heroin because it was more compact and easier to smuggle, with many smokers taking the cost-effective option and turning to injection.[39]

However, there are other drugs in Afghanistan that have the same double-edged nature so characteristic of the opiates, drugs that have been used medicinally and in a more controlled way for social purposes but have increasingly led to health-related, social and economic problems for many users during the conflict and chaos of the past few decades. Various preparations of cannabis are the most obvious.

# 10
# Hashish and *Hakims*

As the National Institute of Mental Health researchers found in the late 1960s, where a drug has a strong associated culture people can consume lots of it without harming themselves. It's when drugs are traded impersonally for profit that they are likely to become lethal.[1]

A son who takes hashish is no son, and the value of two opium eaters is one penny.[2]

Cannabis has been erroneously classified as a narcotic, as a sedative and most recently as an hallucinogen. While the cannabinoids do possess hallucinogenic properties, together with stimulant and sedative effects, they in fact represent a unique class of pharmaceutical compounds.[3]

While there has been much debate about the origins of the cannabis plant, the historical centre for the production of sieved hashish was the central Asian region of Turkestan, stretching from western China to modern Turkmenistan and down through the area that now constitutes Afghanistan. In this part of the world a hashish-making tradition stretches back possibly several thousand years to the time of the ancient Scythians and Persians. It is claimed that 'Afghanistan has the oldest hashish culture still in existence today.'[4] The legend of *Baba Ku* who was sent to earth by God to introduce the euphoriant and medical properties of the cannabis plant and the pleasures of hashish smoking to Afghans and other regional dwellers suggests that this is indeed an ancient drug culture. While over the past century hashish has increasingly become a mass-produced commodity in a burgeoning regional and international trade, Afghanistan 'figures more prominently than any other nation in the tradition of high-quality hashish-making', although this has declined somewhat over recent years.[5]

## CANNABIS CULTIVATION

The cannabis currently cultivated in Afghanistan used to produce hashish is not the more common *Cannabis sativa* but strains of its sister plant *Cannabis indica*, claimed by Lamarck in 1783 as the more intoxicating form of the plant, although no chemical studies had been carried out to determine this at the time. While *Cannabis sativa* is loosely branched and tall, growing up to as much as 15 feet, *Cannabis indica* is a different form of the plant that is usually very densely branched, conical or pyramidal in shape, more broad-leafed and usually no more than three to five feet tall.[6] In the 1950s there were reports of *Cannabis sativa*, called *bhang-dona* by farmers, being cultivated in northern Afghanistan for the medicinal properties of its seeds, while *Cannabis indica* was also grown for hashish production. Other reports from the same period suggest that wild cannabis plants from *sativa* strains were traditionally picked by Afghan *Kuchis* for medicinal use and to process into hashish for sale as part of their seasonal income. When in the 1970s Afghan hashish production rapidly expanded as a result of western market pressures, settled cannabis farmers started to pick the wild cannabis plants to supplement their cultivated crop, thus angering the nomadic *Kuchis* and leading to some violent clashes.

In the 1920s the respected Russian plant explorer Vavilov reported that *Cannabis indica* grew wild along the Kunar river valley in the northeast of the country, while it was *Cannabis sativa* that was cultivated for hashish production near Herat and in Faisabad in Badakhshan. Certainly I have observed *Cannabis sativa* being cultivated for home use in private gardens in Faisabad, as well as the cultivation of datura plants. It has been argued that *Cannabis indica* was considered only as a wild species of the plant up until the 1930s when hashish production was banned in Chinese Turkestan and hashish makers were forced to flee south through the Kunar river valley to Mazar-i-Sharif where they were re-united with their tribesmen who had moved there after the Russian invasion of Turkestan in 1868. During this migration wild *Cannabis indica* seeds were collected and then hybridised with the *Cannabis sativa* cultivated by the resident farmers of northern Afghanistan. Assuming a continuing tradition of mixing different strains of cannabis, 'This type of interbreeding would account for both the vigor and extreme variability which were characteristic of hashish cultivars brought from Afghanistan in modern times.'[7]

Apart from smuggling hashish back to the west, young travellers in the late 1960s and early 1970s also returned with Afghan cannabis seeds that were then hybridised with cannabis varieties from countries like Mexico, Colombia and Thailand, producing powerful strains that eventually formed 'the basic building blocks of modern sinsemilla cultivars'.[8] In other words, much of the extremely potent commercial and homegrown cannabis currently enjoying a market boom in the west has been derived from Afghan strains of the plant. The group credited with originally bringing these strains to the US over 30 years ago was the Brotherhood of Eternal Love, an American drug-smuggling syndicate composed of 'a pseudo-religious group of visionaries, bikers and smugglers' that also manufactured and distributed LSD. Apart from bringing Afghan cannabis seeds to the west they also smuggled large quantities of hashish and hashish oil. The prototype for producing the latter was developed in California in 1970 by a group member called Bobby Andrist who exported the production techniques to Afghanistan where the oil was made on site. Known as honey oil, this was an extremely potent and highly refined form of liquid cannabis that was translucent and golden coloured and sold wholesale in the US for $10,000 a litre.[9] Just as heroin provides a greater value and profit-to-size ratio than opium for smugglers, so hashish oil was a better commodity than hashish for smuggling to the west from Afghanistan.

Meanwhile, over 10,000 miles away from Afghanistan in western Canada the illicit cannabis cultivation industry has recently emerged as the country's most valuable agricultural product, bigger than cattle, timber or wheat. This cannabis, 'boosted by custom nutrients, high intensity metal halide lights and 20 years of breeding', is reputed to be five times as potent as 1970s cannabis sold in the US, although this would not be true of the more potent Colombian and Mexican strains found then. The industry, with an estimated $5 billion wholesale value, has also boosted local economies with sales of air filters and lighting systems and employment for specialised trimmers (reminiscent of Afghanistan's itinerant opium lancers) and cannabis 'growth consultants' remunerated at around $40 per hour.[10] Ironically, this current globalisation of the commercial cannabis market has been due in no small part to the strength and potency of Afghan cannabis and the powerful hybrids derived from its seeds.

Traditionally the cultivation of cannabis and production of hashish in Afghanistan has been a skilled occupation. While many farmers grew small amounts of cannabis for their own use along with their other crops, some families focused almost solely on its cultivation and became renowned specialists, producing the very-best-quality hashish. Until 1973 it was largely a trouble-free occupation, apart from the vagaries of the extreme climate and a shortage of water for the thirsty cannabis plant. It has been claimed that during 1969 and

1970, the government, under official orders from King Zahir Shah, encouraged farmers to use chemical fertilisers to increase production of hashish for export, although some rejected this innovation as the overuse of such fertilisers could acidify the soil and damage crops. However, in 1973, mainly due to pressure from the US, who had given the Afghan government a $47 million grant to stop hashish and opium production, extreme measures were taken to eradicate the cannabis crop in some parts of the country.

When a royal decree making the cultivation of cannabis and production of hashish illegal was posted by the government to village *shuras*, it was largely ignored by families who had grown cannabis for generations, an activity seemingly endorsed by the King only a few years earlier:

Almost all families went ahead and sowed their *Cannabis* crop as always. During July and August, Afghan police stormed into the countryside surrounding Mazar-i-Sharif. Truckloads of police burned *Cannabis* fields, destroyed farmer's homes, threatened and intimidated their families, severely beat field workers and made many arrests.[11]

While this resulted in almost all the cannabis crop in northern Afghanistan being eradicated that year, cultivation resumed the next year after King Zahir Shah had been deposed by his first cousin and brother-in-law Mohammad Daoud. During the rest of the 1970s cannabis cultivation continued apace, although it has been reported that some farmers from the north relocated south to areas around Paktia and Qandahar provinces and that cannabis farms moved further from main roads and inhabited areas to remote farms and inside walled compounds.[12] This process continued after the Soviet invasion in 1979 with areas under cannabis cultivation having to change from year to year to avoid the ongoing fighting.

In the mid-1990s cannabis cultivation was strictly forbidden by the Taliban, as was the production, sale and consumption of hashish, the latter perceived as a serious social vice. As many of the Taliban leaders came from the Qandahar area, they would have been more than familiar with the use of hashish, as this is an area of Afghanistan, along with Mazar-i-Sharif in the north, still famous for its production and consumption of hashish. Other areas of the country now grow cannabis in smaller quantities with one of the more reputedly powerful forms of hashish being produced in mountainous Azro district in Logar province less than 100 km to the southeast of Kabul. In mid-2004 when voters were being registered in Azro for the presidential election the local *shura* would only allow officials into the area if they promised not to damage or destroy the cannabis crop. In 2005, for the first time, UNODC reported on the existence of cannabis cultivation in villages surveyed as part of their assessment of opium cultivation. Seventeen of the country's 34 provinces reported cannabis cultivation although no information was given as to the extent.[13]

However, in a country with a fragile ecosystem, areas of commercial cannabis cultivation have been blamed for contributing to land degradation. One report claimed that cannabis cultivation has had a devastating effect on water supplies, particularly around Mazar-i-Sharif, thus exacerbating the effects of the severe drought. Cannabis growers in the mountains siphoned off water from those few rivers still with water. In the plains, farmers who were rich enough dug boreholes up to 100 m deep to reach the water table, irrigating their cannabis fields and drying up the wells in surrounding villages at the same time. The report claimed that these tactics have contributed to the desertification of areas of north Afghanistan, turning them into dustbowls. A village half an hour to the north of Mazar-i-Sharif is described in the following terms: 'The desert is swallowing Deh Naw whole. Five meter high sand dunes have crashed over the village's mud walls like desiccated tidal waves, burying houses, blocking streets and suffocating the vines and the mulberry, fig and pomegranate trees that once blossomed here.'[14]

## PRODUCTION OF HASHISH

In his definitive work *Hashish!*, Robert Connell Clarke recounts how traditional methods used to produce Afghan hashish from mature cannabis plants have had to change and modernise because of increased market demand from the west. This has also led to a lowering of quality and potency of export hashish. One of the oldest methods used was to pile cannabis flowers on a large clean long-pile carpet that was then rolled up tight and danced on, with an option of placing another carpet pile-down on the bottom carpet before rolling. This process released resin from the flowers that easily stuck to the carpet pile. After unrolling the carpet and removing the plant debris, the carpet was then turned upside down over a piece of thin cloth and beaten to release the resin powder. This powder was then further refined by passing it through a sieve of cloth or metal mesh stretched on a rigid wooden hoop or frame. As with opium, increased refining removes impurities and increases the potency of the drug. Processing the cannabis plant for hashish production is a skilled business:

Taking care to sieve with the correct mesh size, using only a shaking action, and applying no hand pressure to force the resin glands through the sieve, are the two most important considerations when making high quality hashish. Resieving of this carefully collected resin produces *shirac*, the purest and most potent quality of hashish.[15]

Even to produce good-quality hashish this resieving process would have to take place several times.

The light-brown crumbly powder collected from the sieving process is referred to as *girda* that can then be processed into hashish in different ways. While constant kneading by hand is said to produce the best-quality hashish, it is very time-consuming. Another method is to put the *girda* in a goatskin laid on the ground for people to walk over and the sun to heat (the goatskin can also be buried for several years, reputedly increasing potency). When it has 'eaten enough sun' the *girda* is then kneaded or 'cooked' by hand until it becomes black and pliable. Although heat can be applied at this stage, the best *girda* is oily enough not to need a flame. In the 1970s, a similar method for producing best quality hashish was described by an Afridi hashish producer in NWFP in Pakistan to Howard Marks, the notorious English drug smuggler:

When plant first flowers, top is cut and chopped and put into white goatskin in ground. This is first quality but amount is very small. Second flower is cut and put into brown goatskin. This is second quality and amount is much bigger. Third flower is cut and put into black goatskin. When we make hashish we use many bags third quality, some second, and one or two first. Price of first quality is maybe one hundred times that of third quality.[16]

Later Marks commented that 'I wondered which quality went into skins that were both black and white', and described the hashish-making process that he had witnessed in some detail:

The scaffolds were in fact very basic six-feet high cantilevers. On one end of the seesaw was a large, almost perfectly spherical boulder, which was held up about ten feet above the ground by the weight of two Afridi tribesmen holding down the seesaw's other end. Directly underneath the threatening boulder was a large hole in which a fire raged. Almost covering the hole was an enormous cooking pan, like that used to prepare a giant paella. The pan was filled with the contents of the goatskins. Every ten seconds, the two Afridi tribesmen would release the end of the cantilever. The boulder came crashing down on the paella pan, pulverising the resinous chopped plant tops, and was then quickly returned to its mid-air vantage position. Slowly, but noticeably, the pan became full of a piping hot, dark brown goo. This change in molecular structure enabled the plant's full psychoactive potential to be realised. Smoking the stuff straight out of a goatskin didn't work. When the goo became thin enough, it was placed in wooden moulds, each shaped to hold approximately half a kilo.[17]

Marks also reported that with the Soviet invasion of 1980, the supply of Afghan hashish began to dry up and he had to buy Pakistani hashish instead. Some of the refugees who fled into Pakistan were experienced cannabis cultivators and harvesters who now utilised their traditional techniques of hashish production in Pakistan, producing large quantities of high-grade hashish known in the west as 'border hash'.[18]

In Europe poor-quality Moroccan hashish has been referred to as 'soap bar' because it resembles a bar of a particular brand of soap. It may also have been adulterated with wax so that it will burn more easily and impress prospective buyers.[19] Surprisingly, given the supposed quality of hashish produced, similar tactics of adulteration have also been reported in Afghanistan. In late 2002 there was a drug burning ceremony on an open piece of wasteland outside the national stadium in Kabul. The international media were there in force, a group of footballers were practicing nearby, small children were trying to sell bottles of dirty water to the thirsty onlookers and the local police were nominally in charge of proceedings. A bonfire-sized pile of bags of heroin, huge cakes of raw opium and neatly packaged blocks of hashish was doused with five gallons of diesel fuel by a man standing like a Guy Fawkes effigy on top of the bonfire. He then quickly leapt off, threw on a match and with an almighty 'whoosh' the bonfire erupted in a cloud of black acrid smoke, scattering the crowd who had drawn ever closer to it. After a while the black smoke burned off and thick clouds of white smoke wafted downwind alerting those of us with any doubts that at least hashish was being burned. The opium ran like a black oily river into the sandy soil and the dubious heroin sizzled, bubbled and crackled like burning plastic.

Before the match was applied several people had very closely examined the contents of the bonfire, one policeman stuffing two blocks of hashish into the inside pockets of his black leather coat and another taking away a couple of the 50 or so bottles of confiscated Russian vodka that ringed the bonfire and that had later exploded with the intense heat. Journalists split and crumbled blocks of hashish and opium and examined the contents. The hashish was expertly vacuum-packed in slabs of what purported to be British supermarket-branded 'Dried Apricots', a sure sign that this was export-quality hashish. One of my colleagues broke off two lumps of the black resinous hashish and put them in his pocket, not that anybody minded, as most of the journalists were doing the same thing. These samples were then given to two of his hashish-using friends to voluntarily test and it was all they could do to hide their disappointment that no matter how much of it they smoked they couldn't get much of an effect. How could this be? The hashish looked, felt and smelled like good-quality hashish yet was practically inert in effect. The explanation was provided by an Afghan friend who explained that it was not uncommon for old or poor-quality hashish to be reconstituted for sale by mixing 1 kg of fresh hashish with 5 kg or more of the old stuff, enough to give it the proper elasticity and smell, if not the potency.

By the end of 2003 such public drug burnings were much more strictly controlled and policed due mainly to the UK-trained City Gates Police Team, set up to intercept consignments of drugs being trafficked through the roads leading in and out of Kabul. At one subsequent drug burning the only person allowed within 10 m of the bonfire, ringed by the armed police team members, was a masked US soldier taking samples of the drugs presumably for analysis back in the US: at that time Afghanistan still didn't have adequate drug-testing equipment. Meanwhile, adulterated hashish production continues unabated in Afghanistan with a wide range of substances being used to bind inferior cannabis resin powder of low purity and even lower potency. Such additives have included finely powdered sand, candle wax, coconut oil, turpentine, *ghee* (clarified butter), pine tar, henna powder, vegetable lard, mulberry sap and boiled down pomegranate syrup.[20]

## EFFECTS AND USES OF HASHISH

While no conclusive evidence exists, qualities fluctuate in a largely unregulated market and the effects of cannabis and its derivative hashish are probably more subjective than with any other drug. It has been claimed that 'Afghanistan hashish is supposed to cause euphoria exclusively, while Lebanese hashish may on occasion induce depression.'[21] Indeed, the effects of cannabis and its various preparations are complicated and unpredictable which is why it has been classified along with other hallucinogenic drugs as psycho-dysleptic: a substance that changes mood and alters the mind but not in a predictable fashion.[22] This was certainly the case for one Afghan man from Sayed Karam district in Paktia province who recounted the following story:

About thirty years ago I had a job in Qandahar province. During the holidays I smoked a chillum full of very strong hashish then decided to go back to my room. On the way there was a small pipe of water flowing over a concrete floor. I thought it was a big flood and stopped there, although I was surprised how easily other people could cross. After quite a long time and watching many people cross, I rolled up my trousers, took off my shoes and slowly tried to walk across the floodwaters. I was very happy that I was able to do this. When I got back to my house my friends wanted to take me to the hospital, but I said that I just needed to rest. Later my friends told me that I had slept for eighteen hours. After that experience I decided not to use hashish again.[23]

Although, like alcohol, its effects may sometimes be unpredictable, especially for the novice user, one of the reasons why cannabis (and its various preparations) has become such a popular global drug is because it can produce different effects, although not all of them always welcome, for different people. It is also claimed that fat-soluble cannabis suppresses its own withdrawal syndrome due to the slow elimination of THC that makes it a less addictive substance than water-soluble drugs like opium and heroin.

In Afghanistan, cannabis is also known as *bothae faqir* (the hermit's plant) in recognition that it has traditionally been used by Sufi *faqirs*, hermits and less orthodox mullahs, 'with the intention of obtaining religious insight, contact with eternity'.[24] By all accounts, hashish has traditionally been used in most areas of Afghanistan and has been perceived as a venial rather than mortal sin. Like the traditional village drunk in western culture, the hashish 'addict', or *charasi*, is often treated with tolerant scorn and even affection, although some people would not want to be associated with such a person. Many Afghans I have spoken to do not even consider hashish a drug any more, one person saying: 'In your culture you have alcohol, in Afghanistan hashish is our wine.' On the other hand there is a saying in Pashto, believed to originate from Pashtoon women, *charasi sari na sari*, meaning 'The man who smokes hashish is no man.'

Traditionally there has been a widely held belief that cannabis is a cause of insanity, leading many people to avoid it altogether.

Certainly in the ten years between 1960 and 1969, 13 per cent of all patients admitted to the only mental health hospital in the country situated in Kabul were cited as cases of 'pure hashish intoxication', although the psychiatrist in charge also acknowledged that 'There are a lot of chronic or part-time hashish abusers who never need any psychiatric treatment nor show any abnormal or antisocial behaviour.' This psychiatrist personally knew 'a number of these people who have been abusing hashish for more than ten or fifteen years with no ill effect on their jobs or social interaction'.[25] Several Afghans I have talked to recall that during their childhood there was a 'famous *charasi*' living in their village, typically an older man, who was given respect in the community. For some there is still a famous *charasi* living in their village. Different groups in Afghan society, however, have used hashish for different purposes.

The AMRC in Peshawar has a full archive of all film and radio reports produced during the war against the Soviets. One section of film shows a group of *mujahideen* standing in a high-walled compound clustered around a tall straight-stemmed *chillum* smoking hashish. At times it is difficult to see what is happening because of the dense clouds of white billowing hashish smoke generated by the *mujahideen* who seem to have lungs the size of bellows. After they have finished smoking, coughing and spluttering, one by one they slip out of the compound with their AK-47s. Almost immediately the sound of gunfire can be heard, the enemy engaged.

Groups of men with guns still consume hashish in Afghanistan. In 2002, a journalist reporting from Khost in Paktika province where US Special Forces and Afghan government soldiers were hunting al-Qaeda and Taliban, stated that

The men who loiter in the streets carry weapons ranging from Kalashnikovs to rocket propelled grenades. Most of them wear eyeliner, paint their nails deep maroon, and place roses in their hair. It's a sign of a mujahed or holy warrior...the only lodging in town—the Khost Guest House—is manned 24 hours a day by holy warriors strung out on hashish.[26]

### METHODS AND PATTERNS OF CONSUMPTION

Although smoking hashish in a long-stemmed waterpipe or *chillum* has traditionally been the main method of consumption in Afghanistan, rolling hashish into a cigarette has become more common as it is easier, less conspicuous and more mobile than a *chillum*. Hashish is also eaten in the form of *majun,* and sometimes simply sprinkled on food such as a stew or soup, either at the cooking stage or later, as a form of 'salt' or psychoactive condiment. Various other methods that convert apples, plastic bottles or other objects into pipes have also been reported, as has using the 'chasing the dragon' method of smoking, more commonly used for taking heroin. It has been noted that 'This common method of use could be a possible facilitating factor in any later move from hashish use to opium and/or heroin use.'[27]

It is difficult to ascertain individual consumption rates of hashish in Afghanistan as the drug is typically shared with others in a *chillum* or hashish-filled cigarette. Apart from anything else, users report their daily consumption rates in units such as *tolas, paltas,* grams and 'beans' that refer to different weights depending on which part of the country they are measured in. This also applies to measurements of quantities of other drugs. However, there is little doubt, partly because it is relatively cheap and easily available, that large quantities of hashish are consumed by many Afghan users compared to their western counterparts. Afghans seeking treatment in Peshawar self-reported an average daily consumption rate of 16.8 g. While this consumption rate may have been exaggerated by drug users seeking access to treatment and this is likely to refer to the daily amount shared with others, by any standards this is an excessive consumption rate that can lead to a wide range of problems for some users and their families. It has also been suggested that traditionally a *malang,* an Islamic holyman, and his group of followers could smoke 10–15 pipes a day each filled with at least 10 g of hashish, giving an individual daily consumption rate of somewhere between 7 g and 22 g.[28] At the same time, it is unlikely that the majority of Afghanistan's more moderate hashish users would consume more than a daily average of 2–4 g.

Apart from hashish smoke exacerbating endemic respiratory problems like bronchitis, tuberculosis and pneumonia, spending even $5 a month on hashish when a family's monthly income is only $25 can impose severe financial hardship on other family members—it can mean the difference between a child having enough to eat or going without. In February 2002 a report by the WFP noted that money spent on drugs like hashish was a source of household debt that could be 'devastating for households struggling to maintain basic food security'.[29] Ironically the report also noted that hashish production and consumption was not of concern to the authorities in Herat and

Qandahar, but that in Kabul 'there is a growing market for hashish, driven by demand from the ISAF forces', in this case presumably for recreational purposes and not as a precursor to battle.

War-related mental health problems among users can be exacerbated by the habitual use of hashish, as with other psychoactive substances. On the other hand, many users report taking the drug on an occasional recreational basis and experience few problems as a result. Nearly 50 per cent of a group of hashish users interviewed in Kabul in 2003 had started to use hashish 'for enjoyment such as going to parties with friends or to watch films', while others had started either because they had been encouraged by friends or to help them overcome feelings of sorrow and sadness.[30] In a study conducted in 2001 in four districts in rural eastern Afghanistan, it was estimated that nearly 50 per cent of households had a hashish user, although it was likely that most of these households would have more than one user, and that 15–25 per cent of males used hashish regularly.[31] Most hashish users interviewed in the study claimed that they started taking hashish because they had been influenced by others such as friends, fathers or *mujahideen* commanders during the fighting against the Soviets. Of particular concern to key informants like teachers, health workers and local authorities was the increasing number of young men who had started to use hashish recreationally to alleviate boredom and unemployment but ran the risk of ending up as heavy habitual users with related health and socioeconomic problems.

Certainly traditional patterns of hashish smoking have begun to break down under the strain of the social upheavals of the past few decades. The idealised picture of groups of turbaned men sitting peacefully in a *chai khana* in downtown Mazar-i-Sharif sharing and enjoying *chillums* of hashish together, or with young western travellers, now begins to look faded. An Afghan doctor friend suggests that hashish use is now much more common and that any stigma associated with it has all but gone. 'Nobody is bothered about it any more, it is seen like tobacco.' Going on a Friday afternoon picnic after Juma prayers to the Baba Wali shrine in the mountains just north of Qandahar in the summer of 2005, the same doctor noted that most of the many men in the picnic area were smoking hashish and the air hung heavy with its pungent fumes.

While hashish is still seen primarily as a 'male' drug, there are also increasing reports of women using it, often as part of their polydrug use. Out of 50 Afghan refugee women interviewed about their drug taking, 15 said that they had taken hashish mainly to relieve the physical pains of toothache, backache or headache and the emotional pain caused by depression and sadness. One woman said:

I started to use hashish two years ago in Kabul. I used to eat it with cooked meat then I started to smoke it in a cigarette. One of my friends advised me to take hashish. It was after my husband was killed and I became depressed. I liked the effects very much so I continued to use it.[32]

At the same time, these women attributed respiratory problems, headaches, drowsiness and memory loss to their use of hashish.

Such use of cannabis preparations like hashish as forms of self-medication have been common in traditional medicine throughout south Asia where 'It was used as an analgesic and sedative and as a household remedy for many conditions in rural areas.'[33] A report from nineteenth-century India claimed that 'Cannabis indica must be looked upon as one of the most important drugs of India Materia Medica.' At the time cannabis preparations were used for a wide range of medical conditions including colds, brain fevers, convulsions, headache, hysteria, sciatica and tetanus.[34] This was also mirrored in some western countries where cannabis preparations were seen as a panacea for many ailments before they were outlawed during the 1930s. An advertisement by the US pharmaceutical company Eli Lilly in 1913 provided the following list of 'action and uses' for what was referred to as 'Cannabis Americana, or American grown Cannabis Sativa':

Not poisonous according to best authorities, though formerly so regarded. Antispasmodic, analgesic, anesthetic, narcotic, aphrodisiac. Specially recommended in spasmodic and painful affections; for preventing rather than arresting migraine; almost a specific in that form of insanity peculiar to women, caused by mental worry or moral shock. It is the best hypnotic in delirium tremens. Its anodyne powder is marked in chronic metritis and dysmenorrhea; Used with excellent results in habitués of opium, chloral [hydrate] or cocaine. In hysterical cases not calmed by chloral or opium it acts especially well.[35]

Apart from their euphoriant and intoxicating properties, in south central Asia and many other parts of the developing world, hashish and other cannabis preparations have for centuries had the reputation of having medicinal properties and have been used in various lotions, potions and medicines made by traditional healers and hakims. In the west there is still much debate about the medicinal properties of the illegal cannabis plant, although traditional pharmacopoeias certainly extol the positive qualities of the plant. Recent scientific research evidence shows that, among other medical uses, it is clinically useful for treating some symptoms related to multiple sclerosis and effective for reducing intraocular pressure in glaucoma.[36] One study of multiple sclerosis sufferers suggests that their subjective 'reports of pain relief are consistent with previous suggestions that cannabis may be an effective analgesic and could play a more specific role than simple painkillers in managing chronic nervous system pain'.[37] In 1999 the US government's own Institute of Medicine report on medical uses of cannabis indicated that available data showed a potential therapeutic value for pain relief, appetite stimulation and control of nausea and vomiting, for example.[38]

## HAKIMS

Hashish is reputedly one of the ingredients found in preparations made by *hakims* (practitioners of herbal medicine) in Afghanistan and neighbouring countries, although there are many different types of *hakim* to be found throughout south Asia. A report from Pakistan states that many *hakims* now use steroids and veterinary drugs in their preparations but that people are still attracted to such 'quacks' because they charge much lower fees than medical doctors.[39] Genuine modern-day *hakims* derive their medical practice from Unani medicine, first developed by Greeks such as Hippocrates around 500 BC and later spread throughout the Roman Empire. After the fall of the Roman Empire, Unani medicine declined but later re-emerged in Persia where Muslim physicians further developed its principles and translated its texts into Arabic. The founder of Unani medicine is generally recognised as *Hakim* Abu Ali al-Husayn Abd Allah Ibn Sina, better known in the west as Avicenna, who was born in AD 98 in Bokhara, then part of Afghanistan. In the thirteenth century Unani medicine spread to India and other parts of the region.

Currently there are several colleges of Unani medicine in India and Pakistan that provide professional training to *hakims* and award diplomas certifying them to practice. Traditionally a *hakim* would start training at the age of six or seven and only start to practice alone after a period of around 25–30 years studying the complexities of the Unani system of medicine, including the preparation of medicines. The distinction between food and drugs is often blurred in Unani medicine and a substance like sugar or honey is considered to be a potent narcotic medicine. It has even been claimed that 'The *Hakims* of Afghanistan to this day keep sugar under lock and key.'[40] Although sugar hoarding has not been reported by any of the *hakims* I have spoken to, they have all cited honey as a key ingredient in many of their paste-like preparations.

Like other traditional healers, *hakims* have used a wide range of natural ingredients in their medicinal preparations including precious stones, plant material and products derived from animals. The healing of human diseases using animal parts has been described as zootherapy, with ninth-century Muslim physicians describing the medical use of several animals in the area now constituting Iran and Iraq, including camel, dog, horse, rhino, scorpion, snake and wolf. In the area known as the Levant, the land of Israel and parts of present-day Jordan, Lebanon and Syria, seven major products derived from animals have been used in traditional medicine, namely honey, wax, adder, beaver testicles, musk oil, coral and ambergris.[41] However, as the moral stance of modern societies has changed, there has been increasingly limited use of materials of animal origin, such as mummified corpses, silkworm, goat products, stinkbug, scarabees, snail, scorpion and triton, for medical purposes.[42]

## AFGHAN *HAKIMS*

*Hakims* in Afghanistan, as well as herbalists who practice orally-transmitted folk medicine, use many different types of ingredient in their various preparations. These include 215 medicinal plants, 29 per cent of them imported from other countries, identified by ethnobotanists.[43] Psychoactive plants are included in their list: cannabis is categorised as a narcotic; opium as an antitussive, sedative and narcotic; and Datura (*Datura stramonium*, or thorn apple) as a spasmolytic, anti-asthmatic, aphrodisiac and toxic.

One *hakim* from Herat reported that he boiled Datura seeds in water and gave the resultant 'tea', mixed with other ingredients, to opium and heroin addicts for a period of one week to treat their addiction. The same mixture was also given to patients with mild mental disturbances so that they could have 'a calm mind'. The *hakim* also warned that if too much Datura was taken the patient could die, so the dose had to be strictly regulated (for a detailed account of the uses and effects of Datura see Chapter 12). What became clear in talking to this *hakim* was that there are several different types of preparations called *majun* and *burshesha,* some used for purposes of intoxication but most used for medicinal purposes. There is another mixture referred to as *mofarah*, a word derived from Arabic meaning 'that which gives enjoyment or pleasure'. The original *majun* prepared, according to the Herati *hakim*, from Avicenna's original principles, was primarily intended to increase sexual potency and to induce mental calmness. The many ingredients blended with honey into a thick paste included pistachios, almonds, walnuts, dates, rose petals, other flower petals, the bark of a specific type of tree, the brain of a particular bird, the brain of a cockerel, a ram's testicles and flakes of gold, silver, lapis lazuli and other precious stones. For added potency a dried ram's penis could also be added, as could hashish and/or opium if a degree of intoxication was desired. This very expensive type of *majun* is now seldom prepared, principally because it is difficult to find all the ingredients. Other cheaper types are prepared mainly with hashish and opium and can be used for different purposes from suppressing a cough to prolonging male ejaculation. As *burshesha* literally means 'evening paste' this suggests that it is also used primarily for increasing male sexual potency and to enhance sexual performance, or as a sedative to aid sleep. In Hesarak district of Nangarhar province it was reported that *hakims* prepared various types of *burshesha*, including one sold for less than $1 for a 25 g box used for 'chest problems and body pains'. Allegedly there were three main forms of *burshesha* found in Nangarhar, 'Arabic', 'Indian' and 'Afghan', each containing different types and amounts of ingredients, and each reflecting a different interpretation of Avicenna's original recipe.

An Afghan *hakim* sitting with several assistants in his busy shop in the bazaar of the Old City in Peshawar, surrounded by hundreds of jars and faded tins, said that the *burshesha* he made was principally used as an intoxicant and to enhance sexual performance. It contained eight ingredients, including opium, honey, saffron and black pepper. The *majun* that he made, and described as 'Unani Viagra', was explicitly for sexual potency and included hashish, nutmeg, honey, cannabis leaves, cloves, saffron and other plants with mild psychoactive properties imported from Africa. It could be bought as a ready-made paste or in powder form in red and white capsules, giving it the appearance of a pharmaceutical drug. He also recounted that while Datura was 'a magic plant' and could be used to treat many illnesses, it was also very poisonous and if more than the prescribed dose was taken it could result in death. The seeds made into a paste could be applied to boils and were an ingredient in a poultice used for piles in the anus. Datura preparations were also good for sciatica, while the leaves of the plant smoked in a *chillum* would provide relief for asthma sufferers. Scorpions were also used in Unani medicine, although he pointed out that this was only the black scorpion that 'lies under the earth all year and only comes out for one month during the monsoon.' Preparations made from the scorpion included extracted oil that can be rubbed into the skin for paralysis, ash from roasted scorpions mixed with other ingredients and ingested for kidney stones and urinary problems, and a form of *majun* containing honey and other ingredients eaten for kidney stones and other ailments. In 2000, medical researchers from the University of California synthesised a chemical called TRAM-34 based on the characteristics of scorpion venom that could be used to treat disorders like lupus, rheumatoid arthritis and multiple sclerosis.[44]

Another *hakim*, a young Sikh, in the Hayatabad area of Peshawar presented a more professional appearance with his clean white doctor's coat, his framed college diplomas on the wall behind his desk, on which lay a stethoscope and other medical accoutrements and a small consulting room next to his office. He also confirmed that scorpion preparations were used for urinary tract infections, but 'very carefully' as they had toxic properties. This *hakim* bought scorpion oil wholesale from a company that processed it commercially. This company also prepared a form of *burshesha*, allegedly without opium, that had no intoxicating properties. Used mainly for flu and coughs, he nevertheless suggested that it could only be prescribed for five to ten days otherwise the user became dependent on it. He also maintained that *burshesha* made by *hakims* in the tribal areas outside Peshawar contained opium and was primarily used as an intoxicant. Some of the other herbs from India and Iran used in the preparation of *burshesha* also had intoxicating properties. While he claimed that many *hakims* were doing the job 'just for the business and the money', he came from a long line of *hakims* and said 'My heart is in it.'

A Pashtoon *hakim* with a shop in Jah de Maiwand in Kabul who had been trained by a Turkish *hakim* during the time he spent as a refugee in Eastern Europe said that *burshesha* could be used as a painkiller, an intoxicant or to increase male sexual potency. He also jokingly referred to this preparation as 'Afghan Viagra!' Like his fellow-*hakim* from Peshawar he had obviously been keeping abreast of the latest developments in the western pharmaceutical market. Apart from opium and Datura this *burshesha* contained other psychoactive substances among its 62 ingredients, including saffron and the dried testicles of a sea animal called a *saglahoo*, most likely a type of sea otter, imported from Saudi Arabia and other areas of the Middle East. He knew that opium was addictive so would only use it sparingly in his preparations and claimed he would never use hashish because it could lead to psychosis. He would also never use scorpions in his medicines because they could be harmful to health. Like his Sikh colleague from Hayatabad he stressed that 'I care about people's health more than making a profit.'

In such an unregulated and uncontrolled environment as Afghanistan, as well as in neighbouring countries, *hakims* can include any psychoactive substance in their preparations that they decide, as tradition dictates, or as their customers demand. While there are many 'quacks' in the business, there are also many knowledgeable, skilled and respected *hakims* that provide a valuable service for people who have no recourse to modern medicine or who prefer more tried and tested traditional methods to some of the more dubious pharmaceutical products of the modern world. Given the lack of knowledge and understanding of many people regarding the potential harms and risks associated with self-medication of pharmaceutical drugs such as tranquillisers and powerful analgesics, not to mention the risks involved in going to unaccredited or untrained medical 'doctors', it may sometimes be safer for Afghans to retain the services of a good *hakim*.

# 11
# Pharmaceuticals and Chemical Cocktails

In the case of both Afghanistan and refugee communities in Pakistan, there is substantial evidence that a wide range of pharmaceutical drugs is available over-the-counter, without a medical prescription, from 'pharmacies', other retail outlets and even roadside stalls. Many of these drugs are adulterated, spurious, outdated, unregistered and illicitly manufactured in Pakistan and India and then illegally imported into Afghanistan.[1]

Shifting patterns between licit and illicit drug markets have been an ongoing phenomenon in which the distinction between recreational use, self-medication, addiction, prescription or diversion is often more confusing than acknowledged.[2]

Drug safety and effectiveness depend, above all, not on molecular performance, but on the behaviour of pharmaceutical companies, government agencies and professional institutions—and the relationships between them and with users. The Pharmas [multinational pharmaceutical companies] now lead this triumvirate, even while fighting against the odds for their own survival. The Pharmas press their influence everywhere, often creating global conflict between trade and health needs.[3]

## CHEMICAL COCKTAILS

On the streets, parks and other public spaces of Peshawar, the dusty capital of NWFP in Pakistan situated about 50 km from the Afghan border, it is quite common to walk over the comatose bodies of drug users, both Pakistanis and Afghans. There is no way of calculating how many of these men have died over the years. There are no records kept, no official morbidity or mortality rates. It is estimated that over 65 per cent are homeless, often without family contact, and that many are buried or disposed of after they die with few records kept of their passing.

On a wide hard-packed dirt road in Hayatabad, the more Afghan western part of town, where in 2000 the UNDCP, in conjunction with the local NGO Dost Welfare, opened a drop-in daycare centre for street drug users, raised mounds of stones stand as testimony to the dead.

Such unfortunates are simply buried by their fellow users in the street where they live in culverts under the ground, where they buy and use their drugs and where many eventually die. Scavenging dogs disturb the shallow graves and human bones can be seen scattered among the debris littering the street. The daycare centre staff felt compelled to develop a service for these dead drug users by collecting the corpses, washing them, preparing them for a proper Muslim burial and trying to contact their families. This is one of the few treatment centres in the world that provides such a service for dead drug users.

In early 2002 there was a marked increase in deaths among this particular group of street users, those at the extreme end of the problem drug use continuum, due to their consumption of a type of street 'heroin' known as Hungary masala. After confirming that this was 'Hungary masala' and not 'hungry masala', it was ascertained that the main constituent of this particular chemical cocktail was phenobarbitol, imported from Hungary and sold for $135 per kilo. Phenobarbitol was also imported from China although it was deemed to be of inferior quality, costing only $65 per kilo. Other ingredients of the masala were chloral hydrate, heroin wash and *nilo toto*, the poison copper sulphate, added for a bit of colour. Heroin wash is the residue left after the lowest quality of heroin has been produced and copper sulphate is a toxic substance often used as a plant fertiliser. Phenobarbitol is a powerful long-acting barbiturate drug that 'can keep the individual sedated or sluggish for 12–24 hours'.[4] A particular problem with its use is barbiturate automatism, where the user may take a preparation of phenobarbitol, forgets that he has taken it, takes another dose, and then another. Such a cycle can easily be repeated to the point of overdose and possible death.

Chloral hydrate, a quick-acting hypnosedative, produces almost immediate drowsiness and within less than 30 minutes produces a sound sleep that can last up to eight hours. Mixed with alcohol, it constituted the original 'knockout drops' or 'Mickey Finn', has allegedly been used in a number of underworld killings in the US and is reputedly the Mafia's pharmaceutical weapon of choice. First introduced as a surgical anaesthetic in Germany in the 1860s, chloral hydrate was soon being prescribed for insomniacs instead of opium preparations. However, by the late nineteenth century doctors in Europe were warning against the misuse of 'chloral' as it was known, noting cases of accidental overdoses, suicides and dependency. Caution was urged in prescribing the drug: 'whereas many people who had become therapeutically addicted to opiates did not wreck their capacity to fulfil family duties or to work productively, chloral made its *habitués* dysfunctional at home and in workplaces'.[5] Chloral hydrate is still used today in several countries to treat sleep disorders, although its use declined with the introduction of the barbiturates.

Hungary masala was the last psychoactive refuge for those at the sharp street end of the problem drug use continuum. At less than $1 per gram it was cheap and its price never seemed to vary, compared with marked fluctuations in the street price of drugs like heroin and opium. It was also extremely dangerous, especially when sniffed through the nose, which could lead to rapid unconsciousness with all its attendant dangers. In June 2003 it was reported that in Dara Adamkhel district close to the Afghan border, a number of drug addicts died as a result of consuming 'a new sedative drug produced locally as a replacement for heroin', most likely some variant of Hungary masala.[6] Although the type of drug was not named, it was claimed that it had the effect of drying up the body of the user who died the day after taking it. The drug, reportedly produced from 'acid and other chemicals', was sold by shopkeepers in the bazaar in Darra Adamkhel, also noted for its 450 shops selling hashish as well as a wide range of spurious psychoactive pharmaceutical drugs. Darra Adamkhel is also notorious as the main bazaar in NWFP manufacturing copies of a wide range of weapons, including AK-47s, RPGs and pen guns.

By 2004, however, the new staff in the daycare centre in Hayatabad had never heard of Hungary masala, instead they referred to 'Indian masala', another chemical cocktail made with phenobarbitol or other pharmaceutical powders illegally imported from India instead of Hungary or China. Like its predecessor, this new masala was snorted directly through the nose or smoked using the chasing the dragon method inducing almost instant unconsciousness lasting up to an hour, although this was dose-dependent.

Chemical cocktails such as these various masalas constitute cheap poor quality drugs designed and produced solely for impoverished people who cannot afford better quality products. The street drug scene in Peshawar reminded me of an equally destitute people forced to consume poor people's drugs. A bare-breasted Basarwa (Bushman) woman in a settlement in the Kalahari Desert of Botswana, drunk and staggering at nine o'clock in the morning turned her head to spit Clubman Mint liquor into the mouth of the crying infant strapped tightly to her back. This was a scene typical of the cultural and social devastation in many Basarwa settlements caused by over-consumption of home-brewed or cheap proprietary brands of alcohol.[7] Clubman Mint, a sweet, sickly, 40 per cent proof liquor best described as 'alcoholic toothpaste', was one of the preferred drinks in the settlements as it was cheap and strong. Like the illicit drug masalas of Peshawar it was manufactured by unscrupulous, if in this case legal, groups and sold almost exclusively to the poor. The masalas were also redolent of a wide range of illicitly brewed and distilled alcoholic beverages in southern Africa frequently adulterated with additives such as methylated spirits, formalin, anti-malarial drugs, solvents and sulphuric acid from car batteries.[8] Translated names for these beverages such as 'kill me quick' and 'say goodbye to your mother' suggest, as with the drug masalas of Peshawar, 'a potency that goes beyond mere intoxication'.[9] Certainly there is no shortage of pharmaceutical drugs that can be substituted for any of the psychoactive ingredients of these masalas in the unlikely event that phenobarbitol and chloral hydrate become unavailable on the illicit global market in pharmaceutical drugs.

## 'BAD FOR YOU, GOOD FOR US'

The analgesic and anti-inflammatory drug Dipyrone (metamizole) is another heroin additive found in the region and also sold on its own over-the-counter in pharmacies and other retail outlets. It is a drug commonly used for pain relief by Afghan refugees living in Pakistan and is also reportedly used extensively in Afghanistan.[10] Dipyrone was banned in 1979 by the US FDA as being unfit for human consumption because it has been known to cause a serious adverse reaction called agranulocytosis. This reduces the number of disease-fighting white cells in the body, thus making the user more susceptible to life-threatening infections, all too common in an impoverished war-ravaged country like Afghanistan.

Dipyrone has also been banned in several western European countries, Canada, Australia and Japan, and its use has been severely restricted in ten other countries. Known colloquially as 'Mexican aspirin', it has made a comeback in Hispanic communities in the western US. The drug is illegally imported from Mexico or other Latin American countries where it is available in pharmacies without a prescription for just over $1 for 20 capsules. In 1989 the main manufacturer of metamizole, the German pharmaceutical company Hoechst, was severely criticised for designing and sponsoring secret clinical trials in Thailand where children as young as four years old were given the drug, in spite of clear international guidelines stating that 'Children should never be the subjects of research that might equally well be carried out on adults.'[11]

Of even more concern is the fact that in the US the use of Dipyrone as an 'unapproved prescription product' has also been prohibited for use in food-producing animals such as cows and sheep, although it can still be used as an injectable analgesic/antipyretic for horses, dogs and cats. In April 1996, the following statement was made by the chief of the US Milk Safety Branch:

Dipyrone is not approved for use in animals. Dairy farmers, veterinarians and consultants should be aware that the use of dipyrone is illegal drug use...If dipyrone is observed on a dairy farm during a rating or check rating inspection after 1 March 1997, it would be in violation of item 16r(i) of the Pasteurised Milk Ordinance.[12]

In Afghanistan, as well as other developing countries, Dipyrone is still available over the counter and sold in pharmacies for use by human beings. As a reporter in Pakistan stated:

While Hoechst actively promotes its brand Novalgin as relieving all kinds of pain or fever rapidly in all age groups, the dipyrone factor remains a well-kept secret at the cost of millions of users nationwide for whom the substance poses a serious health hazard. In developing countries like Pakistan, patients suffering from agranulocytosis have a very little chance of survival.[13]

More pertinently, as a doctor colleague questioned: 'Why are these drugs banned for you in the west but sold to us here in Afghanistan?'

However, the most commonly and consistently reported analgesic drug used throughout Afghanistan as a heroin substitute, or sometimes as a drug of choice, is pentazocine, marketed as Sosegon, available both in pill form and in liquid ampoule form ready for injecting. In early 2005 an ampoule of Sosegon in Kabul cost between 2 Afs and 20 Afs (less than $0.50) depending on where the drug originated. Although cheap at a maximum cost of less than half a dollar, a user injecting twice a day could spend up to $30 a month on the drug, a substantial sum if the family income is low. In some countries the use of pentazocine has been banned, and in the UK, 'Its prescription is now semi-officially discouraged owing to the extra stress it places on the heart and its tendency to create "hallucinations and thought disturbances".'[14] While Sosegon is used as a heroin substitute, it has also reportedly been used as a powerful analgesic by the physically disabled and war-injured who have been prescribed the drug for their injuries but who continue to purchase the drug over the counter once their prescription is finished and they have become dependent on it. A friend recounted that a Taliban commander who had an arm amputated while fighting against the Soviets had been given Sosegon as a painkiller, continuing to inject himself daily with the drug for several years. After an injury to his good arm he was unable to inject himself so asked one of his men to do it for him. The man refused as he didn't know how to give an injection, whereupon the commander threatened that he would shoot him if he didn't proceed. The man promptly gave the injection.

## ENTER THE BENZODIAZEPINES

While the main focus of the international community and Afghan drug control agencies has been on drugs like opium, morphine base and heroin being smuggled out of Afghanistan, until recently scant attention has been given to the fact that a wide range of psychoactive pharmaceutical drugs are illegally smuggled *into* the country with the potential to cause considerable harm and risk to its citizens. In September 2002 the INCB, referring to the provisions of the 1971 Convention on Psychotropic Substances, and following a request from the Chinese authorities, asked the Afghan government to verify the authenticity of an import order for 5,000 kg (five metric tonnes) of diazepam (Valium) from China. This order far exceeded the 76.6 kg of diazepam required for medical and scientific purposes already established by the Afghan authorities and had been placed by the Gula Khan Pharmaceutical Company with a permit signed and officially stamped by the secretaries of the 'Ministry of Health' and the 'Narcotics Control Board'. However, no such Board existed in Afghanistan and the 'Ministry of Health' was officially the Ministry of Public Health at the time. Such a fraudulent order for a large amount of the tranquilliser diazepam indicates the huge demand for tranquilliser drugs sold openly over the counter without a medical prescription. On the other hand, the diazepam may also have been intended for use as a psychoactive additive in the production of heroin. There have already been several seizures of heroin in Afghanistan adulterated with diazepam.

Valium was first marketed by the Swiss pharmaceutical company Hoffman-La Roche in 1963, along with Librium (chlordiazepoxide), as a drug that relieved anxiety and tension, produced a calming effect and induced sleep if taken at a higher dose. These were the first of many so-called 'minor' tranquillisers, collectively known as the benzodiazepines, developed to replace the barbiturates as the medical professions drug of choice for the relief of a wide range of conditions, particularly depression, anxiety and sleep disorders. By 1975 'an estimated 10–20% of "ambulatory adults" in the US and other western nations were regularly using benzos', and in the UK in 1979, 30 million prescriptions for benzodiazepines were given out by doctors. The many cases of dependence on these drugs were considered as examples of iatrogenic disease (one created and maintained by the medical profession) where doctors provided patients with repeat prescriptions for months or years on end without any further consultations taking place between patient and doctor.[15]

Initially these drugs, along with more than 15 others in the benzodiazepine category, were marketed as being non-addictive and having basically the same effects on the user. However, it soon became apparent from research evidence, although denied at first by the pharmaceutical companies, that the benzodiazepines did create dependence just as their predecessors the barbiturates had done. A clinical study of 13 patients given twice the recommended maximum dose of Valium over a six-week period revealed that six experienced withdrawal symptoms, including one who suffered convulsions. Generally there appeared to be a 'backlash effect' when someone stopped taking a benzodiazepine for insomnia, where the insomnia became worse than before the drug was started and where its continuous use became increasingly less effective with the development of tolerance.

It also became apparent from clinical experience that different benzodiazepines did have some different effects that could potentially lead to harmful consequences, apart from dependence, if the frequency of dosage was not clearly regulated and controlled. While all the benzodiazepines had a long half-life (that is the amount of time it takes to clear a drug from the body), Mogadon (nitrazepam) and Dalmane (flurazepam) both had an exceptionally long half-life which meant that they were cleared from the body very slowly with a resultant accumulation of the drug, particularly in the elderly:

As the body ages, it becomes less efficient, so drugs are broken down and excreted more slowly. With repeated dosing, levels of sleeping pills tend to build up and up until toxic levels are reached. That led to hangover effects the following day and increased the risk of accidents and falls. It also produced toxicity that mimicked states of senility and illness that were easily misdiagnosed.[16]

By contrast, Ativan (lorazepam), a drug readily available in Afghanistan, had a shorter half-life than other benzodiazepines so withdrawal symptoms were experienced sooner and harder and patients who had been under high-dose long-term treatment with the drug were advised to stop gradually to avoid severe withdrawal symptoms, including convulsions and muscle seizures. In 1991 one of the later benzodiazepines, Halcion (triazolam), by that time the best-selling hypnosedative in the world and used mainly as a sleeping pill, was taken off the market in the UK, the Netherlands and several other countries, although it is still available in the US and Canada and throughout south Asia. Because it had a short half-life of two to five hours and there was a recommended 24-hour period between doses some users experienced a 'between-dose withdrawal', basically a rebound anxiety effect. This included symptoms of agitation, amnesia and confused thinking. Like many of the other benzodiazepines it was a drug that had frequently been prescribed at higher doses and for longer periods than necessary. While Halcion is only recommended for short-term use, usually between seven and ten days, in a country like Canada in the mid-1990s the mean duration of its use was estimated at 1.7 years.

Generally there has been concern over the number of people who have become dependent on the benzodiazepines and that long-term use 'also carried risks of cognitive and mental impairment, amnesia and "emotional blunting"'.[17] Currently Afghans who use such drugs have no safeguards or legal redress against their documented side-effects and have little information available about safe dose levels, withdrawal syndromes or the potential for developing dependency.

## VALIUM: THE NEW PANACEA

Valium in particular is commonly used in Afghanistan as a panacea for a wide range of chronic mental health problems such as anxiety, depression, stress and insomnia. It is available almost everywhere except for some remote rural areas of the country where opium is still more likely to be considered the panacea for all ills, although in areas like Badakhshan this may now be changing. Like all other psychoactive pharmaceutical drugs Valium can easily be purchased from pharmacies and other retail outlets in the bazaar. In Kabul City alone there are nearly 5,000 pharmacies. Indeed, the sale of pharmaceuticals is a major commercial enterprise all over Afghanistan where a war-weary population self-medicates on a regular basis with prescription-only drugs sold openly over the counter, mostly without an understanding that the regular consumption of a drug like Valium can lead to dependency within a few months, if not weeks.

The manufacturer's leaflet 'Information for Health Professionals' that should be supplied with every blister pack of 20 x 5 mg tablets of Valium sold in Afghanistan states that while 'the physical dependence potential of benzodiazepines is low in persons taking recommended doses', after long-term treatment with the drug abrupt discontinuation can lead to withdrawal symptoms such as excitation, restlessness, tremors and, in rare cases, convulsions. Even if the leaflet is included, which is unlikely, many Afghans are illiterate and cannot understand the written instructions that are most likely written in the English language anyway. What the long-term effects are for those who self-medicate with Valium and take more than the recommended daily dose is not stated in the leaflet. An Afghan doctor recollected one of his patients from Badakhshan who told him that he had been taking 50 mg of Valium a day for several years, more than double the recommended maximum daily dose of 20 mg, without it adversely affecting him. The doctor did not believe him, whereupon the man swallowed five 5 mg tablets and walked off home to his village in the mountains several miles away.

At a drug conference in Scotland in March 2005 concern was expressed that illicit diazepam smuggled from Pakistan and India or illegally produced in the UK was the third most popular illicit drug after cannabis and heroin, with a detective sergeant from the Strathclyde police drug squad stating that heroin users were taking Valium tablets up to '10 at a time' to cope with the symptoms of heroin withdrawal.[18] It should be remembered that, unlike Scotland, in an illicit unregulated market like Afghanistan there is no guarantee of quality and such drugs are likely to be adulterated with inert substances or may be totally spurious.

A study of 50 Afghan refugee women polydrug users in Pakistan found that many were first introduced to drugs like Valium by visiting a doctor for a range of medical conditions such as body ache, sleep disorders, headaches and psychiatric problems. As the report says, 'Once they understood and had "learned" the effects of these drugs, they were able, if they wanted to or when they needed, to simply buy them to self-medicate whenever they chose.'[19] Others learned of these drugs through neighbours and friends. Many did not even know the name or type of drug they were taking, just that it was a 'red pill' or a 'white pill' that helped them to sleep better, and had no access to any accurate information about possible side-effects.

A qualitative study of women in southern Afghanistan conducted between 1998 and 2001 also showed that women increasingly turned to pharmaceutical drugs to relieve stress and tension, although they generally complained about the lack of good-quality medicines in the country. At the same time traditional home remedies were also used for many ailments: for example, drinking the blood of a rabbit for asthma or wearing a *taweez* (an amulet or talisman) from a mullah to cure and ward off illness. The study concluded that 'The use of strong prescription medicines for minor ailments is frightening. Shopkeepers of medical stores, rarely qualified pharmacists, recommend a range of medicines, often the most expensive, to make their business profitable and to ensure cure.'[20] In the district of Nawsad in northern Helmand province, where 50 women were interviewed, there was a particular problem with the misuse of pharmaceuticals; one woman reportedly self-medicating with 5 mg of Valium daily and another with 15 mg of Tranxene (dipotassium clorazepate). The study emphasised that

Pharmaceuticals have gained a new status in this area of Afghanistan. This is illustrated by the fact that in all of the households visited in Nawsad, medicines are hung on the wall in plastic bags on display like all the other wealth of the household: crockery, cutlery, photographs, pieces of embroidery, carpets, cushions, mattresses, and even shoes in one household.[21]

At the same time, as they had done for centuries, women also used 'poppy water' (opium extracted from poppy pods by boiling) to tranquillise babies or young children who were irritable or could not sleep. But, according to the study, with increasing awareness of healthcare and anti-opium messages now more prevalent, another problem had emerged. Women were beginning to self-medicate their children with antibiotics and codeine-based cough syrups as substitutes for traditional medical use of opium products, risking making children immune to the effects of antibiotics when prescribed by a doctor. In early 1999 a doctor working for the WHO in Afghanistan remarked that 'Codeine-based cough syrups are sold all along the roadside in Jalalabad and are being used indiscriminately.'[22]

In 2001 a Kabul pharmacist talking on BBC Radio claimed that '80 per cent of people with other ailments also ask for tranquillisers, this is about 60 to 65 people every day'.[23] During an in-depth study of problem drug use in Kabul, 80 (52 men and 28 women) out of 200 drug users reported having used pharmaceutical drugs. Their reasons for taking Valium, the most commonly reported drug used with almost 75 per cent of this group having taken it, was typically related to sleep disturbances and anxiety disorders caused by social upheaval and disruption related to war and conflict. The following heart-rending tale reported by one woman was not uncommon:

When I lost my second husband, so I had a lot of sorrow. My father-in-law beat me and said I was unlucky and didn't let me see my daughter who lived with my mother and was injured when a rocket crashed into her house. Because of these problems I started using these tablets (Valium). I used to take two a day, but now I just take one at night otherwise I can't sleep. I started taking them 10 years ago when a doctor prescribed them for me, but then I just started buying them in the bazaar.[24]

Other pharmaceutical drugs reportedly used by this group of drug users were Sosegon, Ativan, Mandrax (methaqualone) and hyoscine, a tropane alkaloid drug derived from plants of the Solanaceae family like Datura, as well as a wide range of non-prescription painkillers such as paracetemol and ibuprofen. Methaqualone, a popular street drug in the UK in the 1960s where it was referred to as 'Mandies' and in the USA in the 1970s and 1980s where it was sold under the trademark *Quaalude*, has been banned in most western countries. Originally synthesised in India in 1955 as an anti-malarial drug, its powerful effects and potential for abuse as a non-barbiturate hypno-sedative were quickly recognised. The leading global consumer of methaqualone is South Africa where it is mixed with herbal cannabis and smoked recreationally in a mixture known as a 'white pipe'.[25] India is the largest producer of illicit methaqualone in the world. In September 2000, over two tonnes of Mandrax powder was seized near Hyderabad, and in February 2001, 1.4 tonnes of Mandrax tablets were seized in Bombay.[26]

There are other more sinister uses for drugs like Mandrax. In July 2003 police in Qandahar reported that 'narcotics', most likely pharmaceutical sedatives, were being injected into fruit that was then given to children. When the children became unconscious as a result of eating the fruit they were kidnapped and then trafficked to Pakistan and the Middle East as 'domestic workers', in other words as forced labour, beggars, camel jockeys or sex workers—or for the removal of body organs. In 2003 it was estimated that over 700 Afghan children had been trafficked to Saudi Arabia alone, while the police reported rescuing nearly 200 abducted children in different areas of the country.[27] The sedating of children for begging purposes is not an uncommon sight even on the more sedate streets of the Pakistan capital Islamabad, and already there is evidence of this happening in Kabul. The first time I saw such a sedated child being carried in an adult's arms it seemed like the comatose bundle was dead. The adult stood at traffic lights trying to solicit money from passing motorists, using the apparently lifeless child as a begging aid.

## INJECTING PHARMACEUTICALS

Apart from the many problems caused by oral ingestion of psychoactive pharmaceutical drugs in Afghanistan, injection of these drugs is also increasingly reported, as it is in the south Asian region generally. In a study based on a sample of 200 drug injectors in Lahore, Pakistan, 'The major reasons cited by the respondents for shifting from smoking heroin to injecting legally procured substances, sometimes in combination with illegal substances, are economics (they are less expensive), better "high" (greater satisfaction) and peer or group pressure to conform.'[28] The study ominously revealed that the majority of the drug injectors had started to inject a combination of legally obtainable pharmaceutical drugs such as sedatives, anti-histamines and anti-vomiting drugs as they 'often complement other drugs used, enhancing their positive effects and minimising the negative side effects'.[29] While only 2.5 per cent injected heroin, 59 per cent injected the analgesic Temgesic (buprenorphine), 58.5 per cent injected morphine, 45 per cent the antihistamine Avil (pheniramine maleate), 31 per cent diazepam and 18 per cent the antihistamine Marzine (cyclazine).

Such a study highlights the risks of decreasing heroin availability and price increase for Afghan heroin smokers who may then move to injecting pharmaceuticals, with all the attendant public health risks, for purely economic reasons. Injecting of pharmaceuticals has already been reported in Afghanistan, particularly in Gardez where Avil, Valium and Sosegon have been injected, as well as heroin and ampoules of morphine smuggled from India via Pakistan. The preliminary results of a study conducted in Kabul during 2005 and early 2006 showed that out of 446 IDUs, 42 per cent had used heroin and 56 per cent had used heroin in combination with Avil.[30] The same study also showed that while 84 per cent of IDUs believed that the price of heroin has increased in the previous six months, 71 per cent believed there was a decrease in purity. Heroin was usually combined with lemon juice, a filter used infrequently, and assistance of the group leader with injecting happened 21 per cent of the time.

A decade earlier, a report from a Peshawar treatment centre of their Afghan client group between 1991 and 1996 claimed that the majority of 231 Afghans reported the consumption of four to six pharmaceutical tablets a day, with 7 per cent reporting that they took 10–15 tablets daily. The main tablets used were Mandrax, Valium, Ativan and Lexotan (bromazepam). Psychiatrists have warned of the abuse potential of Lexotan compared to other benzodiazepines. It has a very rapid onset of action, and with a short half-life can produce relatively severe withdrawal symptoms. Lexotan was discontinued in the UK in 2002. Some addicts from the Peshawar treatment centre also reported using injections of Temgesic, Pethidine, Sosegon and morphine.[31]

Economic reasons for changing behaviour in response to reduced heroin availability and increased street prices have also been found in north east India near the border with Myanmar where drug users have switched to injecting SP (Spasmo Proxyvon), 'a synthetic preparation based on dextropropoxyphene, a non-soluble opioid that tends to stick to the walls of the veins causing abscesses, gangrene, sometimes resulting in the need to amputate limbs'.[32] During 2003 over 100 drug users in Mizoram died as a direct result of injecting SP, with many other cases of undocumented deaths and amputations, according to the North East India Harm Reduction Network.

Apart from morphine-like but purely synthetic opioids like SP (as well as Sosegon) that are increasingly being used as heroin substitutes because of their lower price and regular availability, there is also a growing market in licit opiates diverted to the illicit market. The opium poppy produces a range of natural alkaloids like codeine, morphine and thebaine used in the production of medicines, including semi-synthetic substances such as diamorphine and oxycodone. One example of the latter drug is OxyContin, developed by the Purdue Pharmaceutical Company in 1995 from thebaine-derived oxycodone. While in the clinics and hospitals of the US the number of OxyContin prescriptions had risen 18-fold by 2000 to approximately 5.8 million prescriptions, on the street the drug was dubbed the 'poor man's heroin' or 'hillbilly heroin'. By 2002 it was estimated that nearly 2 million people in the US had used OxyContin for non-medical purposes. While a significant number, it falls far short of the estimated 13 million who had experienced non-medical use of the sister semi-synthetic opiate hydrocodone

(Vicodin). Certainly the DEA has recognised OxyContin as 'a growing problem', while local law enforcement officials have claimed it is 'a national epidemic in the making'. Significant increases in property theft and other crimes attributable to the abuse of OxyContin have been recorded in several areas, particularly in southern states like Virginia and Kentucky.[33]

Though such numbers are difficult to compare with regard to their relevance for heroin prevalence patterns, it is obvious that the dynamics of the licit and illicit markets are connected to some extent...on the streets the distinction between the two apparently distinct markets fades easily.[34]

## OTHER USERS OF PHARMACEUTICALS

Ironically it is not only the locals in Afghanistan who have problems relating to the use of psychoactive pharmaceutical drugs. On 17 April 2002, a US pilot, Major Harry Schmidt (nicknamed 'Psycho' by his squadron buddies), dropped a 500 lb laser-guided bomb—without flight control permission—near Qandahar after deciding that his flight lead Major William Umbach was under attack. The bomb landed only a few metres away from members of the 3rd Battalion of the Princess Patricia's Canadian Light Infantry engaged in a live-fire exercise, killing four soldiers and wounding eight. This incident of 'friendly fire' killings, not the first by the US forces in Afghanistan, was explained away by a US Air Force investigation as due to 'poor airmanship' by the pilots who also ignored standard procedures by not ensuring the area was clear of allied soldiers.[35] The lawyers representing the two pilots, however, alleged that they had been pressurised by the US Air Force into taking dextroamphetamine, a stimulant drug known to military personnel as 'go-pills', resulting in impaired judgement. The lawyers also alleged that pilots were regularly given this drug in order to keep them alert on night flights and during irregular schedules (Schmidt and Umbach were returning from a ten-hour patrol at over 15,000 feet when the incident occurred). The Air Force responded by admitting that low doses of the drug were routinely given to pilots as part of a 'fatigue management program'. While the drug was reportedly taken on a voluntary basis, one of the lawyers commented that if the informed consent form was not signed and the pilot refused the drug then he was officially grounded.[36]

Indeed, a new range of more effective 'fatigue management tools', or eugeroic drugs—meaning 'good arousal'—has already been developed by Lafon Laboratories of France. Adrafinil and its metabolised partner modafinil, marketed under commercial trade names like Provigil and Alertec, constitute a new range of 'smart', 'non-addictive' stimulants that improve short-term memory, attention and concentration, counter depression, lessen mental fatigue and can keep people awake for several days at a time without any apparent adverse effects apart from headache or nausea at therapeutic dosages. It is little wonder that these drugs have been both studied and used by the armed forces of several countries for military operations. As Professor Michel Jouvet, an authority on sleep, has claimed, 'Modafinil could keep an army on its feet and fighting for three days and nights with no major side effects.'[37] The drug has also reportedly been used in some sections of the Belgian, Dutch and US Air Forces and was given to French Foreign Legionnaires on covert operations inside Iraq during the first Gulf war.

## THE PHARMACEUTICAL MARKET IN AFGHANISTAN

Such examples of the burgeoning development, supply and use of psychoactive pharmaceutical drugs, both from the region and elsewhere, potentially spell bad news for Afghanistan, a country where reducing the supply of opium and heroin is likely to have a deleterious effect on demand and may even increase problems related to drug consumption. With few available healthcare facilities and treatment options, as well as largely unregulated and uncontrolled pharmaceutical markets, there is little to prevent an increase in the misuse of already available pharmaceutical drugs and the introduction of new ones such as Spasmo Proxyvon and OxyContin, as well as the 'smart' amphetamines. A compounding problem is that Afghans often rationalise their use of pharmaceuticals as *dawa*, as medicine, while they may also be taking them for their intoxicating effects. In any case, developing a realistic and pragmatic response to an impoverished and depressed woman taking Valium as a psychological survival tool is problematic. While she may become dependent on the drug and cannot sleep without it, if its use is stopped her problems are likely to increase, not decrease, as she now has to face the daily struggle for survival without a chemical crutch, along with suffering the pains of withdrawal.

In Afghanistan the war with the Soviets resulted in the collapse of the existing structure for controlling the availability and use of pharmaceutical drugs. Before 1979 medicines were strictly controlled, at least on paper, with rules and regulations stating that each pharmacy had to apply to the Ministry of Health for registration. A pharmacy also had to be an officially stipulated distance away from another pharmacy and have a locked cupboard to store strong narcotics and intoxicants. In 2004 in Kabul there was one street that contained over 40 pharmacies, many of them next door to each other. Anybody wanting to open a pharmacy before 1979 also had to have a certain amount of capital before they could set up in business and the person selling prescription-only drugs had to be a trained pharmacist. All doctors had to be registered with the Ministry of Health and could only prescribe medicines if they had an official ministry prescription pad. They were not allowed to write prescriptions on their own paper or on plain paper. For every prescription written in a private medical practice, 19 Afs went to the doctor and 1 Af to the ministry. Medicines could not be given without a prescription and could only be sold in pharmacies that were strictly controlled through government monopoly, although there were quite a few 'quack' doctors working in the border areas of the country that would provide any prescription for a fee.

Now the new Ministry of Public Health has started the process of trying once again to control and regulate medicines, although this is a difficult task as it is very easy to smuggle pharmaceutical drugs from neighbouring countries and sell them in a variety of retail outlets. This illicit trade in licit drugs has become well established over the past few decades and is very profitable for those traders engaged in it. By early 2005 the ministry had been able to close down 14 pharmacies in Kabul for selling out-of-date medicines and practising without a licence, although it is unlikely that they will soon have the capacity to effectively regulate all pharmacies acting illegally or selling sub-standard medicines.[38] While it is relatively easy to check whether a pharmacy has a professional licence, it is much harder to determine whether the drugs they are selling are counterfeit, adulterated, illicitly produced or illegally imported. In Herat in February 2005 there were around 80 unlicensed pushcarts in the bazaar selling a variety of pharmaceutical drugs, as well as 150 shop-based pharmacies. After complaints from local people that the medicines sold from the carts were past their expiry date, or not stored in the proper conditions or at required temperatures, the government health department sent teams to locate the expired drugs and burn them. Nevertheless, street vendors selling drugs without a prescription persisted, with one 15-year-old drug seller telling journalists: 'I was selling foodstuff on my cart earlier but as selling medicines is more profitable I started selling medicine.'[39]

## THE GLOBAL PHARMACEUTICAL MARKET

While the global illicit drug trade commandeers media headlines and merits serious policy discussions, it largely goes unreported that the licit pharmaceutical trade depends on dubious trade networks and produces much higher profits, not all derived from legitimate means. The history of the trade has been plagued with well-documented cases of corporate criminal behaviour such as price fixing, bribery and corruption, negligence and fraud in safety testing practices, unsafe manufacturing practices, unethical marketing and dumping counterfeit, expired or banned drugs on the developing world.[40] In 2005 it was revealed that as many experts employed to advise doctors on which drugs to prescribe were in the pay of pharmaceutical companies, there were distinct conflicts of interest. Members of panels responsible for producing clinical guidelines were found to have received payments from the company making the drugs that they had recommended.[41]

Patent protection and brand names have been central to the survival of pharmaceutical companies as the average price, and therefore profit, of a branded drug is at least three to four times more than their generic equivalent. After the antidepressant Prozac (fluoxetine) came off patent in 2001 the manufacturer Eli Lilly lost more than $1 billion in profits per annum as other companies produced generic versions of the same drug.[42] Like several other large multinational pharmaceutical companies, Eli Lilly owes its existence to profits made from morphine and heroin sales, 'in an era which laid the foundations for the self-perpetuating cycles of addiction to these drugs in modern societies'.[43] At the turn of the twentieth century, for example, the pharmaceutical company Bayer promoted heroin using the same successful mass-marketing tactics they had used to sell aspirin—as the panacea for all infant respiratory ailments.

In terms of dumping drugs on developing countries, the large multinational pharmaceutical companies have been guilty of a wide range of malpractices including: exporting the ingredients of a banned drug separately and then reassembling them in a transit country or the country where they are to be dumped; changing the name of a drug that has been withdrawn or had bad publicity in the west; adding inert ingredients to an existing drug to prevent detection by spectrometers and other scanners; and engaging in a tactic called 'the skip' where an unapproved drug is shipped to a third country where it is registered before being exported to its final country of destination as an approved drug. A more common strategy than the skip, however, is simply to spread manufacturing plants worldwide so that the parent company can source drugs for a region from a conveniently located plant in a country that will quickly grant approval to a drug that would not be granted approval in the US or in Europe.

On a legitimate, if unethical, front the big pharmaceutical companies have stridently lobbied through the WTO (World Trade Organization) to impose a uniform global patent regime and to prevent poorer countries from responding to their public health needs by buying or producing cheaper generic drugs. In Pakistan patent laws have to comply with the WTO's TRIPS agreement that fences off intellectual property and has resulted in increases in drug prices and a chronic shortage of essential medicines. By contrast, until January 2005 when it signed up to TRIPS, India did not allow drug patenting so manufacturers of generic drugs thrived as the competition drove down the price of high-quality locally produced drugs and the country emerged as the fourth largest pharmaceutical industry in the world.[44] This expansion of India's pharmaceutical industry also had a downside. In 2003 the WHO estimated that globally up to 35 per cent of all counterfeit pharmaceuticals were manufactured in India, with 11 per cent of all exported pharmaceuticals from India being counterfeit. This represented a large profit for the criminal groups concerned, estimated to be equivalent to 17 per cent of the pharmaceutical industry's turnover.[45] Now that India has made the decision to comply with WTO laws regarding pharmaceutical patents, generic drugs will be outlawed and there will be an added incentive for criminal groups to involve themselves in production of pharmaceutical drugs, many of them spurious, to meet local and international demand.

Certainly the cheap manufacturing costs of many pharmaceutical drugs and the enormous profits involved have made them an attractive proposition for both legitimate and criminal entrepreneurs in developing countries, as well as for the multinationals themselves. While there is a 'culture of denial and secrecy' in the pharmaceutical industry about the problem of counterfeiting, such spurious substances are even being produced in countries like the UK where ingredients, pill presses and duplicate stamps of companies like Pfizer have been imported from India, mainly for making diazepam and Viagra.[46]

In the early 1970s the wholesale price of Valium in the US was 25 times the price of gold, yet the costs for the raw materials were only $87 per kg and the total cost for the final packaged and labelled product was $487 per kg.[47] This meant that the final retail price of $11,000 for the original kilo that produced 100,000 10 mg tablets of Valium was over 120 times the original cost of the raw materials and over 20 times the production costs. It is little wonder that a month's supply of Valium in Kabul can be bought for less than $1, affordable to even the poorest person but still making a substantial profit for the vendor. In 1978 Hoffman-La Roche quoted the Sri Lankan government a price for Valium 70 times higher than the price charged by an Indian pharmaceutical company, this a decade after the company had to make rebate payments of over $5 million to the UK government as reparation for abusing its monopoly of the Valium and Librium markets and making excess profits. Around the same time Hoffman-La Roche gave away over 150 million doses of Valium, as well as around 25 million doses of Librium, among other reasons to prevent the use of competing versions of the drug.[48]

## THE VIRTUAL DRUG MARKET

A newly emerging problem is the purchase of pharmaceutical drugs online over the Internet without a prescription, including psychotropics like tranquillisers, hypnosedatives and analgesics. A wide range of drugs is now advertised in cyberspace with websites displaying varying degrees of responsibility. This has created a virtual marketplace for drug sales, a virtual drug bazaar. Four types of website that have been identified are: legitimate pharmacies (the online equivalent of street shop-based pharmacies) that will only sell on the basis of a valid medical prescription; subscription pharmacies that will access online pharmacies in unregulated areas of the developing world supplying unlimited prescription drugs without a prescription; lifestyle pharmacies that usually require an 'online consultation' form to be completed, although some may sell a range of prescription drugs such as sex-enhancers, painkillers and anti-depressants without a prescription; and no-prescription pharmacies that sell controlled drugs without a prescription, including opioids and benzodiazepines.[49] The global pharmaceutical market is now flexible and expansive enough to enable someone in Kabul to make an online purchase of psychoactive pharmaceutical drugs that will be sent direct to the purchaser by mail or courier.

In response, the INCB has recently called on national governments to clamp down on unlicensed Internet pharmacies and has raised concerns about the lack of age restrictions regarding potential customers and the fear that Internet-sourced drugs could become a major source for abused prescription medications among children and adolescents. In some countries, like the US, this is already the case. In 2005 a national study on teenage drug abuse by the Partnership for a Drug-Free America reported that more teenagers had experimented with prescription painkillers than with ecstasy, cocaine, crack cocaine or LSD. The study claimed that 20 per cent of teenagers (5 million) had abused a prescription painkiller like Vicodin or OxyContin, while nine per cent (2.2 million) had abused over-the-counter pharmaceutical products like cough syrups.[50]

A related problem is the online sale of a range of synthetic psychedelic/hallucinogenic designer drugs, euphemistically referred to as 'research chemicals', usually only known by their laboratory names such as 2-CT-2, AMT and 5-MeO-DMT.[51] These extremely powerful substances can be purchased from Internet websites in China, Japan and India. Similar websites based in the US were shut down in July 2004 in a country-wide sting known as Operation Web Tryp. In September 2005, the DEA announced the culmination of Operation CYBERx having arrested 18 people, including the ringleaders of more than 4,600 rogue Internet pharmacy websites that netted over $50,000 per day in profits from their illegal Internet business.[52] However, underground chemists continue to synthesise new designer drugs that slip through gaps in international drugs legislation and 'online outfits have been able to create a worldwide customer base for designer drugs by subverting the infrastructure laid down by legitimate e-commerce such as international couriers and online credit-card systems'.[53] A related problem is the Internet and retail trade in 'legal highs', the myriad of natural substances with psychoactive effects that have not (yet) been criminalised.[*]

---

[*] A very lucrative 'legal highs' business exists in Europe, for example the sale of preparations produced from the following psychoactive substances: *Salvia divinorum*, a form of the sage plant (banned in Australia and Italy); Fly Agaric (*Amanita muscaria*), the red and white spotted mushroom popularised in *Alice in Wonderful*; and kratom or *Mitragyna speciosa* (illegal in Australia and Thailand). Such substances can easily be sourced from the Internet with one website containing more than 5,000 products of 'drug paraphernalia' and many types of legal high described under the headings 'stimulant', 'visionary', 'relaxant' and 'aphrodisiac'.

Particular concern was raised in the INCB Report about countries like Pakistan that have 'shown a lack of cooperation and of law enforcement action against Internet pharmacies operating from their countries'.[54] It seems unlikely in the near future that Afghanistan will escape an influx of both legally and illegally imported psychoactive pharmaceuticals, both through Internet sales and manual smuggling, to meet the steady demand from a war-weary populace, a significant number of whom are becoming dependent on these drugs. However, while such substances, along with hashish, opium and heroin, remain the most common intoxicants used in Afghanistan, they are by no means the only available psychoactive drugs to which people have access.

# 12
# Masters of the Universe: Other Drugs and Future Dimensions

At a time when religion is fading, family bonds are weakening and society is splintering, designer technology gives young people the false promise of becoming (briefly) 'masters of the universe'.[1]

Alcohol is one of the more potent as well as one of the most widely used of all the psychoactive drugs: paradoxically, it is also the least likely to be recognised as such.[2]

## THE DEMON ALCOHOL

In May 2003 on a 5 km stretch of road from Mazar-i-Sharif to the ancient city of Balkh, once the capital of Bactria with its fabulous treasures of gold, there were three armed checkpoints manned by different militia from *Jamiat-i Islami*, *Jumbesh-i-Milli Islami* and *Hezb-i Wahdat*. The former two displayed large painted portraits of their leaders, Ahmad Shah Massoud and Rashid Dostum. While these armed factions coexisted peacefully at least for the moment, over the previous decade permutations of these three groups, along with several others and various splinter groups, had been bitter enemies as well as uneasy allies if it was in their interests to do so. We passed these checkpoints on our way to talk to opium users in the market town of Aqcha and its nearby communities of Turkmen carpet weavers.

After returning from Aqcha, lunch was served in a commander's compound on the northern side of Balkh, just outside what is left of the ancient city walls. The commander was a good host, very sociable and gregarious with a permanent grin on his face, but it was difficult to find out exactly to which faction he belonged. There were about 30 men there for lunch, eaten communally with fingers while sitting on the floor on plush red *toshacks*. Several armed men hung around, some in uniform. In the yard of the compound there was a chained Alsatian dog, a flock of fat homing pigeons and six strutting peacocks. There was also a group of caged monkeys chattering from behind a wall.

That evening dinner was served on the verandah of the office of a local NGO, with music provided by a band consisting of a tabla player, a *rubab* player and a harmonium player who also sang. The commander who had invited us to lunch was also present, along with the local deputy political leader of a different faction. The issue of whether Afghanistan would be better with a strong centralised government or a looser federalised state structure was discussed before dinner. Then, during dinner, five bottles of Uzbek vodka were suddenly produced and very openly placed on the table and consumed, mostly mixed with a soft drink. Such public display and consumption of alcohol was very unusual, and some of the Afghans there who came from the south of the country were quite shocked at this blatant display of what was, for them, such open use of a banned intoxicant. They were also shocked that measures of vodka were poured into everybody's glass without being asked, although not wanting to offend their hosts they managed to surreptitiously get rid of it from their own glasses before refilling them with a soft drink. Of the 20 or so people present at the party about ten drank alcohol and they easily finished the five bottles of vodka by the end of the evening.

After dinner and relaxing to the music for a while we had to leave as there was a 10 p.m. curfew for international staff. The next day we were told by our Afghan colleagues that after we left the party a heated argument ensued between the commander and the political deputy, with the commander, obviously well under the influence of alcohol, decrying a centralised government and shouting that if anybody was in any doubt about who was in control of the area, who was master of this particular universe, he would use his mobile phone to have his men come over to the party straight away and kill everybody. This was considered by those present as more than an idle drunken threat and it provided a glimpse of the dangers of a drug like alcohol in an environment where people have easy access to guns, as well as the knowledge and experience of using them. And that is not to mention a sense of self bound up in a tribal code of honour that can easily be slighted and just as easily revenged.

By contrast, drug users interviewed in Kabul who had tried alcohol reported few problems with its use, although most had stopped using it because it was too expensive or frequently unavailable, at least at that time. Those who did experience problems all emphasised a lack of self-control and an inclination to violence when they were intoxicated. One man said:

Whenever I am intoxicated with alcohol I don't know what comes out of my mouth. I can't control myself, and one time I broke down a door and some windows. The people in the community don't like me and call me a drunkard. My father always tells me that the use of alcohol is forbidden in Islam.[3]

By all accounts, since the time of Babur there has always been a supply, if fluctuating, of alcohol in the Kabul area. Before the late 1970s mainly the upper classes and the rich took alcohol, although some home brewed forms of alcohol were also sold in the bazaar in plastic bags to anybody who could afford it. With the arrival of the new communist government in 1978, however, the use of alcohol became more common, especially with the communist cadres who saw its consumption as almost a *rite de passage* from the medieval to the modern. This process was inevitably aided by the easy availability of alcohol, where a bottle of Russian vodka cost little more than $1. In parts of northern Afghanistan to this day there is still a plentiful supply of vodka smuggled over the border from the ex-Soviet central Asian republics. In areas like the Shomali plains to the north of Kabul a home-brewed alcohol called *dushawa* is made from fermented wine juice, sometimes with added lime powder, although this is for home consumption only and not generally traded.

From early 2002, however, with an increased foreign presence in Kabul and the opening of several military and civilian exchanges or warehouses solely for foreigners, alcohol has become more and more available to Afghans, bootlegged onto the local market by members of the international community. In early 2005 a small can of Heineken beer sold on street stands in Kabul for 100–110 Afs (just over $2), more than double its retail cost in an international exchange. Beer in particular was reported as being available in many shops in bazaars throughout the city. Nevertheless, people were aware of Islamic injunctions against *sharab* with some reports that people would enter a shop and ask for *zamzam* and not alcohol directly. *Zamzam* is traditionally the water from a holy spring of that name within the Masjid al Haram in Mecca in Saudi Arabia taken by pilgrims on the Haj and brought home in bottles to share with family and friends. Since 2002 people with alcohol problems have also presented at drug treatment centres in Kabul and there are also reports that the bootlegging of alcohol has now spread from Kabul to other provinces, particularly Nangarhar.

On 20 December 2004 the Kabul traffic police division issued a statement claiming that most traffic accidents in the city were caused by drunk drivers, with over 30 traffic accidents every month, although this would seem a gross underestimate and is likely to refer only to those few traffic accidents reported to the police. Indeed the linking of road traffic accidents to alcohol use may be more related to attempts by conservative elements to have customary bans on alcohol reinforced. By all accounts, alcohol is also 'readily available' in many small shops in the capital city and is becoming increasingly popular among young people, even though its use is strictly prohibited under the law. A spokesman for the Supreme Court, Waheed Mojdah, blamed law enforcement agencies for not preventing the problem and thereby allowing an increase in the availability of alcohol and its sale in restaurants in Kabul. He is also reported as saying that *Ulema* and Supreme Court officials have had meetings with President Karzai on the matter, but that members of the Cabinet had allegedly been involved in importing and distributing alcohol in the city: 'There are some people who are keen to discourage Afghan religious ethnic values and try to introduce western values.'[4]

In January 2005 the Interior Ministry closed down three guesthouses in Kabul run by ethnic Chinese because they permitted gambling, sold alcohol and allowed women in the restaurants to be 'improperly attired', a euphemism for prostitution. Both Kabul residents and religious leaders had complained about these activities. While there were over 40 guesthouses and restaurants in the city that had been registered and licensed, only a few were closed. These may have been operating without official registration, but it is interesting that no western-run restaurant and bar was closed although several of them operate in Kabul, all selling a wide variety of alcoholic beverages. Alcohol is now likely to be sold and consumed in some restaurants in a more clandestine fashion, literally 'under the table' from teapots instead of bottles, always an option in some restaurants in neighbouring Islamabad in Pakistan where alcohol is also banned.

## DATURA AND ITS DERIVATIVES[5]

Although alcohol is the main intoxicant found in Afghanistan along with opiates, hashish and a variety of pharmaceutical hypno-sedatives, tranquillisers and analgesics, there have been reports of other substances being used for their psychoactive properties. During an assessment of problem drug use in rural eastern Afghanistan in 2000, there were several reports of the use of *Dantoorah* or *Gul-e-Khapiray*, the local name for the plant Datura, as an intoxicant.

In Sayed Karam district of Paktia province one 49-year-old man reported that

This wild plant becomes ripe in the summer and forms a poppy-like flower. Inside the capsule there are small black seeds. If 8 or 9 are eaten they stimulate a person and make him emotional. The user loses his orientation and cannot identify time and place. Some people use it as a painkiller. To counteract its stimulant effects, people are given valium by the doctor.[6]

Datura was also reported as being one of the active constituents of *burshesha*, a preparation made by local *hakims* and sold for coughs and general body pains, as well as a hallucinogenic additive to hashish. Drug treatment counsellors in Kabul have also come across a few drug users who have smoked a combination of Datura with hashish or tobacco. Unsubstantiated reports from some rural areas have suggested the use of Datura seeds as a poison to kill an enemy or as a means of committing suicide.

Datura, a member of the deadly nightshade *Solanaceae* plant family, grows wild all over Afghanistan and in many other countries of the world. It contains the active ingredients of belladonna alkaloids such as atropine, hyoscymine and scopolamine, substances not controlled under international regulations. While the difference between an intoxicating dose of Datura and a fatal one is allegedly small, like many other toxic psychoactive substances, if used correctly, a constituent drug like scopolamine can be usefully prescribed by a doctor for health problems such as motion-sickness, gastrointestinal disorders and the symptoms of Parkinson's disease.

For centuries various preparations of Datura have been used in traditional medicines in many parts of the world. In China it was mixed with cannabis and wine and used as an anaesthetic for minor surgery. In India it was known as 'the tuft of Shiva' and made into an intoxicating wine. It is also the plant that Avicenna, the Arabian physician and *hakim*, mentioned under the name *jouzmathel* in the eleventh century. In eighteenth-century India a doctor in the service of the East India Company reported a more ritualistic use for Datura:

In Malabar, at the time of the sacrifices in honour of Vishnu, virgins pleasant to behold and richly adorned were brought from the temple of the Brahmins. They came out in public to appease the god who rules over plenty and fine weather. To impress the spectators, these young women were previously given a preparation with a basis of hemp [cannabis] and datura, and when the priest saw, by certain symptoms, that the action of the drugs was about to show itself, he began his invocations. The Devadassy (servants of the gods) then danced, leapt about yelling, contorted their limbs, and, foaming at the mouth, their eyes ecstatic, committed all sorts of eccentricities. Finally the priests carried the exhausted virgins into the sanctuary, gave them a potion to destroy the effect of the previous one, and then showed them again to the people in their right mind, so that the crowd of spectators might believe that the demons had fled and the idol was appeased.[7]

In the New World, several different varieties of the Datura plant have also been developed over the centuries for ritualistic purposes in divination, magic, sorcery and witchcraft, as well as for medicine and healing. *Datura inoxia*, known as *Toloache*, was used by the Aztecs in divination and by other tribes in rain-dance rituals and puberty rites, while 'Californian Indians personified *Toloache* as a great shaman and used it in their vision quests for an animal spirit helper.' It is reportedly still sold in markets in Mexico as an aphrodisiac and traditional medicine.[8] Other Native Americans, such as the Algonquins, used Jimson weed or thorn apple (*Datura stramonium*) for purposes of ritual initiation into manhood.

In South America there are several native tree Daturas that appear to have been cultivated over the centuries specifically for human use and that are unknown in the truly wild state. One variety is known as *borrachero* or *borrachio*, the 'drunken tree'. While the northern Andes region from Colombia to Peru appears to be the centre of the group's origin, their use is known as far south as Chile where the Mapuche Indians have reportedly used preparations made from the tree as a last-resort punishment for unruly children. The Jivaro Indians of the Amazon, who have also used Datura as a preparation for war, say that 'the spirits of their ancestors admonish recalcitrant children during the hallucinations' induced by the drug.

But less traditional uses of Datura are also prevalent in many parts of contemporary South America. While the modern Tarahumares still add the leaves, roots and seeds of Datura to their maize beer, a less benign form of the drug is popularly administered as *burundanga*. This is the practice of using extracts of Datura and the genus Brugmensia to induce retrograde amnesia and submissive behaviour in intended victims of criminal enterprise. Put more bluntly:

It can also induce waking trances where the individual is unaware that the dream they seem to be having is indeed all too real, and persons under the influence of scopolamine can be ordered to release passwords, empty bank accounts, and engage in sexual acts without their consent or even full knowledge.[9]

The use of *burundanga*, which induces scopolamine intoxication, seems to be most prevalent in Colombia with well over 1,000 cases reported each month in Bogota the capital city, where they account for more than half of hospital emergency room admissions. Even a US State Department travel advisory for Colombia has warned its citizens that 'The drug is administered in drinks in bars, through cigarettes and gums in taxis, and in powder form...the drug renders the person disoriented and can cause prolonged unconsciousness and serious medical problems.' As an odourless powder, *burundanga* can simply be blown in the face of a potential victim as it is absorbable through the skin. Datura was one of the main ingredients of medieval witches' 'flying ointment' which once rubbed on the skin and absorbed allowed them to go on hallucinogenic trips symbolised in folklore and fairytales by a witch flying through the air on a broomstick.

A taxi driver in Medellin, more infamous as the regional centre of the cocaine trade in Colombia, says that victims of *burundanga*-induced crime sometimes flag them down in a trance: 'We call them the "disoriented ones". They get in the taxi and you ask them where they are going. They say they don't know. They don't even know who they are. They get in a taxi out of instinct.'[10] In the US, the Northwest Center Against Sexual Assault in Arlington Heights, Illinois, has warned that scopolamine may be the next 'date rape' drug to make its way into Chicago, and an online training course for police in Texas has also warned of the dangers of *burundanga* as a possible 'date rape' drug.[11]

Although current uses of Datura seem to be most prevalent in South America, various preparations made for intoxication and other purposes have been reported elsewhere. In 2002, the International Narcotics Control Board (INCB) reported that the use of the leaves and seeds of *Datura stramonium* mixed with herbal cannabis was 'spreading fast' throughout Central Africa, particularly in Chad and the Democratic Republic of the Congo.[12] Another variety, *Datura metel,* is mixed with cannabis and smoked in parts of Asia and the leaves of *Datura fastuosa*, considered by some botanists as a distinct species, is smoked with cannabis or tobacco in parts of Asia and Africa. Writing in the *American Journal of Psychiatry*, Dr Harold Graff records that 'The smoking of plants containing belladonna alkaloids for their hallucinatory effects has been practiced for centuries by

Arabs, Swahilis, and American Indians.'[13] In Cape Town in South Africa, where Datura is commonly referred to as the moonflower plant, 20 known cases of moonflower poisoning were reported at a local hospital during a five-month period in 2003.

Certainly Datura is a powerful substance with marked psychoactive effects. During controlled customary rituals it has been reported that

Intoxication caused by the drug is characterised initially by effects so violent that physical restraint must be imposed until the partaker passes into a stage of sleep and hallucinations. The medicine man interprets the visions as visitations of the spirits and is supposedly thus able to diagnose disease, apprehend thieves, and prophesy the future.[14]

In modern Colombia it is recognised that scopolamine can make users extremely aggressive, so criminals have mixed it with other drugs like tranquillisers, making *burundanga* yet another type of drug cocktail. Other active ingredients of Datura like hyoscyamine and hyoscine produce a range of physiological symptoms including drying of the mucous membranes, flushing and drying of the skin, alternating slow and rapid heartbeat with palpitations and arrhythmia, vomiting, confusion and dizziness. An overdose of Datura can easily result in unconsciousness, coma and even death. The difference between a dose that will make the user intoxicated and induce hallucinations and one that will result in death is reputedly small. A website providing information about a wide range of psychoactive substances believes it is important to 'Note that an overwhelming majority of those who describe to us their use of Datura (and to a lesser extent, Belladonna, Brugmensia and Brunfelsia) find their experiences extremely mentally and physically unpleasant and not infrequently physically dangerous.'[15]

## METHAMPHETAMINE AND FUTURE POSSIBILITIES

The established use of Datura in Afghanistan, although apparently limited, could potentially increase as it has in other countries, particularly if other drugs become less available and demand for individual psychoactive change continues. At the same time there is always a risk that other intoxicating substances, currently unknown in the country, will also come to be used. In an ever-changing and predominantly predatory global drugs economy, both illicit and licit, significant changes in patterns of drug use can emerge in a country or region in a very short period of time.

In 1989 Bob Stutman, an ex-DEA agent, and Dr Mark Gold, founder of the US Cocaine-800 Helpline, arrived in the UK on a mission to warn of the dangers of crack cocaine and the likelihood of a dramatic increase in its use in the UK. At the time many professionals in the demand reduction field, including myself, thought this unlikely in the foreseeable future as the UK did not have the necessary cultural conditions for its trafficking, such as a violent gun-gang culture and a network of close-knit Hispanic-led criminal groups.[16] By 2003, however, crack cocaine use had become well established in several urban areas of the UK. Even my old university town of Aberdeen in the far northeast corner of Scotland had become a centre for crack distribution, with an estimated 3,000 crack users in the city, many of them also heroin users. Jamaican drug dealers from Wolverhampton in the English Midlands had reportedly targeted Aberdeen for distribution of crack, initially supplying it free with each wrap of heroin sold: 'According to the national criminal intelligence service (NCIS), Aberdeen, often referred to as the "oil capital of Europe", is now the most northern UK outpost of Jamaican and British-born Yardie dealers who have extended their business out of London in the search for new markets.'[17]

While it is unlikely that cocaine use will become popular in Afghanistan in the near future, even given the unpredictable nature of the illicit global drug market, there is another stimulant drug much closer to Kabul that is more likely to emerge in the country—methamphetamine.

In east and southeast Asia methamphetamine has emerged as the major drug of choice, with Thailand the global leader in consumption having an annual prevalence rate in 2001 of 5.6 per cent of the population aged between 15 and 64. In 1993 the prevalence rate was only 0.58 per cent. At that time, 90 per cent of drug users in Thailand seeking treatment were opiate, mainly heroin, users, but 33 per cent were methamphetamine users by 1999. This significant increase in consumption has been due in large part to an increased manufacture of the drug in neighbouring Myanmar. Along with China, Myanmar has become the global leader in methamphetamine production, exporting more than an estimated 700 million tablets to Thailand each year. UNODC estimates that most manufacturing of methamphetamine in Myanmar takes place in remote and inaccessible areas that are outwith central government control. The groups and laboratories that produce methamphetamine tablets are reportedly the same as those that previously manufactured and trafficked in heroin, with traces of opiates being found in methamphetamine tablets originating from the estimated 40 laboratories that once only refined heroin.[18]*

Such changing drug-use patterns could have a serious knock-on effect for Afghanistan. If the continuing eradication of opium cultivation and destruction of heroin laboratories succeeds in Afghanistan then those dedicated to criminal drug enterprises are likely to seek new sources of business and profit that are within easy reach. Given that the structural conditions for the successful manufacture of methamphetamine in Myanmar, remote locations and weak central government, also exist in Afghanistan, there is a distinct possibility of heroin producers in the country transferring to methamphetamine production. The fact that a drug chemist from Myanmar has already reportedly travelled to Afghanistan to provide technical advice on improving the refinement of heroin dramatically increases that possibility.[19] The links and networks have already been established, however loosely. Already the expansion of methamphetamine production westwards from Myanmar has taken place, with reports of possible production on the Indian side of the Indo-Myanmar border, although this may be primarily to gain increased access to precursors as well as a move into a large and lucrative market.

These Indian laboratories, as well as those in Myanmar, have also been reported as producing the high-purity crystalline form of methamphetamine known as *shabu*, or ice, as opposed to the less pure and often adulterated form of the drug popular in Thailand referred to as *yaba* (crazy medicine).[20] Although there are no reliable figures available for methamphetamine manufacture in China, 'based on methamphetamine and ephedrine seizure data as an indicator, potential clandestine manufacturing capacity in China exceeds by far that of other countries'.[21] It is notable that China shares a border of 75 km with Afghanistan at the eastern end of the remote Wakhan corridor, also serving as a land bridge connecting Myanmar with Afghanistan.

---

\*   Ironically one of the factors for the shift from opium to amphetamines in 1998–99 in Myanmar's borderlands under control of the United Wa State Army was the short-term risk of overproduction of opium in Afghanistan.

Generally methamphetamine, brand name Methedrine, is the most potent of the amphetamines, being twice as strong as dexamphetamine (Dexedrine), which in turn is twice as strong as d'l-amphetamine (Benzedrine). Known collectively as ATS (amphetamine type stimulants), the stimulant effect of these drugs soon builds up a tolerance where more and more is needed for the same effect. As such there is a serious dependency potential, and the possibility of what is referred to as amphetamine psychosis for heavy long-term users, although this psychosis usually disappears soon after the body is detoxified from the drug. While methamphetamine, like other stimulant drugs, is frequently stereotyped as a substance that induces aggression and physical violence, this is not always the case. In fact amphetamines can be used to help some tense or insecure people to relax. The main problem with the amphetamines is that they are similar to alcohol—often unpredictable in their effects. While some users may become relaxed and friendly, others can become aggressive and violent.[22] Like heroin, the amphetamines are drugs that can be injected, often with disastrous results. As with alcohol, methamphetamine and guns are unlikely to mix well together. Fortunately in terms of any drug-fuelled contributions to interpersonal violence in Afghanistan, the vast majority of drugs currently consumed are 'downers', drugs that essentially depress the central nervous system, individual responses to particular drugs notwithstanding, and not 'uppers' or stimulants.

As the preface to the *2003 Global Survey of Ecstasy and Amphetamines*, written by the Executive Director of the UNODC, Antonio Maria Costa, says, 'At a time when religion is fading, family bonds are weakening and society is splintering, designer technology gives young people the false promise of becoming (briefly) "masters of the universe".'[23] Certainly a problem with the amphetamines is that they tend to encourage feelings of omnipotence and can act as powerful performance enhancers, producing feelings of well-being and increased alertness, at least in the short term. Little wonder they have been a favourite drug with several social groups since they were first marketed in 1932, including sportsmen and pilots and soldiers on all sides during the Second World War.

### MORE INTOXICANTS

Apart from the possibility of increased use of a freely available hallucinogenic like Datura, an ever more easily available intoxicant like alcohol and the introduction of new drugs to Afghanistan like the methamphetamines, the ubiquitous use of tobacco is often ignored as a type of mild, if highly addictive, intoxicant that contributes to a range of health problems. In the cities it is common to see men smoking imported cigarettes, often counterfeits from neighbouring countries, and in Pashtoon areas in particular the use of *naswar* is common. *Naswar*, sometimes referred to as snuff, is a plug of ground 'chewing tobacco' usually inserted between the gum and bottom lip and left for some time before being spat out. Made from ground tobacco mixed with lime or wood ash, with different users preferring a *naswar* prepared with the ash of a particular tree (presumably as a type of flavour enhancer), it is likely that its habitual use contributes to diseases of the gum and mouth, including cancer. There have also been tales that some forms of *naswar* contain opium but regular *naswar* users refute this. In April 2005 Herat province banned smoking in all government buildings, becoming the first region in Afghanistan to do so after the government signed an international convention banning tobacco consumption in public. Such a move would be unlikely to have any effect on *naswar* users.

There is also reported and verified use of a range of volatile substances like glues and solvents. Sniffing the fumes from shoe polish and paint have been reported in Kabul and in refugee camps in Pakistan, with some users being children as young as ten. One NGO has had 180 referrals to their treatment centre in Kabul for solvent use. A few cases have also been reported of shoe polish being spread on bread and eaten. In 1999, it was reported that in Kabul, 'Shoe polish had been spread on bread, allowing the volatile oil from the polish to seep into the bread. The excess polish was scraped off and the bread then eaten as a "solvent sandwich".'[24] Petrol sniffing has also been reported among young people in Kabul, and in Gardez one man was reported for siphoning petrol from vehicles and drinking it.[25] A mother and her young child in Kabul were also known to drink diesel fuel on a daily basis, while one man reported that he had sniffed eau de cologne every day for the last five years, 'Every morning I take a bottle of cologne and sniff the fumes for half an hour.'[26] In the same study, 'Another person reported smoking dried scorpions mixed with hashish in a chillum.' Perhaps there was some truth in Mullah Akhundzada's assertion that some *mujahideen* fighting the Soviets would smoke scorpion tails when they had no hashish. Maybe this was not a scorpion tale after all?[27]

# 13
# Scorpion Tails

The villagers told me that if I smoked scorpion I would be intoxicated for a week, but this wasn't true. I was only intoxicated for three days![1]

Short of defoliating the entire planet and napalming all of the earth's arable land, the total eradication of drug crops is an unattainable goal.[2]

While global drug policy has declared war on the plant-based intoxicants hashish, cocaine and heroin, it has largely ignored the many other freely-growing plants that can be used as psychoactive mood-altering substances; for example, Datura, Kratom (*Mitragyna speciosa*), Ayahuasca, *Salvia divinorum* and several types of mushrooms and cacti—to name but a few. Currently these have not become culturally popular mainstream 'street drugs' but there is no reason why some of them, or their derivatives, will not do so in the future. Assuming a demand, when the availability and supply of one drug dimishes it opens the door for another to emerge and replace it. There is, of course, no guarantee that the new drug will be any less harmful than the one it has replaced.

## TOADS AND ZOMBIES

However, intoxicants are not only derived from plant material and synthetically derived substances but also from animals, including human beings. In 2003 an assessment of drug use in Maldives found that *minikashi*, exhumed dried human bones, was reportedly mixed with heroin before smoking, although this practice was rare and likely to be symbolic in nature rather than psychoactive.[3] Adrenochrome semicarbazone, derived from adrenaline (technically referred to by its chemical name epinephrine) produced by the human adrenal gland, has been listed as a legal substance with psychoactive properties although it is an esoteric intoxicant whose recorded use is extremely rare.[4]

In the early 1980s Wade Davis, a Harvard ethnobotanist, ventured to Haiti to try and find out the secret of zombies, the so-called living dead. Were they merely fictitious characters or real people who had been induced into a prolonged psychotic state by some type of drug that also had the capacity to cause a deathlike stupor, at least in its initial dose? His first inclination was to look for a toxic and psychoactive plant, and this led him to Datura, 'a plant that has been called the drug of choice of poisoners, criminals and black magicians throughout the world'.[5] Davis found that *Datura stramonium* was known in Haiti as *concombre zombie*, the zombie's cucumber, and was indeed capable of inducing the type of stupor reported as being typical of zombies. But he soon established that the so-called zombie poison likely contained other and much more venomous toxins such as *Diodon hystrix* and *Sphoeroides testudineus*, more commonly referred to as the blowfish (or puffer fish) and the sea toad respectively. These two creatures contain the neurotoxin tetrodotoxin,

one of the most poisonous nonprotein substances known. Laboratory studies have shown it to be 16,000 times more potent than cocaine. As a poison it is, at a conservative estimate, five hundred times stronger than cyanide. A single lethal dose of the pure toxin would be about the amount that would rest on the head of a pin.[6]

Ironically, Davis concluded that while tetrodotoxin from animal sources was the drug that allowed people to be buried alive as the first stage in the process of being transmogrified into zombies, Datura extracts were the likely antidote that amplified the 'physiological template' set by tetrodotoxin and induced a state of 'waking dead', characterised by disorientation, pronounced confusion, complete amnesia and compliance to the orders of others.

Davis also points out that the Japanese are partial to eating four species of puffer fish, all in the genus *fugu* and all violently poisonous, that can sometimes have fatal results. Every year there are up to 100 deaths in Japan due to the consumption of improperly prepared puffer fish. But the art of *sushi* requires the experienced *fugu* chef not to remove all the toxins from the fish. His task is 'to reduce its concentration while assuring the guest still enjoys the exhilarating after effects. These include a mild numbing or tingling of the tongue and lips, sensations of warmth, a flushing of the skin, and a general feeling of euphoria.'[7] In other words, eating correctly prepared fugu brings on a mild intoxication. Davis claims that *fugu* is one of the few substances that 'walks the line between food and drug'.

While it is unlikely that anyone in the modern world would use the gigantic cane toad (*Bufo marinus*) as food, in the late 1980s the media in North America and Australia invoked yet another drug-related

moral panic by reporting that people were ingesting hallucinogenic preparations made from the toxic venom secreted from the
parotoid glands on the toad's back. Most sensationally, this led to
media reports of people simply catching a cane toad then licking its
back to become intoxicated and start hallucinating, although in fact
different powders, pastes and potions prepared from the cane toad
were more likely to be consumed than just licking its bare back. As
Davis says, 'The toad-licking saga revealed more than anything the
extraordinary lengths to which people would go to get intoxicated.'[8]
It also mystified Davis. As an ethnobotanist he could not see any safe
method of consuming secretions of the toad's venomous glands that
contained bufotoxin and bufogenin, both highly toxic substances.
While the glands also secreted bufotenine, a methylated derivative of
serotonin with a definite hallucinogenic quality, there was no known
method of separating the substances. Ingesting the venom would lead
to heart failure long before the effects of the bufotenine were felt.
Davis was also interested in *Bufo marinus* because the archaeological
literature on Central America revealed a significant quantity of the
toad's bones being found in ancient garbage dumps throughout the
area that suggested its use as a ritualistic hallucinogen by the Mayans
and other groups rather than as a survival food.

Nevertheless, Davis also realised that there had been too many
reports of ingesting psychoactive toad preparations for this practice
to be discounted altogether. In fact he had been concentrating on the
wrong toad. Along with his friend, the American 'wellness doctor'
Andrew Weil, he visited the Sonoran desert that stretches from
California through Arizona and into Mexico, to talk to people who
literally 'smoked toad', but preparations made from *Bufo alvarius*,
not *Bufo marinus*. While the two species are physically similar, the
former

is unique within the genus in its possession of an unusual enzyme. O-methyl
transferase, which, among other reactions, converts bufotenine (5-OH-DMT)
to the extraordinarily potent hallucinogen 5-methoxy-N,N-dimethyltrypt-
amine (5-MeO-DMT). The activity of this enzyme leads to the production and
accumulation of enormous amounts of 5-MeO-DMT, up to as much as 15% of
the dry weight of the parotoid glands. Such a concentration of a pure drug in a
living creature is virtually unheard of, and this was no ordinary compound.[9]

While DMT was used along with LSD, psilocybin and other hallucinogenic drugs in the 1960s and still remains a controlled substance
under US federal law, its near relative 5-MeO-DMT is uncontrolled.

Davis ascribes this to the fact that the effects of 5-MeO-DMT are much more powerful than those of straight DMT and never gained street popularity, it is a drug simply 'not for the novice'. Having smoked toad on his trip to the Sonoran desert, he describes it as producing 'an overwhelmingly powerful experience that can be unnerving. It is like taking a rocketship into the void...whereas most hallucinogens, including LSD, merely distort reality, however bizarrely, 5-MeO-DMT completely dissolves reality.'[10] Certainly consuming preparations made from *Bufo alvarius* have never become popularised or entered mainstream western drug subcultures: 'The practice of milking the toxic glands of a living animal, drying the venom on glass, and inhaling a substance that send one into a netherworld of oblivion did not catch on.'[11]

## INTOXICATING PREPARATIONS OF SCORPION

Whether this will be the case with scorpion preparations in Afghanistan remains to be seen, although preparing a scorpion for consumption as a psychoactive drug appears to be a lot less complex than with *Bufo alvarius*. Since Mullah Akhundzada first mentioned the use of scorpions as drugs in 1999, we have come to understand that scorpions are indeed used for their psychoactive, rather than nutritional, properties in Afghanistan. During fieldwork in Azro district of Logar province in 2000 it was reported that 'over 100 people' smoked dried scorpions in a *chillum* or rolled in cigarettes and the use of dried scorpions as an intoxicant was also reported from nearby Hesarak district over the mountains in Nangarhar province.[12]

Then in December 2002 a friend came to Kabul from Bamiyan province where he was coordinator for an international NGO. We started talking about how he had been stung twice by scorpions since arriving in Bamiyan, once by a light-coloured one and again by a black one which had much more serious consequences. On this occasion he was stung on the calf and his leg had swollen considerably, causing a lot of pain. He had also been bitten once in Nigeria by an extremely poisonous scorpion and had to be treated within 90 minutes or death would have occurred. Luckily he was immediately taken to a traditional doctor who bled the wound and applied a curative paste of dried leaves that had been prepared by chewing.

There were many scorpions in Bamiyan. Some Afghans had told my friend that in Khamard district there was a small group of Tartars, under the leadership of a commander associated with *Jamiat-i Islami*, who smoked dried scorpion stings. The sting was taken out of the live scorpion and then dried, ground to a powder, mixed with some leaves, and smoked. The body of the scorpion, still alive, was then hung by what was left of the tail to a door arch and left dangling in the sunlight, supposedly to warn other scorpions against entering the room. In fact his own Afghan colleagues in Bamiyan also hung scorpions in this manner, but did not smoke the removed sting. He thought this treatment of the scorpion was a form of emasculation that symbolised what Tartars traditionally did to enemies they had captured. In smoking the sting from the tail the smoker takes on the power and strength of the scorpion, symbolically or otherwise. Eventually my friend met some of these Tartars who informed him that the scorpion is crushed between two stones and allowed to dry out. The main part of the tail, including the sting, is then ground into a powder and mixed with tobacco and/or hashish and smoked. One stated that when he smoked scorpion he was intoxicated for 'much longer than with hashish', while another said that smoking scorpion kept him awake at night so that he could lead local raids and skirmishes. Yet another told him that it produced very bad headaches. However, despite these accounts from Bamiyan, I still hadn't met someone who could provide firsthand information about consuming scorpion preparations for their psychoactive properties.

Then in February 2003, the UNODC began fieldwork in Kabul to collect data from key informants and drug users about the nature and extent of problem drug use in the city. Twelve fieldworkers were recruited from drug treatment centres in Kabul and trained in ethnographic techniques and interviewing skills. At the end of the first week of conducting interviews, during the daily debriefing session, one of the interviewers remarked that he had talked to a heroin user who had also smoked dried scorpions.

The next day I went to talk to this man to find out more about his use of scorpions. He recounted that in 1991 when he was 36 he had been a soldier in the army in Kunar province where his job was to collect stones from the mountains for road-building. The local villagers told him and his fellow soldiers that they could dry and smoke the large black scorpions they found under the stones. The soldiers then hung the scorpions by their tails to dry in the sun, powdered the whole scorpion, and mixed the powder in a *chillum* with hashish, which was then topped off with a layer of opium. The villagers had told the soldiers: 'If you smoke scorpions you will be intoxicated for a week.' When asked if this indeed was the effect of smoking the mixture, he retorted: 'No! I was only intoxicated for three days!' During these three days he recalled that he found it hard to open his eyes, his head was constantly spinning, and he had continuous visual hallucinations. Altogether he had smoked this mixture between 20 and 30 times. While some of the effects he experienced were undoubtedly due to the hashish and opium mix, it was the intensity and duration of the experience caused by the effects of the dried scorpion that he remarked on. Now he lived in Kabul with his wife and two children and was quite famous in his area as *mar di khuda*, literally translated as 'the man of God' but more likely to mean the strong man or the powerful man. This referred mainly to his generosity. When he worked as a labourer in a cement factory and made some money he bought drugs and always shared them with his friends. However, like many heroin users, he took little home to support his family, and his 14-year-old son had to sell cigarettes on the streets to earn money to feed the family. Since arriving in Kabul he had not smoked any more dried scorpion.

In May 2003, while discussing this book, an Afghan friend recalled that while growing up as a child in Kabul in the 1970s, if a family member was stung by a scorpion it was killed and then bandaged against the wound in the belief that it would suck out its own poison. He also remembered the 1980s when an uncle returned from the Soviet Union with two tubes of ointment, one of which had a scorpion pictured on the side and the other a snake. His mother rubbed the scorpion ointment on her knee to help her arthritis, although she put her hand inside a plastic bag before smearing it on. The tube had warnings not to rub the ointment on with bare fingers, to always wash your hands if you touched it, to ensure it didn't go anywhere near food and to never let it go anywhere near a lesion or an open wound. He assumed that scorpion venom was one of the active ingredients in the ointment. As with *hakims* and Unani medicine, preparations made from scorpions and snakes may contain some healing properties.

In 2002 Joe de Casa, a 61-year-old arthritis sufferer from Northamptonshire in England, was bitten on the hand by an adder, the only poisonous snake found in the UK. Almost immediately he noticed that the snake venom was having 'a miraculous effect' on his arthritic left hand. The constant pain he suffered on the hand had gone completely and this analgesic, or perhaps anti-inflammatory, effect lasted for four weeks. Mr de Casa was reported as saying: 'I would quite like to find another snake and invite him to bite me.' He hoped that scientists would investigate the anti-inflammatory properties of snake venom in the hope of helping other sufferers.[13]

In October 2003 a friend came across a 35-year-old man in Peshawar who claimed to have regularly smoked scorpions since the age of twelve. The man was accompanied to a *hakim*'s shop where he bought two dried scorpions for ten rupees ($0.20) each and then proceeded to crush one of them into powder and rolled it with tobacco into a cigarette. (He also recounted catching live scorpions and drying their tails for at least 24 hours before smoking them.) The effect was instantaneous with the man's face and eyes becoming very red, 'much more than with a hashish smoker' according to my friend. He also seemed very intoxicated but awake and alert, although he stumbled and fell over when he tried to rise from a sitting position. He reported that the smoke tasted 'sweeter' than that of hashish, although my friend said it smelled foul, and the intoxicating effect lasted much longer. The man also claimed that scorpion smokers are prone to anger and are always short-tempered. As a fisherman who had worked on boats out of Karachi, he had been arrested and imprisoned in several countries for fishing illegally, including Sri Lanka, Somalia and Oman. In the many prisons he had spent time in, smoking dried scorpions was 'quite common' as there was no other psychoactive substances available. The man has now returned to Karachi and his fishing boat.

Later I met another man in Peshawar who had smoked dried scorpions, but the more common green ones rather than black ones. He said that the effect was basically like hashish, but made him feel very strong so that he could carry on with his labouring work. It is likely that different types of scorpion have different types of venom with different intoxicating properties, but to my knowledge this has not been investigated. In 2005 a young Afghan heroin user, complete with a bandana round his head and wearing a tie-dyed multicoloured T-shirt, presented himself at a drug treatment centre in Kabul with his 'pet' scorpion lying on his arm. A large green scorpion with yellow legs, it stung him on the arm every day although the centre staff said the effect was 'psychological'. He also had to take analgesics at the same time to counteract the pain of the scorpion sting.

Apart from Afghanistan, the only other documented case of using scorpion preparations for their psychoactive effect that I have heard of comes from India. As part of her university Masters degree thesis, Molly Charles, an Indian researcher, interviewed *sadhus* who used a range of psychoactive substances in their spiritual quest. *Sadhus* are

Hindu mystics, the equivalent of the old Sufi *malangs* of Afghanistan, and several sects 'regularly smoke chillums at bhajans (Hindu devotional meetings) to symbolise their devotional fellowship'.[14] Throughout India, wandering *sadhus* can be seen smoking hashish from clay or stone *chillums*, mainly straight-stemmed conical-shaped pipes grasped in the hands and smoked in the upright position, the mouthpiece often wrapped in a wet cloth to cool the smoke. Charles mentions how the more experienced *sadhus* on an advanced spiritual quest reportedly smoke a *mahachillum* where cannabis, opium, datura, dried scorpion and a preparation made from snake venom are all consumed.

In 2005 an Indian friend who is a *sadhu* told me that a German friend of his had smoked scorpion and described the effects as being 'like a strong mescaline trip': in other words a very powerful hallucinogenic experience. He had smoked the dried stomach of the scorpion after watching it sting itself to death, apparently a common behavioural trait of scorpions, the venom then being distributed more evenly throughout the body.

A scientist colleague conservatively estimates that in Afghanistan there are well over 100 million scorpions. While it may be unlikely that using scorpion preparations as a psychoactive drug becomes a popular pastime, there is obviously not a supply shortage.

To date no cases have been found to substantiate Mullah Akhundzada's claims regarding the use of psychoactive snake prepartions in Afghanistan. Apart from reports of 'the steepings of a snake' used by the ancient Aztecs to increase sexual appetite and physical stamina when prostitutes plied such potions to hapless clients, or legends, even scorpion tales, of hapless men consuming the drug and literally draining themselves and drying up and dying as a result of excess sexual activity, there is little to suggest that snake preparations have been used for anything other than health and medical purposes.[15] In contemporary China, Hong Kong and Taiwan snake bile is still valued as a tonic, characterised by its sweet aftertaste, and served as a special health drink at snake restaurants. The bile of a snake about to be cooked and eaten is typically mixed with some rice wine and consumed before the meal as an invigorating beverage and appetite stimulant.[16]

While toads, scorpions and Datura go mainly unrecognised for their psychoactive properties, apart from the international drug *cognoscente* and a few Afghans and other regional inhabitants, they symbolise the infinite variety and sheer number of available psychoactive substances. To try and control every naturally occurring substance that can be used as a psychoactive drug is the impossible dream, the last policy refuge, of those conducting a war against drugs. Perhaps more than with any other intoxicant, the use of scorpion tails signifies the wide range of psychoactive substances that are sought out by those dedicated to drug consumption or those too desperate to avoid it.

# Postscript

Contrary to what has often been denounced here and there, opium production is more a consequence of Afghanistan's lawlessness, instability and poverty than its cause. Opium production clearly proceeds from poverty and food insecurity, from Afghanistan to Myanmar and Laos, where it is a coping mechanism and livelihood strategy.[1]

It [the opium economy] is the single greatest challenge to the long-term security, development and effective governance of Afghanistan...for the ever-growing numbers of problem drug users in Afghanistan, the drug robs them of ambition and the ability to provide for themselves and their families—and to help re-build Afghanistan.[2]

In January 2006 at a conference in London, President Karzai acknowledged, somewhat optimistically, that it would take at least ten years before opium poppy could be eliminated from Afghanistan. Trying to eliminate the demand for drugs is likely to take a lot longer. For all its complexities demand is also largely a consequence of the country's lawlessness, instability and poverty. While strong religious and spiritual beliefs have helped many Afghans resist the temptation to take drugs, many others have succumbed. Just as the need for survival may override the farmer's firmly held belief that planting opium poppy is *haram* and anti-Islamic, so the drug user overrides Koranic injunctions against the consumption of intoxicants in order to cope with everyday life and to dull physical and/or psychological pain.

In Afghanistan and also globally there appears to be little decrease in the demand for drugs—a demand supplied by the ready availability of a wide, varied and ever-increasing range of psychoactive substances, whether natural or synthetic, animal or vegetable, legal or illegal. In the case of the latter, 'the global retail market for illicit drugs is estimated at US $320 billion. For all the caveats that one may put on such a figure...it is still larger than the individual GDPs of nearly 90% of the countries of the world.'[3]

The UN's optimistic anti-drug campaign, begun in 1998, proclaimed that by 2008 there would be 'A drug free world—We can do it!' seems increasingly unattainable and out of touch with reality—the reality of a world saturated with psychoactive intoxicating drugs of all shapes, sizes and forms. The primary challenge for drug control policy is how to develop practical, realistic and culturally appropriate ways to enable people to live safely with these drugs, to control and regulate their supply and use while minimising the harm caused by them to individuals, families and communities. Laws based on prohibition, frequently draconian in nature, have failed either to prevent an increase in drug cultivation, production and consumption or to deal with offenders in a humane and cost-effective manner, increasing crime and reducing public safety in the process. At a Paris conference in early 2006 on 'Drug Production and State Stability', Professor Alfred McCoy 'explained that "after fighting five drug wars in 30 years at a cost of US $150 billion, Washington has presided over a [fivefold] increase" in the world illicit opium-supply, from 1,000 tonnes in 1970 to between 5,000 and 6,000 tonnes in the mid-2000s'.[4]

There is a basic futility about any war against drugs, especially a war against those who use them. There will always be a supplier willing to meet the demand no matter the risks involved and the penalties incurred. The determined drug user, motivated by a myriad of factors, can always find legal and quasi-legal substitutes available for those substances deemed illegal. The pharmaceutical industry, poorly regulated in much of the developing world, continues to develop and produce drugs that mirror, if not surpass, the effects of many illicit street drugs. Infinitely available in most countries worldwide, in the Islamic tradition alcohol, for good reason, is perceived as one of the most harmful of all the intoxicants. In any case, there are always scorpion tails available, at least in Afghanistan.

Scorpion tales remind us that much of our taken for granted knowledge and understanding of drugs and drug users, as well as drug policies, is frequently flawed and based on uncertainties and unresolved paradoxes. The more knowledge we have, the less we seem able to control problem drug use. There is often no correlation between the level of knowledge about a social problem like drug use and an effective response. While this may be a reflection of a lack of political will or inadequate resources, it can also be accounted for by a lack of understanding of the complex dynamics and relationships between the many factors and conditions that shape the problem in the first place. Moreover the primary problems that underlie drug use such as poverty, alienation, personal insecurity and chronic mental health problems are often neglected or ignored.

While drug use may be the presenting problem, in most cases it is unlikely to stop and enable the drug user to lead a productive and fulfilled life unless the problems that led to it in the first place are acknowledged and tackled. I'm reminded of taking an Afghan colleague to visit a drug treatment centre in the UK where the medical and social welfare services were better than even the best hospital in Afghanistan. He had only one question to ask: 'You have fantastic treatment centres here, lots of resources and the political will to solve the problem, but you say you haven't solved the problem, why not?' Nobody could answer him.

In the case of Afghanistan this is perhaps an easier question to answer. Many of the conditions that contribute to motivations for drug use are unlikely to disappear for most Afghans in the near future, including: high prevalence of chronic mental health problems; impoverishment; food insecurity; repression; social disruption; conflict; violence; and insecurity. Warlords, commanders, militias, pharmaceutical companies, opium farmers, drug traders, untrained doctors, corrupt politicians, insurgents, foreign military and drug users themselves all play a part in creating the jigsaw of problem drug use and the way that we come to understand it.

Inevitably, advisers, politicians and social scientists order and compartmentalise information and research data into neat boxes in order to develop policies, strategies and programmes, but life frequently defies such attempts at compartmentalisation. Many seemingly disparate but interdependent factors contribute to problem drug use, and harmful unintended consequences can result from misguided policies and unrealistic prevention programmes. While this book can only provide the briefest of glimpses into the many factors that impinge on and account for problem drug use in Afghanistan, and other parts of the world, it illustrates the need for a comprehensive and holistic understanding before any effective and realistic solution can be developed. Most importantly, Afghanistan reminds us that 'Fragmenting countries show the integrating ones the dark side of their common present.'[5]

Despite some positive developments and successes since the Bonn agreement of December 2001, by the time this book went to the publishers in mid-2006, Afghanistan was a country still deeply mired in political flux, escalating violence, poverty and growing social inequalities—starkly reflected in the contrast between the ostentatious newly-built villas of the rich and the war-battered slums and squatter settlements of Kabul, still without basic services such as electricity and running water. Many of those refugees who had returned in hope to their country after the Taliban had been 'defeated' by US-led forces in November 2001 were desperate to leave again, this time as economic migrants.[6] There are still little available sustained employment and income-generation opportunities, despite over $8 billion already spent on reconstruction efforts.[*]

With threats of forced eradication of opium poppies over the next few years and few viable alternative livelihoods, the poorer farmers are likely to join the exodus of economic migrants or join the growing ranks of the disaffected. In London in early 2006 international donors pledged $10.5 billion to Afghanistan over a five-year period in a wide-ranging reconstruction programme known as the Afghan Compact, but perhaps failed to recognise that in Afghanistan time and commitment are more valuable commodities than money when it comes to reconstructing and developing the country. The elusive Taliban are still resurgent, with some Afghans even wishing for a return to the dubious peace and security that they viciously established between 1995 and 2001. As Taliban commanders, free of the pressures facing vote-catching western politicians, are frequently quoted as saying: 'The Americans have the clocks, but we have the time.'[7]

In the summer of 2006 over 3,000 UK troops were sent to Helmand, a major drug production and trafficking region, adding to the country's already volatile political-military mix of commanders, warlords, commanders and warlords-turned-politicians and government officials, US forces, NATO forces, the Taliban, other armed groups and various units of the newly trained Afghan national army and police, many of whom formerly belonged to militias. The excursion of foreign troops into the country will inevitably be time limited. Their presence dictated more by the interests of western politicians than the needs of the Afghan people. While the London conference set out a roadmap for Afghanistan's long journey towards peace and stability with such milestones as wiping out all illegal armed groups by 2007 and creating a respected national army by 2010, this is currently a road blocked by increasing numbers of insurgents, other armed groups and disaffected Afghans.

There has been an international emphasis and focus of resources on drug supply reduction and the development of effective law

---

[*] An investigative report released by CorpWatch in May 2006 graphically describes how much of this reconstruction money has been spent with little accountability and many opportunities for graft and abuse, for example large open-ended contracts were granted without competitive bidding or limited competition to politically connected corporations doing comparative work in Iraq, such as Kellog, Brown and Root, The Louis Berger Group and DynCorp. Indeed a good percentage of this reconstruction money never leaves the western countries where such multinationals are based.

enforcement initiatives and alternative livelihoods for poppy cultivators in the rush to stem the flow of narcotics out of Afghanistan and into the west. However, in the longer term excessive drug consumption and the myriad of problems that it brings to such an impoverished and war-traumatised populace may prove just as big a barrier to human and socioeconomic development as the cultivation and production of illicit drugs. Put another way, some decades from now when opium cultivation in Afghanistan has finally been eliminated and the law enforcement advisors and rural development consultants have all moved on to new cultivation and production countries, for demand reduction specialists it will be 'business as usual' with Afghans who will be using drugs that, like scorpion tails, we can hardly even imagine.

Meanwhile, in central Kabul, a man called Abdul Shah sits slumped against the wall of a small mosque by the side of the river. With all his family killed in the fighting over the past 25 years he has no home to go to and now lives in a hole in the river bank. He returned to Afghanistan two years ago after 15 years in Iran where he first started to smoke heroin. Now he is an injector of the drug and has just had a hit. One of his fellow-injectors sticks a cigarette in his mouth the wrong way round and vainly tries to light the filtered end. He catches my eye, sways a bit, shrugs his shoulders and grins sheepishly. It is the classic glassy-eyed look of the intoxicated, a global expression. Abdul Shah and his compatriots have never heard of anyone smoking scorpion tails but, yes, they say, if there was nothing else available on the street of course they would try it.

# Notes

## PROLOGUE

1. *National Geographic*, April 2002.
2. Sirdar Ikbal Ali Shah, 1928, *Afghanistan of the Afghans*, Quetta: Nisa Traders.
3. Rory Stewart, 2004, *The Places in Between*, London: Picador, p. 180.
4. UNDCP, 2001, Community Drug Profile No. 4: 'An assessment of problem drug use in rural Afghanistan: the GAI target districts', Islamabad: UNDCP Afghanistan.
5. Lowell Thomas, 1998, *Beyond the Khyber Pass*, Lahore: Vanguard Books, p. 222.
6. Idries Shah, 1986, *Kara Kush*, Glasgow: Fontana/Collins, p. 131.
7. M. Masood, A. Coste and S. Turbot, 2003, 'Reaching People in the Field', *Afghanistan Monitor: An Independent Journal of Humanitarian Accountability*, Issue No. 1, 15 July 2003, p. 18.
8. Robert D. Kaplan, 2001, *Soldiers of God: With Islamic Warriors in Afghanistan and Pakistan*, New York: Vintage Books, p. 243.
9. UNICEF, 2003, 'Afghanistan: Multiple Indicator Cluster Survey 2003', Central Statistics Office Transitional Islamic Government of Afghanistan and UNICEF Afghanistan Country Office, Detail Table, December 2003, p. 86
10. BBC News, 13 December 2004.
11. Ibid.

## 1 INTRODUCTION

1. Peter L. Bergen, 2001, *Holy War, Inc.: Inside the Secret World of Osama bin Laden*, London: Weidenfeld & Nicolson, p. 12.
2. Ismail Khan, Governor of Herat, quoted in *New York Times Magazine*, 1 June 2003, p. 101.
3. Peter Marsden, 1998, *The Taliban: War, Religion and the New Order in Afghanistan*, London: Zed Books, p. 11.
4. Jason Elliot, 2000, *An Unexpected Light: Travels in Afghanistan*, London: Picador, p. 27.
5. Barnett R. Rubin, 1996, *The Fragmentation of Afghanistan: State Formation and Collapse in the International System*, Lahore: Vanguard Press.
6. *Kabul Weekly*, 30 July 2003.
7. *Kabul Weekly*, 6 August 2003.
8. Council on Foreign Relations and the Asia Society, 2003, 'Afghanistan: Are we losing the peace?', Chairman's Report of the Independent Task Force on India and South Asia, New York: Council on Foreign Relations, p. 12.
9. *Daily Times*, 19 November 2004.

10. *Asia Times*, 21 September 2005.
11. Martin Ewans, 2001, *Afghanistan: A New History*, Richmond: Curzon Press, p. 92.
12. Ibid, p. 95.
13. Asne Seierstad, 2003, *The Bookseller of Kabul*, London: Little, Brown.
14. *Observer*, 21 September 2003.
15. *Toronto Star*, 17 November 2003.
16. *Observer*, 21 September 2003.
17. Pamela Constable, 'Pageant flap bares depth of tradition for Afghans: Rights advocates fear conservative backlash', *Malalai: A Social and Cultural Magazine for Women*, Issue 17, November 2003, p. 3.
18. Ibid.
19. *Christian Science Monitor*, 9 May 2005.
20. *Independent*, 28 April 2005.
21. Human Rights Watch, 2003, '"Killing you is a very easy thing for us": Human Rights Abuses in Southeast Afghanistan', New York: Human Rights Watch, Vol. 15, No. 5, July 2003.
22. Agence France Presse (AFP), 21 October 2005.
23. IWPR (Institute for War and Peace Reporting), 4 February 2006, downloaded from http://e-ariana.com/ariana/eariana.nsf/allDocs/6BCF5D6E882439F68725710C003B68FA? OpenDocument
24. BBC News, Kabul, 19 June 2006, downloaded from http://news.bbc.co.uk/1/hi/world/south_asia/5096004.stm
25. Barnett R. Rubin, Humayun Hamidzada and Abby Stoddard, 2003, 'Through the Fog of Peace Building: Evaluating the Reconstruction of Afghanistan', New York: Center on International Cooperation, June 2003, p. 7.
26. *IRIN*, 20 June 2006.
27. *Guardian Review*, 29 June 2002.
28. Martin Ewans, *Afghanistan: A New History*, p. 9.
29. George Forster, 1808, *A Journey from Bengal to England through the Northern part of India, Kashmir, Afghanistan and Persia, and into Russia by the Caspian Sea*, quoted in ibid., p. 27.
30. John Prebble, 1981, *The Lion in the North: A Personal View of Scotland's History*, London: Penguin Books, p. 283.
31. Frank L. Holt, 2005, *Into the Land of Bones: Alexander the Great in Afghanistan*, Berkeley and Los Angeles: University of California Press, p. 81.
32. Ibid., p. 82.
33. G. Whitney Azoy, 2003, *Buzkashi: Game and Power in Afghanistan*, Illinois: Waveland Press, pp. xiii–xiv.
34. Anne Marlowe, 'The hypocrite of Kabul', available on: www.salon.com
35. International Narcotics Control Board, 2005, Report of the International Narcotics Control Board for 2004, New York: United Nations.
36. LEAP (Law Enforcement Against Prohibition) available on: www.leap.cc/about/index.htm
37. *Scottish Daily Mail*, 13 April 2006.
38. *Guardian*, 28 April 2006.

39. Mental Health Foundation, March 2006, 'Cheers? Understanding the relationship between alcohol and mental health', available on website: www.mentalhealth.org.uk/page.cfm?pageurl=cheers_keyfindings.cfm
40. See LEAP Drug War Distortions, available on website: www.drugwardistortions.org/distortion2.htm

## 2 SCORPION TALES

1. Cindy Fazey, 2002, 'Estimating the World Illicit Drug Situation—reality and the seven deadly political sins', *Drugs: Education, Prevention and Policy*, Vol. 9, No. 1, p. 95.
2. Alfred McCoy, 'Interim Draft Report: Historical Review of Opium/Heroin Production', Schaffer Library of Drug Policy, undated.
3. Robin Room, 2003, 'The Cultural Framing of Addiction', *Janus Head*, Vol. 6, No. 2, p. 221.
4. Olivier Roy, source unknown.
5. *Scotsman*, 19 October 2002.
6. Sandy Gall, 1988, *Afghanistan: Travels with the Mujahideen*, London: Hodder & Stoughton, p. 66.
7. Chris Johnson and Jolyon Leslie, 2005, *Afghanistan: The Mirage of Peace*, London: Zed Books, p. 73.
8. Peter Marsden, source unknown.
9. L. Dupree, 1980, *Afghanistan*, Princeton, NJ: Princeton University Press, p. 43.
10. Michael Bhatia and Jonathan Goodhand (with Haneef Atmar, Adam Pain and Mohammed Suleman), 2002, 'Profits and Poverty: Aid, Livelihood and Conflict in Afghanistan', unpublished paper, final draft August 2002, p. 1.
11. UNDP, 2005, *Afghanistan: National Human Development Report 2004*, United Nations Development Programme Afghanistan and the Islamic Republic of Afghanistan, Kabul: UNDP, p. 264.
12. *Kabul Weekly*, 5 December 2002.
13. A. Pain and J. Goodhand, 2002, 'Afghanistan: Current employment and socio-economic situation and prospects', Working Paper No. 8, Geneva: ILO Recovery and Reconstruction Department, March 2002.
14. Azarakhsh Mokri, 2002, 'Brief Overview of the Status of Drug Abuse in Iran', *Archives of Iranian Medicine*, Vol. 5, No. 3, p. 184.
15. National Research Council, *Informing America's Policy on Illegal Drugs: What We Don't Know Keeps On Hurting Us*, Washington DC: National Academy Press, 2001, p. 2.
16. Danish Karokhel, 2003, 'Corruption probe nets millions', *Afghan Recovery Report* No. 53, 21 March 2003, Institute for War and Peace Reporting.
17. WHO, 1964, WHO Technical Report Series No. 273: 'Expert Committee on Addiction-Producing Drugs', Thirteenth Report of the WHO expert Committee, Geneva: World Health Organization.
18. WHO, 1994, 'Lexicon of Alcohol and Drug Terms', Geneva: World Health Organization.
19. EMCDDA, 2000, 'Annual Report 2000', European Monitoring Centre on Drugs and Drug Abuse (EMCDDA), Lisbon.

20. Advisory Council on the Misuse of Drugs, 1982, *Treatment and Rehabilitation*, London: HMSO.
21. J. Westermeyer, 2004, 'The Importance and difficulty of drug research in developing countries: a report from Kabul as timely reminder', *Addiction*, Vol. 99, Issue 7, p. 803.
22. UNDCP, 2001, Community Drug Profile No. 4: 'An assessment of problem drug use in rural Afghanistan: the GAI target districts', Islamabad: UNDCP Afghanistan.
23. UNODC, 2003, 'The Opium Economy in Afghanistan: An International Problem', New York: United Nations, p. 73.
24. Cindy Fazey, 2002, 'Estimating the World Illicit Drug Situation—reality and the seven deadly political sins', *Drugs: education, prevention and policy*, Vol. 9, No. 1, pp. 95–96.
25. UNDCP, Community Drug Profile No. 4: 'An Assessment of problem drug use in rural Afghanistan—the GAI target districts'.
26. Ibid.
27. Arnold S. Trebach, 2002, 'What we need is a world drug reform report', Book Review of United Nations Office for Drug Control and Crime Prevention, World Drug Report 2000, Oxford University Press, Oxford, 2000, *International Journal of Drug Policy*, Vol. 13, Issue 3.
28. Personal communication, UNODCCP Official, Vienna 2000.
29. Carla Rossi, 2002, A critical reading of the World Drug Report 2000, *International Journal of Drug Policy*, Vol. 13, Issue 3.
30. Quoted in Prof. Carla Rossi's comments on the UNDCP reaction to her critical review of the World Drug Report 2000, downloaded from: http://coranet.radicalparty.org/pressreview/arlacchi1.php
31. Neil Hunt, 2004, 'A review of the evidence-base for harm reduction approaches to drug use, Forward Thinking on Drugs: A Release Initiative', London: Release.
32. Ibid.
33. Ibid.
34. Martin Jelsma, 2003, 'Drugs in the UN system: the unwritten history of the 1988 United Nations General Assembly Special Session on drugs', *International Journal of Drug Policy*, Vol. 14, Issue 2, p. 182.
35. Amy Gibson, Louisa Degenhardt, Carolyn Day and Rebecca McKetin, 2005, 'Recent trends in heroin supply to markets in Australia, the United States and Western Europe', *International Journal of Drug Policy*, Vol. 16, Issue 5, pp. 293–299.
36. Narcotics Drugs Quarterly Supplement No. 3, 2001, Vienna: United Nations.
37. *AARP, The Magazine*, downloaded from: www.aarpmagazine.org/health/prisoners_pain.html
38. *Asia Times*, 1 February 2006.
39. UNODC, 11 April 2005, 'Points of discussion on licit cultivation of opium poppy in Afghanistan', Kabul: UNODC Country Office for Afghanistan, p. 2.
40. *New York Times*, 13 July 2005.
41. Press release, 'Afghan Government says the licit cultivation of opium poppy will not be possible for the time being', Islamic Republic of Afghanistan Ministry of Counter Narcotics, Kabul, 26 September 2005.

42. *Gulf News*, 20 December 2002.
43. *Indo-Asian News Service*, 27 January 2006, downloaded from: http://stop-thedrugwar.org/chronicle/420/southasia.shtml
44. Commission on Narcotic Drugs, 1995, 'Economic social consequences of drug abuse and illicit trafficking: an Interim report', Vienna: UN Economic and Social Council.
45. UNODC, 2002, 'Afghanistan Annual Opium Poppy Survey 2002', Kabul: United Nations Office on Drugs and Crime.
46. US Department of State, 2003, 'International Narcotics Control Strategy Report', Bureau for International Narcotics and Law Enforcement Affairs, March 2003.
47. UNODC, 2004, 'Afghanistan Annual Opium Poppy Survey 2004', Kabul: United Nations Office on Drugs and Crime.

### 3   A NATION IN ANGUISH

1. Ashraf Ghani, Minister of Finance, Kabul, April 2003
2. Carl Robichaud, 2006, 'Remember Afghanistan? A Glass Half Full, On the Titanic', *World Policy Journal*, Vol. XXIII, No. 1.
3. K. Klave, 1999, 'Drugs, addiction, deviance and disease as social constructs', *Bulletin on Narcotics*, Vol. 21, Nos 1 & 2, p. 50.
4. Richard Davenport-Hines, 2002, *The Pursuit of Oblivion: A Social History of Drugs*, London: Phoenix Press, p. 125.
5. Andrew Weil, 1973, *The Natural Mind: A New Way of Looking at Drugs and the Higher Consciousness*, Boston: Houghton Mifflin, p. 17.
6. J. Ahtone (ed.), 1985, 'Proceedings of a Workshop on the Afghan refugees health programme', 19–21 November, Islamabad.
7. Zohra Rasekh, Heidi Bauer, M.Michele Manos and Vincent Iacopino, 1998, 'Women's Health and Human Rights in Afghanistan', *Journal of the American Medical Association*, Vol. 280, No. 5.
8. A. Rahman and A. Hafeez, 2003, 'Suicidal feelings run high among mothers in refugee camps: a cross-sectional survey', *Acta Psychiatrica Scandinavica*, Vol. 108, Issue 5, p. 392.
9. Jill S. Williams, 2002, 'Depression, PTSD, Substance Abuse Increase in Wake of September 11 Attacks', *NIDA Notes*, Vol. 17, No. 4.
10. Center for the Advancement of Health, Press release, 22 October 2004, downloaded from: www.cfah.org/hbns/news/september10–22–04.cfm
11. Quoted in Richard Davenport-Hines, *The Pursuit of Oblivion: A Social History of Drugs*, p. 85.
12. Charles W. Hoge, Carl A. Castro, Stephen C. Messer, Dennis McGurk, David I. Cotting and Robert L. Koffman, 2004, 'Combat Duty in Iraq and Afghanistan, Mental Health Problems, and Barriers to Care', *New England Journal of Medicine*, Vol. 351, No. 1.
13. Charles Medawar and Anita Hardon, 2004, *Medicines out of Control? Anti-depressants and the Conspiracy of Goodwill*, Amsterdam: Aksant Academic Publishers, p. 221.
14. *IRIN News*, 12 February 2003.

15. Barbara Lopes Cardozo, Oleg O. Bilukha, Carol A. Gotway Cranford, Irshad Shaikh, Mitchell I. Wolfe, Michael L. Gerber and Mark Anderson, 2004, Mental Health, Social Functioning, and Disability in Postwar Afghanistan, *Journal of the American Medical Association*, Vol. 292, No. 5.
16. Ronald Waldman and Homaira Hanif, 2002, 'The Public Health System in Afghanistan', Issues Paper Series, Afghan Research and Evaluation Unit [AREU], May–June 2002.
17. Judy A. Benjamin, 2002, 'A study on the situation of women and girls in Afghanistan—Post-Taliban Afghanistan: Changed Prospects for Women?', UN Coordinators Office, Afghanistan, February 2002.
18. IWPR, 15 August 2004 downloaded from http://e-ariana.com/ariana/eariana.nsf/allDocs/0B369F
19. Pharmaciens Sans Frontieres, 'Activity report 2001'.
20. Mark Van Ommeren, 2003, 'Validity issues in transcultural epidemiology', *British Journal of Psychiatry*, Vol. 182, No. 5.
21. D. Macdonald, 2001, 'Death, destruction and depression—understanding Afghanistan', *Druglink*, Vol. 16, Issue 5.
22. Ronald Waldman and Homaira Hanif, 'The Public Health System in Afghanistan', p. 12.
23. P. Bracken, 2002, *Trauma: Culture, Meaning and Philosophy*, London: Whurr Publishers.
24. Jo de Berry, 2002, 'Agency viewpoint: Are Afghan children traumatised?', *Crosslines Afghanistan Monitor—An Independent Journal of Humanitarian Accountability,* Issue No. 2, pp. 10–11.
25. *IRIN News*, 1 July 2003.
26. Shon Campbell, 'Lost Chances—the Changing Situation of Children in Afghanistan 1990–2000', cited in Jonathan Walter, 2003, 'Children of War', *The Crosslines Afghanistan Monitor: Independent Journal Monitoring Afghanistan's Recovery*, Issue No. 3, p. 4.
27. *Observer*, 25 May 2003.
28. *Newsweek*, 16 May 2005.
29. Michael von der Schulenberg, Afghanistan: Peace in a Glasshouse, 28 July 2002, Vienna, unpublished.
30. David B. Edwards, 2002, *Before Taliban: Genealogies of the Afghan Jihad*, Berkeley: University of California Press, p. 295.
31. *Reuters*, 24 August 2005.
32. Peter L. Bergen, 2001, *Holy War Inc.: Inside the Secret World of Osama bin Laden*, London: Weidenfeld & Nicolson, p. 53.
33. Robert Schultheis, 2002, 'We are all free', *Coloradan*, Vol. 7, No. 3.
34. UNICEF, 2003, 'Afghanistan: Multiple Indicator Cluster Survey 2003', Central Statistics Office Transitional Islamic Government of Afghanistan and UNICEF Afghanistan Country Office, Detail Table, December 2003, p. 94.
35. 'Afghanistan—the world's guilty secret', *Amnesty Journal*, Jan/Feb 1996.
36. 'Amnesty International Report 1999: Afghanistan', Amnesty International.
37. 'Human Rights Watch World Report, Asia: Afghanistan, 2002', New York: Human Rights Watch.

38. *News International,* 24 October 2002.
39. 'Human Rights Watch World Report, Asia: Afghanistan, 2002'.
40. *Kabul Times,* 2 October 2002.
41. *Independent,* 18 January 2005.
42. UNDP Country Development Indicators, 1995.
43. UNDP, 2000, Helmand Initiative: Joint Strategy Development 2nd Draft, Helmand Planning Group, Islamabad, May 2000.
44. Ahmed Rashid, 2000, *Taliban: Islam, Oil and the New Great Game in Central Asia,* London: I.B. Taurus, p. 105.
45. Musa Khan Jalalzai, 2002, *Women trafficking and prostitution in Pakistan and Afghanistan,* Lahore: Dua Publications.
46. Anne E. Brodsky, 2003, *With all our strength: The Revolutionary Association of the Women of Afghanistan,* London and New York: Routledge, p. 142.
47. Ibid., p. 111.
48. William Maley, 2002, *The Afghanistan Wars,* London: Palgrave Macmillan, p. 238.
49. Chris Johnson, William Maley, Alexander Thier and Ali Wardak, 2003, 'Afghanistan's political and constitutional development', London: Overseas Development Institute, p. 29.
50. *Christian Science Monitor,* 24 April 2006.
51. *BBC News World Edition,* 9 August 2003.
52. David Macdonald, 2000, 'The war on drug users in Afghanistan', *Aina: UN Afghanistan Magazine,* Summer Issue 2000.
53. UNDCP, 1999, Community Drug Profile No. 1: 'Problem Drug Use in Afghan Communities—An Initial Assessment', Islamabad: UNDCP Afghanistan Programme.
54. *The Times,* 4 October 2001.
55. Joint Reintegration Programme Unit in Afghanistan, 2000, Greater Azra Initiative—Joint Reintegration Programme in Afghanistan 1999 to 2000, Islamabad, p. 4.
56. Afghanistan Weekly Situation Report, 8–14 September 2002
57. *The News,* 9 May 2002.
58. UNICEF, Afghanistan: Multiple Indicator Cluster Survey 2003, p. 78.
59. UNEP, 2003, Afghanistan—Post-Conflict Environmental Assessment, Nairobi: United Nations Environment Programme.
60. *IRIN News,* 22 June 2004.
61. Associated Press, 14 March 2006, downloaded from: www.e-ariana.com/ariana/eariana.nsf/allDocs/FA21F20583816295872571310083A239?OpenDocument
62. Government of Afghanistan, 2002, Strategic Directions for Livelihood and Social Protection in Afghanistan, Kabul: Livelihoods and Vulnerability Analysis Unit.
63. *Xinhua,* 28 September 2004.
64. *New York Times,* 12 December 2004
65. UNDP, 2004, 'Afghanistan: National Human Development Report', United Nations Development Programme Afghanistan and the Islamic Republic of Afghanistan, Kabul: UNDP, p. 276.
66. Human Rights Watch, 2002, 'Fatally flawed—Cluster bombs and their use by the United States in Afghanistan', New York: Human Rights Watch.

67. Uranium Medical Research Centre, 2002, 'Afghan Field Trip No.2 Report: Precise Destruction—Indiscriminate Effects', September/October 2002, Washington.
68. BBC News, 22 May 2003.
69. Observer, 25 May 2003.
70. Barnett R. Rubin, Abby Stoddard, Humayun Hamidzada and Adib Farhada, 2004, 'Building a New Afghanistan: The Value of Success, The Cost of Failure', New York University: Center on International Cooperation in conjunction with CARE, p. 25.
71. Private Eye, Issue 1107, 28 May–10 June 2004.
72. Associated Press, 27 April 2003.
73. Sue Lautze, Neamat Nojumi and Karem Najimi, 2002, 'Food Security, Malnutrition and the Political Economy of Survival: A Report from Kabul, Herat and Qandahar', WFP, p. 27.
74. Reuters, 25 August 2003.
75. Independent, 10 February 2006.
76. Kabul Times, 27 August 2003.
77. Adam Pain and Jonathan Goodhand, 2002, 'Afghanistan: Current employment and socio-economic situation and prospects', In Focus Programme on Crisis Response and Reconstruction Working Paper No. 8, Geneva: ILO.
78. Frank L. Holt, 2005, Into the Land of Bones: Alexander the Great in Afghanistan, Berkeley and Los Angeles: University of California Press, p. 145.
79. Washington Times, 5 January 2004.
80. Sunday Times, 12 March 2006.

## 4   OPIUM CULTIVATORS

1. UNODC, 2003, 'Strategic Study No. 9: Opium Poppy Cultivation in a Changing Policy Environment—Farmer's Intentions for the 2002/03 Growing Seasons', Kabul: UNODC, p. 24.
2. Islamic State of Afghanistan—'Second Quarterly Review Under the Staff-Monitored Program and the 2004 Article IV Consultation', Kabul: IMF External Relations Department, 3 November 2004.
3. Chris Johnson and Jolyon Leslie, 2004, Afghanistan: The Mirage of Peace, London: Zed Books, p. 112.
4. IBC Report on the Province of Nangharhar undertaken in 1905 by Captain Johnson on behalf of the British Indian Government.
5. Imperial Gazetteer of India: Afghanistan and Nepal, 1999, Lahore: Sang-e-Meel Publications, p. 30.
6. Alexander Cockburn and Jeffrey St. Clair, 1999, Whiteout: The CIA, Drugs and the Press, London: Verso, p. 262.
7. UNODC, 2003, 'The Opium Economy in Afghanistan: An International Problem', Office on Drugs and Crime Vienna, New York: United Nations, p. 88.
8. Alfred W. McCoy, 2003, The Politics of Heroin: CIA Complicity in the Global Drug Trade, Chicago: Lawrence Hill Books, p. 468.

9. United Nations Office on Drugs and Crime Update, 2002, Vienna: UNODC, p. 11.

10. Adam Pain and Jonathan Goodhand, 2002, 'Afghanistan: Current employment and socio-economic situation and prospects', InFocus Programme on Crisis Response and Reconstruction Working Paper No. 8, Geneva: ILO, p. 12.

11. Adam Pain and Sue Lautze, 2002, 'Addressing Livelihoods in Afghanistan', Kabul: Afghanistan Research and Evaluation Unit.

12. Peter Sloane, 2000, 'Helmand Initiative: Joint Strategy Development Draft Report', Islamabad: UNDP, p. 20.

13. David Mansfield, 2004, 'What is Driving Opium Poppy Cultivation? Decision Making Amongst Opium Poppy Cultivators in Afghanistan in the 2003/4 Growing Season', paper for the UNODC/ONDCP Second Technical Conference on Drug Control Research, 19–21 July 2004.

14. David Mansfield, 2005, 'What is Driving Opium Poppy Cultivation? The Pressures to Reduce Opium Poppy Cultivation in Afghanistan in the 2004/05 Growing Season', a report for the Afghanistan Drugs Inter Departmental Unit of the Foreign and Commonwealth Unit, London: FCO.

15. Ibid,. p. 1.

16. UNODC and Government of Afghanistan Counter Narcotics Directorate, 2003, Afghanistan Opium Survey 2003.

17. David Mansfield, 2002, 'The Economic Superiority of Illicit Drug Production: Myth and Reality—Opium Poppy Cultivation in Afghanistan', paper prepared for the International conference on alternative development in drug control and cooperation, Feldafing, January 7–12, 2002, p. 3.

18. Chris Johnson and Jolyon Leslie, *Afghanistan: The Mirage of Peace*, p. 113.

19. David Mansfield, 'The Economic Superiority of Illicit Drug Production: Myth and Reality—Opium Poppy Cultivation in Afghanistan', p. 4.

20. Ibid., p. 5.

21. UNDCP, 2000, Strategic Studies series No. 6: 'The Role of Women in Opium Cultivation in Afghanistan', Islamabad: UNDCP Afghanistan Programme, p. 39.

22. UNDCP, 1999, Strategic Studies series No. 5: 'An Analysis of the Process of Expansion of Opium Poppy to New Districts in Afghanistan', Islamabad: UNDCP Afghanistan Programme, p. 17.

23. Barnett R. Rubin, 1996, *The Fragmentation of Afghanistan: State formation and Collapse in the International System*, Lahore: Vanguard Books, p. 34.

24. UNDCP, 1999, Strategic Study series No. 3: 'The Role of Opium as a Source of Informal Credit', Islamabad: UNDCP Afghanistan Programme, p. 7.

25. David Mansfield, 'The Economic Superiority of Illicit Drug Production: Myth and Reality—Opium Poppy Cultivation in Afghanistan', p. 6.

26. Personal communication, law enforcement officer, Kabul 2004.

27. David Mansfield, 'The Economic Superiority of Illicit Drug Production: Myth and Reality—Opium Poppy Cultivation in Afghanistan', p. 6.

28. UNDCP, 1998, Strategic Study series No. 2: 'The Dynamics of the Farmgate Opium Trade and the Coping Strategies of Opium Traders', Islamabad: UNDCP Afghanistan Programme, p. 12.
29. David Mansfield, 'What is Driving Opium Poppy Cultivation? The Pressures to Reduce Opium Poppy Cultivation in Afghanistan in the 2004/05 Growing Season', report for the Afghanistan Drugs Inter Departmental Unit of the Foreign and Commonwealth Unit, UK Government, London, p. 258.
30. W. Byrd and C. Ward, 2004, 'Afghanistan's Drug Economy: A Preliminary Overview and Analysis', Draft Technical Annex 2, Washington: World Bank.
31. *The Economist*, 16–22 August 2003.
32. *Washington Post*, 23 February 2003.
33. Chris Johnson and Jolyon Leslie, *Afghanistan: The Mirage of Peace*, p. 114.
34. Ibid. p. 126.
35. UNIDATA, 1992, 'Afghanistan: Badakhshan Province—a socio-economic profile', Kabul: UNIDATA—A Project of UNDP/OPS & UNOCA.
36. Judith Barrand, 2003, 'Empowering Women, Fighting Poppy: Red Gold Rising', *Afghanistan Monitor: An Independent Journal of Humanitarian Accountability*, Issue No.1, p. 11.
37. *Kabul Weekly*, 8 December 2004.
38. *Newsweek*, 4 October 2004.
39. David Mansfield, Forthcoming, 'Economical with the truth: The limits of price and profitability in both explaining opium poppy cultivation in Afghanistan and in designing effective responses', in Adam Pain (ed.), *Reconstructing Afghanistan: What Crisis in Agriculture and Food Security?*, Bloomfield, CT: Kumarian Press.
40. Ibid., p. 18.
41. Barnett R. Rubin, 2004, 'Road to Ruin: Afghanistan's Booming Opium Industry', New York University: Center on International Cooperation, p. 14.
42. William Byrd and Christopher Ward, 2004, 'Drugs and Development in Afghanistan', Social Development Papers: Conflict Prevention and Reconstruction Paper No. 18, Washington: World Bank.
43. UNODC, 2003, Strategic study No. 9: 'Opium cultivation in a changing policy environment—farmer's intentions for the 2002/2003 growing season', Kabul: UNODC, p. 11.
44. Ibid.
45. Associated Press, 22 November 2002.
46. *Pajhwok Afghan News*, 11 May 2006.
47. Reuters, 10 May 2006.
48. *Independent*, 13 April 2005.
49. 'Asia: Afghan Opium Eradication Campaign Off to Violent Start', *Drug War Chronicle*, Issue 382, 15 April 2005, downloaded from website: http://stopthedrugwar.org/chronicle/382/afghanistan.shtml
50. AFP, 17 April 2005, downloaded on 18 April 2005 from website: http://e-ariana.com/ariana/eariana.nsf/allDocs/

51. Jan Koehler and Christoph Zurcher, 2005, 'Conflict Processing and the Opium Poppy Economy in Afghanistan', PAL Internal Document No. 5, Jalalabad/Berlin: GTZ, Jalalabad/Berlin, p. 14.
52. Agence France-Presse, 18 March 2006.
53. *New York Times*, 27 May 2005
54. Barnett R. Rubin, 'Road to Ruin: Afghanistan's Booming Opium Industry'.
55. A Transform Briefing paper, undated, 'The War on Drugs Final Solution: Biological Warfare'.
56. Paul Rogers, Simon Whitby and Malcolm Dando, 1999, 'Biological Warfare against crops', *Scientific American*, June 1999.
57. *New York Times*, 12 December 2004.
58. This section, apart from a few minor changes, has been reprinted from *The International Journal of Drug Policy*, Vol. 16, Issue 2, David Macdonald, 'Blooming flowers and false prophets: the dynamics of opium cultivation and production in Afghanistan under the Taliban', pp. 93–97, 2005, with permission from Elsevier.
59. G. Farrell and J. Thorne, 2005, Where have all the flowers gone?: 'Evaluation of the Taliban crackdown against opium poppy cultivation in Afghanistan', *International Journal of Drug Policy*, Vol. 16, Issue 2, p. 82.
60. UNDCP, 2001, 'Afghanistan Annual Opium Poppy Survey 2001', Islamabad: United Nations Drug Control Programme.
61. Barnett R. Rubin, 2004, 'Road to Ruin: Afghanistan's Booming Opium Industry'.
62. B. Lintner, 2001, 'Afghanistan Taliban Turns to Drugs', *Far Eastern Economic Review*, 11 October 2001.
63. William Maley, 2002, *The Afghanistan Wars*, London: Palgrave Macmillan, p. 236.
64. Peter Marsden, 1998, *The Taliban: War, Religion, and the New Order in Afghanistan*, London: Zed Books, p. 140.
65. A. Meier, 1997, Afghanistan's drug trade. *Muslim Politics Report*, Vol. 11, Nos. 3–4.
66. Ahmed Rashid, 2000, *Taliban: Islam, Oil and the New Great Game in Central Asia*. London: I.B. Tauris Publishers, p. 118.
67. Asa Hutchinson, 2002, 'Narco-Terror: The International Connection between Drugs and Terror', speech given at the Institute for International Studies, Washington, 2 April 2002. Downloaded from: www.usdoj.gov/dea/speeches/s040202p.html
68. UNDCP, 1999, Community Drug Profile No. 1: 'Problem drug use in Afghan communities: an initial assessment', Islamabad: UNDCP Afghanistan Programme, p. 7.
69. B. Lintner, 'Afghanistan Taliban Turns to Drugs'.
70. Pete Brady, 2002, 'The geopolitics of Afghani hash', *Cannabis Culture*, No. 35.
71. Afghanistan's new militant alliances, 17 April 2006, downloaded from: http://news.bbc.co.uk/1/hi/world/south_asia/4915692.stm
72. William Maley, *The Afghanistan Wars*, p. 236.
73. IRIN, 2003, IRAN: Interview with Antonio Maria Costa, head of the UN Office for Drug Control and Crime Prevention, 5 December 2003,

Teheran. Downloaded from: www.irinnews.org/report.asp?ReportID=38
247&SelectRegion=Central_Asia&SelectCountry=IRAN
74.  B. Lintner, 'Afghanistan Taliban Turns to Drugs'.
75.  Personal communication, UN official, Islamabad, 2000.
76.  World Bank, 2001, 'Brief Overview of Afghanistan's Economy', 5 October
2001: downloaded from: http://lnweb18.worldbank.org/SAR/sa.nsf/
Attachments/96/$File/afOvervw.pdf
77.  David Mansfield, 'What is Driving Opium Poppy Cultivation? The
Pressures to Reduce Opium Poppy Cultivation in Afghanistan in the
2004/05 Growing Season'.

## 5   HEROIN PRODUCERS AND TRAFFICKERS

1.   Alfred W. McCoy, 2003, *The Politics of Heroin: CIA Complicity in the Global
Drug Trade*, Chicago: Lawrence Hill Books, p. 470.
2.   Ahmed Rashid, 2000, *Taliban: Islam, Oil and the New Great Game in Central
Asia*, London: I.B. Tauris, p. 123.
3.   Personal communication, law enforcement official, Kabul 2004.
4.   Alfred W. McCoy, *The Politics of Heroin: CIA Complicity in the Global Drug
Trade*, p. 469.
5.   Amir Zada Asad and Robert Harris, 2003, *The Politics and Economics of
Drug Production on the Pakistan-Afghanistan Border*, Aldershot: Ashgate,
p. 37.
6.   Ibid., p. 147.
7.   Michael Chossudovsky, 2004, *The Spoils of War: Afghanistan's Multi-Billion
Heroin Trade*, California: Center for Research on Globalization.
8.   Alfred W. McCoy, *The Politics of Heroin: CIA Complicity in the Global Drug
Trade*, p. 500.
9.   Ibid., p. 512.
10.  Barnett R. Rubin, 'The Political Economy of War and Peace in
Afghanistan', Sweden, 21 June 1999: downloaded from: http://institute-
for-afghan-studies.org/ECONOMY/political_economy_of_war_peace.
htm#Transnational%20Networks
11.  International Crisis Group, 2003, 'Afghanistan: The Problem of Pashtoon
Alienation', Kabul/Brussels: ICG Asia Report No. 62, Kabul/Brussels,
p. 15.
12.  Barnett R. Rubin, 1996, *The Fragmentation of Afghanistan: State Formation
and Collapse in the International System*, Lahore: Vanguard Books,
p. 256.
13.  Alexander Cockburn and Jeffrey St. Clair, 1999, *Whiteout: The CIA, Drugs
and the Press*, London: Verso, p. 256.
14.  Barnett R. Rubin, *The Fragmentation of Afghanistan: State formation and
Collapse in the International System*, p. 257.
15.  Michael Griffin, 2001, *Reaping the Whirlwind: The Taliban Movement in
Afghanistan*, London: Pluto Press, pp. 147–9.
16.  Alexander Cockburn and Jeffrey St. Clair, *Whiteout: The CIA, Drugs and
the Press*, p. 257.

17. Tom Carew, 2000, *Jihad! The Secret War in Afghanistan*, Edinburgh and London: Mainstream Publishing, p. 198.
18. Ibid., p. 201.
19. Adam Pain and Jonathan Goodhand, 2002, 'Afghanistan: Current Employment and Socio-economic situation and prospects', InFocus Programme on Crisis Response and Reconstruction Working Paper No. 8, Geneva: ILO, p. 14.
20. Ahmed Rashid, *Taliban: Islam, Oil and the New Great Game in Central Asia*, p. 119.
21. Alexander Cockburn and Jeffrey St. Clair, *Whiteout: The CIA, Drugs and the Press*, p. 260.
22. Ibid., p. 260.
23. Ibid.
24. Bob Woodward, 2002, *Bush at War*, New York: Simon and Schuster, p. 35.
25. Alfred W. McCoy, *The Politics of Heroin: CIA Complicity in the Global Drug Trade*, p. 521.
26. Ibid., p. 525.
27. Ibid.
28. AFP, 28 April 2005.
29. Transnational Institute, 2005, 'Downward Spiral: Banning Opium in Afghanistan and Burma', Drugs & Conflict Debate Papers No. 12, Amsterdam: Transnational Institute, p. 11.
30. Associated Press, 24 October 2005.
31. *Daily Outlook Afghanistan*, 16 May 2005.
32. *Guardian*, 31 January 2006.
33. *Drug War Chronicle*, 3 February 2006, 'Afghan Opium Conundrum: Four years on the West searches for answer': downloaded from: http://stopthedrugwar.org/chronicle/421/conundrum.shtml
34. *Sunday Telegraph*, 5 February 2006.
35. Dirk Kurbjuweit, 'A Schizophrenic War—Germany turns a blind eye to Afghanistan's growing opium trade', *Spiegel*, 21 August 2005, downloaded from: www.e-ariana.com/ariana/eariana.nsf/allDocs/0047680E0F87CDE587257064004474C6
36. Aina television, Sheberghan, 21 March 2006.
37. Dave Macdonald, 1997, 'Barriers to reconstruction and development: A brief view of corruption and economic crime in Southern Africa', in Kempe Ronald Hope (ed.), *Structural Adjustment, Reconstruction and Development in Africa*, Aldershot: Ashgate.
38. International Narcotics Control Strategy Report, 2003, Bureau for International Narcotics and Law Enforcement Affairs, Washington DC: State Department.
39. Christopher Ward and William Byrd, 2004, 'Afghanistan's Opium Drug Economy', SASPR Working paper Series, Washington: World Bank, pp. 25–39.
40. BBC News, 6 January 2006, downloaded from: http://news.bbc.co.uk/1/hi/world/south_asia/4585188.stm
41. *Sunday Telegraph*, 5 February 2006.
42. *Khaleej Times*, 15 October 2005.

43. Associated Press, 14 March 2006.
44. Amir Zada Asad and Robert Harris, 2003, *The Politics and Economics of Drug Production on the Pakistan-Afghanistan Border*, Aldershot: Ashgate.
45. *The News*, 27 May 2003.
46. AFP, 22 August 2003.
47. Alfred W. McCoy, *The Politics of Heroin: CIA Complicity in the Global Drug Trade*, p. 509.
48. UNODC, 2005, 'Afghanistan Opium Poppy Survey', Kabul: UNODC Country Office for Afghanistan.
49. Robert Fisk, 2005, *The Great War for Civilisation: The Conquest of the Middle East*, London: Fourth Estate, p. 18.
50. *Pajhwok News*, 15 July 2006.
51. UNODC, 2003, 'The Opium Economy in Afghanistan: An International Problem', New York: United Nations, p. 55.
52. Personal correspondence, Professor Gerry Stimson, 2006.
53. Personal communication, international law enforcement official, Kabul, 2002.
54. UNODC, 2005, 'Afghanistan: Counter Narcotics Law Enforcement Update No. 4', Kabul: UNODC Country Office for Afghanistan, Kabul.
55. Reuters, 1 December 2004.
56. DEA News Release, 3 April 2003.
57. *Australian*, 20 March 2003.
58. *Asia Times*, 25 May, 2006.
59. UNODC, 2005, 'World Drug Report Volume 1: Analysis', Vienna: UNODC, p. 49.
60. Pierre Arnaud Chouvy, Michel Koutouzis and Alain Labrousse, 'Background to the drug routes', paper presented at Ministerial Conference on the drug routes from Central Asia to Europe, Paris, 21–22 May 2003.
61. Pierre Arnaud Chouvy, 2003, 'Opium smuggling routes from Afghanistan to Europe and Asia', *Jane's Intelligence Review*, Vol. 15, No. 3.
62. Chris Johnson and Jolyon Leslie, 2004, *Afghanistan: The Mirage of Peace*, London: Zed Books, p. 116.
63. *Financial Times*, 10 January 2004.
64. Voice of the Islamic Republic of Iran, Mashad, in Dari 13.30 GMT, 2 January, 2004.
65. Personal communication, law enforcement official, Kabul, 2005.
66. 'China: Country Brief, Drug Intelligence Brief, Drug Enforcement Administration', US Department of Justice, February 2004.
67. *The Hindu*, 3 October 2005.
68. *People's Weekly World*, 25 February 2005. It should be noted that some websites reported this quotation as 'Daddy, there's a lot of drugs here. The officers are dealing in drugs. I don't like it. I talked to all my friends and told them "Don't use drugs" because it's really terrible here.'
69. Ibid.
70. Ibid.
71. William Byrd and Christopher Ward, 2004, 'Drugs and Development in Afghanistan', Social Development Papers: Conflict Prevention and Reconstruction Paper No. 18, Washington: World Bank.

## 6   OUTLAWS AND WARLORDS

1. Lowell Thomas, [1925] 1998, *Beyond the Khyber Pass*, Lahore: Vanguard Books, p. 25.
2. Chris Johnson, William Maley, Alexander Thier and Ali Wardak, 2003, 'Afghanistan's political and constitutional development', London: Overseas Development Institute, p. 11.
3. Ali Ahmed Jalali, Minister of the Interior who resigned from his post in September 2005, downloaded from: www.carlisle.army.mil/usawc/Parameters/06spring/jalali.htm
4. ICG, 2003, 'Afghanistan: Judicial Reform and Transitional Justice', *Asia Report* No. 45, Kabul/Brussels: International Crisis Group.
5. Barnett R. Rubin, 1996, *The Fragmentation of Afghanistan: State Formation and Collapse in the International System*, Lahore: Vanguard Books, p. 264.
6. IRIN News, 20 May 2003.
7. Chris Johnson, et al., 'Afghanistan's political and constitutional development', p. 27.
8. J.P. Ferrier, [1858] 2002, *History of the Afghans*, Lahore: Sang-e-Meel Publications, p. 287.
9. Barnett R. Rubin, *The Fragmentation of Afghanistan: State Formation and Collapse in the International System*, p. 42.
10. Martin Ewans, 2001, *Afghanistan: A New History*, Richmond: Curzon Press, p. 55.
11. Ahmed Rashid, 2000, *Taliban: Islam, Oil and the New Great Game in Central Asia*, London: I.B. Tauris, p. 57.
12. Said Hyder Akbar, 2005, *Come Back to Afghanistan: My journey from California to Kabul*, London: Bloomsbury, p. 53.
13. Christopher Kremmer, 2002, *The Carpet Wars: Ten Years in Afghanistan, Pakistan and Iraq*, London: HarperCollins Publishers, p. 35.
14. Martin Ewans, *Afghanistan: A New History*, p. 99.
15. Cited in: Christina Lamb, 2003, *The Sewing Circles of Herat*, London: Flamingo, p. 127.
16. *Ariana News*, 11 November 2004.
17. *Washington Post*, 9 April 2003.
18. *Washington Post*, 7 April 2003.
19. Ibid.
20. *Bloomberg*, 22 March 2004.
21. Conrad Schetter, 2002, 'The "Bazaar Economy" of Afghanistan: A Comprehensive Approach', in Christine Noelle-Karimi, Conrad Schetter and Reinhard Schlagintweit (eds), *Afghanistan: A Country without a State?*, Lahore: Vanguard Books.
22. UNDP, 2005, 'Afghanistan: National Human Development Report 2004', United Nations Development Programme Afghanistan and the Islamic Republic of Afghanistan, Kabul: UNDP, pp. 102–3.
23. Eric Hobsbawm, 2000, *Bandits*, 4th edn, London: Weidenfeld & Nicolson.
24. Anne Baker and R. Ivelaw-Chapman, 1975, *Wings over Kabul*, London: William Kimber, p. 40.

25. Ahmed Rashid, *Taliban: Islam, Oil and the New Great Game in Central Asia*, p. 25.
26. Michael Rubin, 2002, 'Who is responsible for the Taliban?', *Middle East Review of International Affairs*, Vol. 6, No. 1, p. 11.
27. Chris Johnson and Jolyon Leslie, 2004, *Afghanistan: The Mirage of Peace*, London: Zed Books, p. 123.
28. Ahmed Rashid, 'Disarming Afghanistan's warlord militias', *Far Eastern Economic Review*, 29 July 2004.
29. *IRIN*, 11 Jan 2006, downloaded from: www.irinnews.org/report.asp?Rep ortID=51036&SelectRegion=Asia
30. International Crisis Group, 2003, 'Afghanistan: The Problem of Pashtun Alienation', ICG Asia Report No. 62, Kabul/Brussels: International Crisis Group, pp. 17–18.
31. BBC News, 20 July 2004: downloaded from: http://news.bbc.co.uk/1/hi/world/south_asia/3909503.stm
32. AFP, 27 March 2005.
33. Robert D. Kaplan, 2001, *Soldiers of God: With Islamic Warriors in Afghanistan and Pakistan*, New York: Vintage Books, p. 184.
34. Quentin Outram, 1997, 'It's Terminal Either Way: An analysis of armed conflict in Liberia 1989–1996', *Review of African Political Economy*, Vol. 24, No. 73.
35. *Kabul Times*, 26 February 2003.
36. *Asia Times*, 17 September 2004.
37. Personal communication, international NGO coordinator who lived in Bamiyan province for two years, June 2004.
38. Human Rights Watch, 2003, '"Killing you is a very easy thing for us": Human Rights Abuses in Southeast Afghanistan', New York: Human Rights Watch Publications, Vol. 15, No. 5.
39. Ibid., p. 24.
40. Ibid., p. 36.
41. Ibid., p. 38.
42. International Crisis Group, Afghanistan: 'The Problem of Pashtun Alienation', ICG *Asia Report* No. 62, p. 14.
43. Jonathan Goodhand, 2002, 'From Holy War to Opium War? A Case Study of the Opium Economy in North-Eastern Afghanistan', in Christine Noelle-Karimi, Conrad Schetter and Reinhard Schlagintweit (eds), *Afghanistan: A Country without a State?*, Lahore: Vanguard Books.
44. *Kabul Times*, 30 April 2003
45. Ibid.
46. *New York Times*, 9 February 2004.
47. *Gulf Today*, 7 June 2004.
48. *Pajhwok Afghan News*, 28 August 2005.
49. *Guardian*, 31 March 2005.
50. *Los Angeles Times*, 21 May 2005.
51. Ibid.
52. Bashir Babak and Sayed Yaqub Ibrahimi, 'When Cops become robbers', IWPR, 1 May 2005, downloaded from: http://eariana.com/ariana/eariana.nsf/allDocs/227489560BA0BF6987256FF4004AF877
53. Afghaniyat Newsgroup, 23 February 2005.

54. *New York Times*, 20 February 2006.
55. Afghan News Network, 23 February 2003.
56. Institute for War and Peace Reporting, 2002, 'Afghan Recovery Report: Disarmament Drive'.
57. Ibid.
58. David B. Edwards, 2002, *Before Taliban: Genealogies of the Afghan Jihad*, Berkeley: University of California Press, p. 104.
59. Barnett R. Rubin, 1996, *The Fragmentation of Afghanistan: State Formation and Collapse in the International System*, p. 48.
60. Steve Coll, 2004, *Ghost Wars: The Secret History of the CIA, Afghanistan, and Bin Laden, from the Soviet Invasion to September 10, 2001*, New York: The Penguin Press, p. 66.
61. Ibid.
62. BBC News World Edition, 22 February 2003.
63. International Crisis Group, 2005, 'Afghanistan: Getting Disarmament Back on Track', Update briefing: Asia Briefing No. 35, Kabul/Brussels, International Crisis group, p. 3.
64. Associated Press, 30 May 2006.
65. Ibid.
66. Gulf News, 8 August 2004.
67. IRIN News, 1 November 2004.
68. Personal communication, UN colleague's letter of resignation, 2003.
69. Human Rights Watch, '"Killing you is a very easy thing for us": Human Rights Abuses in Southeast Afghanistan', p. 17.
70. *New York Times*, 30 January 2005.
71. International Crisis Group, Afghanistan: 'The Problem of Pashtun Alienation', ICG Asia Report No. 62, p. 16.
72. Bob Woodward, 2002, *Bush at War*, New York: Simon and Schuster, p. 213.
73. *The Economist*, 10–16 June 2006.
74. Human Rights Watch representative, quoted in Duncan Campbell and Suzanne Goldenberg, 'They said this is America...if a soldier orders you to take off your clothes, you must obey', *Guardian*, 23 June 2004.
75. BBC News, 24 August 2005, downloaded from: http://news.bbc.co.uk/go/pr/fr/-/1/world/south-asia/4180692.stm
76. *Irish Sun*, 28 August 2005.
77. An Open Letter to US Secretary Donald Rumsfeld, Human Rights Watch, 13 December 2004.
78. Ibid.
79. BBC News, 27 July 2005.
80. *Cheragh*, 13 January 2005.
81. Associated Press, 22 February 2005.
82. *Guardian Weekend*, 19 March 2005.
83. *The New York Times*, 23 April 2005.
84. *Seattle Times*, 24 April 2005.
85. John McCarthy, 'Expanding private military sector faces structural change and scrutiny', *Jane's Intelligence Review*, February 2006.
86. *Rolling Stone*, 5 May 2005.

87.  Barnett R. Rubin, 2004, 'Road to Ruin: Afghanistan's Booming Opium Industry', New York University: Center on International Cooperation, p. 19.
88.  William Byrd and Christopher Ward, 2004, 'Drugs and Development in Afghanistan', Social Development Papers: Conflict Prevention and Reconstruction Paper No. 18, Washington DC: World Bank.

## 7  DRUG USE IN AFGHANISTAN'S HISTORY

1.  Zahirud-Din Muhammad Babur, *Babur-Nama*, translated from Turki by Annette S. Beveridge, 2002, Lahore: Sang-e-Meel, p. 16.
2.  Ibid., p. 212.
3.  Sir George Scott Robertson, [1896] 2001, *The Kafirs of the Hindu-Kush*, Lahore: Sang-e-Meel, p. 559.
4.  *The Economist*, 22 December 2001—4 January 2002.
5.  Zahirud-Din Muhammad Babur, *Babur-Nama*, p. 373.
6.  Ibid., p. 393.
7.  Ibid., p. 608.
8.  Ibid., p. 386.
9.  J.P. Ferrier, [1858] 2002, *History of the Afghans*, Lahore: Sang-e-Meel, p. 173.
10.  Ibid., p. 171.
11.  R.C. Mitford, [1881] 1999, *To Caubul with the Cavalry*, Lahore: Vanguard Books, p. 115.
12.  J.P. Ferrier, *History of the Afghans*, p. 319.
13.  Ibid., p. 290.
14.  Frank A. Martin, [1907] 1998, *Under the Absolute Amir of Afghanistan*, Lahore: Vanguard Books, p. 89.
15.  Charles Masson, [1842] 2004, *Narrative of Various Journeys in Afghanistan, Balochistan and the Punjab: Including a residence in these countries between 1826–1838 Vol. 2*, Kabul: Shah Books, p. 179.
16.  T.L. Pennell, 1908, *Among the Wild Tribes of the Afghan Frontier*, London: Seeley & Co., p. 239.
17.  Lowell Thomas, [1925] 1998, *Beyond the Khyber Pass*, Lahore: Vanguard Books, p. 166.
18.  Ibid., p. 56.
19.  Ibid., p. 60.
20.  Ibid., p. 58.
21.  Ibid., p. 59.
22.  Morag Murray Abdullah, [1930] 1990, *My Khyber Marriage—Experiences of a Scotswoman as the Wife of a Pathan Chieftain's Son*, London: The Octagon Press Ltd.
23.  Memoona Hasnain, 2005, 'Cultural Approach to HIV/AIDS Harm Reduction in Muslim Countries', *Harm Reduction Journal*, Vol. 2, No. 23.
24.  Marjorie Jewett Bell, 2004, *An American Engineer in Kabul*, (2nd Reprint), Kabul: Iraj Books, p. 108 (first published in 1948 by the University of Minnesota, North Central Publishing Company, St. Paul).

25. Colombo Plan Secretariat Drug Advisory Programme, 'Understanding Drug Addiction from the Islamic Perspective—A Guidebook', October 2005.
26. Dato' Zainuddin A. Bahari, 2005, 'Understanding Drug Addiction from the Islamic Perspective', paper presented at Mullah Symposium on 'Role of Religious Leaders in Drug Demand Reduction', Kabul, 25–26 July 2005, p. 8.
27. Peter Levi, 2000, *The Light Garden of the Angel King: Travels in Afghanistan with Bruce Chatwin*, London: Pallas Athene, p. 115.
28. Ibid., p. 80.
29. Ibid., p. 155.
30. H.W. Bellew, [1864] 2001, *A General Report on the Yusufzais*, Lahore: Sang-e-Meel Publications, p. 215.
31. Asad Hassan Gobar, 1976, 'Drug Abuse in Afghanistan', *Bulletin on Narcotics*, Issue 2.
32. Ibid.
33. Ibid.
34. *Sydney Morning Herald*, 13 October 2001.
35. Kathleen Trautman, 1972, 'Spies Behind the Pillars, Bandits at the Pass', quoted in Bijan Omrani and Matthew Leeming, 2005, *Afghanistan: A Companion and Guide*, New York: Odyssey Books, p. 596.
36. David B. Edwards, 2002, *Before Taliban: Genealogies of the Afghan Jihad*, Berkeley: University of California Press, p. 11.
37. Rory Stewart, 2004, *The Places in Between*, London: Picador, p. 303.
38. UNODC, 2003, Community Drug Profile No. 5, 'An assessment of problem drug use in Kabul City', Kabul: UNODC Country Office for Afghanistan.
39. UNDP, 2005, 'Afghanistan: National Human Development Report 2004', United Nations Development Programme Afghanistan and the Islamic Republic of Afghanistan, Kabul: UNDP, p. 41.
40. Amnesty International, Afghanistan: 'Women still under attack—a systemic failure to protect', 30 May 2005: downloaded from: http://web.amnesty.org/library/index/engasa110072005
41. Ibid., p. 40.
42. *Kabul Weekly*, 23 February 2005.
43. Dr Farid Bazger and Andrew T. Young, 'Survey of Groups at Risk of Contracting Sexually Transmitted Infections and HIV/AIDS in Kabul', Kabul: ORA International, April 2005.
44. *Khaleej Times*, 8 March 2005.
45. Personal communication, police officers in Kabul, 2003 and 2004.
46. *Pajhwok news*, 26 March 2006.
47. Robert O'Brien and Sidney Cohen, 1984, *The Encyclopedia of Drug Abuse*, New York: Green Spring Inc., p. xi.
48. E.L. Abel, 1980, *Marihuana: The First Twelve Thousand Years*, London and New York: Plenum Press.
49. Tom Carew, 2000, *Jihad! The Secret War in Afghanistan*, Edinburgh and London: Mainstream Publishing, p. 217.
50. Henry S. Bradsher, 1999, *Afghan Communism and Soviet Intervention*, Oxford: Oxford University Press, p. 249.

51. John K. Cooley, 1999, *Unholy Wars: Afghanistan, America and International Terrorism*, London: Pluto Press, p. 128.
52. Diego Cordovez and Selig S. Harrison, 1995, *Out of Afghanistan: The Inner Story of the Soviet Withdrawal*, New York: Oxford University Press, p. 54.

## 8   NEIGHBOURS AND REFUGEES

1. Idries Shah, 1987, *Kara Kush*, Glasgow: Fontana Books, p. 492.
2. UNODC, 2005, 'World Drug Report Volume One: Analysis', p. 54.
3. UNODC, 2003, Community Drug Profile No. 5: 'An assessment of problem drug use in Kabul city', Kabul: UNODC Country Office for Afghanistan, p. 31.
4. Barnett R. Rubin, 1989, 'The Fragmentation of Afghanistan', *Foreign Affairs*, Vol. 68, No. 5.
5. Amir Zada Asad and Robert Harris, 2003, *The Politics and Economics of Drug Production on the Pakistan-Afghanistan Border*, Aldershot: Ashgate.
6. UNHCR, 2000, *The State of the World's Refugees*, Oxford: UNHCR/Oxford University Press, p. 119.
7. David Turton and Peter Marsden, 2002, 'Taking Refugees for a Ride: the politics of refugee return to Afghanistan', Issues Paper Series, Kabul: AREU (Afghanistan Research and Evaluation Unit).
8. Ibid., p. 19.
9. Ibid., p. 2.
10. Ibid., p. 3.
11. Amnesty International, 2003, 'Afghanistan—Out of sight, out of mind: the fate of the Afghan returnees', London: Amnesty International, p. 3.
12. Ibid., p. 4.
13. Ibid., p. 13.
14. UNHCR, Lubbers warns against speeding up refugee returns to Afghanistan, 17 January 2005, downloaded from: http://e-ariana.com/ariana/eariana. nsf/allDocs/F140159A
15. CIA World Factbook, downloaded from: www.odci.gov/cia/publications/ factbook/geos/af.html
16. A. Ghanizadeh, 2001, 'Shiraz University students' attitude towards drugs: an exploratory study', *Eastern Mediterranean Health Journal*, Vol. 7, No. 3.
17. *Guardian*, 27 October 2005.
18. Alfred W. McCoy, 2003, *The Politics of Heroin: CIA Complicity in the Global Drug Trade*, Chicago: Lawrence Hill Books, p. 468.
19. Ibid., p. 468.
20. Ibid., p. 469.
21. M. R. Moharreri, 1976, 'Out-patients treatment of opium addicts: report of a pilot project in Shiraz', UNODC *Bulletin on Narcotics*, Issue 3.
22. Alfred W. McCoy, *The Politics of Heroin: CIA Complicity in the Global Drug Trade*, p. 470.
23. E. M. Razzaghi, A. Rahimi, M. Hosseni, S. Maddani and A. Chatterjee, undated, 'Rapid Situation Assessment of Drug Abuse in Iran 1998–1999',

Short Report, Tehran: Ministry of Health Islamic Republic of Iran and UNDCP.

24. Azarakhsh Mokri, 2002, 'Brief Overview of the Status of Drug Abuse in Iran', *Archives of Iranian Medicine*, Vol. 5, No. 3.

25. A. William Samii, 2003, 'Drug Abuse: Iran's "Thorniest Problem"', *The Brown Journal of World Affairs*, Vol. X, Issue 2.

26. Ibid., p. 21.

27. Gary Reid and Genevieve Costigan, 2002, 'Revisiting "The Hidden Epidemic": A Situation Assessment of Drug Use in Asia in the Context of HIV/AIDS', Australia: The Centre for Harm Reduction, the Burnet Institute, p. 103.

28. Azarakhsh Mokri, Brief Overview of the Status of Drug Abuse in Iran.

29. UNODCCP, 2002, 'Drug Abuse in Pakistan: Results from the year 2000 National Assessment', New York: United Nations, p. xii.

30. Ibid., p. 4.

31. UNDCP, 1998, 'Pakistan: Status of Knowledge of Drug Addiction in Pakistan', Islamabad: UNDCP Regional Office for South West Asia, p. 4.

32. Personal communication, UNDCP fieldworker, 2000.

33. Amir Zada Asad and Robert Harris, 2003, *The Politics and Economics of Drug Production on the Pakistan-Afghanistan Border*, Aldershot: Ashgate Publishing.

34. UNDCP, Pakistan: 'Status of Knowledge of Drug Addiction in Pakistan', p. 7.

35. Soros Foundation, 2000, 'Summary of Fact Finding Mission to Tajikistan International Harm Reduction Development Program', Open Society Institute, Soros Foundation. Downloaded from: www.eurasianet.org/policy_forum

36. A. Wodak, S. Sarkar and F. Mesquita, 2004, The globalisation of drug injecting, *Addiction*, Vol. 99, Issue 7, p. 800.

37. *New Scientist*, 26 July 2005

38. UNODCCP, 2001, 'Rapid Situation Assessment on Drug Abuse in the Central Asian Countries', Regional Report.

39. WHO, 2005, 'Uzbekistan: Summary Country Profile for HIV/AIDS Treatment Scale-up'. Downloaded from: www.who.int/hiv/HIVCP_UZB.pdf

40. UNDCP, 1999, Community Drug Profile No. 1: 'Problem Drug Use in Afghan Communities—An Initial Assessment', Islamabad: United Nations International Drug Control Programme Afghanistan, p. 8.

41. T. Zafar, H. Brahmbhatt, G. Imam, S. ul-Hassan, S.A. Strathdee, 2003, 'HIV Knowledge and Risk Behaviours Among Pakistani and Afghani Drug Users in Quetta, Pakistan', *Journal of Acquired Immune Deficiency Syndromes*, Vol. 32, No. 4.

42. UNDCP, 2001, Community Drug Profile No. 4: 'An assessment of problem drug use in rural Afghanistan—the GAI target districts', Islamabad: United Nations Drug Control Programme Afghanistan, p. 17.

43. *Guardian*, 27 November 2003.

44. UNODC, Community Drug Profile No. 5: 'An assessment of problem drug use in Kabul city', p. 15.

45. UNDCP, 1999, Community Drug Profile No. 2: 'Opium and other problem drug use in a group of Afghan refugee women', Islamabad: United Nations Drug Control Programme Afghanistan.
46. UNDCP, 2000, Community Drug Profile No. 3: 'A comparative study of Afghan street heroin addicts in Peshawar and Quetta', Islamabad: United Nations Drug Control Programme Afghanistan.
47. Ron Synovitz, 'AIDS Statistics unknown due to social repression', 11 July 2002, downloaded from: www.reliefweb.int
48. Tariq Zafar et al., 'HIV Knowlege and Risk Behaviors among Pakistani and Afghani Drug Users in Quetta, Pakistan'.
49. A Report by Nai Zindagi: 'Graphic Presentation of Data relating to Afghan clients accessing services at Nai Zindagi, Quetta, Pakistan', undated.
50. Ulrich Kohler, 1995, UNDCP 'Assessment and Strategy Formulation Mission Afghanistan', 23 May–20 July 1995: A Report, p. 25.
51. A. Wodak, S. Sarkar and F. Mesquita, The globalisation of drug injecting.

## 9  A TALE OF TWO OPIUMS

1. Amir Zada Assad and Robert Harris, 2003, *The Politics and Economics of Drug Production on the Pakistan-Afghanistan Border,* Aldershot: Ashgate, p. 31.
2. Personal interview, Badakhshan resident, 2003.
3. Andrew Tyler, 1986, *Street Drugs,* London: Hodder & Stoughton, p. 275.
4. The Colombo Plan Secretariat Drug Advisory Programme, 'Understanding Drug Addiction from the Islamic Perspective—A Guidebook', October 2005, p. 19.
5. Louis Dupree, 1973, *Afghanistan,* Princeton NJ: Princeton University Press, p. 673.
6. Barbara Hodgson, 2000, *Opium: A Portrait of the Heavenly Demon,* London: Souvenir Press.
7. Andrew Tyler, *Street Drugs,* p. 305.
8. The Royal College of Psychiatrists, 1987, *Drug Scenes: A report on drugs and drug dependence by the Royal College of Psychiatrists,* London: The Royal College, p. 59.
9. Nina Kerimi, 2000, 'Opium Use in Turkmenistan: a historical perspective', *Addiction,* Vol. 95, Issue 9, p. 1323.
10. Ulrich Kohler, 1995, 'UNDCP Assessment and Strategy Formulation Mission Afghanistan', 23 May–20 July 1995: A Report.
11. United Nations Environment Programme and Food and Agriculture Organisation of the United Nations, 2003, 'Afghanistan: Wakhan Mission Technical Report', Geneva: UNEP and FAO, p. 38.
12. Ibid.
13. Peter Sloane, 2000, 'Helmand Initiative: Joint Strategy Development Draft Report', Islamabad: UNDP, p. 20.
14. Dave Macdonald and Louis Molamu, 1997, 'Between a Rock and a Hard Place: Alcohol and Basarwa Identity in Contemporary Botswana—the Cultural Reality', in Andre Bank (ed.) *The Proceedings of the Khoisan*

*Identities and Cultural Heritage Conference*, Institute for Historical Research, University of the Western Cape, p. 332.

15. N. Scheper-Hughes, 1995, 'The Primacy of the Ethical: Propositions for a Militant Anthropology', *Current Anthropology*, Vol. 36, No. 3, p. 416.

16. Asad Hassan Gobar, 1976, 'Drug Abuse in Afghanistan', *Bulletin on Narcotics*, Issue 2.

17. ORA International Central Asia, 1998, 'Taking up the Challenge', ORA Annual Report 1997/98, p. 8.

18. Marc Theuss, G.E. Poole and Falak Madhani, 2005, 'Addiction in the Border Regions of Badakhshan, Afghanistan: Range, Trajectory and Impacts', unpublished report, p. 1.

19. Personal interview, Badakhshan resident, 2003.

20. Asad Hassan Gobar, 'Drug Abuse in Afghanistan'.

21. WFA, 1994, 'National Drug Addicts Survey in Afghanistan : Opium in the Hindu Kush', Wak Foundation for Afghanistan, p. 5.

22. Personal interview, Badakhshan doctor, 2003.

23. Personal correspondence, David Mansfield, 2006.

24. UNDCP, 1999, Community Drug Profile No. 1: 'Problem Drug Use in Afghan Communities—An Initial Assessment', Islamabad: UNDCP Afghanistan, p. 7.

25. Robert O'Brien and Sidney Cohen, 1984, *The Encyclopedia of Drug Abuse*, New York: Green Spring Inc., pXIV.

26. UNDCP, 1999, Community Drug Profile No. 2: 'Opium and other problem drug use in a group of Afghan refugee women', Islamabad: UNDCP Afghanistan, p. 11.

27. Ibid., p. 12.

28. Ibid., p. 13.

29. Frank A.Martin, [1907] 1998, *Under the Absolute Amir of Afghanistan*, Lahore: Vanguard Books, p. 312.

30. Ulrich Kohler, 1994, 'UNDCP Assessment and Strategy Formulation Mission Afghanistan', 23 May—20 July 1995: A Report, p. 13.

31. Amir Zada Assad and Robert Harris, 2003, *The Politics and Economics of Drug Production on the Pakistan-Afghanistan Border*, Aldershot: Ashgate.

32. *Independent*, 28 September 2002.

33. The Scottish Executive, 2005, 'Substance Misuse Research: Low Level Heroin Markets—A Case Study Approach'.

34. UNDCP, 2001, Community Drug Profile No. 4: 'An assessment of problem drug use in rural Afghanistan—the GAI target districts', Islamabad: UNDCP Afghanistan, p. 14.

35. UNODC, 2003, Community Drug Profile No. 5: 'An assessment of problem drug use in Kabul City', Kabul: UNODC Country Office for Afghanistan, p. 13

36. Ibid., p. 15.

37. Ibid., p. 13.

38. M.S. Kumar et al., 2000, 'Rapid assessment and response to injecting drug use in Madras, south India', *International Journal of Drug Policy*, Vol. 11, Issues 1–2.

39. J. Westermeyer, 1976, 'The pro-heroin effects of anti-opium laws in Asia', *Archives of General Psychiatry*, Vol. 33, No. 9.

## 10   HASHISH AND HAKIMS

1. Patrick Matthews, 2000, *Cannabis Culture: A Journey through Disputed Territory*, London: Bloomsbury, p. 222.
2. Old Pashtoon proverb.
3. Commonwealth of Australia, 1994, Monograph No. 26: 'Legislative options for cannabis use in Australia', Australian Government, Department of Health and Ageing.
4. Robert Connell Clarke, 1998, *Hashish!*, Los Angeles: Red Eye Press, p. 41.
5. Ibid., p.42.
6. Richard Evans Schultes, William M. Klein, Timothy Plowman and Tom E. Lockwood, 'Cannabis: an example of taxonomic neglect', in Vera Rubin (ed.), 1975, *Cannabis and Culture*, The Hague: Mouton Publishers.
7. Robert Connell Clarke, *Hashish!*, p. 124.
8. Ibid., p.126.
9. S. Tendler and David May, 1984, *The Brotherhood of Eternal Love*, London: Panther Books.
10. *Forbes Magazine*, 10 November 2003.
11. Robert Connell Clarke, *Hashish!*, p. 118.
12. Ibid., p. 119.
13. UNODC and the Ministry of Counter Narcotics, Government of Afghanistan, 2005, 'Afghanistan: Opium Rapid Assessment Survey', March 2005, p. 8.
14. Alex Perry, 2002, 'Wasted: the drought that drugs made', *Time Asia*, Vol. 160, No. 15.
15. Robert Connell Clarke, *Hashish!*, p. 130.
16. Howard Marks, 1998, *Mr Nice: An Autobiography*, London: Vintage, p. 291.
17. Ibid., p. 293.
18. Ibid., p. 250.
19. Patrick Matthews, *Cannabis Culture: A Journey Through Disputed Territory*.
20. Robert Connell Clarke, *Hashish!*, p.131.
21. Alvin B. Segelman, R. Duane Sofia and Florence H. Segelman, 'Cannabis sativa L. (Marihuana): VI Variations in Marihuana Preparation and Usage—Chemical and Pharmacological Consequences', in Vera Rubin (ed.), 1975, *Cannabis and Culture*, The Hague: Mouton Publishers.
22. Patrick Matthews, *Cannabis Culture: A Journey Through Disputed Territory*.
23. UNDCP, 2001, Community Drug Profile No. 4: 'An assessment of problem drug use in rural Afghanistan—the GAI target districts', Islamabad: UNDCP Afghanistan, p. 18.
24. Asad Hassan Gobar, 1976, 'Drug Abuse in Afghanistan', *Bulletin on Narcotics*, Issue 2.
25. Ibid.
26. Guy Raz, 2002, 'Khost City: Wild at Heart', *Crosslines Afghanistan Monitor—An independent Journal of Humanitarian Accountability*, p. 9.

27. UNDCP, 2001, Community Drug Profile No. 4: 'An assessment of problem drug use in rural Afghanistan—the GAI target districts', Islamabad: UNDCP Afghanistan, p. 18.
28. Robert Connell Clarke, *Hashish!*, p. 143.
29. Sue Lautze, Neamat Nojumi and Karem Najimi, 2002, 'Food Security, Malnutrition and the Political Economy of Survival: A Report from Kabul, Herat and Qandahar', WFP, p. 27.
30. UNODC, 2003, Community Drug Profile No. 5: 'An assessment of problem drug use in Kabul City', Kabul: UNODC Country Office for Afghanistan, p. 19.
31. UNDCP, Community Drug Profile No. 4: 'An assessment of problem drug use in rural Afghanistan—the GAI target districts'.
32. UNDCP, 1999, Community Drug Profile No. 2: 'Opium and other problem drug use in a group of Afghans refugee women', Islamabad: United Nations Drug Control Programme Afghanistan, p. 16.
33. A. Dhawan, (undated), 'Traditional use, in South Asia: A Drug Demand Reduction report', New Delhi: UNDCP Regional Office for South Asia.
34. Richard Davenport-Hines, 2002, *The Pursuit of Oblivion: A Social History of Drugs*, London: Phoenix Press, p. 65.
35. Robert Connell Clarke, *Hashish!*, p. 260.
36. Anna Porcella, Chiara Maxia, Gian Luigi Gessa and Luca Pain, 2001, 'The synthetic cannabinoid WIN55212-2 decreases the intraocular pressure in human glaucoma resistant to conventional therapies', *European Journal of Neuroscience*, Vol. 13, Issue 2, p. 409.
37. 'Summary of findings from the MRC Cannabinoids in MS Trial (CAMS)', *The Lancet*, 8 November 2003.
38. Janet E. Jov, Stanley J. Watson Jnr., and John A. Benson Jnr., 1999, *Marijuana and Medicine: Assessing the Science Base*, Washington DC: National Academy Press.
39. *News on Sunday*, 25 August 2002.
40. 'Unani Origins', downloaded from: www.unani.com/avicenna
41. Efraim Lev, 2003, Traditional healing with animals (zootherapy): medieval to present-day Levantine practice, *Journal of Ethnopharmacology*, Vol. 85, Issue 1.
42. Ibid., p. 116.
43. C. Younos, J. Fleurentin, D. Notter, G. Mazars, F. Mortier and J.M. Pelt, 1987, 'Repertory of drugs and medicinal plants used in traditional medicine of Afghanistan', *Journal of Ethnopharmacology*, Vol. 20, Issue 3.
44. 'Immune Suppressant Drug Based on Scorpion Venom Action', MS news articles July 2000, downloaded from: www.mult-sclerosis.org/news/Jul2000/DrugScorpionVenom.html

## 11 PHARMACEUTICALS AND CHEMICAL COCKTAILS

1. UNDCP, 1999, Community Drug Profile No. 1, 'Problem Drug Use in Afghan Communities—An Initial Assessment', UNDCP Afghanistan Programme, Islamabad, p. 9.

2.  Transnational Institute, 2006, 'Drug Policy Briefing No. 18: International drug control: 100 years of success?' TNI comments on the UNODC World Drug Report 2006, Amsterdam: Transnational Institute, p. 2.
3.  Charles Medawar and Anita Hardon, 2004, *Medicines Out of Control? Antidepressants and the Conspiracy of Goodwill*, Amsterdam: Aksant Academic Publishers, p. 88.
4.  A. Tyler, 1986, *Street Drugs*, London: Hodder & Stoughton, p. 105.
5.  Richard Davenport-Hines, 2002, *The Pursuit of Oblivion: A Social History of Drugs*, London: Phoenix Press, p. 97.
6.  *The News*, 2 July 2003.
7.  Louis Molamu and Dave Macdonald, 1996, 'Alcohol Abuse among the Basarwa of the Kgalagadi and Ghanzi Districts in Botswana', *Drugs: Education, Prevention and Policy*, Vol. 3, No. 2.
8.  Dave Macdonald, 1996, 'Drugs in Southern Africa: an overview', *Drugs: Education, Prevention and Policy*, Vol. 3, No. 2, p. 131.
9.  N. Giesbrecht, 1989, 'Alcohol issues and recent experiences in Southern Africa', *Contemporary Drug Problems*, Vol. 16, No. 2. p. 106.
10. UNDCP, 1999, Community Drug Profile No. 1: 'Problem drug use in Afghan communities: an initial assessment', Islamabad: UNDCP Afghanistan Programme, p. 9.
11. *New Internationalist*, April 1989.
12. Dipyrone Update, AABP Newsletter, January and July 1996.
13. *Pakistan Economist*, 10–16 August, 1996.
14. Andrew Tyler, *Street Drugs*, p. 285.
15. Charles Medawar and Anita Hardon, *Medicines Out of Control? Antidepressants and the Conspiracy of Goodwill*, p. 37.
16. Ibid., p. 34.
17. Ibid., pp. 41–2.
18. *Herald*, 31 March 2005.
19. UNDCP, 1999, Community Drug Profile No. 2: 'Opium and other problem drug use in a group of Afghan refugee women', Islambabad: UNDCP Afghanistan Programme, p. 14.
20. Anna M. Pont, 2001, *Blind Chickens and Social Animals: Creating spaces for Afghan women's narratives under the Taliban*, Portland ORE: Mercy Corps, p. 67.
21. Ibid.
22. Personal interview, WHO doctor, Islamabad 1999.
23. UNDCP, 2001, Community Drug Profile No. 4: 'Assessment of problem drug use in rural Afghanistan—the GAI target districts', Islamabad: UNDCP Afghanistan, p. 6.
24. UNODC, 2003, Community Drug Profile No. 5: 'An assessment of problem drug use in Kabul City', Kabul: UNODC Country Office for Afghanistan, June 2003, p. 21.
25. Dave Macdonald, 1996, 'Drugs in Southern Africa: an overview', *Drugs: Education, Prevention and Policy*, Vol. 3, No. 2.
26. DEA, 2002, 'Drug Intelligence Brief: India Country Brief', US Drug Enforcement Administration, May 2002, downloaded from: www.dea.gov/pubs/intel/02022/02022.html

27. UNDP, 2005, 'Afghanistan: National Human Development Report 2004', United Nations Development Programme Afghanistan and the Islamic Republic of Afghanistan, Kabul: UNDP, p. 40.
28. UNDCP and UNAIDS in Pakistan, 1999, 'Baseline Study of the Relationship between Injecting Drug Use and Hepatitis C among Male Injecting Drug Users in Lahore', December 1999, p. 16.
29. Ibid., p. 15.
30. Personal correspondence, Dr Catherine Todd, Kabul 2006.
31. ORA International, 1999, 'Nejat Centre: the first five years—Research of data collected from 1991–1996', p. 20.
32. Martin Jelsma, 2005, 'Learning lessons from the Taliban opium ban', *International Journal of Drug Policy*, Vol. 16, Issue 2, p. 99.
33. DEA, 2001, 'Drugs and Chemicals of Concern—Action Plan to Prevent the Diversion and Abuse of OxyContin', Drug Enforcement Administration, June 22, 2001; downloaded from: www.deadiversion.usdoj.gov/drugs_concern/oxycodone/oxycodone.htm
34. Martin Jelsma, 'Learning lessons from the Taliban opium ban', p. 101.
35. *News (Pakistan)*, 3 January 2003.
36. *Guardian*, 4 January 2003.
37. Modafinil, the ultimate stimulant, downloaded from: www.modafinil.org/
38. *Pahjwok News*, 6 January 2005.
39. *Pahjwok News*, 20 February 2005.
40. John Braithwaite, 1984, *Corporate Crime in the Pharmaceutical Industry*, London: Routledge & Kegan Paul.
41. Rosie Taylor and Jim Giles, 'Cash interests taint drug advice', *Nature*, No. 437, 20 October 2005.
42. Charles Medawar and Anita Hardon, *Medicines Out of Control? Antidepressants and the Conspiracy of Goodwill*, p. 88.
43. John Braithwaite, *Corporate Crime in the Pharmaceutical Industry*, p. 206.
44. *New Internationalist*, November 2003.
45. *Indian Express*, 14 August 2003.
46. Bad Medicine, BBC2 TV, 12 July 2005.
47. John Pekkanen, 1973, *The American Connection*, Chicago: Follett, p. 81.
48. Michael Gossop, 1982, *Living with Drugs* (2nd edition), Aldershot: Wildwood House, p.64.
49. Christopher Littlejohn, Alex Baldacchino, Fabrizio Schifaw and Paula Deluca, 2005, 'Internet Pharmacies and Online prescription Drug Sales: a cross-sectional study', *Drugs: Education, Prevention and Policy*, Vol. 12, No. 1.
50. Associated Press, 21 April 2005.
51. An account of the effects of a drug like 5-MEO-DMT is provided in Chapter 13.
52. DEA News Release, 21 September 2005, downloaded from: www.usdoj.gov/dea/pubs/pressrel/pr092105.html
53. *Guardian*, 26 May 2005.
54. Press Release UN Information Service Vienna, 2 March 2005, 'Internet pharmacies ramping up sales of illicit drugs', INCB Annual Report.

## 12   MASTERS OF THE UNIVERSE

1. Antonio Maria Costa, Executive Director of UNODC, UNODC Vienna, 2003, 'Ecstasy and Amphetamines—Global Survey 2003', New York: United Nations.
2. Michael Gossop, 1987, *Living with Drugs* (2nd edition), Aldershot: Wildwood House, p. 70.
3. UNODC, 2003, Community Drug Profile No. 5: 'An assessment of problem drug use in Kabul City', Kabul: UNODC Country Office for Afghanistan. p. 28.
4. *Pajhwok News*, 22 December 2004.
5. Much of the information in this section has been compiled from the excellent *Vaults of Erowid*, a website providing comprehensive and responsible information about a wide range of psychoactive substances. Downloaded from: www.erowid.org/psychoactives/psychoactives. shtml
6. UNDCP, 2001, Community Drug Profile No. 4: 'An assessment of problem drug use in rural eastern Afghanistan—the GAI target districts', Islamabad: UNDCP Afghanistan, p. 22.
7. Cited in R.J. Bouquet, 1950, 'Cannabis', *Bulletin on Narcotics*, Issue 4, p. 18.
8. Lester Grinspoon and James B. Bakalar, 1981, *Psychedelic Drugs Reconsidered*, New York: Basic Books.
9. Downloaded from: www.earthops.org/burundanga.html, 22 November 2003.
10. Downloaded from: www.amarillonet.com.shtml, 22 November 2003.
11. Downloaded from: www.shout.net, 22 November 2003.
12. International Narcotics Control Board, 2003, *Report of the International Narcotic Control Board for 2002*, New York: United Nations, p. 35.
13. Dr Harold Graff, 1969, 'Marihuana and Scopolamine "High"', *American Journal of Psychiatry*, Vol. 125, Issue 9.
14. Downloaded from: www.erowid.org/plants/datura/datura.shtml
15. Downloaded from: www.erowid.org/plants/datura/datura_dose.shtml
16. *Druglink*, Vol. 21, No. 1, January/February 1990.
17. *Guardian*, 14 June 2003.
18. UNODC Vienna, 2003, 'Ecstasy and Amphetamines—Global Survey 2003', New York: United Nations, p. 96.
19. Personal communication, law enforcement official.
20. UNODC Vienna, 'Ecstasy and Amphetamines—Global Survey 2003', pp. 95–7.
21. Ibid., p. 100.
22. Andrew Tyler, 1995, *Street Drugs*, London: Hodder & Stoughton, p. 82.
23. UNODC Vienna, 'Ecstasy and Amphetamines—Global Survey 2003', p. iii.
24. UNDCP, 1999, Community Drug Profile No. 1: 'Problem Drug Use in Afghan Communities: An Initial Assessment', Islamabad: UNDCP Afghanistan, p. 12.
25. UNDCP, 2001, Community Drug Profile No. 4: 'An assessment of problem drug use in rural Afghanistan—the GAI target districts', Islamabad: UNDCP Afghanistan, p. 22.

26. UNODC, 2003, Community Drug Profile No. 5: 'An assessment of problem drug use in Kabul city', Kabul: UNODC Country Office for Afghanistan, p. 24.
27. Ibid., p. 25.

## 13    SCORPION TAILS

1. Personal interview, scorpion smoker, Kabul, 2003.
2. Taras Grescoe, 2006, *The Devil's Picnic: A Tour of Everything the Governments of the World Don't Want You to Try*, London: Macmillan, p. 303.
3. UNDP, 2003, 'Rapid Situation Assessment of Drug Abuse in Maldives', Male: UNDP Maldives, p. 23.
4. Adam Gottlieb, 1973, *Legal Highs: A Concise Encyclopedia of Legal Herbs and Chemicals with Psychoactive Properties*, Manhattan Beach, CA: Twentieth Century Alchemist.
5. Wade Davis, 1985, *The Serpent and the Rainbow*, New York: Simon and Schuster Inc., p. 35.
6. Ibid., p. 118.
7. Ibid., p. 121.
8. Wade Davis, 1998, *Shadows in the Sun: Travels to Landscapes of Spirit and Desire*, Washington DC: Island Press/Shearwater Books, p. 222.
9. Ibid., p. 226.
10. Ibid., p. 227.
11. Ibid., p. 237.
12. UNDCP, 2001, Community Drug Profile No. 4: 'An assessment of problem drug use in rural Afghanistan—the GAI target districts', p. 22.
13. BBC News, 5 May 2002.
14. Robert Connell Clarke, 1998, *Hashish!*, Los Angeles: Red Eye Press, p. 109.
15. Inga Clendinnan, 1991, *Aztecs: An Interpretation*, New York: Cambridge University Press.
16. Subhuti Dharmananda, 'The Medicinal Use of Snakes in China', May 1997, downloaded from: http://www.itmonline.org/arts/snakes.htm

## POSTSCRIPT

1. Licensing Afghanistan's opium: Solution or fallacy?, *Asia Times*, 1 February 2006.
2. President Karzai, 'Preface to the National Drug Control Strategy', Ministry of Counter Narcotics, Islamic Republic of Afghanistan, Kabul, January 2006.
3. UNODC, 2006, 'World Drug Report 2005: Volume 1 Analysis', Vienna: UNODC, p. 2.
4. *Asia Times*, 1 February 2006.
5. Barnett R. Rubin, 1996, *The Fragmentation of Afghanistan: State Formation and Collapse in the International System*, Lahore: Vanguard Books, p. 5.
6. *Observer*, 5 February 2006.
7. *Washington Post*, 27 May 2006.

# Index